Real World Software Configuration Management

SEAN KENEFICK

APress Media, LLC

ISBN 978-1-59059-065-2   ISBN 978-1-4302-0792-4 (eBook)
DOI 10.1007/978-1-4302-0792-4

Trademarked names may appear in this book. Rather
than use a trademark symbol with every occurrence of a
trademarked name, we use the names only in an editorial
fashion and to the benefit of the trademark owner, with
no intention of infringement of the trademark.

Borland, CodeWright, StarBase, and StarTeam are
either registered trademarks or trademarks of Borland
Corporation in the United States and other countries.
Screenshots are used with permission.

cmReady is a trademark of cmReady Systems,
Incorporated.

IBM, Rational, ClearCase, ClearQuest, Atria, DB2, and
OS/2 are either registered trademarks or trademarks of
IBM in the United States and other countries.

InstallShield, Developer, Professional, Express, and
AdminStudio are either registered trademarks or trademarks of InstallShield Software Corporation, in the
United States and other countries. Screenshots are used
with permission.

Kinook and Visual Build are either registered trademarks
or trademarks of Kinook Software, Inc., in the United
States and other countries. Screenshots are used with
permission.

Merant and PVCS are either registered trademarks or
trademarks of Merant, Inc., in the United States and
other countries. Screenshots are used with permission.

Microsoft, Visual SourceSafe, Access, Office, Visual
Studio, Visual C++, Visual Basic, SQL Server, and
Windows are either registered trademarks or trademarks of Microsoft Corporation in the United States and
other countries. All operating systems listed, including
Windows 95, Windows 98, Windows NT, Windows 2000
and Windows XP, are copyrighted by Microsoft Corporation. Screenshots are used with permission.

MKS and Source Integrity are either registered trademarks or trademarks of MKS, Inc., in the United States
and other countries.

Oracle, Oracle8i, and Oracle9i are either registered
trademarks or trademarks of Oracle Corporation, in
the United States and other countries.

Screenshots for SourceGear Vault are used with
permission.

Sun, Java, and Solaris are either registered trademarks
or trademarks of Sun Microsystems, Inc, in the United
States and other countries.

Wise Solutions, Wise for Visual Studio .NET, and Wise for
Windows Installer are either trademarks or registered
trademarks of Wise Solutions, Inc. Screenshots are used
with permission.

Technical Reviewer: David Birmingham

Editorial Board: Dan Appleman, Craig Berry, Gary Cornell,
Tony Davis, Steven Rycroft, Julian Skinner, Martin Streicher,
Jim Sumser, Karen Watterson, Gavin Wray, John Zukowski

Assistant Publisher: Grace Wong

Project Manager: Tracy Brown Collins

Copy Editor: Kim Wimpsett

Production Editor: Janet Vail

Compositor: Diana Van Winkle, Van Winkle Design Group

Illustrator: Cara Brunk, Blue Mud Productions

Proofreader: Nancy Sixsmith

Indexer: Kevin Broccoli, Broccoli Information Managment

Cover Designer: Kurt Krames

Manufacturing Manager: Tom Debolski

The source code for this book is available to readers at
http://www.apress.com in the Downloads section.

Dedicated to Scott Vouri and Paul Higgins,
who gave me a chance when they didn't have to do so.

Contents at a Glance

Contents

Part Two

Part Three
The Tasks

Chapter 7   In the SCM Lab

Chapter 8   Basic Builds

Chapter 9   Builds for Windows .NET

Foreword

BY DAVID BIRMINGHAM

WHEN GATHERING THE TECHNICAL TALENT and tools to put together solutions in an increasingly competitive and demanding marketplace, timelines are tighter, money is thinner, and your solution group is under the constant temptation to push solutions out the door with a minimum of formal procedure getting in its way. It's not easy, quick, or cheap—and lack of attention to at least a minimum of infrastructure can convert your cool n-tier solution to an n-*tear* solution in no time flat.

Not one for heavy-handed procedures and tedious ISO compliance, but knowing that some infrastructure process and forethought is indispensable, I like Sean Kenefick's approach. It has the kind of balance and flexibility that will serve most teams. If we had unlimited time to stand around white boards, wait on other team members to fix broken software that keeps us from running free, or carefully train even novice programmers on the disciplines of source control—we wouldn't need automated tools or procedures just to protect us from each other.

Imagine a line of world-class runners in lanes on a track. To win, they need to stay focused and pour their energy out at high speed. They also know that to keep from getting disqualified, they need to stay in their own lanes. It's for safety, too—two people tripping over each other and spilling out at nearly 20 miles per hour can irreversibly damage a human body. We must keep the runners moving and keep them safe—protecting them from each other.

Software Configuration Management (SCM) and its tools and procedures help developers stay focused and keep their processors burning at high temperature. A track meet needs lots of people to stay organized, but a good SCM can do everything virtually—but not without the cooperation of the team. If the team begins to see the SCM as being in the way, the team has lost sight of the big picture in exchange for short-lived success. One developer "crossing the line" can cause others to stumble. If this continues, the team can't possibly win the race.

Software development is as much about the process as the technology. I recall one developer coming into my office, closing the door, and seriously suggesting we dismiss the entire testing team for our project. "They are only in the way," he claimed. "Nothing we do is good enough for them." Experienced developers see the irony in this statement. If the testers represent the end users, they are doing you a favor. Don't take it personally; just fix the problem.

In another setting, three developers pushed out a breathtaking amount of functionality at a speed that absolutely astounded the customer. It was rock solid and production strength. These three people understood the process of software development, cross-tested their own work, and by sheer force of will maintained the discipline to stay focused, collaborate, and close issues at high speed. Their anticollision strategy was to stay in the same room and coordinate everything on the fly—and it worked for them because as a team they had long-since gelled into a group that could complete each other's sentences. But that kind culture is rare— so rare that the need for SCM is ever-present to mitigate the lack of collaboration, the pace of the project, the size of the team, and clashing personalities or the ever-present need to insert, remove, or swap out technologists at a moment's notice.

The consistency of process also frees your developers from having to deal with the oh-so-tedious aspects of software versioning, building, configuring, and other largely administrative activities of software delivery. One developer told me he felt constrained by the use of a version control system. Why does he need to check things into a central repository if nobody else is working on it but him? Administrative thinkers understand this need, but technologists—especially inexperienced ones—just don't. If you've put together a team of software developers and have no infrastructure in place, you'll be surprised how many developers want to join your team. Then you'll be appalled at how little they can get accomplished.

SCM also protects you from rogue behavior. The "active rogue" is easier to identify and control because he's out in the open and often very verbal. The "passive rogue" is pretty much anyone on your team who will sacrifice quality when the heat starts to rise. Face it, when crunch time comes, you need a process in place that keeps your people from being tempted to put in quick fixes that ultimately become time bombs for someone else to fix—or for the user to encounter after delivery. What's that—you added a new table to the database on your local machine, but it never made it to the central server? And you upgraded to Widgets 4.0 to solve a problem, but everyone else is still using Widgets 3.0? You checked in a bunch of software before leaving for a long weekend but didn't bother to see if it would even compile cleanly?

In most cases of failed software projects—at least those that are funded and staffed to be successful—the failure rests in the inability to keep all of the developers in their own tracks and not stepping on each other. The SCM has a huge responsibility in designing the infrastructure but requires significant support from the project's leadership.

Sean makes excellent points about how to navigate the sticky political issues and help people stay focused. An SCM is ideally part administrator, part technologist, part cheerleader, part diplomat, and part police officer, and must never lose self-control or a sense of humor. If your SCM is gruff, insensitive, sarcastic, or has any problems in actively (and enthusiastically) interacting with people on various levels, you've got a more serious problem than having no SCM at all. Sean describes the flexibility and congeniality required of an SCM, and you'll see his personality come out in the pages you're about to read.

Whether you're an administrator, a business analyst, a technologist, on the testing staff, or in any of the myriad roles on a software development project, you'll see some wisdom in the ability of simple processes and infrastructure to put—and keep—wind in your sails and some fun back into the project lifecycle. And who doesn't need more of that?

David Birmingham
CEO, Virtual Machine Intelligence

Foreword

BY MICHÈLE LEROUX BUSTAMANTE

ONCE UPON A TIME, when the Internet was in its infancy and before there was Component Object Model (COM), I was responsible for the development of installation software for several boxed imaging solutions. It was during that time that I would learn to appreciate and respect the art of configuration management; because my job came last, I was always late. Now, to be clear, I was late because the software was almost always late getting into my hands, which meant my timeline on the white board schedule was compressed to meet our shrink wrapping schedule (which comprised an assembly line of our staff, stuffing and wrapping boxes). So, at the kick-off of my installation development schedule, my office was lined with developers, managers, and a Chief Technical Officer (CTO) hovering and offering to bring me food, water, and coffee as I completed the work.

Even a simple installation program is critical because it is the first experience a customer has with your software. It will either make or break their ability to run the software successfully. Yep, that's important, and if you've ever written an installation for "release," then you know the intricate details involved that could drive even the best developer mad! A great deal of pressure comes with the responsibility of software deployment, and this pressure increases when you introduce other configuration management concepts such as source control, versioning, and automated production builds. This can be even further complicated when the technologies are complex.

Happily, I was fortunate to have left my installation days behind me by the time we introduced COM components into our evolving imaging solutions. Just in the nick of time, too! In the days of early COM (or OLE Automation 1.0), versioning and deployment headaches were almost insurmountable, especially when you had to deal with some legacy 16-bit applications and perform thunking from 32-bit components!

Eventually, I left imaging and animation to work on document management solutions. That is when I met the author of this book, Sean Kenefick, and learned how a professional configuration management expert gets the job done. Our document management solution was a classic client/server enterprise application that leveraged both proprietary and third-party databases, included email server configuration for workflow, and was built using distributed COM architecture (DCOM). Sean, determined to make his job as enjoyable as possible, set out to automate the build, versioning, and deployment process to a desktop shortcut icon.

And so it was.

Our nightly builds were automated such that the dedicated build machine had a desktop icon that would pull the latest source code from Visual Source Safe, build all components using a script that properly arranged the build order to handle component dependencies, assign an incrementing version to all build output, label source safe directories with this version stamp, and create a versioned directory with the resulting CD image. I was an immediate admirer of this, given my prior experience where source control was a nightly backup to tape and where developers built and tested their own components.

From a business perspective, this automated process was critical. Implementing source control ensured the company had the latest source from all developers. Automating the build process from that source ensured the correct source was used to build components and disciplined developers to avoid "breaking" the build by checking in partially completed work. Versioning provided us with historical footprints that could be reviewed when features were broken between builds but also made it possible for development and Quality Assurance (QA) teams to record in which build they discovered defects. This automated build process completely streamlined our ability to update development and QA servers with the latest build.

A core set of tasks simply must have process and automation in the back-office of a development environment. You must have source control to protect your company's code assets and to provide versioning and rollback functions. You must have a streamlined build process that will build components from their source and organize the distributable components and other content for deployment. You must also have an automated deployment process that can be relied upon to accurately update the destination of the deployment be it a CD installation, a Web download, or a script that deploys updates to a hosted environment.

We've come a long way in 10 years. To think I used to build floppy disk installations that required "jamming" close to 1.44MB of information on each disk to reduce the overall disk count. In fact, I remember using tools that required me to hand pick the files to make this possible! Ughh! Nowadays, people download entire CD footprints over the Web. And although this traditional CD installation is still alive and well, there are many more things to consider today such as Web deployment, automatic version updates over the Internet, and application hosting.

Today, a configuration manager, along with development teams and managers, must come together on the right deployment model for an application. Application versioning is no longer as simple as a component stamp or a source control directory. So, new distribution channels, component architectures, and version update technologies now make it necessary for application developers to assist configuration managers in forming the correct software architecture to complement the deployment plan and to remove the need for intervention for automatic updates. Similarly, when working in a hosting environment, developers and Information Technology (IT) staff must join forces with configuration managers to construct an effective process that will allow companies to maintain service levels while updating production sites.

These concepts truly cross platform boundaries. During the time I was Chief Information Officer (CIO) of a 24×7-hosted operation built on Java 2 Enterprise Edition (J2EE), I had the opportunity to work with Sean once again. This time, he was brought in to build an entire process for configuration management that would be responsible for streamlining the deployment of code from development, to QA, and finally to production. When you work in a 24×7 environment and are ultimately responsible for the safe deployment of production updates, you realize how incredibly important it is to be able to roll back changes, deploy accurate updates, and have well-documented procedures and configuration steps. We had to be able to rebuild a production machine immediately if we lost one or if there was a problem with a deployment. I could not have imagined entrusting this process to anyone but Sean because in my years of experience he was the only person I knew who had a passion for and truly had perfected this art form.

Configuration management is as much about process as it is implementation. In large organizations, many of the tasks that fall under the umbrella of configuration management are distributed among several individuals and/or departments. Sean's book focuses on the core tasks of the "CM guy," but he also injects his vast practical experience with process and management into the content he delivers in each chapter. He will teach you how to automate build scripts, how to deploy applications over the Web, and how to build traditional installation applications using some of the common tools available today for multiple platforms. More important, he will inspire you to take pride in the perfection of this art that is in many cases the center of a successful software development operation. You won't find a better source of information on this subject or a more passionate author willing to share his vast experience!

Michèle Leroux Bustamante
Associate, IDesign
http://www.idesign.net

About the Author

Sean Kenefick is one of the founders of cmReady Systems, a company specializing in software configuration management services and collocation/hosting solutions. Prior to that, he was the director of network operations at ConfirmNet Corporation and the manager of client applications at Motiva Software. He has taught programming languages through the University of California at San Diego Extension program since 1997.

In his spare time, he enjoys reading, biking, and tinkering with the six computers lying around his house. He lives in San Diego, California, with a dog named Gus, a cat named Sable, and four unnamed goldfish.

Sean can be reached via skenefick@cmready.com or through the cmReady Web site at http://www.cmready.com.

About the
Foreword Writers

David Birmingham, also the technical reviewer of this book, is an independent consultant for Metamorphic Software Corporation in Dallas, Texas. David has successfully deployed a wide range of large- and medium-scale software solutions in varying complexity—promoting products, services, and methodologies to help technical groups gain and keep a foothold in the marketplace. David has embraced software configuration management and its supporting products in various forms, and hopes the reader will find value and success in applying the concepts of this book. David, his wife, and three children live and play just north of Dallas, Texas. See his book, also from Apress, *Software Development on a Leash* (Apress, 2002). David can be reached at dbirmingham@metamorphicsw.com.

Michèle Leroux Bustamante is an associate of IDesign, a Microsoft regional director, a member of the International .NET Speakers Association (INETA), and an author. At IDesign, Michèle contributes her diverse background to .NET training and high-end corporate consulting. She focuses on the C# language, ASP.NET, and Web Services and also provides guidance to technology executives. Michèle is also a frequently published writer and international conference speaker. For more information, visit http://www.idesign.net or subscribe to her newsletter at http://www.dotnetdashboard.net.

Acknowledgments

THANKS TO EVERYONE I've worked with at Apress including the straight-shooting but always supportive Karen Watterson, technical reviewer David Birmingham, copy editor Kim "Willy-Nilly" Wimpsett, and production editor Janet Vail—all of whom were forced to read this manuscript again and again. Special "monster thanks" to project manager Tracy Brown Collins who always kept me pointing in the right direction. I'm also going to miss emailing her every day.

I'd also like to acknowledge some of the folks I've worked with professionally, without whom I could not (or would not) have written this book. Specifically, I'd like to mention Paul Higgins and Scott Vouri (to whom this book is dedicated), Barry Knuttila, Andrea Ames, Jose Cepeda, and Michèle Leroux Bustamante (who got me the gig in the first place).

I'd also like to thank (and apologize to) the friends and family who suffered in silence as I worked every weekend, holiday, and vacation day for the past two years: Jerry and Beverly Kenefick (also known as Mom and Dad), Kellee and Riley Bergendahl, Jeff Pierick, and Mike Ellis (though he rarely suffered silently). Thanks for the support!

But most important, I want to savor this moment with Audrey Oberman—the rock who keeps me sane.

Introduction

UNLESS YOU WORK FOR EBENEZER SCROOGE, everybody typically wins when your company is successful. Stock options are suddenly worth cash. Paychecks increase at review time. Companies can offer better benefits, such as 401(k) matching and optical care. It's definitely in your best interest for your company to succeed.

With that it mind, building your product and presenting it to the marketplace could be considered the most important job in the company. But there's a whole lot more to releasing a product than coming up with the artwork for the box. Someone has to make sure the right version of the software gets copied to the CD-ROM or deployed to the Web. Then he or she has to make sure customers aren't being exposed to the next Melissa virus.

But more important, long before the customer ever sees the box, this same person has to watch over the building blocks of the product to ensure that nothing goes wrong long enough for the software to be placed on the final CD-ROM. The person is the team goalie: Behind every corner lurks disaster that can destroy a company's chance for success, and he or she has to block fate's kicks.

Who is the person who bears all this on his or her shoulders? Meet the Software Configuration Manager (SCM).

Who Is the Software Configuration Manager?

Oddly enough, sometimes the most junior programmers are thrust into this position. With the best intentions, and oftentimes learning on the job, these apprentices take the burden of ensuring that the programmers' output is constantly available and that the product can be built and installed.

It may seem strange that companies push this highly important job onto their most inexperienced personnel. But in the fast-paced world of software engineering, these same managers must meet what many consider to be impossible deadlines while supervising a staff of very large egos—they can be forgiven for trying to cut corners. Especially now, after we've entered a new century and all the paradigms in the software engineering world have changed.

Companies no longer have the luxury of hiring on whims. Where managers used to search unsuccessfully for months trying to attract qualified candidates and even created positions for good people when they were chanced upon, now companies must make do with the staff they have. Companies that frivolously spent money on the "whatever-it-takes" theory of software development have gone the way of the dinosaurs. In today's market, only the frugal survive.

Companies in the know crave and desire high-end SCMs (also known by the *configuration manager* moniker) while software engineers currently face the worst job market they've experienced in memory. A good SCM can still get calls from recruiters two or three times a month.

And then there are the companies that seem to not know any better. For these companies, the junior employees are still given the arduous task of making sure all their coworkers stay employed.

What Are the Possibilities for the SCM Today?

When I started in the software engineering industry, I worked for a small video card driver creation company in San Rafael, California. Immediately upon joining the programming staff as the most-junior employee, the basics of SCM were put in my hands: administering the source database, building the products, and creating an installation for its deployment.

A few years later, I was offered a job in San Diego as the senior SCM for a product development house. They chose me more for my programming background than my SCM skills. I was wary about taking the job—after all, in many companies, configuration managers are considered (along with quality assurance and technical support) to be second-class citizens. I was also worried about not being challenged by the position.

But hey—it was a job in San Diego. I took it.

And I've never looked back. I think the experience I gained at that company has given me opportunities I might never been afforded if I stayed in mainstream programming. I find myself in a niche that is not easily filled. And I find myself constantly challenged to keep up with technologies I might never have explored if I had stayed a C++ programmer.

In this market, at least here in California, programmers pound the pavement looking for marginal positions. But SCMs are still high in demand. Recently a recruiter called me so I could consider two open positions he had. Because I was happy in my current situation, I politely declined. "Well, have you got any friends with similar experience levels? You must know someone," he said. Unfortunately, I couldn't help him. In fact, when I was a manager looking for a strong SCM candidate, I went through eight months of interviewing—and found only one person who was properly qualified for the job. He turned me down because he was offered much more money from a competing suitor.

Second-class citizens? No way! Smart companies understand the necessity for strong SCM. And that need will never go away.

So, Why a Book on SCM?

I decided I wanted to write a book that would help people who, like I was, have been thrown into a role that's totally foreign to them. Many of them have no formal programming experience and, worse, have no one to guide or mentor them. Almost all of their abilities come from learning them on the job. I'm hoping this book might aid them in their work tasks.

Who Should Read This Book?

When I started in the SCM role, I searched for a book that might help me understand the basics of this new position; instead, I found plenty of books that covered small parts of the job, but none that encompassed the fundamental tasks and tools I was going to have to master. Time has moved on, but there still seems to be a dearth of such basic resources for the new SCM on the job.

Because the SCM position can be thrust upon not only programmers, but also quality assurance and technical support personnel, this book is designed as a "start-from-scratch" manual. It describes the rudimentary aspects of the position as well as strategies that can help you avoid the typical "newbie" pitfalls. More experienced SCMs may find that this book will "round out" many of their skills as well as detail specifics tasks that they may want to integrate into their processes.

This book is extremely well-suited for those working in basic software engineering houses. However, you may be building critical medical or engineering software. Maybe you're programming a rollercoaster's functions or integrating software into an airplane cockpit. If so, this book will give you an excellent foundation for your job—but there are other rules and laws you must follow that are outside the scope of this book. You'll want to explore other reference material for your particular situation.

How This Book Is Organized

This book is divided into three parts, each made up of several chapters.

Part One, "The Role," is a fundamental primer for the SCM role. In it, you'll find a description of the role itself, as well as basic information regarding source control and the tools used to implement it:

- **Chapter 1**: "Getting to Know the SCM Role"

- **Chapter 2**: "The SCM and the Software Development Process"

- **Chapter 3**: "All About the Source"

Part Two, "The Tools," includes overviews of many source control tools, as well as detailed chapters on the two most popular freeware tools:

- **Chapter 4**: "Source Control Tools"

- **Chapter 5**: "CVS"

- **Chapter 6**: "SourceSafe"

Part Three, "The Tasks," outlines the responsibilities that are a part of the SCM job. These chapters cover how to care for your source database and include techniques for building your product. Furthermore, this part discusses specific strategies for different operating systems and compilation tools. You'll also find information on Web deployment and product releases:

- **Chapter 7**: "In the SCM Lab"

- **Chapter 8**: "Basic Builds"

- **Chapter 9**: "Builds for Windows .NET"

- **Chapter 10**: "Installations"

- **Chapter 11**: "Deployment and Build Afterthoughts"

Conventions Used in This Book

This book uses certain style conventions to help you understand certain phrases.

A constant-width font indicates code examples:

```
such as this
```

A constant-width font in a sentence `such as this` denotes commands or keywords that might be case-sensitive when used. It also denotes Web addresses.

Italics indicate new terms and important concepts.

The ➤ symbol denotes a menu hierarchy. For example, select File ➤ Open Project indicates that you should select the File menu and then select the Open Project command.

Unfortunately, book pages are only so wide. A small arrow at the end of a code line indicates single code lines that have been split into multiple lines merely to fit the confines of the printed page:

```
A Constant Width Font with an Ending Arrow ↵
    and a Following Indented Line
```

Part One

The Role

CHAPTER 1

Getting to Know the SCM Role

BEFORE TAKING ON a new role in any organization, it's important to understand what makes the Software Configuration Management (SCM) role necessary. Surprisingly enough, you can see the need for SCM in many aspects of the world around you.

Consider these real-life scenarios where configuration management might be handy:

You're writing a term paper on English history when you decide that your section on Henry VIII is unnecessary and delete it. Two days later, your teacher tells you that extra credit will be given to anyone who includes a section on corpulent philanderers. Now you'll be up all night writing that section again.

You work with several coworkers on the same document. You and Bryan each get the same copy of the document and make separate changes. You copy your document back to the network, and then Bryan copies his. Three days later, only Bryan is getting credit for getting his work done—his document overwrote the one you copied to the network.

You work on a document using a new version of a word processor. Your boss finds that he can't open it using the version of the software installed on his machine.

You finish your sales document for a customer. You need a similar document for a second customer—and then a third and a fourth. Then you realize that you misspelled your name in the header in each one. You have to open all the documents separately and correct your name four times.

On your Web site, you link to another site describing the best movies of the year. The guy who owns the movie domain suddenly decides to make more money by placing an online casino at that address instead. Because you didn't test the basic functionality of your site, your customers start showing up in bankruptcy court.

Annoying as these problems are, I hope that you're lucky enough not to run into them often. Software developers, on the other hand, face these daunting trials daily.

Again, these are real-world problems—but the trials developers face can be much more dramatic. As this chapter progresses, you'll look at similar problems related more to the software world and see how good SCM control can help.

Configuration Management in the Real World

You might be surprised at the pervasiveness of the term *configuration management* throughout the business world. The definition of the term can be boiled down to the following statement: Configuration management is a deliberate process that ensures the delivery of a high-quality and predictable product.

Some of the tasks involved in the configuration management process might include (but certainly aren't limited to) the following:

- Recording the state of an object at any given time

- Detailing what makes up the object

- Specifying the environment in which the object exists

- Documenting any changes made to the object

Soon you'll see how the previously listed processes help keep consumer prices down and, more importantly, can keep you and the ones you love safe. Most manufacturing companies use configuration management processes to ensure the quality and safety of their products.

The basic premise of configuration management is to break down large objects into the smallest chunks possible and then to record the changes and environment in which the part is made. In a configuration management system, a *part* is made of smaller parts that are combined to create it. Each smaller part is also made up of even smaller parts until a base object is reached that has no other parts that make it up. For instance, Figure 1-1 displays a primitive automobile configuration.

Part			Quantity
Automobile			1
	Engine		1
		Carburetor	1
		...	...
		Fuel Pump	1
		...	...
	Frame		1
	Axle		2
		Tire	2
		Tire Screw	8

Figure 1-1. A primitive automobile configuration

This display of parts and their subparts is a simple bill of materials. The automobile is made up of an engine, a frame, and two axles—though the chances of this poorly equipped automobile running on the highway aren't very good. Further down, you can see that each axle is made up of two tires and eight tire screws. Because tires and screws are single objects made up of one material (rubber and metal, respectively), they're known as *base objects* that have no subparts. By tracking these small items—and every other separate piece that "makes up" a product—manufacturers are able to more efficiently produce, and then reproduce, their products. The following are some advantages to this system:

Manufacturers know exactly what quantity of materials is necessary to create the object. For instance, how much steel is required by this car? The total can be tallied by noting how much of the metal is required by each of the base parts and then adding the numbers together.

They know what's necessary to re-create any parts should it become necessary. It's much easier to re-create that blue paint job if you understand which dyes make up the paint.

They can swap out parts as necessary. If Shop 312 has run out of fuel pumps, the company can continue production with another pump of similar size and make.

Different groups at different plants can work on different parts. The team creating the exhaust pipe in Cleveland doesn't need to know anything about the team working on the headlamp in Atlanta. In fact, companies can even buy parts from other companies, and the assembly workers can ignore their origins when building the final product. The purchased products are simply treated as base objects.

They can more easily root out problems after assembly is complete. If the car malfunctions and it's known that the only change was to the fuel pump, there's a high probability that the problem can be fixed quickly.

They will schedule more efficiently. If the manufacturer can determine how many parts must be created versus those available in stock, it has an edge in knowing when the completed item will be ready.

You might be asking: What does this automobile have to do with software? Everything! Even though software isn't a tangible object you can hold in your hand, most of the same principles and rewards can be applied to it.

Programming 101

Computers are funny things. They seem pretty powerful to us, but in reality they're extremely limited. They don't speak our language. They can't reason. And they're only able to do exactly what they're told to do. If they're told to make a mistake, they'll make that mistake over and over again until told otherwise. They can't learn as we do unless we tell them how to learn.

Computer processors only understand two things: on and off. So programmers, or *software developers* as they're often called, use electrical impulses to communicate in that language. To indicate on, you send an electrical pulse to the processor. To indicate off, you send nothing. You use those same pulses to tell your screen how to show fonts or pictures or to save your files on your hard drive. In fact, it all boils down to this: To a computer, everything is a jumble of zeros and ones—the numbers that represent off and on, respectively. This is the binary number system.

Binary numbers are the building blocks of all software. All data and commands break down to them. But before you start giving software programmers more credit than they deserve, I'll tell you a secret: They don't actually string binary numbers together to create software. If they did, simply putting up a message box would take weeks of work.

Instead of speaking binary directly, programmers use tools called *compilers* to translate instructions into machine language. First, they write a series of commands in English-like languages using a text editor similar to a word processor. This text is often referred to as *source code* or just *source* or *code*. When programmers want to see their commands in action, they run the text through a compiler. The compiler spits out what's known as *object code*—binary files that mean nothing to humans but that tell the computer, in its own language, exactly what to do.

To use a specific programming language, programmers must use that language's compiler. You might be familiar with the names of some of the more popular languages and their compilers: Java, C/C++, Basic, COBOL, Fortran, Assembly. Most compilers must be bought like any other software; however, some are available as freeware. Programmers use different languages depending on the cost of the compiler and the functionality they want to create—and each language has its own set of features and syntax. Because many of the languages have similar properties, programmers typically use a language because it's familiar to them or because it's more efficient for certain tasks.

Once the compiler has created sets of object code, these sets are put together into an executable that an end user can click and run. You use a linker so you can "link" object code from several different languages into one executable.

WORD OF THE DAY

ac'rō·nym, *n.*

And you thought that *OLE* should be used only in bullfights and flamenco dancing.

There are many generally accepted laws in the computing world. One of the most well-known laws is Moore's law, which states that the speed of processors will double once every 18 months.

And then there are the unwritten rules that everyone seems to know but never talks about. For instance, a widely followed but unspoken rule is that developers should always test their work—but they should never be tasked with the final approval for the quality of their own code. This is an important rule, and future chapters cover it in more detail.

Another one of these unwritten rules is the law of acronyms: As a technology grows in usage and importance in the computing world, it's referred to by its initials or given a Three-Letter Acronym (TLA) by which it's known throughout the industry and the general public.

Okay, so maybe it's not a *serious* law. But the truth is that you aren't really living in the software world if you don't see that most technologies can be boiled down to a three-, four-, or five-letter abbreviation or acronym.

You've probably heard most of these: ASCII, XML, ADO, HTML, DOS, Unix, Linux, J2EE, COM, DHCP, DNS, FTP, TCP/IP, UDP....

Frankly, this list is like the number pi—it would go on forever if I could bring myself to type it all. But did you know that HTML actually stands for *Hypertext Markup Language*? Or that DOS could mean the *Disk Operating System* or a *Denial of Service* network attack depending on its pronunciation? By the by—in case you didn't know—HTML and DOS (Denial of Service) are both abbreviations. And DOS (the operating system) is an acronym. Each letter of an abbreviation is spoken, but an acronym is pronounced as if it were a single word.

It's like learning another language—but here's a hint: The next time a developer throws out a mouthful of acronyms at you, excuse yourself for a moment and check out http://www.whatis.com. This advertising-supported Web site can give you the full names and definitions of thousands of terms—many of which you've heard but don't necessarily know what they are.

You'll then see that Object Linking and Embedding (OLE) has little to do with the bulls in Spain.

Are You a Native of These Here Parts?

A huge barrier that has confronted development houses is that of *portability*. Different computers use different processors, and each of these processors follows distinct rules ranging from the amount of data it can read at one time to the way data must be processed. Operating systems, such as Microsoft Windows and Sun Microsystems Unix, marry themselves to certain processors and their respective advantages.

To run software on more than one operating system, it must be compiled for each operating system. Unfortunately, that code must be prepared for that compilation; oftentimes developers must make a great number of changes in order to integrate with a new processor. This is known as *porting* code to different *platforms*. It's also known as creating code *native* to an environment.

As you can guess, this presents a huge challenge for companies. They must weigh the amount of work and time it will take to complete the task against the possible rate of return. That's the reason why you find certain software for Windows that doesn't seem to exist for Unix and vice versa.

One way to get around this problem is to create languages that are operating system *independent*.

Let me introduce HTML—one of the most popular languages used. The entire World Wide Web is built completely around it. If you've never seen HTML before, right-click your favorite Web site in your Internet browser and choose View Source. Here's an example:

```
<html>
    <body>
        <h1>My Web Page</h1>
        <p>Hello world!</p>
    </body>
</html>
```

HTML doesn't seem to follow the rules of which I spoke in the previous section. HTML has no need of compilers or linkers. Instead of being generated into machine language before the code is delivered to an end user, this process takes place when the code runs. This difference makes HTML both a *markup language* and an *interpretive language*.

When you click a hyperlink in your Internet browser, it downloads a copy of the HTML script that it is supposed to run. The browser then interprets the instructional *tags* it finds in the HTML scripts and displays text and pictures accordingly. The <body> directive in the previous code is an example of a tag.

Other languages also share this distinction. Active Server Pages (ASP), PHP: Hypertext Processor (PHP), and Java Server Pages (JSP) are *scripting* languages similar to HTML. Instead of running directly in your browser, however, they run on Web servers before a dynamically created Web page is sent to the end user. This allows companies to hide much of their proprietary code.

It's important to note that Java isn't a scripting language—however, it's still considered an interpreted language. This explains much of its popularity. It's still compiled, but each operating system knows how to deal with Java components when the Java Runtime Environment (JRE) is installed. This allows developers to compile applications only once and then copy that same binary file to any operating system that supports Java. Led by Sun Microsystems, a consortium of industry leaders have tried to make life easier for thousands of developers by advocating Java. Microsoft has tried to create a similar set of cross-platform languages with its .NET initiative—though the .NET Framework is available only for the Windows operating system at the time of this writing.

The Software Configuration Management Dilemmas

To understand how good SCM can simplify your life, you must first understand the problems that you're trying to solve.

Throughout the rest of this chapter, I'll identify issues that you might face in the real software development world if you didn't have any kind of SCM processes in place. At the same time, I'll list solutions or "golden rules" that you can apply to lessen the impact of these problems. Further chapters will detail how you can implement these rules.

The Source Control Dilemma

When architected, most software products are broken down into parts and sub-parts of functionality—just like the automobile used as an example in Figure 1-1.

Imagine that Bob's Software Company is building a suite of office products. Bob, the owner, has spent many months researching the software market and has come up with what he considers to be a winning project. He and his marketing team have spent a great deal of time documenting the product's functionality so that it will both meet the market need and differentiate itself from those of his competitors. Then he hired several talented software developers to work on his project.

The functionality of Bob's Office Software might naturally be broken down into discrete parts and then farmed out to specific groups of programmers to create the software (see Figure 1-2).

Bob's Office Software Employee Assignments	
Task	Employee(s)
Database	Joe, Brad, Mark, and Sheila
Spreadsheet	Larry, Frank, and Rob
Word Processor	Jenny, Louise, and Tom
Toolbars	Fred
Spelling	Mac

Figure 1-2. Bob's Office Software breakdown and development staff

You can see that Fred and Mac are pretty lucky. They get to work by themselves on their own parts of the product. In theory, they can use whatever coding language they want, and they don't have to worry about "playing well with others." Keep in mind, however, that they're still susceptible to disasters—such as accidentally deleting source or having a hard drive crash.

But Joe, Brad, Mark, Sheila, and the other teams have bigger problems. Even though they break up the different functionality of their components into separate source code files, it's likely that they'll all need to work in more than one of the files at one time or another. Maybe Mark will overwrite Sheila's changes. Maybe Joe will cause the program to malfunction by effecting a change that he didn't quite understand. Maybe Sheila will arbitrarily decide that Joe's section is no longer needed and permanently delete it. Worst of all, maybe Brad will suddenly decide that he wants to be a drummer in a punk band. Joe, Mark, and Sheila will have to figure out what he was doing and attempt to continue his work after he starts touring across Europe.

Here's a classic example of the "two-steps forward, one-step backward" mentality. A larger team means having more people to complete the work. But because software development is often more about communication than the technology itself, working in a larger team can increase the probability of unrecoverable disasters.

These kinds of challenges present themselves all the time in the programming world. Regardless of whether the code is written in an interpreted or natively compiled language, SCM can add a certain degree of control to the equation. Furthermore, if all else fails, SCM provides mechanisms for recovery. The previously mentioned problems can (for the most part) be solved by using good SCM.

GOAL 1: *You must provide your developers with a way to work efficiently on your product while protecting the source from accidental changes and unexpected disasters.*

The Build Dilemma

For Bob's Office Software, the development team has been working together for a while now, and each group is ready to provide a first draft of their respective subcomponents. This process is called *building the product*. Because of the chaos that ensues when individual developers each build their own components, the process takes eight hours. However, after they've filtered their source code files through their compilers and linkers to create executable code, they bundle the executables together, and Bob excitedly tries to run the set of programs on his machine.

The words *Chapter 11* clearly float through his mind as he tries (and fails) to use the product for the first time. He's very unhappy because the product doesn't work, and he financed this company by taking mortgages on his home and maxing out his credit cards.

Some of the problems he has run into are as follows:

- Each group of engineers built its components on different operating systems using different sets of languages and compilers. Now the components don't understand each other, and several won't run at all on the proposed product operating system.

- None of the developers documented their source code—also known as *commenting*—so other developers had a rough time understanding the intended logic when attempting to fix bugs.

- Rob's executable won't run at all. "It works on my machine!" he exclaims and leaves for the night.

GOAL 2: *You must formulate and achieve consensus on a set of standards for developers to follow so that the executables created will run correctly on required platforms and problems can be fixed quickly.*

- Tom was out sick on the day of the build. He took all his source home with him on his laptop the night before. This results in the entire Word Processing subcomponent being left out of this version.

- Brad's band has been offered a recording contract in Norway. As much as they've tried, Joe, Mark, and Sheila weren't able to determine the source code necessary for inclusion of his component in the build; they must re-create Brad's assigned functionality from scratch.

GOAL 3: *You must provide a mechanism for developers to share their code both among themselves and with those who build and support the product.*

- There's a bug in Frank's code, but he can't reproduce it with the source that's on his machine. "I've made a lot of changes since I built the executable seven hours ago," he says. "Must mean that I fixed it."

- There are no toolbars. "What do you mean?" asks Fred. "I think that I'm pretty sure. I mean, I'm absolutely certain that I compiled from the right source! It can't be my fault!"

GOAL 4: *You must centrally build the product to ensure that what has been compiled can always be re-created from source code files.*

The Deployment Dilemma

Bob certainly isn't thrilled with the progress that his team has made in creating Bob's Office Software. But he has to meet certain dates to be successful with the product launch. He decides that Ralph and José in the quality assurance department should try and test the product as it is. Just as their department name indicates, their job is to ensure the quality of the product before it's distributed to the public.

It seems that Bob is to be thwarted at every turn. He tries to remain calm as Ralph and Jose explain the diabolical forces that keep them from completing their assigned tasks:

- Ralph finds that he can't even install the product. He asks Bob to send an engineer over to help him. Bob quickly realizes that profits will suffer if he has to send an engineer to each end user's house in order to install the product.

GOAL 5: *You must provide a method for transferring the software to an end user's machine.*

- Once the product is successfully installed, Ralph and Jose complain that it's unsuitable for testing—they immediately find bugs so overwhelming that it's impossible to test the product for more than a few minutes before it crashes.

GOAL 6: *You must conduct preliminary testing on the product to ensure that it meets a minimum set of agreed-upon requirements before passing it to the quality assurance team.*

- Whoa—is that the I LOVE YOU worm? The nasty virus was on one of the developer's machines and has now propagated once more by sending itself to all of Ralph's and Jose's business contacts.

GOAL 7: *You must scan the product for dangerous anomalies before allowing it to be sent to customers.*

- After many unexpected bugs and great confusion, Frank realizes he copied an old version of his executable to the installation directory instead of the new version he compiled—Ralph and Jose have been testing outdated software for six hours.

GOAL 8: *You must provide the quality assurance team and other interested parties with descriptions of the files you build and a method to confirm that information.*

- Ralph is unable to determine whether he's installed the newest build of the product onto a test machine or whether it's a previous version. He must reinstall everything just to make sure.

- Jose thinks that a bug he previously reported is fixed; however, he can't remember the exact steps he took to find it. Unfortunately, he can't check on the previous version of the software because the directory containing it was overwritten during the new build process.

GOAL 9: *You must create unique labels for every version of the software that's built and ensure that the labels are displayed in the software itself.*

GOAL 10: *You must allow the team access to previous versions of the software.*

- After copying the Internet version of the product to the test Web site, a stray click during a routine spell check displays a picture of Mac's pet lizard Marie eating a mouse named Elroy.

GOAL 11: *You must be aware of all the files you make available to your customers.*

The Versioning Dilemma

Finally, after many months of trials and tribulations, Bob's team releases version 1.0 of Bob's Office Software. The aftermath of champagne toasts and heart-warming speeches finds the team ready to work on the new version of the software.

Bob finds that things aren't quite as rosy as he may have thought:

- Within days, customers call the technical support department with fairly serious bugs that require immediate attention. In the same amount of time, his development team has completely changed the architecture of the product in preparation for version 2.0.

- Bob's team has another copy of the source for the previous version, but they find it tedious and extremely accident-prone to make bug fixes in both versions of the software.

GOAL 12: *You must provide a mechanism that allows your developers to work on more than one product version at time while minimizing the need to make redundant changes in more than one place.*

GOAL 13: *You must provide patches to the current product while the new version is in development.*

The Golden Rules of Software Configuration Management

Let's close this chapter by repeating the goals outlined earlier. These goals are attainable and will greatly increase your productivity when building your software:

1. You must provide your developers with a way to work efficiently on your product while protecting the source from accidental change and other disasters.

2. You must formulate and achieve consensus on a set of standards and rules for developers to follow so that the executables created will run correctly on required platforms and problems can be fixed quickly.

3. You must provide a mechanism for developers to share their code both among themselves and with those who build and support the product.

4. You must centrally build the product to ensure that what has been compiled can always be re-created from source code files.

5. You must provide a method for transferring the software to an end user's machine.

6. You must conduct preliminary testing on the product to ensure that it meets a minimum set of agreed-upon requirements before passing it to the quality assurance team.

7. You must scan the product for dangerous anomalies before allowing it to be sent to customers.

8. You must provide the quality assurance team and other interested parties with descriptions of the files you build and a method to confirm that information.

9. You must create unique labels for every version of the software that's built and ensure that the labels are displayed in the software itself.

10. You must allow the team access to previous versions of the software.

11. You must be aware of all the files you make available to your customers.

12. You must provide a mechanism that allows your engineers to work on more than one product version at a time while minimizing the need to make redundant changes in more than one place.

13. You must provide patches to the current product while the new version is in development.

Summary

You should now have a good grasp of what comprises SCM and the important role it plays in the development cycle. You've seen real-world examples of the problems faced every day by team members of software development groups. These problems may seem exaggerated in the terms of this text; however, encountering even one of the problems discussed in this chapter can bring the development process to a stop and cause your company to hemorrhage cash and effort.

The chapter also discussed the basics of how software is made and how computers actually work. You should begin to see the complications you might run into during the development process and how much risk there is in creating computer software. Even so, it's still amazing what we can get away with as software developers. What other industry would be allowed to ship products with the flaws allowed for software (and then charge for the updates that fix them)? Would you be happy with a chair that wouldn't let you sit in it periodically? How about a television that frequently shut off for no apparent reason?

CHAPTER 2

The SCM and the Software Development Process

WHEN DEVELOPING CODE, software companies all have processes that they follow—sometimes referred to as *Standard Operating Procedures* (SOPs) or sometimes thought of as *rituals* (or *ruts*). A *development process* is generally considered a list of rules and guidelines that team members follow in order to build a quality product. This process might boil down to a single developer writing, compiling, and publishing all of the code that makes up a company's offerings. At the other extreme, it can be a complicated, inflexible checklist that provides little room for variance or creativity. Regardless, both methods attempt to achieve the same goal (though some with less efficacy): providing the highest quality software at the lowest possible cost of production.

The Software Configuration Manager (SCM[1])—official or de facto—can be a significant contributor to this endeavor. Often described as the "hub of the wheel," the SCM can be the common link between members of the software development team. The SCM often becomes the conduit of information between the developers and the other members of the team.

This chapter discusses the many possible roles an SCM can play in any development organization. But as previously stated, there are as many ways to develop software as there are coffee houses in San Francisco. There's no such thing as a perfect process that fits every dynamic—and although some or all of this chapter's information may be applicable only in part (or not at all) to your organization, you may find it interesting to see how versatile the SCM role can be.

Of course, if your company only has four employees, you might find that it's overkill to try and come up with an extremely detailed development process. Read this chapter anyway if you want to see how your company may evolve.

---

1. Watch out! The initials SCM can stand for both software configuration management (the practice) or a software configuration manager (the position) depending on its context.

The "Who's Who" of the Process

It can be argued that every person in a software development company is part of its process—and to some degree that's true, right down to the receptionist and bookkeeper. But there are groups of people who play a more important role in the development of software; each has a distinctive purpose and, in reality, are all equal in the eyes of the Fates—it's tough to release software without any one of them. The following sections detail these groups in the order of their contribution to the development process.

 NOTE *Because of slightly different job responsibilities, companies may have different names for the groups in these sections. In fact, some of these groups may coexist in the same department, the same person, or not at all. In other words, your development environment will surely differ! On the other hand, creating quality software in a timely manner depends on these functions taking place. You'll find that someone at your company probably fulfills each of these tasks even if a particular job title doesn't exist.*

Marketing

Though it's hard to believe, most software companies are in it for the money.[2] This is absolutely true—don't bother trying to deny it. Sure, there are folks out there who build software in an effort to better humanity—and this trend is expanding through the open-source movement—but this tends to be the exception and not the rule.

But even if you aren't in it for the money, there are some basic tenants you must follow when creating software:

- Software is created to solve problems or to make life a little easier for end users.

- The marketplace determines the worth of the solution. If you're combating a widespread problem and there are few competing products available, you can be very successful; on the other hand, if there's a glut of products that solve the same problem, you might be in trouble unless you somehow differentiate yourself from the pack.

---

2.   Yes, that was sarcasm.

Enter the marketing team. These folks determine if it makes sense to solve the pinpointed problem by analyzing the competition, hosting focus groups, and trying to determine just how much you might charge for the product in relation to the cost of its manufacture. Developers often question the need for such tactics, but here's the cold hard truth: It's difficult to create a product without the answers to some questions:

- Is there a need for your product's functionality in the real world?

- Are there existing products that provide the functionality you plan to sell? If so, what are its features? How will your product be superior?

- Who are your customers? Are they technically savvy? How important to them is the feature set versus the ease of use?

- When must your product be available? Is there a window of opportunity? For instance, a Y2K software checker isn't necessarily a big seller four years after the turn of the century.

- How you will sell your product? Over the Internet? In stores?

- At what price can you sell your product and still remain competitive?

Imagine trying to develop a software application without this information. You won't even know what the functionality of the product is! Creating an underlying vision for the product and a blueprint of what it should do is an all-important job. Normally, this task falls into the hands of the marketing department (and, to a lesser extent, the sales team).

The marketing department doesn't necessarily design or architect the technical aspects of the product—they aren't all that concerned with dialog boxes and menu items. They rarely get into the "how"; their real goal is to inform the developers of the "why" and the "what."

Project Leadership/Program Management

Once marketing has finished its analysis and the company decides to go ahead with the creation of your product, someone must track the job while it's in progress. This is the person who dictates the "when" of the product—using information that the marketing group has provided, the project manager creates schedules and manages the team. In many cases, the project leader actually reports to the head of the marketing group.

The project manager role is the one most likely to differ substantially between different companies. The other groups may have slight differences in their job descriptions, but most of their common functionality is fulfilled in the same manner. But this position's responsibilities can be very different depending on whether you call the person the project leader, program manager, product manager, or one of myriad other possibilities.

At one company, a person in this position might work in a nonauthoritative secretarial capacity—they simply track schedule changes and keep meeting notes while other managers oversee the day-to-day tasks of the team. At other locations, the project manager is the most powerful (for lack of a better word) position in the process—this person manages and rates the performance of every person working on the project regardless of their department. At other companies, two or three positions may fulfill different responsibilities concerning the management and scheduling of the project.

The one thing that all of these people have in common is that they attempt to keep the group on schedule. While tracking the development schedule, they often have to reset expectations to the rest of the company when the schedule slides or needs updating.

Architecture

Once marketing has defined a product and a project leader/secretary has been chosen, this group takes over. The architect's first task in fulfilling the vision is to choose the technologies with which the product will be built and design how it will actually work.

In most cases, there's but a small group of people—and sometimes just a single person—who architect a product. In smaller companies, a group of senior engineers might fulfill this role. Larger companies often hire dedicated resources for this position.

The architect takes the information provided by marketing and attempts to plot out the product from a technical perspective. This often includes mapping out the functionality of components that make it up, determining how it'll scale, and mocking up the interfaces that will allow different components to communicate with each other.

Without a strong architecture planned in advance, the development team will often flounder as it tries to code and plan at the same time—a sure way to miss scheduled dates.

Development/Engineering

I dislike using the moniker *development* for this group because every group mentioned in this chapter is integral to the development of quality software. However, the term has become ubiquitous in the industry to indicate the group of people that actually code the product. They might also be known as the *engineering* or *programming team*.

Once the product is architected by senior developers and approved by the other development process members (with the heaviest weight of the approval coming from the marketing representative), the actual creation of the product takes place by divvying up its functionality and assigning the separate pieces to be built by software engineers.

Okay—this isn't nearly as easy as I just made it sound. In reality, many battles will be fought (and lost) while the application is created. Cries of "That will take too long! We have to do it all and do it faster!" and "What do you expect with our current staff level? Get rid of some features! (And we want a pinball machine!)" will emanate through the building for weeks at a time.

When all is said and done, however, marketing and development always come to an uneasy compromise, and the work continues.

Software Configuration Manager

I'll discuss the specifics of the SCM role in the development process a little later in this chapter. Suffice for the time being to say that SCMs protect the source and the build product as necessary.

In the early stages of the development process, remember to tell your loved ones that you'll miss them and that you'll try to see them as often as you can.

Documentation/Training

As often-overlooked members of the team, the brave souls who write the documentation for the product must meet many of the same deadlines as the software engineers—but in a fraction of the time and generally at the last minute. In many cases, they write manuals, training materials, help files, and tutorials on software that doesn't exist—also known as *vaporware*—using only the functional specifications and empty promises to create the all-important customer documentation. Later, once the software is actually available, the writers compare their text against the actual use of the finished product before the documentation can go out the door.

NOTE *Let's all take a moment to reflect on the huge debt we owe to folks who thanklessly toil in order to provide publications such as* Real World Software Conf...*I mean, such as the documentation provided in software applications.*

Quality

The sometimes (and quite unfairly) denigrated position of quality assurance/control is actually one of the most important roles in the development process. Sure, the software wouldn't exist without someone coding it...but then again, when's the last time you heard of nonexistent software actually erasing hard drives and causing a company to go under?

Buggy software can do just that. Your company's reputation—arguably its most valuable resource after the source and its employees—will dictate whether customers choose to invest in the future products that your company might produce. The quality team ensures that the product safely does what it says that it's going to do.

In one of the worst-case scenarios, the quality team must fulfill this job after other groups have used up more than their scheduled time. As the executives scream and yell (and many times plead), the unpopular quality engineer must point out the basic flaws in the product that make it unsuitable for release.

Friendship rings may not be exchanged during the testing phase of the product, but the quality team gets the dubious reward of protecting the company's investment, reputation, and well-being.

Release Management

Release management is a task that's likely to fall under the guidance of the SCM, especially in smaller companies. This person is responsible for delivering the finished product (and several iterations along the way) to customers, both internally and externally.

This might mean mastering the product on removable media such as DVD or CD-ROM and then delivering those masters to a duplication house. In a different scenario, the duplication of the media itself might take place on site by members of this group. Or perhaps the release manager will simply make the software available on a Web or File Transfer Protocol (FTP) site. The methodology doesn't matter—what does is that they get the goods to the customer.

Technical Support

The technical support representative has the task of supporting the software once it's out the door. If the other groups have done their duties extremely well and the gods are smiling, the tech support representative's job is cushy. On the other hand (and in every case I've ever heard), if the product is buggy, sophisticated, or aimed at a nontechnical audience, your overworked technical support representative will live minute by minute with irate customers and stomach ulcers.

NOTE *Try to imagine the last time you used a software product that wasn't buggy, sophisticated, or aimed at a nontechnical audience. I think you get the picture.*

Admittedly, there are many nightmare scenarios associated with being a technical support representative. On the other hand, they're often the folks who are the most knowledgeable about the product. While developers and quality engineers are focused on the varying functionality of the product, technical support might be the only group that has a firm grasp of the product's entirety. I remember a meeting we had once at a company I worked for in San Diego. The development manager was explaining a new feature in a product that we all knew fairly intimately. Suddenly, he began to search his brain and wonder aloud how an obscure existing feature currently worked. All eyes turned to Bill, our tech support manager. He grinned and told us exactly how it worked and how well the customers liked the feature. Unfortunately, he then took the opportunity to tell us about features that didn't make customers feel quite as good.

WORD OF THE DAY

cŏn·sen'sus, *n.*

The problem with meetings.

As companies increase in size, so does the amount of time it takes to make decisions. In meetings that seemingly last forever, wistful dreams of cyanide tablets travel from participant to participant. "I could be *building* it instead of talking about it," a developer will surely grumble.

Worse, many meetings end only when everyone agrees—the horror of consensus. In many companies, there may not be one firm voice who becomes the decision maker during times of dispute. Many believe that the marketing representative should be the final customer of the development process and therefore have the final say on any changes made to the product or schedule—but that's only one opinion, and it certainly isn't shared by everyone in the software industry. When this voice is lacking, consensus becomes the only way to effect change. And consensus can take a lot of time to achieve.

As an SCM, choose well the meetings in which you'll participate. You have many important tasks to accomplish and schedules that must be met...don't let meetings suck all the usable time out of the day. There are times, of course, when you won't have a choice on which meetings you'll attend. But there will be other times when joining a meeting is at your discretion. Think carefully about the topics of each meeting and how the meeting affects (or doesn't affect) your duties and join them only when necessary. Also, look at the person who is moderating these meetings before accepting invitations. Moderators who force the group to stay focused and timely can help meetings become useful and informative. In the other case, try to avoid meetings thrown by wimpy moderators who don't have the gumption to cut people off.

It's generally considered acceptable to bail out of a meeting in progress once your topic of interest has been exhausted. A polite "If there's nothing else for me, I have a lot to do—please call me back in if you need me." is a sufficient exit line. If your desk is more than a few hundred feet away from the meeting room, you may want to avoid the offer to return. Better than a surprise exit, inform the moderator before the meeting begins that you'll need to leave after your contribution has been made—this allows the moderator to change the meeting's agenda as required to ensure that all topics that might concern you are discussed before you leave the room.

If, for some reason, you're unable to bail from a meeting, don't grumble or doodle. Instead, help the meeting move along by contributing enthusiastically and cheerfully—especially if your boss is the moderator.

Understanding the Development Process Cycles

Now that you have a general idea of the folks who come together to build the software, let's look at the process itself. Again, there are many different development processes—but the following sections discuss the one I've often seen put to use successfully. Figure 2-1 displays the development process cycles in a graphical format. Notice how the circle perpetuates itself forever—that's because when the first version of a product has completed, the cycle continues with future versions.

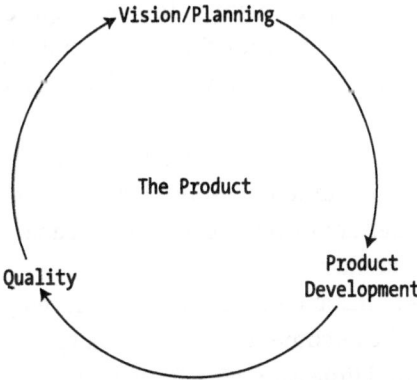

Figure 2-1. The software development process cycles

Cycle 1: Vision and Planning

The first step to any job is coming up with a plan. During the vision and planning phase, detailed plans and schedules for the application are developed. This cycle is considered "owned" by the marketing group members because most of the main tasks fall on their shoulders during this time.

What Happens Now?

In the case of software, this cycle normally splits up into two parts. First, the marketing department takes a general product idea and researches to determine if it makes sense for the company to produce. As discussed earlier in the description of the marketing group, a document is produced that provides answers to questions relating to the product market and users.

As part of this information flow, the marketing group develops use-case scenarios about how the consumer will use the product. The development team, particularly the architects, studies these scenarios and other information regarding the necessary features, and then someone produces a document outlining how all these feature sets will conceivably work in the product. This document is often called a *Functional Requirements Specification* (FRS)—but your terms may differ!—and it exists as a direct response to the original vision/use-case document. Either the marketing or development groups might be responsible for writing this document depending on how the company divvies up the duties. The writer will describe features from the customer's perspective—in many cases, only the user interface is detailed. After receiving the FRS, an architect might create a "down-and-dirty" document detailing the technical specifications of the product for the development team's private use. In addition, developers might code an example or proof-of-concept application, known as a *prototype*, to ensure that the product is technically feasible and has the ability to fulfill the functionality detailed in the FRS.

Once development and marketing has created these specifications, documenters and testers review them and provide their own papers detailing how they'll approach their jobs in the process. After the different groups have created these specifications, the development, documentation, and quality teams each provide a proposed schedule for their particular tasks.

Many of these steps may be staggered—for instance, it might be that development tasks have been scheduled long before the documentation and quality teams turn in their respective specifications and time estimates. Both of these teams may need to review the development contributions before they can commit to either task or schedule.

What You Should Expect As the SCM

The SCM usually plays a limited role during this time. In most cases, the SCM works with the product architect to inventory new components and map out plans for a new source tree. The source outline, however, is rarely subjected to the group scrutiny that other vision/planning documents go through.

If the SCM is providing an installation or is responsible for distributing the product, he or she may have to write an FRS that details how these jobs will be fulfilled. In the case of the installation, the FRS should, at the least, detail the complete user interface to be presented to the consumer. Included in the document should be screenshots of every dialog box—oftentimes mocked up using photo imaging software—and any details that might be necessary so the entire development process group understands how the customer will use the setup program. Be sure to provide a second technical specification detailing what changes the installation will make to the operating system—see Chapter 11, "Installations," for more information regarding these steps.

Once the SCM has written these specifications, he or she must provide a schedule for the completion of the tasks outlined in the documents. The following are some things to keep in mind when scheduling:

- In the weeks before your schedule is due, make a note of your everyday tasks and the approximate amount of time they take. As you develop your schedule, be sure to subtract this amount of time right from the top.

- Don't forget the emergencies! How often do they happen? How much time do they take?

- Will you have to create a build for this project? If so, remember to schedule it in with your other tasks. See Chapter 8, "Basic Builds," and Chapter 9, "Builds for Windows .NET," for more information.

- If you're using unfamiliar tools, keep the learning curve in mind when scheduling. What might seem simple often becomes more difficult when new tools are utilized.

- Unless you're an experienced scheduler, always pad your estimates with a little extra time. But let's keep this our little secret—I don't want frenzied managers filling my inbox with hate email.

- Leave time for testing your work and fixing obvious defects.

- Make sure that there's plenty of "turn-around" time for when the quality team finds defects (*bugs*) in your code. And don't kid yourself—they *will* find bugs.

- Always schedule the items that have the most risk value first; for instance, you may have great InstallShield experience but have no idea how to create a needed Windows service—make sure you work on the service first. By planning the "unknown" at the beginning of the cycle, you can quickly reset expectations should you run into one of the all-too-common stumbling blocks.

- My own personal rule (and the one I consider the most important): Always put dreaded tasks earlier in the schedule. Get them out of the way quickly, and you'll find that the fun stuff is all that's left.

Finally, as part of the planning phase, make sure that all other groups have you covered in their functional specifications and schedules. For instance, the installation may need help or README files that the documentation team must provide. It'll also need to be well tested, and the quality group needs to understand its dynamics. As you review their specifications, be generous with notes and suggestions.

Where's the Give?

How many times have you heard this exchange?

Big-Shot Marketing Guy: "We need this by October 30."

Developer: "Well, okay. But then I'll need more programmers."

Big-Shot Marketing Guy: "We can't afford more programmers."

Developer: "Then I'll have to cut down on the feature set."

Big-Shot Marketing Guy: "Can't cut down the functionality."

Developer: "Then I can't make October 30."

Big-Shot Marketing Guy: "You *have* to make October 30. And you *have* to do it with your current staff. And you *can't* cut out any functionality."

This sort of conversation is ubiquitous in the software industry. The business side demands software by a certain date with a set amount of features and staff and simply won't budge. And then—scary but true—many development groups just give in and tell the business side what they want to hear.

Unfortunately, this ensures an unrealistic schedule with missed milestones. And it won't just be a few days missed, either.

Thus, you must discuss the physics of software development. Of the three objects discussed in the previous fictional exchange—time, staff, and feature set—only two can be constrained while maintaining the integrity of the schedule. For instance, to make an October 30 deadline, the business side must agree to hire more programmers (or—yikes!—force the current employees to work more hours) or lose some functionality of the release. To constrain to the current feature set, the company must increase the staff or move the date. Otherwise, you're set for the big game of tug of war as displayed in the following figure.

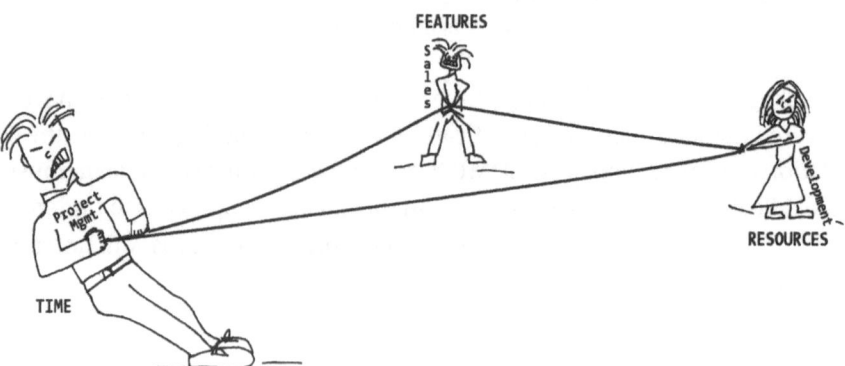

You get the picture: Each group pulls the Time-Features-Resources rubber band toward its own goal.

But even if the development manager is told to hire staff, it's simply not that easy. People have to be interviewed, hired, and trained—oftentimes an extremely time-consuming task. When I was a hiring manager in the late 90s, I consistently had three open positions. I'd fill one, and another would open up. In most cases, it's just easier to move a date or lose some functionality.

Always remember to adhere to the physics of software development when creating schedules. Don't be bullied into accepting an unreasonable schedule—you'll be the one who suffers when you can't fulfill your obligations. No matter what your objections might have been when you reluctantly gave in, this conversation will certainly be heard:

You: "Well, I said early on that it wasn't really doable...."

Big-Shot Marketing Guy: "What are you talking about? You agreed to it! If it wasn't a reasonable schedule, why didn't you say so three months ago?"

You (but don't say it out loud): $%@#!

The Big-Shot Marketing Guy is exactly right. Don't be afraid to ask "Why?" when asked to meet a hard date. And just say no to coerced and artificial schedules!

Cycle 2: Product Development

The second step in the development process is to build the product. This cycle is usually owned by development.

What Happens?

As the name of the cycle implies, the developers and writers start creating the product and its assorted documentation. In most cases, milestones were set in the vision/planning phase that dictate when sets of features will be "interface complete." This means that both the user interface and any underlying Application Programming Interfaces (APIs) are finished and ready for other groups to test and document. The interfaces will be considered *frozen*—development can't change these interfaces unless there's a compelling reason to do so. By the same token, other groups can't request changes to these interfaces after the freeze without schedule change allowances for development.

During this cycle, another milestone is set to indicate when the quality group can begin to test the product. This normally falls in the last third of the cycle—or at least after the interfaces are frozen. It takes time for the product to mature, and it's wasteful to test it while it's still in great flux.

The development or quality groups often create a *smoke test*[3] to determine the worth of testing the product. If basic functionality doesn't work as expected, it's crazy to spin the wheels testing it. Does the product open? Can a document be saved? Do all the menu items actually do something? The key words here are *expected functionality*—it doesn't necessarily mean that the whole product has to be ready to go. The smoke test simply proves that development has fulfilled its promise to deliver certain functionality at a usable level.

It can be argued that this task should fall into the hands of the quality department. Personally, I disagree. When developers check in their code, there should be a reasonable expectation that they have tested the code and that it's working as designed. Developers should *unit test* their code by quality checking and running test scripts on their own systems. The smoke test is an additional way for the development group to check itself before passing the baton to other groups.

What You Should Expect As the SCM

This is where the ball really gets rolling for the SCM. The previous planning and scheduling that you completed in the first cycle comes to life—and if you've planned things correctly, everything runs smoothly. More times than not, however, you find a few items that you missed along the way. Make sure to reset expectations if you find you're not going to be able to somehow make up the time.

The first course of action for the SCM is to create the new source trees that were planned with the architect and make them available for use to the developers. If you're unfamiliar with this terminology, refer to Chapter 3, "All About the Source," for more information. In addition, the SCM prepares build scripts (see Chapter 8, "Basic Builds," and Chapter 9, "Builds for Windows .NET," for more information). It's also time to make builds available to any interested parties once they're complete—for instance, quality and documentation might need access to newly created builds. It's likely that these builds will be scheduled to take place at even intervals—for instance, in the beginning, a build might take place every week or so. As the "freeze" date approaches, this frequency generally increases to a couple of times a week or once a day.

If working on installations, the developer will have milestones to meet in relation to the completion of functionality. Perhaps a basic installation that simply bulldozes over preexisting data will be scheduled for a certain time, and an ability to upgrade previous installations will be scheduled some time later. Demonstrations of the user interface (and the tweaking of it after hearing opinions) will be

---

3. I've been told that the term *smoke test* originates from hardware designers who labeled their circuit boards ready for testing when they were plugged in and didn't start smoldering. How true this yarn might be, I'm not sure—but it sure makes for great computer mythology.

necessary for the documentation and quality groups as they fulfill their own tasks. Technical support may also be interested in these demonstrations.

All code written by the SCM should be thoroughly self-tested before it ever goes to the quality group. Try to break your software in any way possible. You're not doing anyone any favors by pushing buggy code to the quality team. In fact, you'll find it less time consuming (and much less humiliating) to find your own defects than to have them travel through the quality control process. Remember that your code is a reflection of you—developers who don't test their code develop an unpleasant reputation that isn't necessarily rewarded at bonus time. Worse, as a senior management member once said to me, folks who don't test their code are the most likely to get laid off when things get slow.

Cycle 3: Quality Assurance/Improvement

The third step in the development process is to test the built product. This cycle is usually owned by quality.

What Happens?

The quality group generally starts testing the product after the user and program interfaces have been frozen. One of the first tasks the quality group takes on is to ensure that the functionality provided by the development team matches what was mapped out in the various specifications. After this confirmation, the quality group begins to test for defects using prewritten and approved test plans. These tests may be performed automatically or may involve manual steps.

As defects are found, they're tracked in a special database that allows the developers and quality members to work together to ensure that appropriate bugs are fixed. Many SCM source control tools have integrated defect-tracking systems available to them—see Chapter 4, "Source Control Tools," for more information.

The quality group ranks bugs as they're added to the tracking tool. This allows developers to prioritize which fixes should take place first. Sometimes the project leader or a senior development team leader ranks the bugs instead of a quality representative. As developers fix the bugs, they take special care to avoid adding a new bug to previously working functionality. This type of bug is known as a *regression* and is especially dreaded. Because every change to the software increases the risk of breakage, each published build of the product generally goes through a pass where all functionality is thoroughly tested in order to search out newly introduced regressions.

From development to testing and then back to development, these cycles continue until the software is *stable* or considered worthy for release to the consumer. As the release date approaches, special care must be taken to fix only the bugs that are considered highly important—also known as *showstoppers*. Otherwise, one of those deadly regressions might be introduced to a stable code stream. A showstopper can be defined as a bug that makes a product not usable or appear defective. For instance, a regression that causes a memory fault when the About menu is clicked would probably be considered a showstopper. On the other hand, a bug that's unlikely to be harmful or seen by the end user might be put off until a later release. As bugs are found, a select group of decision-making individuals representing the development process groups (in the past, my companies called them the *Bug Triage* group) often gather to evaluate the importance of bugs and whether applicable fixes are both worth the time and any risk of regressions.

What You Should Expect As the SCM

Bugs.

And did I say bugs? If the SCM has created any code for the product, including installations, a good deal of time should have been added to the schedule for fixing bugs and regressions as the product is stabilized.

Some bugs are tougher than others, so in the later stages of the cycle, be sure to reset expectations when a change to your code presents a high risk for regressions. In addition, always inform the quality group which portions of your code have had heavy work and merit hardier testing.

As the cycle progresses, the SCM might build more often but publish these builds less frequently to the quality group. This allows the quality group to thoroughly test the product and gives the developers time to turn around bugs. In addition, the SCM will probably run frequent smoke tests to ensure that obvious defects are found and fixed before the quality team receives the build. Because the quality team is the one that decides what makes a build worthy for testing, it will generally be the team to dictate what functionality the smoke tests will cover.

Lastly, after the quality team releases the build for consumer use, the SCM prepares the build for the deployment team or, alternatively, performs the deployment. This might mean posting the code to a Web/FTP site, creating a gold CD and driving it to a duplication lab, or using burners to copy the code on site.

Understanding the Different SCM Positions

In addition to the usual source management duties applicable to the SCM, job recruiters tend to look for one of two kinds of people when filling open-source configuration management positions: the button pusher and the button creator.

The Button Pusher

The button pusher usually joins a company with a well-established process, build scenario, and source tree. Their job is to run jobs that were architected and created by other people. This person is often junior in nature and may report to a more senior SCM. In a smaller shop, this person may run scripts and processes created by a developer, previous employer, or outside contractor.

This SCM isn't really in a position to make decisions or change policies regarding process or configurations. Many people prefer to work in this type of environment because they fulfill a fairly routine set of tasks—such as completing simple administrative functions on the source tree or running and documenting existing builds—without the necessity of completing other more harrowing tasks. They may consider this position to be a stepping-stone job to development or another more interesting position.

On the other hand, this type of position tends to not afford a person with a great deal of freedom or salary. The tradeoff for a limited number of routine tasks and regular hours often tends to be the insidious trap that an easy job with a satisfactory salary will always provide—frankly, you won't have any motivation to go out and find a more enjoyable position.

Another variation of the button pusher is a junior developer who is tasked with maintaining the source and builds in addition to his or her usual engineering duties. I'd hesitate to even call this person an SCM—the developer is simply completing a duty about which he or she probably hasn't much choice or interest. This person will likely invest little effort when other interesting tasks are available.

The Button Creator

The button creator is empowered to enforce development policies, create builds using programming or scripting, and schedule builds and deployments. The person in this position is much more likely to attend meetings and manage other SCM employees.

For obvious reasons, I term this position the "strong" SCM position. It should be noted that with the extra responsibility and challenge that this position affords can come a great deal of stress. It can be exasperating to juggle the creation of installations, builds, and source control trees. There are times when a single problem may occupy your time for days at a time—all the while, your regularly scheduled tasks still need to be completed.

But even if you approach this position as a stepping stone to development, be sure to do the job well, and people will notice. How many managers do you know would want to promote the button pusher to a development position when someone like the button creator is around?

NOTE *Beware! If you do the job too well, they'll never want to let you out. If you're simply fulfilling the SCM position until another job is offered to you, be sure to get promises (preferably written, but an email will do) that provide for your future. Otherwise, the "You're too valuable where you're at" quote will be thrown at you. Personally, I'd advise you to stick it out in the SCM world. It's a niche market, and it pays well. Remember that there are lots of (very experienced) developers out of work right now.*

Which Should You Be?

I hate to preach, but my mother always said that a job worth doing is worth doing well. Regardless of the choice you make, be sure to fulfill your responsibilities professionally with respect for the other members of the team. This doesn't mean that you can't ever make mistakes—but it does mean that you should always be trying for that "A" in effort in every task you undertake.

If you're just starting out and have a limited amount of time to invest in learning this field, the button pusher position might be right for you. On the other hand, if you want to jump in (and then watch the water flow over the sides of the tub), try for the button creator position. Be honest with your management about your skill level, but make sure it knows how willing you are to take on the extra responsibility. The desire to be accountable (when not taken to extreme) is typically viewed as an attractive attribute. Frankly, the SCM position can be difficult to fill—your managers may be so grateful you took on the job that they'll give in to your every demand.

Be aware that your personality type matters. A strong SCM will often be expected to battle on schedules and other matters. A shy person who has trouble with confrontation may find the button creator position to be fraught with intimidation. And vice versa—a strong personality may find the button pusher position too passive and boring. That's not to say that it's not possible for an introverted person to be happy and satisfied in the strong SCM role—but think about it before you stick your feet in the water.

The Jan Brady Syndrome

Always outshone by a well-seasoned older sister (the development group) and the demands of a younger sister (the quality group), the Jan Brady of the software world must work harder and smarter than everyone else to get noticed.

Believe it or not, if you give it your all, you'll find yourself rewarded in the end. I remember a Chief Executive Officer (CEO) once taking me aside and whispering in my ear that the company couldn't have survived without my specialized contribution.[4] In the meantime, however, get ready for some of the more unglamorous aspects of the SCM position:

> Because the SCM tends to be a loner (especially in small companies or because of departmental locations), no one else really understands the duties of the position and can't always appreciate your most treasured achievements. Be proud of yourself when no one else can be![5]

> When the build breaks or obvious regressions are found, the finger always gets pointed first at the SCM. Shields up, Mr. Spock! Make sure you've done your due diligence and you've completed quality work. And then (sweetly) point to someone else.

> The engineers can get tired of regulations regarding the source and builds. As the messenger, the SCM may be the target for this frustration.

> The quality group gets tired of lousy releases coming out of development. As the funnel who provides the builds, the SCM may, again, be the target of this frustration.

> Get used to being in a position where you must force your will upon others without any direct authority. Make sure you have formalized agreements (and immunity) with the head of the department before implementing new rules that won't be popular.

> Who's going to turn out the lights at night? Take a guess. The SCM has to stay until the build completes—often after all the developers have gone home.

---

4. Of course, it's possible that he took everyone aside and whispered the same thing, but I sure watched for it and didn't see it happen.

5. In fact, some managers have told me that it pays to sometimes "toot your own horn"—especially if your hard-earned accomplishments might go unnoticed.

Understanding the SCM's Most Important Relationship

There are unusual times when the SCM group is formed as its own department in a company. This model tends to be the exception and not the rule. Instead, most SCMs will find themselves strongly attached to the development group. It's a natural fit because the SCM protects the source, institutes check-in policies, and builds the product.

I'd argue that the SCM should also form a strong allegiance with the quality group. Although the SCM position is rooted in the development group, many of its tasks—such as releasing code and smoke testing—could conceivably fall into the realm of quality.

The "Doorway" in the "Wall"

Ah. The Quality-Development Wall. And people thought the Berlin Wall was a tough one to crack. Sure, the wall is metaphorical—but that doesn't mean it doesn't exist.

Your workplace may differ. It might be that your developers and quality engineers lunch together daily and battle over a foosball table. If so, your team is lucky. Because here's the truth of the matter: A quality engineer's job is to tell the world when a developer has made mistakes.

Sure, they don't phrase it that way. And it sounds very ugly. But that's the crux of the position—and, believe me, it's an *extremely* important job. Unfortunately, the job description alone can create a chasm between the development and quality groups. Perhaps you've heard a developer make a disparaging comment about "the wanna-be programmers down the hall" or a quality engineer complain that only a can of Raid could possibly kill all of the bugs in a certain developer's code. The relationship between the two groups can get so rocky—especially during the last crucial development process cycle—that communication slows down to a trickle.

And now put yourself right in the middle of these two groups. Because that's where SCMs will often find themselves. The SCM becomes the doorway in the wall—open the door and product, build notes, and test instructions flow through. Acrimony might flow through as well, but what's an SCM to do?

Embracing the Double Agent Within You

It's natural to develop a "home-team" loyalty to the development group. But it's also important to remember that you can best serve your group by making sure the company continues to generate revenue through the manufacture of quality merchandise. A tough-love approach to your own department is sometimes in order.

Try to think of yourself as the development department's personal quality engineer—a double agent of sorts. To effect this, you may run smoke tests that qualify a minimal amount of functionality in builds. Or you may install builds on department test machines so engineers can check their code integration. You may even compile a list of build notes and testing instructions to pass to the quality department. Sometimes you'll hear yourself berating an engineer when you hear the excuse that "it works on my machine."

In this respect, along with your other source regulations, you may be viewed as a departmental turncoat. Wear the moniker proudly. Because you fulfill this sacred responsibility, the developers are more secure in their employment position.

Quality-Driven Releases

Where does the buck stop during a release process? Where do you draw the line between getting the product out the door and fixing all of the defects that might be found? Many people believe (as do I) that the quality and product managers should work together as the final approver of the release.

Yes, the developers have contributed a lot to the product and deserve to have their voices heard, but it's marketing that should be the final advocate for the customer. What may seem important to you might be considered trivial to the end user—and, more importantly, the converse is also just as true. The marketing group representative must collate information about the state of the product and make an informed decision about when to release it.

And who can provide such information? You guessed it. The quality manager seems to always track the pulse of the product. Is it ready to go out the door? Is it weeks away? Is it days away? In a quality-driven release schedule, the marketing representative and the quality manager can come up with the all-important answers.

Of course, there may be times when getting the product out is more important than quality. I personally believe that this is self-defeating—as discussed earlier, releasing an "unfinished" product can affect how the world perceives your company. On the other hand, if it's a choice between closing the doors of the company and having some serious bugs in the product, you've got to do what you've got to do. Many developers write their code in such a way that, in a pinch, they can "stub" off functionality and push it off to a future release. This can be an ideal compromise when a product must go out the door before certain functionality is stable.

What does this have to do with the SCM? Simply put, pinpoint the final arbiter for the release of product and be sure to inform that person of any risks or problems that might exist within your duty area near release time. You don't want to be the one responsible if the product is found to have a severe defect two days before or after it's released. Never assume that the arbiter knows about problems simply because other coworkers do.

A Sample Development/Quality Process

You've learned about the development process in a general sense. Each of the cycles—vision/planning, product development, and quality—have subprocesses associated with them that the members of the team can follow to ensure that nothing falls between the cracks.

The following is a sample script of the development/quality relationship sub-process during the testing cycle. If your department doesn't currently have an existing written process for this specific task, feel free to adapt this to your needs.

NOTE *This section's intent is to provide an example of a written process. This particular subprocess is specific to the relationship between development and quality during the testing cycle. It's a subprocess of the actual "big-picture" software development process; other aspects of the development cycle, such as planning, aren't included. Those missing aspects, of course, will have sub-processes of their own.*

ANOTHER NOTE *Many steps in this example process may involve tasks that are discussed in more detail in future chapters.*

1. The development manager, lead developer, or project manager assigns tasks to particular developers.

2. The developer gets source as necessary from the source control system.

3. The developer changes source as necessary to fulfill obligations made to development or project managers.

4. The developer thoroughly tests code on his/her machine and is confident that reasonable defects have been found and corrected.

5. The developer checks in code to the source control system.

6. If code is new and requires compilation, the developer informs the SCM to add the component to build.

7. The SCM "burns down" test machines to original precode release state.

8. The SCM labels and versions the source, builds the product, and deploys to development test environment. An automated (if possible) smoke test is run to ensure functionality works as designed.

    a. If the build doesn't pass the smoke test, the problems are fixed and another build (or patch) is completed. Go to step 7.

9. The SCM deploys code to the development test environment. Developers are invited to check the integration of their code on this machine.

    a. If a serious problem is found, it's fixed and another build (or patch) is completed. Go to step 7.

10. Development, the project manager, or the SCM informs the quality manager of build readiness.

11. The quality manager assigns the testing task to the appropriate quality engineer.

12. The quality engineer tests code and enters defect reports as necessary. Other groups may also enter defects as this time as well as entering Requests for Changes (RFCs) in functionality.

13. If there are defects or RFCs (hereafter collectively referred to as *defect*), then the following happens:

    a. The defect gets tracked in the defect tracking system.

    b. The defect is assigned to development or the project manager, and the status is set to *assignment pending*.

    c. When necessary, the Bug Triage committee comes together to determine the severity of bugs and whether they should be addressed in this release or at all. Should a Bug Triage committee not be used, the quality manager and lead developer together determine severity of defect.

   d. If the defect doesn't meet criteria (duplicate, works as designed, requested feature too much work for inclusion, and so on), the defect is assigned to the quality manager for closure or reassignment to the next release.

   e. Development, the product manager, or Bug Triage assigns the defect to the appropriate developer.

14. The defect enters the development process and is fixed by developer. (Go to step 1.)

15. When coding for the defect is complete, the developer sets the status in the defect tracking software to be *Completed, Developer Testing.*

16. The developer thoroughly unit tests his or her code on development test machines.

17. Developer sets the status of the defect to be *Ready for Verification by Quality.*

18. If the defect was reported by quality, then the developer assigns the defect back to originating quality engineer.

19. If the defect was reported by any other entity, then the following steps take place:

   a. The developer assigns the defect to the quality manager.

   b. The quality manager assigns the defect to the quality engineer.

20. The quality engineer verifies that the defect was fixed to specification.

21. If the defect isn't correctly fixed or has caused a regression, then the following steps take place:

   a. The defect is reassigned to development or the project manager.

   b. The development project manager reassigns the defect to the developer.

   c. This process loops until the quality engineer verifies that the defect has been properly addressed.

22. The quality engineer closes the defect once verified.

Becoming the Release Manager

After the bug fixing begins and the SCM starts building the product more often, he or she is often put into the role of release manager for both end users and internal customers. But don't shoulder this responsibility completely—you can spread the joy around make this job a little easier.

First, make sure that the development team members feel empowered. They should know—either directly from you or from higher up on the food chain—that getting a build to quality or out the door is a group effort. Everyone is responsible for the success or failure to achieve that goal.

The first step in making that happen is to ensure that the developers stay in the building until the quality group has accepted the build. In small companies with smaller products, this is perfectly reasonable. Of course, if this process ends up taking days instead of hours, the SCM and the development manager should negotiate how and when the developers will be available during the build process. This might include pass-around pagers or being "on call" for the SCM as necessary.

TIP *Start your builds earlier in the day, and you'll increase the chance of finishing the job before the whistle blows in the late afternoon or early evening.*

Developers might argue that their jobs end when the build begins, but this is an absolute fallacy. What happens when a component doesn't build? Or if a bug is found during smoke testing? Ideally, of course, the developers check their work on test machines after the build has completed (see the best practices section in Chapter 7, "In the SCM Lab" for more information). But even if it means that they're playing pinball in the kitchen or hanging out with a basketball in the parking lot, every developer who has code included in the build should be compelled to be available until the product has been accepted by the quality group.

This whole process leads to the all-important release to customers. Build yourself a checklist for when this magic time approaches so you won't forget important things to complete, such as virus checking the software. Refer to Chapter 11, "Deployments," for more information.

I can't describe the satisfaction you'll feel by being the last person to "touch" the software before it goes out the door—it's a great feeling. When you're finished, be sure to send out a celebratory email or run to the kitchen to join the party.

Summary

This chapter's purpose was to tell you about the software development process and how the SCM fits into it. The SCM can fit into the process in many different ways.

First, the chapter covered the different groups that make up the development team:

- Marketing

- Product/program management

- Development

- Software configuration management

- Documentation

- Quality

- Release management

- Technical support

Then you learned about the three cycles of the development process and how the SCM fits into each of these cycles:

- Vision/planning

- Product development

- Quality

Lastly, the chapter discussed some of the challenges that the SCM will face during the development process and how the position can act as an interface between the development and quality groups. It discussed the different kinds of SCM positions and spoke about the release of the software to both internal and external users.

After reading this chapter, you should have an understanding of how the software development process works and how you might choose to apply yourself to it at your company.

All About the Source

WHENEVER YOU HAVE something precious, you want to keep it somewhere safe. You keep your money in the bank. Perhaps you have jewelry locked away in a safe deposit box. You tuck your children into bed snugly and then lock the doors to your house.

It's an uncertain world, and there are thousands of circumstances waiting to separate you from your valuables. You are under constant threat from theft, fire, tornadoes...the list goes on and on. Good software configuration management can help you protect your company's most important assets from disasters such as these.

And better yet, you can take that safety net one step further. How would you like to be protected from bad decisions? Imagine this scenario: You invest $10,000 in the stock market. Your stock plunges. Now imagine getting into your time machine and stopping yourself from making that original investment—no strings attached.

A good source control system allows you to do just that. By taking "snapshots" of your code at certain intervals in its development, you'll always be able to travel back in time. For instance, if your product stops working after a bug fix, you'll be able to compare the differences between the current version and a previous version to help troubleshoot the problem.

To take advantage of this functionality, you'll need to get your hands on a source control database and its corresponding set of tools. Chapter 4, "Source Control Tools," discusses several available systems. But before getting to the specifics of the tools, let's use this chapter to discuss the fundamentals shared by each of the software configuration management databases.

Organizing Files with the Source Tree

The organization of files on your hard drive makes your life much easier. It would be difficult to find a particular file if everything on your hard drive was lumped into one location. And worse, you'd only be able to use filenames once—and just think of how many README files exist on your computer now!

Operating systems solve this problem by allowing the creation of directories (also known as *folders* on some operating systems) that can collect related files together. Again, it wouldn't have been flexible to lump all of those directories at your root—so the hierarchical directory structure was created. This allows the user to place directories inside of other directories.

Whether you're using Windows, Macintosh, Linux KDE, or pretty much any operating system graphical interface, this type of hierarchy is presented to you in what is known as a *tree*. The tree allows you to navigate to and from different files on your hard drive using a mouse click—in much the same way that you can move from your sister to your first cousin Julie in your family tree. This graphical tree has different names depending on the operating system—such as the Explorer in Windows or the View in Linux's KDE.

What you see, however, isn't how the operating system truly stores those files—it wouldn't be efficient from the computer's perspective. Instead, depending on your operating system, files are stored in a table more akin to a spreadsheet or a database. For instance, you've probably heard of the File Allocation Table (FAT), which was used by the Disk Operating System (DOS) and older Windows operating systems to keep track of the files on x86 machines. Other file systems you may have heard of are the New Technology File System (NTFS) for Windows and the Hierarchical File System (HFS) for some other operating systems such as Macintosh and Linux.

Understanding the Tree and Its Trunk

You can apply the same paradigm to the tool you choose to use for source control. This tool is typically made up of two parts—a database that holds the source and a client that allows the source tree to be traversed and acted upon in a graphical way.

The source control tool's database is like a virtual hard drive that keeps track of files and their attributes and then displays them in a way that makes their organization easy to manage. Depending on the features of your tool, it's possible that this database may conveniently appear as another drive on your computer.

Although there are many similarities between your file system and your source control database, there are also several important differences: First, a good source control system will never allow you to permanently remove files from its database. Instead, it will mark them as hidden—this allows you to recover files long after they've been "deleted." Second, in most cases, the source control tool's database will be self-contained for easy backup and administration.

NOTE *Unfortunately, secure as they are, source control tools aren't the software equivalent to a human superhero. By saying that good tools don't allow permanent deletions of files doesn't mean that a typical operating system command won't accidentally wipe these files—and years of work— off of a disk in an unrecoverable way. Care and a strong security model should always be used on machines that house a source database.*

In addition to these qualities, source control tools go one step further. They allow you to save multiple versions of the same file.

To understand this better, it's important to see that the source code that makes up your software goes through many drafts before it's complete enough to be released as a product. New features are added, bugs get fixed, functionality is scrapped—the reasons for updating code are too numerous to mention. You can compare it to creating a large manuscript using a word processing document. It will go through many drafts and iterations before it can be sent to a publishing house. And imagine this: After deleting a huge chunk of text in the word processing document and saving it, what if the operating system had saved the previous version of the file and now allows you to open it?

For the time being, this may be a pipe dream for operating systems, but it's a reality for source control tools. Suddenly the file system has hit the third dimension. Not only does it keep track of directories and files; it keeps track of every version of these files that has ever existed!

This allowance for the coexistence of multiple drafts is called *version control* or *revision control*. It allows developers to revert to more stable code or thumb through previous drafts of the same file in order to retrieve deleted information. Unlike the pipe dream mentioned previously, however, these drafts aren't updated to the source control database automatically every time a file is saved—that would create enormous overhead on the tool. Instead, this update task falls into the hands of the developer working on the code. When he or she has fixed a bug in a source file, this new version is *checked in*, which tells the source control tool to add the file's changes to its database.

Let's check out some examples that demonstrate how important version control is to software development in the real world. Keep in mind that every source control database is different—though they all share similar features—and the steps taken to fulfill tasks may slightly differ.

You may remember that previous chapters talked about the company making Bob's Office Software and some of the problems the team encountered. But things are looking up at Bob's Software Company—Bob has bought a new source control tool, and the team is ready to start following proper software configuration management procedures in their development process.

The first thing that the new software configuration manager or product architect does is break down the product into the smallest possible parts, as discussed in the first chapter. These parts, or *projects* as we'll call them, represent all the components that make up the product. A tree is created on a typical computer's hard drive in a temporary location with each component project separated into its own directory. This directory contains all the source files required to build the project component. Once these project directories are created, they're typically separated into logical family groups on the file system—for instance, projects for the client Graphical User Interface (GUI) might be added to a parent directory called *client*, as displayed in Figure 3-1. In the case of Bob's Office Software, a similar tree might indicate where the word processor and spreadsheet projects reside.

Figure 3-1. A generic file system example of a source tree

 NOTE *Please keep in mind that this chapter is a high-level overview of source control tools. Breaking down a product for builds and for its addition to source control is described with much more detail in Chapter 8, "Basic Builds," and Chapter 9, "Builds for Windows .NET."*

Now let's discuss how the developers at Bob's Software Company might actually use their new source control tool. Jenny, a member of the development team, is writing a new C-language component for Bob's Office Software suite. She starts writing the code on her own computer and stores it on her local hard drive. At some point, Jenny will reach a point of completion—a relative state that might indicate it's ready to be deployed or, more often, that she's no longer comfortable keeping the only copy of the source on her hard drive.

In Listing 3-1, take a look at Jenny's first version of source that she put into a file called ENTRY.CPP.

Listing 3-1. Jenny's First Version of Source

```
#include <stdio.h>

void main()
{
    printf("Welcome to Bob's Office Software!");
}
```

This is a simple program whose only function is to display the text *Welcome to Bob's Office Software!* Don't worry about understanding what the code is doing—the goal here is to understand its relationship to the source control tool.

Because Jenny has worked long and hard on this code—okay, it's actually pretty simple, but for the sake of this example, let's pretend she did—she's ready to add this file to the source control system. Depending on the tool she uses, she either navigates to a drive that's masquerading as the source control database or engages the source tool's client through an operating system command. She might create a new project called *Entry* and then add the file to the project's location in the source control database. The tool might render the file to appear as in Figure 3-2.

Figure 3-2. Jenny's addition to the source control database

Because this is the first time code has ever been put in the database, Jenny has added the code to the *trunk* of the tree. In this example, you're going to work linearly with Jenny's source. This means that every change she wants to make to the ENTRY.CPP file will be for the main release of product. Later, as if working in separate dimensions, Jenny will be able to work on the file for two different releases, each with their own set of changes and functionality. For the time being, however, you're only concerned that she's added her code to the "first" dimension—the database's trunk.

Making File Revisions

Jenny has returned the next day, ready to continue her programming. After reading her functional specification, she finds that she needs to ask her user for a name—thereby personalizing the user's welcome.

She's ready to make these changes. But remember—she already added a version of the file to the source control database yesterday. In order to add new changes to the file, she must let the source control tool know she's planning on working on the file by fulfilling a process called *checking out*. This command will copy the file from the source control database to Jenny's file system and then mark the file as "being edited" to other developers who might be interested. If she doesn't want any other developers to work on the file at the same time, she can set it to be *exclusively locked*. When a file is exclusively locked, the source control database will no longer let other developers edit it. She can then make her changes and put the new version of the file into the source control tool's database. She has now added a new *revision*. Listing 3-2 displays her changes.

Listing 3-2. Jenny's Contribution to the Release

```
#include <stdio.h>
void main()
{
    char szName[128];
    printf( "Please enter your name: " );
    gets( szName );
    printf("Hello %c!  Welcome to Bob's Office Software!", szName);
}
```

Because there are now two versions of the same file in the source database, the tool must have a way to differentiate between them. Source tools generally have a numbering scheme for the revisions of files, so let's say that this tool keeps tracks of revisions and assigns them a number that increments as Jenny adds new versions of the code. For example, the first file she added was identified by the number 1.1. The next revision she adds would be numbered 1.2, followed by 1.3, 1.4, 1.5, and so on…. Whichever revision is the latest to be added on the trunk is called the *tip*. The tip can also refer collectively to the latest revisions of all files on the trunk.

NOTE *The period in the revision identification number (for example, 1.5) is often used as a delimiter between branches and revisions. The later "Branches" section covers just that.*

To keep the size of the source control database as small as possible, a good source tool will track only the differences between the two revisions (also known as the *delta*) instead of storing an entire copy of the new ENTRY.CPP. Unfortunately, many tools can store only the deltas for text files—binary files such as JPGs or EXEs must have each of their revisions stored in their entirety. This is another excellent reason to avoid storing binary files in your source control database whenever possible.

NOTE *This chapter is a high-level overview of source control tools. Many specific strategies, including how to deal with binary files and other best practices, are described with more detail in Chapter 7, "In the SCM Lab."*

Checking In and Checking Out: The Source Control Motel

Several days later, Jenny goes on a long-deserved vacation to Peru. Unfortunately, as soon as she leaves the building, Mickey finds a bug in her code. Instead of using the %s specification in her printf statement, she has mistakenly entered a %c. Mickey must somehow get the file from the tip, fix the bug, and quickly put out a new version of the software.

Because the programming team is using a source control database, this isn't a problem. These tools are designed for collaborative use among a team of programmers. As long as the software configuration management administrator has given him the proper security rights, Mickey can make changes to the ENTRY.CPP file.

The ability to get files and add revisions is generally known as *checking out* and *checking in* source—and every source control database will have some sort of mechanism to fulfill this functionality (though the terminology may differ).

The steps Mickey will take are as follows:

1. Mickey starts the source control database client and enters a user name and password as necessary.

2. He selects the filename from the tree and checks it out. This tells the database that he's working on the file and will copy the latest version of it (in this case, 1.1) to his local hard drive. Depending on the tool, checking out a file will also exclusively lock it for Mickey's use.

3. Mickey changes %c in Jenny's code to %s. He's careful as he makes his changes. He doesn't want his fix to cause another problem. As discussed in Chapter 2, "SCM and the Software Development Process," if his fix, in fact, does break another part of the product, it is called a *regression*.

4. Mickey checks the file back into the database. This creates a new version, 1.2.

The new version of the software with the fix can now be built and distributed as necessary. If, when Jenny returns, she finds that Mickey has incorrectly changed her code, she can either check in a new version or *revert* to her previous version, 1.1. She must be careful when reverting—some tools will delete the 1.2 revision of the file permanently. More sophisticated tools have a numbering scheme that allows the new revision to appear deleted even though it's still safely stored in the database.

But wait a minute…what happens if two people need to check out the same file at the same time? That's an excellent question. In many cases, the tool allows only one person to check out a file at a time. For instance, with this tool, when Mickey checks out ENTRY.CPP, it becomes exclusively locked by default, and no one else can check in another revision until he has checked his in. Some tools may allow more than one developer to check out the same file at the same time. The benefit is that more than one person can work on a piece of code at a time. The disadvantage is that one person will always have to manually or programmatically weave their changes into the version checked in by the other.

What's in a Label?

As you can imagine, source databases grow quickly. It's not uncommon to have tens of thousands of files and their revisions in a single source control database. That's pretty daunting in itself, but now consider this scenario: Three months ago, the team released version 1 of Bob's Office Software. Suddenly, a call comes into tech support: Bob's word processor has a bug that erases users' hard drives. The team has to fix this bug—and fast. But they've been working fervently on version 2, and all the files have changed significantly.

That leads to a mad scramble. Scores of revisions have been added to the database, and no one is really sure which ones actually made up the release version. Some files have 20 revisions, and others have been checked in only twice. Trying to figure out what revision every file was at a certain date and time can be difficult. It's conceivable that the software configuration manager has created a spreadsheet with revision numbers for each release listed on it, but that would be a full-time job all by itself.

The team will be relieved to know that their source control tool has a feature called *labeling*, which can be used for future releases. When you create a label, you take a snapshot of the tip (the collection of the latest versions of all files discussed earlier). This label is like a list of all of the files in the source control database and their current revisions, as displayed in Figure 3-3. Many tools additionally allow you to adjust which revision numbers of files are part of a label. Some even let you create a label from an earlier time and date.

Label	entry.cpp	entry.h
Build 1	1.7	1.5
Build 2	1.13	1.5
Release 1	1.18	1.7

Figure 3-3. The source control database keeps track of releases by mapping file revisions using labels.

To make this easier to conceptualize, imagine a label being a long piece of rope that attaches revisions of documents together, as displayed in Figure 3-4.

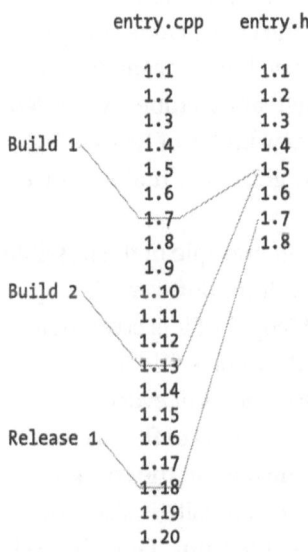

Figure 3-4. The rope that attaches revisions together is a label

Understanding Branches

But now that you can see which revisions of files actually were released to the customers, what can you do about the hard drive erase bug? How can the team continue working on the new features of version 2.0 while still supporting existing customers of version 1.0? If you simply fix the bug using the tip, you may accidentally include version 2.0 code and features!

So far, you've only worked in a single dimension—all of the files have been in one project destined for a single release. *Branching* the source gives you the flexibility you need to support two lines of code. It allows programmers to work on two "versions" of the same source at the same time. Branching normally occurs once a major milestone has been achieved, but this can vary greatly among development teams. There may often be times when you'll want to branch pieces of all your code or subsets of it for one reason or another.

 NOTE *Branching correctly can be a huge challenge, and some companies have determinedly found ways to live without it. I'll talk about branching in this section because it's a common software configuration management duty. However, it's perfectly reasonable if your team decides that branching doesn't fit into your development process. You and the developers should get well used to using any new source control tool before ever considering a branching strategy.*

Let's look at branching from the view of the folks developing Bob's Office Software, had they chosen to do so three months ago. After the champagne stopped flowing, the team split up into two groups. Most of the developers began to implement features for Release 2.0 of the software. But several team members were dedicated to fixing bugs found in Release 1.0. Periodically, new builds of Release 1.0 with these fixes go out to consumer. This second team is given the "maintenance group" moniker.

The source was then branched. Figure 3-5 displays an example of the possible branching strategy used by developers working on Bob's Office Software. A snapshot of the Release 1.0 code was taken, and a simulated "copy" of it is created in the source control database. This copy is often displayed as a new folder in the source tree. To the developer, this looks as if there are two copies of every file—but this is an illusion. Instead, the new branch points to the revisions of files as they were right when the branching command occurred. As the files on the trunk change, the source control tool hides it on the branch. The opposite is also true—files may change on the branch, but the tool hides this on the trunk. Only the revisions that were created on a branch will appear in that branch.

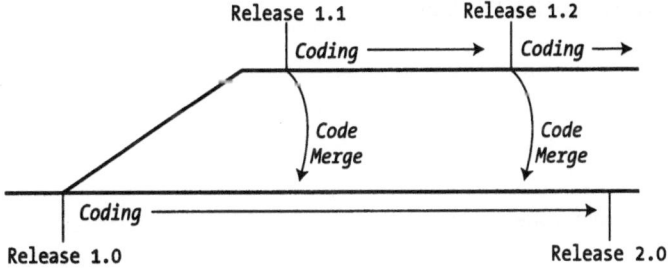

Figure 3-5. Source code branch example

For example, if the maintenance team checked out the previous example ENTRY.CPP when it was version 1.45 and checked it into the new maintenance branch, it might be numbered 1.45.1. The version number now also reflects the *parent branch* of the version (version 1.45 in the trunk) as well as the version created from the parent (the final 1). If the document in the new branch never changes, the source control database will simply continue to point to the original version of the file *as it was when it was branched*.

As the team fixes bugs, the source control tool lets the developers check in files to the Release 1.0 branch without a fuss. A new version is saved, and the "pointer" to the file for the branch is updated to reflect the change.

And then things get a little complicated. If the maintenance team only checks in bug fixes to the Release 1.0 branch, those fixes will never find their way to the second release of the product. Imagine the uproar of Bob's customers if bugs that were fixed by a maintenance patch suddenly appeared again in the more expensive Release 2.0 of the product!

To get around this problem, the defects corrected by the maintenance group in the Release 1.0 branch must also be integrated into the Release 2.0 branch. This process is called *merging* branches.

Luckily, any files in the main branch that haven't been touched since Release 1.0 are easily updated. The developer can simply check in the file, and the source control tool updates the file without complaint.

It gets more difficult when changes have been made to both the Release 1.0 branch and the Release 2.0 branch. Let's look at the previous example of ENTRY.CPP. When the product was branched at Release 1.0, the code looked as it does in Listing 3-3.

Listing 3-3. The Release Version of ENTRY.CPP

```
#include <stdio.h>
void main()
{
    char szName[128];
    printf( "Please enter your name: " );
    gets( szName );
    printf("Hello %s!  Welcome to Bob's Office Software!", szName);
}
```

The marketing group has decided that the welcome sentence isn't obsequious enough, and Mickey, now a member of the maintenance group, has been given the responsibility of adding another sentence to the welcome screen. He makes his change, as displayed in bold in Listing 3-4, and checks it into the Release 1.0 branch.

Listing 3-4. Mickey's Changes to ENTRY.CPP in the Maintenance Branch

```
#include <stdio.h>
void main()
{
    char szName[128];
    printf( "Please enter your name: " );
    gets( szName );
    printf("Hello %s!  Welcome to Bob's Office Software!  Thanks for purchasing ↵
        Bob's Office software.", szName);
}
```

Meanwhile, Jenny had been hard at work on the features for Release 2.0. Listing 3-5 displays her changes to ENTRY.CPP in bold. Keep in mind that she is working with a different revision of the ENTRY.CPP file—Mickey's change doesn't yet exist on her branch.

Listing 3-5. Jenny's Changes to ENTRY.CPP in the Maintenance Branch

```
#include <stdio.h>
void main()
{
    char szName[128];
    char szIntials[4];
    printf( "Please enter your name: " );
    gets( szName );
```

```
    printf("Hello %s!  Welcome to Bob's Office Software!\n", szName);
    printf("Please enter your initials: ");
    gets( szInitials );
    printf("From now on, you can add your initials to a document by pressing ⏎
        <CTRL>-D.");
}
```

Jenny checks in her changes to the Release 2.0 branch and then moves on to other new features. But Mickey is faced with a conundrum: He needs to make sure his bug fix gets into the trunk of the code. When checking in his changes to the Release 2.0 branch, he must also preserve the changes that Jenny has made.

Luckily, the source control database provides tools for just this problem. He chooses to check in his code to the Release 2.0 branch—but this time, the tool complains. It tells him that a newer version of ENTRY.CPP has already been checked into the Release 2.0 branch. In other words, his version of the source file is *stale*—he needs to compare his changes to Jenny's, create a new file with the combined changes, and check that one in instead.

This sounds like a daunting task—and it certainly can be in large files with many changes—but in this case, both his and Jenny's modifications were rather simple. In some scenarios, the changes made to the file are so removed from each other that the source control tool can automatically merge the files together and display the changes before the new file is checked in.

For Mickey, however, the tool will find a *conflict*: a set of changes between the files that either involve the same lines of code or are too close to each other for the tool's comfort. Mickey is therefore given the task to manually merge the files together. This task can be difficult and time-consuming—the reason that some companies prefer not to use the branching mechanism of their source control tools.

Using a tool provided by the source control database, Mickey compares the two files. After determining that Jenny's fix is still relevant after his change is introduced, he manually merges the file together, as displayed in Listing 3-6. Mickey's changes are in bold, and Jenny's previous changes are italicized.

Listing 3-6. Mickey's Merged ENTRY.CPP *File*

```
#include <stdio.h>
void main()
{
    char szName[128];
    char szIntials[4];
    printf( "Please enter your name: " );
    gets( szName );
    printf("Hello %s!  Welcome to Bob's Office Software!  Thanks for purchasing ⏎
```

```
        Bob's Office software.\n", szName);
    printf("Please enter your initials: ");
    gets( szInitials );
    printf("From now on, you can add your initials to a document by pressing
        <CTRL>-D.");
}
```

After Mickey completes the merge, he checks the new file into the Release 2.0 branch. What happens when Jenny tries to check in further changes to the file? She might be told that the revision of the file that she has on her hard drive is stale, and she'll have to merge the files much like Mickey did. More than likely, though, she'll check the source database and get Mickey's changes before she again starts working on the file.

<hr />

Which Version Should Be the Trunk?

Branching isn't nearly as cut and dried as it seems. So, the first release of your product has gone out the door. Now it's time to come up with a strategy where the developers can fix defects on the first release while still allowing for the addition of new functionality to the second release.

It might seem logical to create a new Release 2.0 branch from the trunk and maintain the first release on the trunk. If you choose this approach, you'll have to continually create new branches atop the last ones as shown in the following figure.

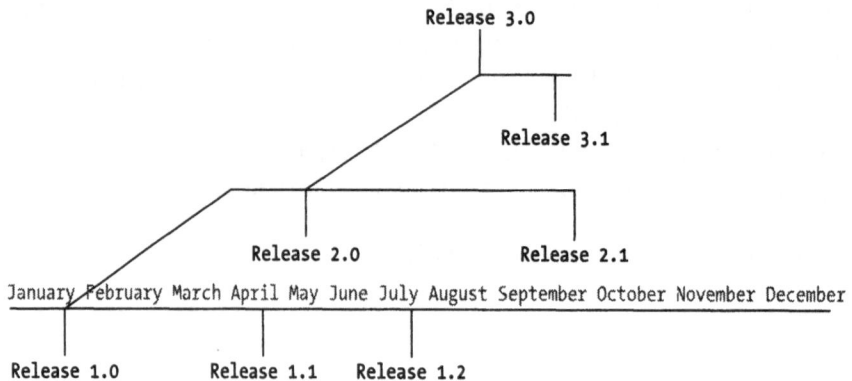

There are several reasons why this isn't the best approach:

1. Users never know where the "tip" of the code is. What's the latest version of ENTRY.CPP? Developers are going to have to figure out where the tip is on their own.

2. A new branch has to be created for every release regardless of whether a maintenance version is planned.

3. If a developer works on code for a future release before the current one is out the door, he or she has to copy over all that work to the new branch. This is time-consuming and error-prone.

4. Working on two branches concurrently is difficult—but now imagine having three or more releases at the same time. What a nightmare! Which version of the code do you start working in? Which branches would you merge to, and which ones would you leave be?

Instead, explore the idea of always using the trunk of the source tree for all major releases, as shown in the following figure.

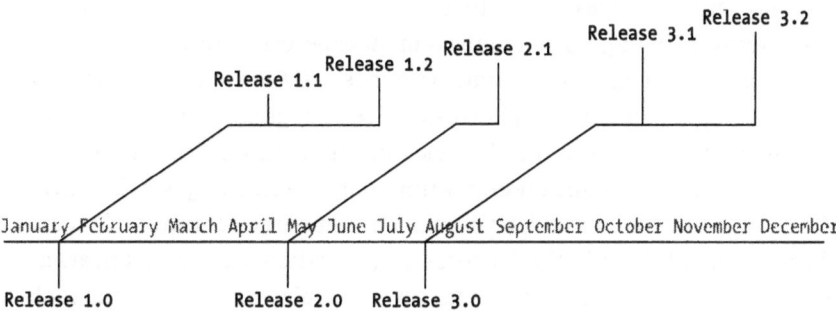

Using this approach, all users know where the "latest" code can be found because it's always in the trunk. Releases without maintenance never need to be branched. Most important, the branches stay flat and close to the trunk—allowing for easier merging.

As a footnote, keep in mind that no matter what anyone says or plans in the software world, business needs change frequently and might dictate unexpected releases. Always be flexible in architecting your branches. For instance, you may not think that a maintenance branch will ever be necessary—but that won't satisfy your boss when the sales department is breaking down his or her door for an interim release to satisfy hungry customers.

Using branches in this manner is known as working in a *parallel* development environment versus that of a *serial* one where all releases exist in a single branch and are completed one at a time. Parallel development is often necessary for working on different versions of the software at the same time—however, there are many other uses for branches that may not be obvious from the outset.

For example, let's say it's time for a preliminary build of the Release 2.0 branch that will be used internally for testing. It's quite possible that the development manager may instruct developers to only check in small bug fixes that won't affect the stability of the branch. Jenny needs to continue to add large new features during testing, but if she checks in her work, there's a good chance she might break existing functionality. Should she stop working?

There isn't any need to stop functionality development while the release is tested. Instead, a new branch can be created in which she and other team members can continue to work while the release is stabilized. This branch would be completely separate from both the Release 1.0 and Release 2.0 branches, and any change she makes won't affect either of them. Once the development manager gives her the okay and she has thoroughly tested her code, she can merge her new functionality into the Release 2.0 branch.

Many software configuration management experts recommend that *all* changes be made in their own separate branches and then added to their parent branches only after being thoroughly tested. This can greatly enhance the stability of the main branch. Of course, this has a serious tradeoff—quick fixes are no longer quick, and every change requires time-consuming merges. I find this kind of strict change control too rigid; if you must use this kind of strategy, I recommend you use it only later in the process—such as when the product nears a release milestone and must be frozen for several weeks. Of course, some tools can help make this scenario more acceptable.

Sharing Files Between Branches

You're going to find that there are times when a single component will be shared between several branches. For instance, in the case of Bob's Office Software, it's clear that the spell checker may not have to be changed often—its functionality is complete after its first release, and only defect fixing will take place throughout its life.

Some source control tools have a feature that will allow you to "share" the same file throughout a number of branches. In the current scenario, the spell checker files would be shared in both the tip and the Release 1.0 maintenance branch. If any of its files are changed in one branch, those modifications will appear automatically to all branches. This is analogous to the link functionality in the Unix operating system.

This may seem like a great solution—and, certainly, it's tempting to be able to make changes in only one place. Why? Well, if the files exist unshared in two or more branches, any changes have to be propagated to each version of the file. This can be both time-consuming and error-prone. Whether the developer physically makes the change in all the files or a merge takes place, mistakes can happen that may show up later as a regression. But this is a double-edged sword. If a developer makes what he thinks is a harmless change in a shared file on one branch, all the other branches containing the file may suddenly have a regression.

So what's the solution? You're presented with a "six-of-one, half-dozen-of-the-other" kind of scenario. Sometimes, especially in the software configuration management world, you'll find that the best solution is to come up with a third option.

When designing your source database, take a good look at the components that make up your release. Are all the components really one "product?" More than likely, you'll find that some components stand completely on their own—they don't share any code with other portions of the product and could, in theory, be deployed on their own. The previously discussed spell checker is an excellent example of a free-standing project. If you're working in the Windows environment, you might find that the spell checker is shipped as several Dynamic Link Libraries (DLLs) and a binary data file containing the correct spellings of words.

In this scenario, version 1.0 of the spell check tool can ship with Release 1.0 of Bob's Office Software and can also be shipped unchanged with Release 2.0. When you fix defects in the spell check's code, you update its release number, and this new version will ship with any new releases of Bob's Office Software. You create labels for the products and their revisions just as the source control tool would a file.

Keep these ideas in mind:

Every "component" should have its own version number. Releases of software will include several of these components. You'll have to keep track of what makes up a release—this methodology will be discussed more thoroughly in future chapters of this book.

Sharing files between branches should be the exception and not the rule. And it's best not done at all. If you find that you're sharing files that form a component, consider splitting the component out into its own project.

Advocate the componentization of the product during the design phase to your architects. As a software architect once told me, products "should be designed for delivery."

Developers will always choose the path of least resistance when it comes to your development process. When they ask you to share files between branches, always ensure that the reasoning is sound. There are few circumstances where file sharing should actually be necessary.

WORD OF THE DAY

in·val'u·å·ble, a.

Watch out for the bus.

You may be shocked to hear that software developers are disproportionately injured and killed by runaway buses.

"Well," you might hear a developer manager say, "If Bill were hit by a bus tomorrow, then Ken would need to know what was going on so he could take over the project."

No, the manager isn't being cavalier about Bill's life. It's actually not even true that buses kill software developers more frequently than other people. It's true, however, that the large vehicle is often used as an example during risk management discussions. It's often easier to use the bus metaphor than list all the reasons an employee might not be around tomorrow—such as a better job offer or the loss of an appendage. There must always be plans in place for when someone is unavailable to work.

Regardless of the reason, it's imperative that you watch out for the bus in your role as software configuration manager. Especially in a small company, software configuration managers often become indispensable to the team. He or she is the only one who knows all the passwords, how to build the product, and how to unlock files when someone goes out of town.

You may think that's great job security. It is indeed—and you'll certainly feel it every time you make a request for vacation or attempt to be sick. Whenever software configuration managers plan to go away for more than a day or two, development managers begin to twitch and speak in tongues. Unless you provide the ability for other people to do your job in your absence, you'll feel enormous pressure to always be available to the team.

Lastly, at the end of the day, you probably like the people with which you work. If you were to be offered a great job or win the lottery, you'd want to leave with a clear conscience and make sure your friends are in good hands. "Watching out for the bus" will give you the luxury of sleeping easy at night.

Exploring Strategies for Control

This chapter has gone over some fairly general software configuration management concepts so far. Branching, labeling, versioning—every source control database is going to have functionality that can complete these tasks.

But a source control tool can only go so far. There's a point where a human being must use his or her judgment in order to secure releases in a timely manner. The rest of this chapter is dedicated to concepts that go beyond the scope of your source control tool.

Naming Your Releases

Tiffany from the marketing department has just rushed into Bob's office. Bob's Office Software Release 2.0, she says, must absolutely go out the door by the end of the month in order to meet a necessary marketing window.

Bob clutches his heart. Release 2.0 is two weeks behind schedule. There's no way his team will be able to pull it all together in the time available. No sweat, says Tiff. All the market really wants is the ability to use formatting styles…a feature that's already complete and ready to go.

Bob breathes a sigh of relief. Jerry, the software configuration manager on the project, however, is horrified. All of the documentation, all of the design documents, all of the labels…*everything* reflects the name *Release 2.0*. If this one feature goes out now as Release 2.0, then the rest of features will have to deploy as version 3.0…. Every employee now knows exactly what comprises Release 2.0 (now suddenly Release 3.0) and the former Release 3.0 (now Release 4.0). The confusion will be extraordinary. How will Jerry get himself out of this mess?

Unfortunately, there's not much Jerry will be able to do. He's stuck—he'll put in hours of work to deal with this problem. And the team will suffer endless confusion as they try to sort it all out. But if he had planned correctly, Jerry could have skirted around this roadblock fairly easily.

Most software development companies have internal names for their releases. These names become associated with certain bundles of functionality rather than with release dates. In this way, development teams can easily change schedules, components, and order of releases without unproductive misunderstandings.

You may have heard of some of the more famous internal names. Remember when Windows 95 was known as *Chicago*? Or that Windows 2000 was once named *Cairo*? Microsoft decided on famous cities for the internal names of its operating systems. What do famous impressionist painters, North American rivers, and the crew of *Star Trek* have in common? They're all themes used for development in companies for which I've worked.

What you choose for your themes doesn't really matter—though it's best to keep them in good taste. In theory, these names shouldn't be publicized, but all too often they end up in marketing materials…. Customers may stay away from products named after serial killers or adult video stars. What does matter is that diverse themes be applied to all of your different products and that all members of the team use the monikers.

Let's take a look at the previous example. Perhaps Jerry chose a monster theme for the internal names of the products. The functionality for the next release (what we've referred to as Release 2.0) is called *Dracula,* and the following (Release 3.0) is *Wolfman.* Tiffany suddenly rushes into the room and says that formatting styles must go out the door by the end of the month. No problem, says Jerry. He'll pull out the files that comprise the feature into its own release and name it *Frankenstein*. It can go out in two weeks. Dracula and Wolfman's functionality—and names!—remain unchanged, and the two releases will go out as previously scheduled.

Of course, Jerry doesn't get off scot-free. He'll still have to spend a small amount of time changing the version numbers for the products before they go out the door—but that's just another good deed that goes unnoticed. Because nobody was confused by the schedule change, no one has noticed the efficiency of his internal names.

NOTE *Ideally, each product that a company develops should have its own moniker theme. If they're also released together in a separate suite, that logical gathering should also have a naming convention.*

The development team usually owns the internal naming of products. Themes and names should be chosen early in the design stage, and the theme should have many choices to it—smaller releases tend to pop up when you don't expect them. Had Jerry chosen to use states as his theme (such as California and Nevada), he might have been forced to use American territories such as Guam or Samoa in the unlikely scenario that he had more than 50 releases.

Lastly, make sure that the name sticks to a bundle of functionality and not to a date. A name shouldn't change because the schedule does—even if the order of product releases changes. It's tempting to base names on release dates rather than by functionality, but then the solution doesn't solve a problem. By using internal names consistently, communication regarding releases requires much less effort.

Securing Your Source

So you've added your code to the source control tool's database. But what happens to it now? Who keeps it safe? Remember—your company's source code is its most important asset. It should be treated like cash.

Of course, you would put cash in a bank. They build banks to be strong and secure. But what would happen to the bank if nobody cared for it? After a few months, the vault locks start rusting and sticking. After a few years, the masonry crumbles. Wood warps.

Without proper care and maintenance, the bank falls apart, and your money can be stolen or destroyed. You can apply this same analogy to your source control tool's database. And the chore of maintaining your source will fall upon you. The first and most important step in this maintenance program is to decide who has the rights to read, change, and administer your source tree.

NOTE *Chapter 7, "In the SCM Lab," includes a section on calendaring the maintenance of your source control database.*

So…who does have rights? Every development shop is different, so you'll want to check with the management of the teams with which you work. But the following are some things to remember:

Anyone who has read rights to your source control database also has the ability to copy that source to removable media and remove it from your premises.

Generally, the nontechnical divisions of your company don't need access to the source—even at a read-only basis. It would be unusual for a sales or marketing team member to want to see code. In fact, you should question a request to do so.

In small companies, it's usual that the entire development team (meaning those who write code) has read-write access to the full tree. You'll quickly regret being too draconian with rights—not so much because of the criticism with which you'll have to deal, but more because you'll be the one who has to change the access level whenever a developer actually needs to get to source that's currently off limits.

Nontechnical folks tend to be oblivious (even more so than developers) to considerations of disk space and the correct types of files to check in. In fact, I've seen folks dump tens of megabytes of useless garbage into the source database because they didn't know any better. This can be irreversible if you have a tool that doesn't allow true deletions. If you're going to allow nontechnical people to check in and out, make sure you spend some time on education or create a separate tree just for them.

Unless there are compelling reasons to do otherwise, it's best that the documentation and quality team members should have write access only for their specific areas—for instance, when quality wants to version their test scripts. In general, they should have only read access to the product source. This may get some complaints; oftentimes, the best response to the complaint is the question, "Why do you need any other kind of access?" No one should have access to the source without good reason.

Administration rights to the database should be limited to the software configuration manager and one other person who can act as a backup. You may decide that some tasks are not "administrative" as much as utilitarian. For instance, if you need to create a branch for every single change, it's ridiculous to allow only the software configuration manager this ability. However, if branching should occur only when releases are completed, you may want this right to be limited in nature. Think about your policies and set your security levels accordingly.

A strong development process isn't an excuse for lax security. Just because you've told your fellow employees the rules doesn't ensure that they'll follow them. Once a security policy has been agreed upon, use the operating system and source control tool's inherent security capabilities to enforce it.

Security isn't a one-person decision—remember that you're part of a team, and, frankly, sometimes others know better. Try to be flexible about rights whenever possible. If someone asks for changes, don't refuse outright. Query them for an explanation and, if it makes sense, change the rights accordingly. If you're not convinced, however, there's no need to roll over. Take it to the development managers and have the decision made through consensus. In fact, many companies protect the software configuration manager by placing this decision-making responsibility solely on the shoulders of development managers. Then the software configuration manager is "just following orders" when denying rights to other employees.

Becoming the Source Janitor

I'm not going to preach here—but your source will stay healthy only if you treat your source database well. Be sure to read the maintenance instructions that come with your tool and be consistent about following the directives. Many source databases will have diagnostic and repair tools that should be run against them every so often to check that all is functioning properly.

Recovering from Catastrophe: Backups and Archives

When you lose data, it is often gone forever. You'll want to make sure that you have plans in place for catastrophes and how to recover from them quickly.

Backing up the source is the single most important thing you can do in relation to catastrophe prevention. With a good backup strategy, you'll be able to recover from almost anything that nature, a bad hard drive, or a careless developer can throw at you:

- Depending on the size of your source base and your backup medium, it's smart to plan on a full backup taking place once every 24 hours.

- Backups should occur in off-hours—especially because you may need to freeze or shut down the source during the time at which it's being backed up to tape.

- Be aware of what you're backing up; you'll want to back up the source database and all of its configuration files. All good source tools will provide instructions for making sure the database is backed up properly.

- Don't just leave it to your network administrator. Your number-one priority is to protect the source—make sure you have tangible evidence that the source is being backed up.

- Consider keeping the developer's working folders on a network share that's backed up nightly. This has the double problem-solving ability of protecting the developer's work in between check ins and providing access to the code should the developer be absent.

Chapter 7, "In the SCM Lab," also discusses backup and recovery strategies.

Outside the Subnet

One of the beauties of working in the software industry is the ability to work wherever it makes the most sense. This might be at a desk in a cube, at a kitchen table (as I'm doing now), or on a white sandy beach in Maui armed with a daiquiri and true determination.

In order to facilitate all of these possible scenarios—including having to make source available to different office locations—creating access for the outside world must be taken into consideration.

The Internet

The obvious choice is to hook the source machine to the Internet. Unless you're working on an open-source project, however, this can be problematic because of the security considerations that must take place. This sort of connection should be handled by someone in your company who is knowledgeable about the Internet and its nastier security holes. A great way to accomplish this task is to set up a Virtual Private Network (VPN) to your subnet. Using firewalls and other devices, your network experts can allow developers to access the source through the Internet from outside the office.

VPN is tempting and seems to be a fairly safe venture. It's important to keep in mind that nothing is 100-percent safe on the Internet. New security vulnerabilities show up daily, and no operating system is immune. There is no safety nowadays from pesky crackers who want to wreak havoc wherever possible.

 NOTE *It's a little off the topic here, but many people confuse the terms* hacker *and* cracker. *In the development world, someone who is an expert and extraordinarily gifted with computers is known as a* hacker. *Journalists often quote the word with a negative connotation, using it to describe destructive people who break into "secure" sites to cause damage. To set the record straight, hackers with bad intentions are really called* crackers.

Because Telnet and File Transfer Protocol (FTP) are clear text and therefore notoriously unsafe, another Internet possibility is the use of Secure Socket Shell (SSH) and Secure Copy (SCP). These tools provide a popular way to get command-line access and copy files on Unix and Linux systems without the need to set up VPN. Adding these tools to Microsoft machines can be tricky but is definitely possible—especially with the use of Cygwin. SSH and SCP are generally considered to be very secure. There are those who argue that FTP and Telnet can be safely used within a VPN environment, but this is simply not true. Because passwords are unencrypted when passed through network packets using those protocols, a disgruntled employee or contractor can easily gain access to your source tree using widely accessible network-sniffing devices.

NOTE *Employees and those you allow in your building are and remain the largest risk in protecting your source using secrecy. They have access to the code and can easily take it with them at any time on any type of media. This is the Achilles heel to trying to secure proprietary source and is therefore one of the main arguments used by proponents of the open-source movement.*

Dialing for Source

A less risky method, though still not absolutely safe, is to set up Remote Access Services (RAS) dial-in access where developers must use a modem to access the source. In this scenario, the source machine wouldn't be accessible to any part of the network that had external access via the Internet. It's still possible, however, for someone to infiltrate your vault. Anyone who knows the dial-in phone number is a possible risk—including disgruntled former employees or crackers who attempt to find random data lines through trial and error.

In this day and age, this scenario will probably not be acceptable unless you're working for a government or financial institution. Connections through modems are slow, and many home computers no longer come with the necessary hardware.

Creating a Small World

There may be cases when you'll have two or more different office locations where teams of developers code. This isn't uncommon. One of the small companies for which I worked had an Ireland office with a full-time developer. My first development house had 15 people in a California office and five people in Florida.

In these situations, you may want to consider setting up a dedicated connection via your favorite telecommunications company. Of course, these can be quite costly. Another solution is to look at your source control database tool—many of them have built-in multilocation functionality that can be used over a dedicated line or on the Internet. If you think you'll have multilocation development, coming up with a strategy early on will make it much easier for you in the long run.

Living in Denial

The truth of the matter that there are only two ways to be absolutely safe from external crackers—you can set up expensive dedicated lines or deny access to outside locations altogether. In most cases, you'll find that allowing people to work from outside the office is more important than the slight risk you take when using VPN or other connection methods.

Summary

This chapter covered the basics of source control and its administration.

First, it discussed the similarities between operating system file systems and source control databases. It's easy to see that source control takes the file system a few steps further—in fact, as the price for hard drive storage continues to plunge, I wouldn't be surprised if version control became a standard file system feature in the future. Imagine being able to see every draft of a Word document you ever saved!

You then took a general look at some of the features available in most source control tools. You saw how revisions of source files can be collected together for a release (or for any other reason) using labels. You also learned about serial and parallel development—and the necessity for branching in the software development world.

After you finished looking at the source database, you took a quick look at some strategies to make the software configuration manager's life easier. You learned about creating monikers for branches of the source tree, securing and backing up the source, and allowing external access to the database.

In the following chapters, you'll take a closer look at some of the tools. You'll see some of their benefits, and you'll learn about what you should watch. You'll also learn specifically about CVS and SourceSafe, two of the most popular tools.

Part Two

The Tools

Part Two

The Tools

CHAPTER 4

Source Control Tools

FIRST WE LIVED THROUGH the operating system wars. Then came the browser wars. And now—the Software Configuration Management (SCM) tool wars? It's true—the competition for customers in the SCM tool market is fierce. And choosing the right tool is one of the most important tasks a manager can complete. Why? Because making the wrong choice can be disastrous. The tool can be very expensive—and finding out after you've bought it that it isn't going to fulfill the necessary job requirements can cause big problems.

This chapter helps you make an informed decision about which tool might be the most appropriate for your environment. These are all fine tools—but because each is aimed at different market segments, they all have their advantages and disadvantages depending on your situation.

You'll explore the following tools in this chapter:

- Borland StarTeam

- CVS

- IBM Rational ClearCase

- Merant's PVCS

- Microsoft Visual SourceSafe

- MKS Source Integrity

- Perforce

- SourceGear Vault

Although this definitely isn't a comprehensive list of all of the tools available, it covers most of the market. Keep in mind that it doesn't include content management tools such as Vignette and TeamSite. Although I'll spend a short amount of time talking about the differences between a source control tool and a Web content management tool, discussing specific content management tools is beyond the scope of this book.

Some of the specific topics that I'll cover for each tool are as follows:

- Ease of installation.

- Ease of administration.

- Ease of general use—will your developers find it intuitive and friendly?

- Scalability—Can it grow with your product? Can it be used in different locations? Is it appropriate for use with small products?

- Available features, such as branching and promotion.

- Integration with related tools, such as bug trackers.

- Price point.

Version Control vs. Content Management

Content on Web pages changes frequently to provide the most up-to-date and accurate information to the end user. For instance, how often would you visit CNN.com if it contained only last week's news? The SCM tools of yesterday (and some of today) aren't necessarily well suited to this fast pace—though many of them are attempting to morph into Web-friendly tools. You'll find that in sites where content changes frequently, the following are true:

- The main contributors are often writers and not developers.

- Content goes through an editing process not applicable to regular source code.

- Designers who lay out the pages must be able to see their work in progress in relation to the changes made by other team members.

Enter the content management tool. Many companies quickly saw the need (and, of course, the opportunity) for new systems that provide typical source control functionality, but are optimized for a publishing environment. An example of a handy new feature might include the ability to create templates for business logic so that nontechnical authors can simply drop new text into an existing layout as necessary. Another feature might allow for a virtualized staging area where code can immediately be integrated with other development changes before it is checked into the source management database.

It's important to keep in mind that features that are necessary to provide a robust content management solution don't always mesh well with the features of a strong application source control tool. For instance, content management tools may not include a branching mechanism—it may be considered unnecessary for Web solutions. They're often living documents that are constantly updated and don't need to be split from a baseline point.

All books have a focus and, unfortunately for you Web shops out there, this book concentrates on configuration management for software applications. Content management is a whole different beast and belongs in a book all its own. For that reason, this chapter won't cover tools such as Vignette and Interwoven TeamSite.

Choosing the Right Tool

Finding the right source control tool for your environment can be difficult and time-consuming. Why does it take so long? Let's face it—you could go out and purchase the software today. But as mentioned earlier, if you don't do the proper due diligence, you could be making an expensive mistake. So, instead, let's take a few minutes to talk about the process you might want to follow when purchasing a new SCM tool.

Step 1: Map Out the Next Year

The tool you buy should be acceptable for use only for the upcoming year. And in that same vein, you don't want to pay for a lot of bells and whistles that just aren't necessary for the development road you have ahead of you.

For instance, if you're a Microsoft-centric shop with the plan to release a first-time product nine months from now, SourceSafe is the probably both the easiest and most cost-efficient tool choice you can make. On the other hand, if your company is moderately sized and has a few product lines under its belt, you may want to consider one of the proprietary tools that handles branching more appropriately.

Whatever the case, look at your company's road map and, if necessary, consult with your lead developer or architect to help you determine what the upcoming year will mean to your source control needs.

Step 2: Set Expectations and Prepare Your Environment

In many cases, the decision to research new tools is based on how difficult and tedious the current one is to use. In fact, you may find that you can't get a new tool budgeted until the current one is found to be completely unworkable. And after your team has reached that point, the pressure to finish the process quickly will be sudden and heavy.

Honestly, depending on your tool choice, you should generally expect to take two to three months to evaluate, bid on, purchase, and set up a new source control tool. Obviously, choosing a freeware tool can significantly shorten this period because the bulk of the previously mentioned time is wasted waiting on phone calls, visits, and price quotes from salespeople. A freeware tool also frees you from the price negotiations that you're sure to have with your Chief Financial Officer (CFO) and managers. Be sure to set the proper time expectations to the development group and the management team before you start and refer often to that agreed-upon date when you start getting "pushback" from the team.

If you belong to a new shop and your team doesn't currently have an SCM tool in place, consider trying one of the freeware tools while you undertake the proper due diligence required for this kind of purchase. You may even find that the freeware tool is adequate for your needs! Don't necessarily judge the value of a tool based upon its price.

Step 3: Determine Your Needs

Why is it that your team needs a new tool? Is it because you need a sophisticated branching scenario? Or perhaps because you want your developers to work in a virtualized source tree? Regardless of the reasons, you need to come up with a list of features that are important to you.

Start by examining your company's current development process to get a good understanding of what features you might need. For instance, if you have a stringent process, you may want to make sure your tool features strict controls that are difficult to circumnavigate. Keep in mind that most experts agree that your process should be pretty well defined before you try to decide what kind of tool you might use.

As you come up with your list, it's smart to divide it into three sections:

- Features/scenarios that you can't live without. Keep in mind that this applies to other people, too. Work with your lead developer or architect to ensure that you have a good grasp on the necessary feature sets.

- Features/scenarios that you shouldn't live without, but could in a pinch.

- Features/scenarios that are really nifty, but aren't necessary and might not be practical to purchase at the current time.

This list will come in handy as you narrow down your choices. A lot of basic functionality—such as checking files in and out—is going to be standard in all the tools, so try to focus on features and benefits that differ between the SCM tools vendors. Examples include the following:

- Which platform(s) will you be supporting? Does the tool provide a solution for each of these platforms?

- Does the tool integrate with your shop's Integrated Development Environment (IDE)? Borland, Macromedia, and Microsoft all provide IDEs that can integrate with source control systems.

- Can you automate the tool? In most cases, it's imperative that you can accomplish all actions without opening a Graphical User Interface (GUI).

- How stable is the company putting out the tool? Does the product have market penetration? Are there companies providing third-party utilities? How long has the company been around, and will it still be around next year when you need an update?

- Does the tool have any outside dependencies? Some tools require an outside database—such as Microsoft SQL Server or Oracle 9i—that can cost you in addition to the tool's basic price.

- Is there an ability to use the system via a remote location?

- Scalability and performance—will this tool be the right one for the next year?

- What is the tool's security and process models? Do they fit the needs of your organization?

WORD OF THE DAY

sŏ·lū·tion, *n.*

No tool can magically fix a bad process.

If I only had a dollar for every time I've seen it: A development team grows from three to 30 overnight. And then the bugs come. And the schedule gets missed. And upper management seethes behind closed doors.

What's a development manager to do? The first thing that comes to mind is to get a new source management solution! That will solve all the problems, right?

Not necessarily. One of the first (and most important) things to do when deciding on a new tool is to determine if you really need one. In many cases, what you may really need is a new process. It's time to determine whether your process is broken.

Making this determination isn't as easy as it sounds. First, the allure of a new tool can be overwhelming—who doesn't like to buy new things? And then there's the office politics.... Discussing a broken process can be difficult when people inherently want to blame a tool (or worse, someone else) rather than a set of procedures. Here's an example:

Bob: "I think our process is broken."

Rick: "Why?"

Bob: "Brenda wasn't able to [*make her date/fix her bug/unit test her code*] because the process is [*too strict/too lenient/not specific enough*]."

Rick: "Okay, so Brenda knows what she did wrong. It's because the tool is terrible. I know it. You know it. Everybody knows it, and we're trying to work with it. Stop beating up on Brenda."

Bob: "I'm not blaming Brenda. I'm blaming the process."

Rick: "Oh, okay. I hear you. Yeah, you're right. Phil wrote the process...it must be *his* fault."

Take a look at the problem and try to determine what will really effect a solution. For instance, if your product constantly releases with nasty defects, it may be because developers are allowed to sneak in code fixes with impunity right until the release date. Is the team constantly missing the schedule? Maybe it's because not enough time is spent planning the release.

Tools can definitely help you improve your process if you choose to let them. But they won't fix it—especially if you haven't pinpointed what the problems really are.

Step 4: Determine Your Budget

This is usually an easy step—mostly because the answer is completely out of your hands. You'll get a directive from the money men: "Don't spend more that $20,000," your manager might say.

NOTE *If your management gives you a firm resounding "zero" when you put in your budget request, consider skipping this chapter and moving directly to the freeware tools discussed in Chapters 5 and 6—the CVS and SourceSafe chapters, respectively. Do you really want to read about features that you won't be able to buy?*

In some cases, you might be asked to provide a guesstimate of how much a tool will cost so the accounting group can work the numbers. In this case, skip to the next step and then revisit this step after exploring each tool's features and cost. Keep in mind that buying expensive software is much like a buying a new car—you never really know the price until the paperwork is in front of you. Use list prices only as a guide—many vendors will significantly lower the price depending on the time of year or their need for market penetration.

As you think about your budget, consider other tools you might want to integrate into your source control tool—for instance, a bug-tracking system. Adding these on will often mean an increased cost if they aren't built into the tool.

Step 5: Narrow Your Search to Three or More Choices

It's wise to heartily evaluate and then get bids on at least three tools to ensure that you've chosen the correct one for your environment. This will prove to yourself and the powers that be that you've done your research and have justified the expense.

TIP *In most cases, especially in this post-tech-boom time, your CFO will be resistant to spending money on a tool with functionality that isn't always quite grasped by nontechnical folks. To present a well-balanced view to the money minders, be sure to include a freeware tool in your comparisons so your management understands what features the developers will lose if nothing is budgeted to a new system.*

To narrow down your choices, review the tools that meet the feature set and budget decided upon in steps 3 (the section "Step 3: Determine Your Needs") and step 4 (the section "Step 4: Determine Your Budget") of this process. Surf the Web to research each product. As you visit their sites, start checking off the features on your list. If you're lucky, a price range might be listed on the site, but this would be unusual because of the complex nature of SCM tool pricing. In most cases, you'll have to call a salesperson (and get ready for the heavy sales banter) to get an approximate cost.

Most of the products will have a per-seat price cost based upon the number of developers on your team and may also include a server cost. If you find yourself calling around, I advise you to let the salesperson know that you're only in the preliminary stages of a purchase and aren't interested in a heavy-sell job. Tell them you'll call back in a week or so after narrowing down your choices—many salespeople will respect you for being upfront with them. If you want, feel free to ask them to quickly tell you how their tool differs from the others on the market.

In addition to doing research on the Web, refer to magazines or other sites that might have reviewed the products or offered comparisons between them. A simple Google search can give you a much better understanding of a tool's advantages and disadvantages.

Finally, be sure to talk to the developers. Many of them will have worked at different locations and used different tools—they might have strong opinions, both positive and negative, about a tool they've used in the past. This can be valuable to you as you start to narrow down your choices. But keep an open mind... many years (and many versions) may have passed since the developer last used the tool. Try to get specific questions that you can ask the tool salespeople.

NOTE *This probably goes without saying (but I'm going to anyway)—think hard before offering to "create" your own tool for in-house use. You'll quickly find that the cost for its development and administration will greatly outweigh any cost you might have paid to an outside vendor. My mother always told me to avoid reinventing the wheel.*

Step 6: Invite the Sales Representatives to Visit

Once you've narrowed down your choices, it's time to take a look at the tools. In many cases, evaluation versions are available for download on the tool's company Web site. Sometimes, though, it makes more sense to invite sales representatives to visit you so you can see a demonstration of the tool in action and be able to ask questions on the fly. Of course, if you choose a freeware tool or an inexpensive one available at Costco, this step is unnecessary.

But even if salespeople pay you visits, you still want to take some time to evaluate the products on your own. You're preparing to spend a lot of money; be sure and communicate that fact to the salesperson so they readily make technical resources available should you have questions or problems.

Be aware (though, again, this may go without saying) that a salesperson's primary goal is to sell stuff. The line between what you need and what they want you to buy can often be blurry. Don't let salespeople tell you what you need—your feature list should already be completed by this step. If, during the sales process, you do learn of features you missed, be sure to add it to your list and update other tools' checkboxes appropriately. Worse, don't let your salesperson bully you. You're the customer, and no information you ask for should be considered by the salesperson to be an unreasonable request. It's their job to provide you with whatever you might need to make an informed decision.

As you speak to the salesperson, be sure to ask how their product differentiates itself from the others. If it's "superior technology," get a detailed explanation of how or why it's superior. If it's a simpler GUI or administration, get a demonstration and be sure to ask the other tool's salespeople to do the same for a proper comparison.

Lastly, as you discuss price with your salesperson, be sure to ferret out any hidden costs that might be associated with purchasing the tool. Many software companies now force you to purchase a maintenance program with any sale—which can significantly increase your price. In addition, many tool companies make much of their revenue through the sale of their "services," so watch out for any consulting time that might be tacked on to the price.

Step 7: Enlist the Developers

After meeting with the salespeople, you should have a good idea about which tool might be right for you and your company. Once you've narrowed down your choice, it's time to let the developers play with the tool and offer opinions. It's tempting to simply make the choice for them—after all, you're the one who has done all the research!—but you'll suffer later if they don't feel like they've been a part of the decision. And the truth is that it's more their tool than your tool. Remember, the developers are your primary customer—the more enthusiastic they are about a given tool, the easier it'll be to sell its cost to management.

Set up a common test machine with an evaluation version of the software and fill the repository with a small source tree. Then send out an email inviting the developers to try it out. In your mail, be sure to list the primary features of the tool, what differentiates it from other tools, and what struck you about it to make it your number-one choice.

 TIP *Use this same email to make sure the developers know that now is the time for their opinions. They should be told that once the tool is bought, there's no going back…this may well be their only chance to (productively) express their thoughts regarding the tool.*

The developers will probably (and rightly so) have questions and concerns about the tool. Try to alleviate these by answering questions honestly while avoiding a defensive posture. You all have the same goal: You're trying to find the best tool for your shop. If you're cornered by a developer about the tool, don't get flustered. Simply call the salesperson and ask the proper questions—it's their job to make people feel good about a sale, and they'll want your developers to be happy, too.

If the developers have concerns that aren't addressed by the tool's manufacturer, consider choosing another. It's important to note, though, that there's no tool that can be everything to everyone—you have to draw the line somewhere.

Step 8: Buy It!

You found it. You researched it. Everybody likes it. It's time to buy it. As you do, the following points are some things to keep in mind:

Timing is everything: Completing the sale a short time before the end of the month, quarter, or company's fiscal year end can get you a good deal. Salespeople often have quotas they must meet in order to get bonuses (or just to keep their jobs!) and are often willing to make large concessions to get a sale "booked" by a particular date. Using this technique can be a double-edged sword—you may lose the luxury of properly evaluating all the tools on your list if a salesperson throws a "drop-dead" date at you.

Ask for extras: What else will they throw in if you play hard to get? Don't worry—no one will like you any less (well, it doesn't really matter if they do anyway), and all they can do is say no. Can you get a training session for your developers? Can you get a consultant to come out and help you set up the repository? Free maintenance for a year? A few extra licenses? Hold them off for a couple of days so the salesperson sweats a bit. And be sure to try out one of my favorite lines: "You know, I'm sold—but my boss thinks I should be getting more for this kind of money. If you just threw in [*insert your chosen freebie here*], I'm sure she'd go for it." Car salesmen do it to you—it's time you passed that joy onto others.

Get it in writing: What kind of guarantee can you get on the product? Don't laugh—I bought a $50,000 source control tool and negotiated a 100-percent, satisfaction-guaranteed, no-questions-asked, 90-day return option with it. Many companies will offer 30 days, but that's not a long time to get a tool set up and in running condition. A longer guarantee protects your investment and ensures that the salesperson will jump when you call with problems. If you choose to go this route, make sure to *get it in writing*. I'd like to say that one more time to make sure you understand it completely: *Get all guarantees in writing.* Otherwise, you're depending on the vendor's good faith—a mistake that can cost you should you decide that the tool isn't working for you.

TIP *Sometimes the quickest way to get the support you need is through your salesperson. If you find that you're getting the run-around in technical support, try pinging your salesperson with an "I'm packing up the box for return now" email. You'll get the attention you need quickly.*

Start with the evals: If you find that it's taking longer than you'd like to get a purchase order through your CFO's office, ask your tool vendor for an evaluation version with a switch that can be "flipped" when you enter a license key into the appropriate dialog box. This will allow you to get started with it while the money men play their games.

TIP *Use your mileage credit card to pay for the tool. Your turnaround time for the purchase will be much faster, and you could earn a free trip to Hawaii. Don't forget to be reimbursed by your company.*

Promotion: How the Source Gets to the Head of the Pack

Surprisingly enough, I'm not talking about your career. Instead, I'm talking about a process that allows you to create transition states for your source.

Transition states? Sounds confusing. In actuality, it's pretty straightforward. In most development cycles, source goes through different stages based on certain milestones. For example, when the functional specifications have all been written and developers start to create the code, the source is in the "development" stage. As the source progresses and is compiled into usable builds, it gets promoted to new states. It's almost like labeling a label—Build 2.04.165 can easily be marked as "in QA" as it's tested. Some of these states might include:

- In development
- Interface complete
- In QA
- Development bug fixing
- Beta
- Release candidate

What's the purpose? It allows team members to quickly find the source for certain builds as they progress through the development cycle. Other uses might include the triggering of actions, such as emailing the team leader for authorization to release a build to quality. In high-end tools, role security can change based on promotional states. For instance, as source is in a "release candidate" state, perhaps only development managers can check in code for bug fixes—handy functionality if you find you're changing security based on the build's status in the development cycle.

If you find that perfect source control system that just doesn't support promotion, there are third party-tools, such as TestTrack Pro, that allow you to mimic promotional states. It may be cost-effective to use an inexpensive tool such as this with a freeware source control system.

Up until a few years ago, *promotion* was *the* key buzzword for SCM tool sales. Nowadays, *workflow* has replaced it as the feature to get. As you investigate tools, be aware that although promotional states tend to be similar from tool to tool, the bells and whistles that accompany them can vary.

Exploring the Tools

In the beginning, most SCM tools were proprietary in nature and existed individually on mainframe computers at one specific location. The first widely available SCM tool was a Unix product called the *Source Code Control System* (SCCS). Developed by Bell Laboratories in the late '70s, this tool allowed users to lock source files so developers didn't write over each other's code. As files changed, new versions of them were added to a repository—thereby preserving the previous versions of the same files. A few years later, an engineer at Purdue University introduced the Revision Control System (RCS), which furthered the SCCS tool by providing an easier interface and storing the delta of changed files instead of complete copies.

These are the forefathers of all of today's tools. Surprisingly enough, the basic paradigm for creating and editing source in modern SCM tools remains much the same as it did 30 years ago. Of course, as one would hope, feature sets and the backend technology have been greatly enhanced. Today's tools range from simply providing basic SCM functionality to those that provide an end-to-end software development process solution. Your weighty task is to determine which tool might be right for you and your team.

So let's get started. The following sections are designed to familiarize you with the basics of several source management tools. Two of the tools (namely CVS and Microsoft SourceSafe) are detailed more completely in future chapters. Keep in mind that products are updated often and bugs can be fixed—even if you use the information in this chapter as a baseline, you should still spend some time researching these tools on your own.

The legend for the price point is as follows:

- **$**: Free or less than $100 per user.

- **$$**: Low cost; expect to pay an average of a few hundred dollars per user.

- **$$$**: Medium range; expect to pay an average amount of $1,000 per user.

- **$$$$**: High end; expect to pay an average amount that's quite a bit more than $1,000 per user.

- **$$$$$**: Expect to pay a whole lot of money.

Borland StarTeam

- **Current version (as of this writing):** 5.2.

- **Supported operating systems:** Server: Windows 2000 Server (SP3), Windows NT 4.0 Server (SP6a), or Sun Solaris (7.0/8.0). Client: Windows NT, 2000, or XP for native client application or any operating system that has installed Java Runtime Environment for interpreted client.

- **Dependencies:** Third-party database.

- **My testing environment:** Windows XP Professional (SP1) and Microsoft Access from the Office 2002 suite (SP2).

- **The company tagline:** "Borland StarTeam provides an automated and comprehensive software configuration management (SCM) system for supporting the management of assets and application lifecycle tasks, all from within a single repository."

- **Price point:** $$$.

- **Evaluation:** Available at http://www.borland.com.

In October 2002, Borland acquired a small SCM tool manufacturer headquartered in Santa Ana, California, called *StarBase*. Its product, StarTeam, is heralded as an end-to-end development lifecycle tool that allows every member of the development process team to participate in creating software.

Three versions of the server are available. The entry-level server, StarTeam Standard, provides for basic configuration management services along with an embedded defect tracking tool and integration with Windows Explorer. In addition to these features, your off-site development teams can rest easy—StarTeam allows the connection of remote clients to each of its servers through both the standard client and Web client via an internal network or the Internet itself.

 CAUTION *Exposing your source through the Internet is enticing but can be dangerous—especially if you're trying to protect your intellectual property through secrecy. Be sure to analyze this possibility thoroughly with both network and StarTeam experts before attempting this functionality.*

The higher-end models of the server have all the features of the standard version but add a little more functionality related to the software lifecycle management, such as promotion, the ability to synchronize status with Microsoft Project, and the ability to publish and review requirements documents. In addition, you'll have to shell out a little more for the expanded servers if you want to use the Sun Solaris operating system as the server base. An interesting aside: With Borland's continued investment in Linux tools, I bet that a Linux version of the tool is in the works.

StarTeam's marketing group emphasizes the tool's "traceability" as one of its major features. Developers are assigned tasks within the tool. Once they've completed these tasks and checked in the new code, the source becomes "linked" to the original task request so a manager or quality engineer (or SCM builder!) can quickly see what source makes up the new feature. As defect and change requests flow through the tool, all source changes are also linked—this allows the project management team to determine at a glance how an added change might affect the stability of the build. StarTeam provides a security model that allows rights to be dictated through the user's role at the company—for instance, a quality engineer might be allowed to view source but not to modify it. Role-based security makes life a whole lot easier when adding or changing users.

From an installation perspective, if you're using Windows, you'll be pretty happy with StarTeam.[1] Using standard InstallShield setup programs, the server is installed inside of ten minutes. The client software takes even less time. Be sure as you install, however, to follow the StarTeam white papers, which will guide you in creating a scalable and efficient database.

StarTeam requires a third-party database in which it keeps all of its *metadata*—the information maintained about labels, versions, and users. The currently supported databases are Microsoft SQL Server 7 and 2000, Microsoft Access, IBM DB2, and Oracle 8i and 9i.

StarTeam provides a mechanism for transferring existing SourceSafe or Merant's PVCS source databases to a StarTeam server—all the file histories and labels are saved in the new database just as they were created. This can be a time-consuming process, however, so you'll want to be sure to budget some time for this task.

Like several other tools described in this chapter, StarTeam is a view-based SCM tool. A *view* is similar to a branch in that only certain versions of files are displayed to a user. The difference is that the branching mechanism is completely seamless to the user. As files are checked in and out of the view, new branches for the files are created as necessary behind the scenes by the tool. This view-based

---

1. I haven't had the opportunity to test the Solaris version of the StarTeam server.

behavior makes life much easier for the developers as they embark on bug fixes or new versions of the software. You can see the StarTeam client and its view-based look in Figure 4-1.

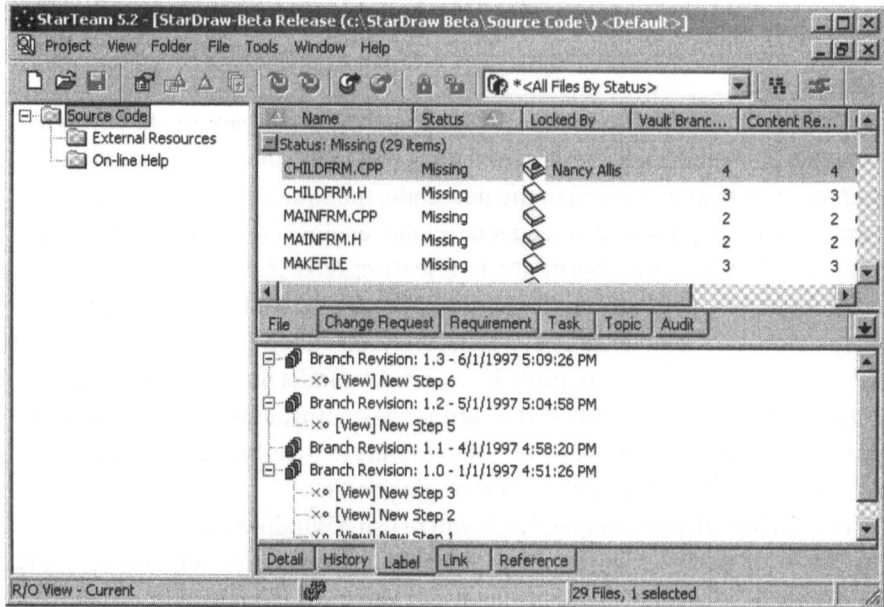

Figure 4-1. The StarTeam Windows client

The tool is fairly pretty simple to use from an end user's perspective. Some functionality, such as the combination of "get" and "check out" into one command, takes a little getting used to, but most of the tool is fairly straightforward and intuitive. All of the product's features are integrated in the one client—for instance, the defect tracker is simply another tab in the upper window.

The usual administration tasks are required—creating new projects, adding groups and users, and ensuring that the backups are properly configured. Borland recommends that no users be logged into the system while backups take place. Be sure to back up whichever SQL database you're using for the system at the same time—its data is as important as the source files. In addition to these tasks, the SCM will also need to create and manage views as well as perform periodic automerges when branching takes place.

All in all, StarTeam is a fine product that falls squarely in the middle of the tool price scale.

CVS

- **Current version (as of this writing):** 1.12.

- **Supported operating systems:** Server: Most flavors of Unix/Linux, Windows NT. Client: Most flavors of Unix/Linux, Windows, VMS, and OS/2.

- **Dependencies:** None.

- **My testing environment:** Windows XP Professional (SP1) and Red Hat Linux 8.0.

- **The company tagline:** CVS isn't produced by a single company—it's open-source software, after all—but the Free Software Foundation site states that "CVS is a version control system and important component of Source Configuration Management (SCM). Using it, you can record the history of sources files, and documents. It fills a similar role to the free software RCS, PRCS, and Aegis packages."

- **Price point:** $.

- **Evaluation:** Available at http://www.cvshome.org.

If you're anything like Bob Barker, you'll be pretty hip for CVS—the price is definitely right. CVS, also known as the *Concurrent Versions System*, began its life in 1986 as a set of Unix scripts written by Dick Grune. Quickly embraced by the open-source community, it morphed into the binary tool we know today.

Like any other open-source tool, the code necessary for creating the tool is freely available for download—you can update it or make any changes to it that you'd like. You can find it at http://www.cvshome.org. If you choose to redistribute any of your changes, be sure to check out your responsibilities that are spelled out in its GNU license (http://www.gnu.org).

CVS extends the change management functionality that has been available in the Unix world since the early 80s in the Revision Control System (RCS) program. In addition to this basic functionality, however, CVS added a client/server mechanism that allows for multiple locations using the Internet to coordinate source. Since then, CVS has been ported to Linux, Windows, and OS/2.

There's a learning curve with CVS—both from a client and a server perspective. Some of that is because of it being a command-line tool. In the past few years, several open-source GUI CVS clients have popped up, but they also suffer from a lack of intuitiveness.

I'll discuss CVS and some of its available GUI tools with much more detail in Chapter 5, "CVS."

IBM Rational ClearCase

- **Current version (as of this writing):** 2002.05.00.

- **Supported operating systems:** Server: Most flavors of Unix/Linux, IBM mainframes, and Windows NT. Client: Most flavors of Unix/Linux, Windows, VMS, and OS/2.

- **Dependencies:** None.

- **My testing environment:** Windows XP Professional (SP1).

- **The company tagline:** "Rational's software configuration management (SCM) solution helps project managers and all team members manage change throughout the development lifecycle."

- **Price point:** $$$$$ (for the standard product; a "lite" version is also available for a lower price or as a bundle with other products).

- **Evaluation:** Talk to a salesperson about getting an evaluation—only demos and presentations are available online.

ClearCase, arguably one of the most scalable tools featured in this chapter, began its existence at Atria software in 1990. What a difference a decade makes…. Atria merged with Pure Software in the early 90s, which merged with Rational in 1997, which was bought by IBM in 2003. Now there's a complicated lineage.

 NOTE *Because the IBM purchase took place only recently, this section refers to Rational as the parent of ClearCase when discussing the timeline of feature additions.*

ClearCase managed to get a large hold on the existing SCM market because it was the first major player to be able to store data on multiple servers while appearing to users that it's all emanating from one location. Source files and directories are stored in repositories called *Version Object Bases* (VOBs). ClearCase provides the ability to link file versions to views—essentially a moveable label that appears to end users as a flat-file system. ClearCase administrators create and maintain *config specs* that detail which revisions of files are attached to the view.

An extension to the ClearCase product, the MultiSite add-in allows the support of parallel development in different geographic locations. To work in this manner, each location has a replica of the same VOB, which periodically is synced to the locations. The downside to this, of course, is that periodic merging must take place when the VOBs are synced. Keep in mind, however, that several other tools allow for similar geographic development functionality without the need to sync source databases.

ClearQuest, the IBM Rational defect tracking software, can ship with ClearCase to provide an integrated work environment. The bug tracker can be entirely customized to include personalized entry forms and defect types. Both the Visual Basic and Perl languages are supported to further customize fields and actions. As bugs are fixed, ClearCase source files can be added as attachments, allowing project managers and quality to get an idea of how the change might affect the overall product.

In the last couple of years, Rational has been positioning its development tools as an end-to-end lifecycle solution. It recently introduced the Unified Change Management (UCM) model, which, acting as a superset to the usual SCM model, ties the planning, schedule tracking, and defect reporting processes together with the original ClearCase source control model. The use of this model is described with great detail in the software's documentation.

This UCM model provides the promotional ability that other tools introduced in the late 90s. See the sidebar "Promotion: How the Source Gets to the Head of the Pack" for more information on promotion. The UCM model also allows for the "code streams" in which developers work—much like a local directory, but existing on the server. All activity in this code stream is merged and checked in as a "change set" to an integration stream. After the integration stream is stabilized, it's merged into the main branch of code. This idea of integration using branches isn't new—but the UCM model allows it to be configured more easily than from scratch.

ClearCase is known for its difficult administration. Many of the other tool vendors mention this in their sales talks (though Rational representatives downplay the accusation). It should be noted, however, that the ClearCase and ClearQuest products ship with no fewer than 12 books, which stacked together measure almost a foot tall.[2] The administration guide itself is more than 500 pages—views must be created, a license server and a registry-type server must exist, tweaks must be completed to ensure performance...the list goes on.

In addition to its main application client, ClearCase integrates with most of the large development IDEs, including Visual Studio.

If you've got the money and the need, Rational ClearCase is definitely a powerhouse. Although most developers are pleased with its abilities, be prepared to spend some time with the administration and config spec creation. Rational

---

2.   Think this is an exaggeration? I just measured 'em—they're sitting next to my desk right now!

ClearCase is a valuable tool—but you're going to spend some money if you want to use it. A "lite" product, which can exist only on one server and has several other limitations, is available for a significantly lower price. It's sometimes even bundled with other IBM tools such as Rational Rose.

Merant's PVCS

- **Current version (as of this writing):** 7.5.1.0.

- **Supported operating systems:** Both the client and the server support most flavors of Unix/Linux and Windows.

- **Dependencies:** None.

- **My testing environment:** Windows XP Professional (SP1).

- **The company tagline:** "PVCS Professional gives teams the power to organize and manage software assets, track and communicate issues, and standardize the software development process."

- **Price point:** $$$.

- **Evaluation:** Talk to a salesperson about getting an evaluation—only demos and presentations are available online.

Meet the granddaddy of commercial SCM. Polytron Software created the Polytron Version Control System (PVCS) in the late 80s as a DOS alternative to the afore-mentioned RCS.[3] PVCS became a GUI tool during the reign of Windows 3.1, and now that its company has gone through countless mergers and acquisitions to become Merant, PVCS Version Manager has emerged as the number-one market leader for paid SCM tool seats.[4]

Often bundled with bug tracking and automated build tools as PVCS Profession, the Version Manager provides the basics—exclusive checkout, labeling, branching—all with a robustness that comes from years of being in the game. Its backend is written in Java, which is interpreted by the included open-source Tomcat application server. The client is available both in Web format and as a Java application, displayed in Figure 4-2. The Java client can, in theory, run on any operating system that has a Java Runtime Environment (JRE) installed.

---

3. See the "CVS" section earlier in this chapter.

4. Not to be confused with the number-one market leader in SCM tool *dollars*: IBM's Rational ClearCase. ClearCase tends to be more expensive than PVCS.

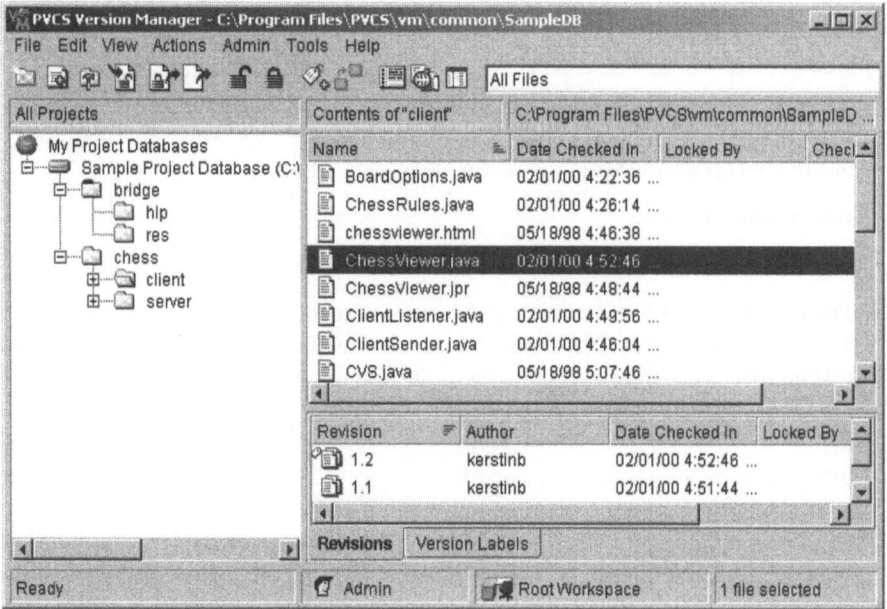

Figure 4-2. The PVCS Version Manager client

The Merant team touts that its easy out-of-the-box experience is its main selling point. Its client is fairly intuitive, but one can see that this is because almost every developer who worked on PCs in the late '80s or early-to-mid '90s used PVCS as their primary source control tool.

The GUI has, of course, evolved significantly since then. In addition to the standard features available to all of the tools, PVCS supports promotional state security, Internet accessibility from multiple geographic locations, and strong integration with other PVCS products.

For higher-end customers, the PVCS Dimensions product is available as a step up from the current Version Manager. More of a workflow management tool, the Dimensions product supports the change management process with strict promotional state security and the ability to track and trace all changes. Dimensions might be the product to consider (along with IBM's Rational ClearCase and MKS Source Integrity) when building software that must go through rigorous accountability—an example might include code to be used in airplane cockpits or in medical equipment.

Merant's stated growth plan—from PVCS Professional to PVCS Dimensions—allows companies to start small and work their way up, both from a conversion perspective as well as from a cost perspective.

Microsoft Visual SourceSafe

- **Current version (as of this writing):** 6.0d.

- **Supported operating systems:** Server and client: Windows.

- **Dependencies:** None.

- **My testing environment:** Windows XP Professional (SP1).

- **The company tagline:** "A developer can use Microsoft Visual SourceSafe with any type of file produced by any development language, authoring tool, or application. Using it enables users to work at file and project levels while also promoting file reuse. Its project-oriented features increase the efficiency of managing day-to-day tasks associated with team-based software and Web content development."

- **Price point:** $.

- **Evaluation:** Not available as an evaluation. It does, however, come bundled with versions of Visual Studio.

Another tool for the cost-conscious, Microsoft Visual SourceSafe is the low-end leader for the Windows operating system. Lacking many of the bells and whistles of the other tools, it can still do the job for small projects and teams working in the Windows environment. Figure 4-3 displays the SourceSafe client.

Most of the basic functionality—versioning files, viewing the delta between revisions, labeling the source—is in the package. The notable exception from the list of "basics" is SourceSafe's fairly pitiful branching mechanism. This makes it a tool that's quickly outgrown when you start new versions of applications.

On the other hand, you can't argue with the cost. SourceSafe is bundled with almost every version of Visual Studio. In addition, you can buy it for less than $500 in a shrink-wrapped package. It was designed to be used with Windows, but several third-party vendors have ported the application to other operating systems. You'll have to pay for that perk, though.

Unfortunately, nothing comes for free: SourceSafe databases are notorious for corrupting. In contrast to some of the other transactional tools, the SourceSafe client actually carries out all business logic while attaching to a server file share. This scenario relies on other clients not performing on the same file at the same time—which every now and again does happen. When it does happen, however, this corruption is limited in most cases to the loss of history for one or several files.

The bottom line is that SourceSafe is easy to use, easy to administer, and easily available—a combination that makes it a win for many organizations. I'll discuss SourceSafe with much more detail in Chapter 6, "SourceSafe."

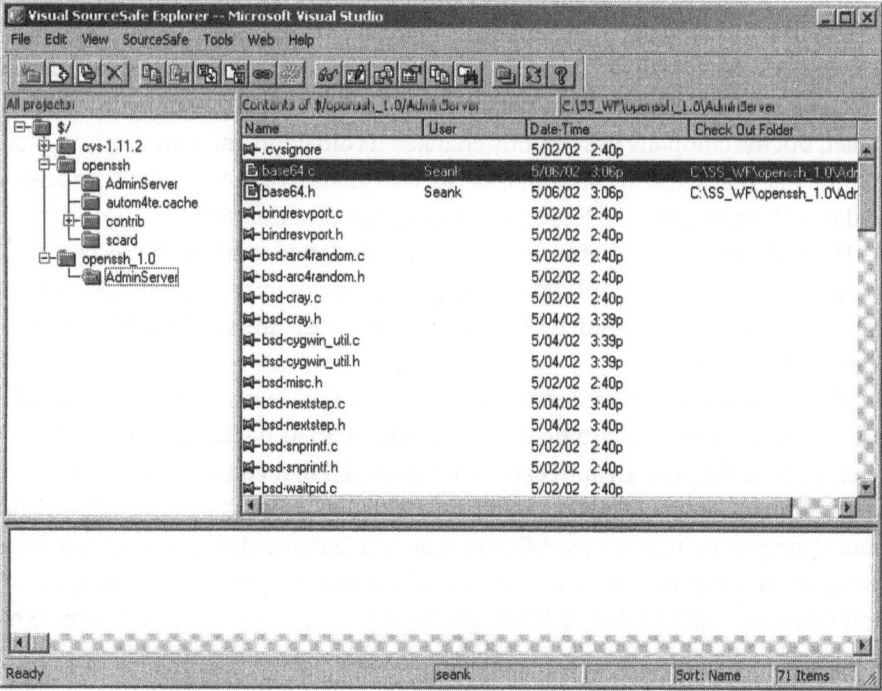

Figure 4-3. The Microsoft Visual SourceSafe client

MKS Source Integrity

- **Current version (as of this writing):** 8.3.

- **Supported operating systems:** Server: Windows 2000/XP and many flavors of Unix/Linux. Client: Windows and most flavors of Unix/Linux.

- **Dependencies:** None.

- **My testing environment:** Windows XP Professional (SP1).

- **The company tagline:** "MKS Source Integrity Enterprise Edition is the best-of-breed, enterprise choice for comprehensive, cross-platform software configuration management. Its platform transparent, advanced multi-tiered architecture is scalable in local and distributed environments, and its flexibility allows for high quality integrations into other leading IDEs and developer productivity tools."

- **Price point:** $$$$$.

- **Evaluation:** Talk to a salesperson about getting an evaluation—only demos and presentations available online.

Though not widely known as such, MKS (which stands for *Mortice Kern Systems*) was also one of the forefathers of the SCM commercial market. In 1987, it introduced a Unix product called *MKS-RCS* that provided a superset of the functionality provided by the standard RCS tool. Over the years, it has been a smaller player in the SCM market, but the company has recently changed its direction and now wants to pick up some market steam. In 2001, MKS decided to focus its attention on the process of building software versus the less encompassing job of simple SCM.

The product isn't for everyone—and it isn't designed to be. MKS has positioned itself as a high-end solution for large companies. It sees only the Merant Dimensions and IBM's Rational ClearCase products as direct competitors in its sphere of influence.

What makes this tool so different from some of the lower-end tools? The MKS folks stress that it begins with their architecture. With its backend written completely in Java, they use an application server model that can stand alone or be used with products such as WebLogic or WebSphere. Using this model allows MKS Source Integrity to increase its ability to scale while maintaining a comparatively low cost of administration. Some tools require a full-time employee just for its administration; MKS prides itself on needing approximately "a half-day a month" for the same tasks. This depends, of course, on the scale of the project.

In addition to the basic version control features, Source Integrity also provides a workflow management tool that allows companies to define and strengthen their current development processes. In fact, it's this feature that the company says really differentiates its product from the others. Large companies can propagate their current processes throughout the organization—even when portions of their code are outsourced or written in multiple locations. Event triggers and automatic notifications play a central role in these processes.

Most of the high-end tools allow users to access the same code at mirrors of source repositories in different geographic locations. Unlike its rivals, however, the MKS server architecture allows this ability without requiring a "sync up" at specific intervals. This alleviates worries about having to possibly merge a large amount of code every time a sync takes place.

An optional component to the system is a tracking tool that allows users to manage tasks associated with the development of software. This tool goes beyond the usual bug tracking tool—any piece of the process can be tasked out to any team member and then tracked as one might with defects. There's also integration with management programs, such as Microsoft Project.

In addition to its Java and Web clients, MKS has integrated with most of the large development IDEs, including Visual Studio, Borland JBuilder, and Rational Rose.

This is a tool designed for larger organizations. Although the tool provides a great deal of strong functionality, it doesn't come cheap. If you're working in a small shop, this sort of product might be overkill for your particular needs.

Perforce SCM System

- **Current version (as of this writing):** 2002.2

- **Supported operating systems:** The server runs on Windows, most flavors of Unix/Linux, and Macintosh, among others. The client runs on a huge variety of systems including Windows, most flavors of Unix/Linux, OS/2, and Macintosh—even Amiga and Cygwin!

- **Dependencies:** None.

- **My testing environment:** Windows XP Professional (SP1).

- **The company tagline:** "Perforce is the undisputed high-performance solution in Software Configuration Management. Built from the ground up to provide full-functioned source management with a light footprint, Perforce responds so quickly that developers never doubt using it. Simply put, Perforce never makes users wait."

- **Price point:** $$$.

- **Evaluation:** Available for evaluation at http://www.perforce.com.

"It's fast." That's how one of the representatives from Perforce responded when asked what differentiates their product from the competition. This may not seem like a big deal, but when it starts taking your build script an hour or more to download source from the server, you'll start to see the value in this virtue.

Honestly, there are few tools that have as dedicated a following as the Perforce offering. Known as a "developer's tool," Perforce was designed with the software writer in mind. From day one, its most important goal was to be a fast tool that's easy to use. Frankly, the only arguments I've heard about not using Perforce have stemmed from the fact that it's not a free tool—and not because of any lack of features.

From a client perspective, Perforce supports an amazing amount of operating systems. Some of these are supported only with a command-line tool, but that's still pretty good when you realize that some of these operating systems aren't supported by any other leading tools vendor. In comparison with other tools, using the GUI client, as displayed in Figure 4-4, can be a bit strange. The Perforce terminology is a little unusual, and the basic premise of the product has strayed from the usual paradigm. This aside, most of the basic tasks, including branching and merging, can be mastered inside of an hour or so. The help is a little lacking, especially when discussing branching, but the FAQs on the Perforce Web site are informative.

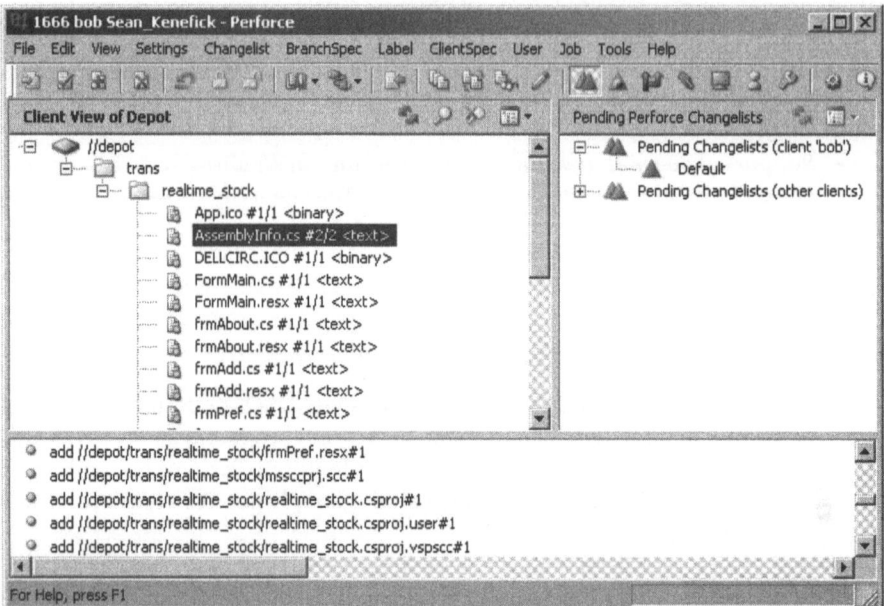

Figure 4-4. The Perforce client

Much like StarTeam and SourceGear, Perforce stores all of its metadata using a transactional database model. Don't worry—the database is included in the software. A major difference between the tools, however, is that Perforce adds rollback capability to groups of checked-in files in place of the usual model. For instance, if I were to fix a bug that required me to change eight files, I would check them in as a group. If one of those files were to have a conflict of some kind, Perforce gives me the opportunity to roll back the checkin of *all* of the other files in the group—thereby not contaminating the source tree with a partial bug fix. These "groups of changes" are numbered in such a way that anyone, from a quality engineer to an SCM preparing a build, can quickly see what files make up a bug fix or a component.

Another way that Perforce is different from the competition is in its branching model. Called *interfile branching*, its idea is to copy branched files to a new location instead of tracking versions inside the file itself. This unique change means that the files evolve separately, but can be merged or not merged at the whim of the user. This is quite different from the usual branching mechanism that relies upon a tight connection between the branched files—even when files are branched, one must always plan to merge back into the main line. A handy side effect of interfile branching is that any file can be merged into another as if it were originally branched from it. This allows the SCM and developers to merge changes in any way they like.

As with the other tools, Perforce provides a command-line interface for use in automated builds. A nifty added feature is the "echo mode," a way to fulfill tasks in the GUI client and have the system echo its command-line equivalent back at the user. This allows scripts to be built quickly without the need for a lot of research.

The last distinction I'd like to make about Perforce is that it doesn't have a sales team. You heard that right. The company places evaluation software on the Internet and then lets customers, mostly through word of mouth, come to them. The technical support team provides both pre- and post-sales support and, once bought, the software is simply downloaded onto the client machine.

SourceGear Vault

- **Current version (as of this writing):** 1.0.3.

- **Supported operating systems:** Server and client: Windows.

- **Dependencies:** SQL Server 2000 or higher, IIS 5.0 or higher, and .NET Framework 1.0 or higher on both server and client.

- **My testing environment:** Windows XP Professional (SP1).

- **The company tagline:** "SourceGear Vault is a version control system for Windows developers, with full integration into the Visual Studio .NET environment. It is implemented entirely on the .NET platform and uses SQL Server 2000 for its repository storage. Vault is the only version control system designed specifically to offer a seamless transition from Visual SourceSafe. SourceSafe repositories are imported with no lost data, including history. The user interface resembles SourceSafe Explorer, and all SourceSafe features are present, including Share and Pin."

- **Price point:** $$.

- **Evaluation:** Available at http://www.sourcegear.com.

How about an introduction to the newest kid on the block? SourceGear Vault officially debuted in February 2003. Why—oh why?!—would I even consider a 1.0 product in this chapter of well-respected SCM tools? There are actually several good reasons.

As you may know, SourceGear has provided the SourceOffSite module for SourceSafe since 1997. It also sponsored and administered the development of open-source CVS for several years—pretty much a charity gig—until OpenAvenue took over for them. With the knowledge the company has garnered from both of these tasks, it has tried to capture the benefits of SourceSafe while addressing what can be considered its most glaring faults. See Chapter 6, "SourceSafe," for more information regarding SourceSafe's problems.

Almost all of the current SourceSafe functionality is included. The omission of keyword expansion will be addressed in the next version of the software; it may have already been released by the time you're reading this. Although SourceSafe databases can't be accessed directly by the SourceGear Vault client, they can be imported via a provided tool—history and all. This can be a time-consuming process, however, so budget some time.

In a nutshell, SourceGear provides a low-cost step up from Visual SourceSafe. If you know the Microsoft product, you already know (for the most part) SourceGear Vault. As displayed in Figure 4-5, SourceGear Vault shares most of its user interface with SourceSafe. The major differences between the two products are that Vault supports a true database backend with transactional capability— meaning that clients don't write over each other and cause data corruption like they do in SourceSafe—and the added support of true branching and merging. The planned future of the product includes a Unix client and the integration of a low-cost defect tracking program called FogBUGZ provided by Fog Creek Software.

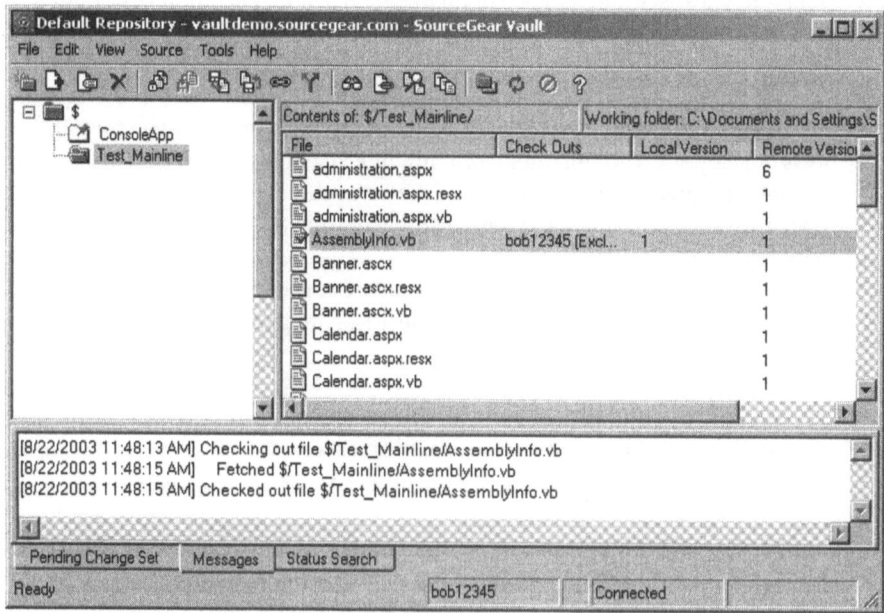

Figure 4-5. The SourceGear Vault client

The most positive aspect of SourceGear Vault is its remote accessibility over the Internet. Built entirely using the .NET Framework, the server installs itself as an addition to Microsoft's built-in Internet server (IIS). This means that, using a Secure Sockets Layer (SSL) and Challenge/Response security model, clients can remotely access the server over typical Web ports.

Sound great? Just keep in mind that this is a version 1.0 product—something the SourceGear marketing folks were quick to point out to me. If you need a better branching model than SourceSafe provides and you want to save some money, you may be okay with this. On the other hand, it might be a deal breaker—and who could blame you for thinking so? After all, your company's source is its most valuable asset.

Summary

This chapter discussed some of the most popular software configuration management source control tools. Some of them—or none of them—might be the right fit for your organization. The tools included the following:

- Borland StarTeam

- CVS

- IBM Rational ClearCase

- Merant's PVCS

- Microsoft Visual SourceSafe

- MKS Source Integrity

- Perforce SCM System

- SourceGear Vault

I discussed the importance of ensuring that your tool fits into your development process and how to determine what features are important to you and your company. I also discussed the difference between a content manager and a typical source management application.

You should now have a good idea of which tool might be right for you. For more information about tools, refer to Chapters 5 and 6 where I discuss the freeware tools CVS and SourceSafe, respectively. I'll discuss basic use-case models as well as strategies you might apply to ensure the integrity of your source.

CHAPTER 5

CVS

WHEN DISCUSSING SOURCE CONTROL TOOLS, you can't go far without talking about CVS, also known as the *Concurrent Versions System*. It began its life in 1986 as a set of Unix scripts written by Dick Grune and has slowly evolved with the help of the open-source community into the tool we know today. CVS extends the change management functionality that has been available in the Unix world since the early 80s in the Revision Control System (RCS) program. In addition to this basic functionality, however, CVS added a client/server mechanism that allowed for the coordination of source using multiple locations on the Internet. In the passing years, CVS has been ported to Linux, Windows, and OS/2.

Is it the easiest of tools to use? One might say no—it tends to have a higher learning curve than some of the tools on the market. On the other hand, once you've used it for a couple of days, you'll find that it doesn't seem to be that much more difficult to use than the others. And let's face it—it's been around for years. I'd lay three-to-one odds that several of your programmers have worked with it in the past—especially in non-Windows shops. If you do run into problems, an untold number of folks worldwide use CVS—simply query Google with the issue and immediately see thousands of related answers appear in your browser.

So, when evaluating CVS, the big questions come down to price, stability, and functionality. Let's get the first question out of the way—you can't argue with the price. Whether you've got five developers or 5,000 of them, CVS is Gnu's Not Unix (GNU) open-source software and will stay so for the life of the product. From a stability perspective, CVS has demonstrated its strong constitution for many years on many projects. And although it's not considered the most flexible tool on the market (okay—perhaps that's an understatement), CVS still provides all of the basic Software Configuration Management (SCM) functionality in a tight, easy-to-install package. By hooking up with an open-source defect tracker such as Bugzilla (http://bugzilla.mozilla.com) using the CVSzilla integration, your team can quickly have a robust, no-cost SCM solution.

By utilizing a variety of security models, you can set CVS up as a multilocation source database, which allows users in various geographic locations to work on the same source trees. In addition to this functionality, CVS can automatically detect the end-of-line characters on the client's operating system.[1] Unix, Linux,

---

1. See the later section "Binary Files in the Repository" if you don't know how the end-of-line character differences in operating systems can make life difficult.

or Windows—developers can seamlessly code in whichever operating system they prefer without affecting their coworkers.

Sounds great, does it? Before you run to your computer to download the software, let's take a couple of moments to discuss the downsides of both CVS and open-source software in general.

Open-source software is usually much less expensive than proprietary products, that's true, but you'll quickly find that other, less-tangible costs often balance things out in the long run. For instance, you may find that you're forced to use a time-consuming workaround to enable functionality that comes packaged in a proprietary product. Or you may find a nasty bug that you simply can't live with—in the open-source world, you may be required to report or fix that bug yourself. These expenses add up, so don't underestimate the value of your time when considering open-source products.

With that in mind, let's talk about some of the peskier disadvantages of CVS. The following are a few you may want to consider.

CVS's foremost flaw—the one on which most of its other problems are based—is that it hasn't been meaningfully architected for 20 years. As new functionality is desired by the market, the CVS code steam is hacked apart and then glued together again to meet current users' needs. This has led to large ugly inconveniences that won't be fixed in the near future (or ever, in most cases).

For instance, directories and files can't easily be renamed in CVS. Because the tool continues to exploit the ancient RCS storage for storage, only the contents of files—and not their relationships to other files—are maintained. When moving a file, it actually must be "copied"—and the history from before the move stays with the old location, and all future history is placed in the new location. It's simply not possible to move or rename objects that have already been checked into the tree without leading to the confusion and ire of other developers on the project. On a related point, this also means that directories and file properties can't be versioned in CVS as they are in other tools.

CVS is also not a transactional database, so it can't fulfill checkins on an *atomic* level—files that are selected together for checkin aren't treated as a single entity. Instead, each file is committed separately. If a single file in a group checkin fails to update, the source can possibly become destabilized because of the partial commit.

Frankly, building the product with RCS under the hood has created some serious limitations. Arguably, the most annoying problem with CVS is its treatment of binary files. Because versions of binary files are always transmitted to users in their entirety, CVS slows down significantly when nontext files are used in source trees. In addition, if binary files aren't appropriately marked as such, they run the risk of being corrupted by CVS's automatic end-of-line and keyword expansion features.

Lastly, and some would argue most importantly, is that using CVS relies on an established process and human discipline. If you're looking for a tight security model that dictates how and when the developers should access the source, CVS probably isn't for you. CVS does have functionality that can help your group stay in tune with each other, but it tends to be voluntary and must be fulfilled by the developer as part of a process.

As with any other tool, you'll have to decide whether CVS is a good solution for your group. If it's not, refer to Chapter 4, "Source Control Tools," for information on how to evaluate other SCM systems. On the other hand, if you want to move ahead with CVS, this chapter is for you—it'll give you a good idea of how to fulfill basic SCM functions from both CVS's command-line interface and the affiliated Graphical User Interface (GUI) tools.

 NOTE *A couple of years ago, the Tigris open-source group decided to write a new version of CVS from scratch without using RCS as its base. The new product, Subversion, contains most of CVS's current feature set and user interface—as well as the ability to commit atomically and to version directories and metadata. You can find out more about Subversion at* `http://subversion.tigris.com`.

WORD OF THE DAY

non·prŏ·prī'e·tăr·y, *a.*

When *free* doesn't mean free.

A leader in the open-source world is the GNU Project—a group that launched in the mid-80s to develop a knockoff of Unix that would be freely distributable. The GNU operating system is still available today (with, interestingly enough, a Linux kernel as its core), but GNU is known nowadays more for the breadth of its free software offerings.

But what is "free software" anyway? It may not be quite what you might think it is. The GNU Project describes free software as "a matter of liberty, not price. To understand the concept, you should think of 'free' as in 'free speech,' not as in 'free beer.'"[2] This is a significant difference—because it might mean that you have to pay money for open-source software!

The basis for freedom, according to GNU, is the accessibility to the software's source. This access allows you to run, modify, inspect, or distribute any software created under the GNU General Public License (GPL) once you've procured it. In other words, if you download a GPL product, you have the right to its source for whatever purpose upon which you may decide—as long as the GPL always applies to the code should you ever decide to distribute any updates.

CONTINUED

---

2.   The GNU "free software" definition, located at `http://www.gnu.org`

CONTINUED

And therein lies the rub. Did you see it, or did you miss it? That's right—in order to get the freedom dictated by the GPL, you must first obtain a copy of the product. In some cases, that might mean—gasp!—having to buy it. According to the GPL, companies can charge you a distribution fee for binary versions of software—whether it is a dollar or a million dollars. If you do buy the distribution, however, the manufacturer of the software must also make its source available to you (though they're allowed to charge another nominal fee for this service). Of course, access to the source may be of little comfort if you had to spend a million dollars to get it.

The good news is that once you've got the code, you can do pretty much what you want with it. You can change it, put it on 20 computers, or simply just give it away to your neighbor. Using this knowledge, you might be able to figure out other ways of procuring software at a lesser cost than the distributor might be charging…copy it for free from someone who has already bought it, split the cost of the purchase with a friend, or start a software co-op for the product that costs a million dollars. You need only 10,000 people to chip in $100 bucks, and it's yours!

Can proprietary source products ever be free? According to the GNU folks, some software that distributes without cost isn't really free. As an example, take a look at Microsoft's Internet Explorer or SourceSafe…although these products may not cost you anything to install, you're surely not free to modify or distribute the code in any way you'd like. You might be asking what the manufacturer gets out of offering these products without cost to end users. In many cases, the widespread use of these types of proprietary freeware products can lead to the adoption of more expensive products. An example of this scenario is that the use of SourceSafe gets more people to buy Visual Studio. In other cases, the freeware product might have limited functionality—but once users try out it out, they're tempted with offers of a more feature-rich version of the software.

As you delve into the open-source world, be aware that products can be distributed with more than one license. For example, Lindows.com ships a suite of tools for use with Linux based on both GPL and proprietary components. The GPL components are GPL licensed—but the portions of the code Lindows created or licensed itself have their own "family" license, which bars you from sharing the product with a friend.

This entire discussion begs the question of whether free is better than proprietary in the software world. There are good arguments for both sides. For instance, proprietary software vendors say that allowing people to view and change code leads to flaw exploitation by hackers. On the other hand, open-source advocates contend that multiple-eye inspections might lead to those same flaws' fixes before the software is released for general use. Another argument by proprietary vendors is that there can be no future in open-source software—by its nature, this type of software is architected by community consensus, and changes to it are often more by hack than by design. This can lead to subpar user interfaces and code that's difficult to manage. Of course, the open-source advocate then plays his trump card—feel free to change whatever part of the product you don't like.

Installing CVS

CVS is available as a binary executable for Windows and Red Hat Linux 8.0 at http://www.cvshome.org. Like other open-source tools, the code necessary for creating the tool for other platforms is also freely available for download. In addition, you can update or make any other changes to it that you like. Of course, if you choose to redistribute any of your changes, be sure to check your responsibilities to the GNU GPL at http://www.gnu.org. See the previous "Word of the Day" sidebar for more information about the GNU license.

Server Requirements

Before you install the tool, you should be aware of its requirements, easy as they are. CVS has been around for a long time and thrives on the outdated machines you might have considered tossing in the trash.

The source repository itself is just a directory on the machine. Plan on providing three times as much hard drive space as the size of the current source tree. For instance, if you think the tip of the source will be about 10 megabytes (MB) in size, you want to dedicate about 30MB of hard drive space to the CVS repository. Although processor speeds and RAM amounts aren't specifically stated, the CVS group advises that 32MB of RAM "can handle a fairly large source tree with a fair amount of activity."[3]

CVS clients are able to run on any computer that can handle the parent operating system. In other words, don't worry about the systems requirements for the client.

Network and Security

CVS offers some flexibility in its ability to be used in both intranet and Internet settings. Table 5-1 displays a quick run-down of the models available for use when setting up a CVS repository.

---

3. *Version Management with CVS* by Per Cederqvist—the official CVS manual located at http://www.cvshome.org

Table 5-1. CVS Network and Security Models

Network	Model	Description
Intranet	Localhost	The client and the source repository are located on the same machine. Users call the CVS command executable or a local CVS GUI client to access source. In the Unix-flavored environments, multiple users can access the same source repository when logged into the machine.
Intranet	Network Share	The source repository is stored on a network drive and made available to clients via a Windows share, Samba (the tool used to expose Unix shares to Windows), or the Network File System (NFS). This should be considered an intranet-only scenario because of the serious security flaws associated with sharing directories.
Intranet/Internet	Remote Protocol	The source repository is stored on a machine behind a firewall. Users access the source via a remote protocol such as Remote Shell (RSH) or Secure Shell (SSH). This is the only remote location method that's detailed in this chapter.
Intranet/Internet	CVS Client/Server with Password Authentication	To access source, the CVS executable on client machines makes direct connections to the CVS server using an optional password vault. There's no need to expose a network share or force users to use a remote protocol. By default, passwords are sent to the server in clear text, so it's important that developers not use login passwords. Kerberos password authentication can be utilized to secure the server—however, each client machine must be installed with the Kerberos version of the CVS software before a connection can be made. Please note that using CVS in this manner requires that the executable be built with special parameters. For more information, refer to the CVS site at http://www.cvshome.org.

NOTE *Because this chapter doesn't discuss the client/server model, I won't cover its applicable CVS commands—such as those for logging into the server. In addition, some commands discussed in this chapter may require extra parameters for use in the client/server model. See the CVS site at* http://www.cvshome.org *for more information about these parameters.*

Creating a CVS Executable from Source

Although you can download an already created version of the CVS executable for many operating systems, you may choose to build it yourself so you can modify the product or create it for a rare Unix system. Choosing to do so isn't as difficult as you may think. Many people prefer to build their own versions of code so they can inspect it for security defects or hacks before installation. In addition, because there are so many flavors of Unix and Linux, many applications are available only as a source distribution—the overhead of providing binaries for every supported operating system is just too overwhelming.

CVS is just one executable, so it'll be fairly easy to install after you build it. If you do choose to build it instead of downloading the binary, go to the CVS download page at http://www.cvshome.org and grab whichever version of the source you plan to install.

NOTE *You may need to have root access to the build machine to fulfill some of these commands. See your system administrator if you're unsure of your security rights.*

Building CVS for Unix-flavored operating systems: The first step in building the executable for Unix systems is to uncompress the source into a working folder. If you've downloaded a GZIP tar ball of source, you can do this by typing the following on a shell command line in the same directory where the archive exists:

```
gzip -d -c [cvs.gz] | tar xvf -
```

The [cvs.gz] listed previously should be substituted with the name of your distribution file. And be sure not to forget the dash at the end of the command! You might uncompress the GZIP archive for the most current version of CVS (as of the time of this writing) by typing the following:

```
gzip -d -c cvs-1.11.5.tar.gz | tar xvf -
```

Continued

The archive will decompress into its own directory—most likely named for the distribution of the source. In my case, the directory is named *cvs.1.11.5*. Change into that directory by typing the following:

```
cd cvs.1.11.5
```

Now you follow the standard source compilation and installation procedures that most Unix-flavored programs provide:

```
./configure
make
make install
```

This may take a few minutes, but after running these three commands, the result should be the installation of the CVS binary to the /usr/bin directory.

NOTE *Depending on the network model you choose for your CVS server, such as the client/server model, there may be additional steps to creating your CVS executable. See the "Network and Security" section of this chapter to determine which model is right for your team.*

Building CVS for Windows: The first step in building the CVS executable for Windows is to uncompress the source into a working folder. Create a working folder and then, using your favorite unzipping utility, uncompress the source into that directory.

A Visual Studio project file is included with the source distribution. The project file was created in a much older version of Visual Studio, and you may be prompted to update it as it opens—don't worry…it'll still work. Once opened, simply choose to build the project. Regardless of the debug configuration you select during the build process, you'll find the built WINDEBUG\CVS.EXE executable in the directory in which you opened the project file.

Once created, simply copy the executable to an appropriate location for use. Many people drop it into the Windows directory so it's automatically found when called from the command line.

NOTE *The Windows version of CVS.EXE provided by the CVS organization doesn't include support for several security models available on other platforms; however, you can find an open-source Windows client/server version of CVS at* http://www.cvsnt.org. *See the "Network and Security" section of this chapter to determine which model is right for your team.*

Understanding the Repository

Before discussing the creation of a source repository, let's talk about its basic makeup and properties.

CVS source repositories are simply a hierarchical set of files located in a common directory. At the root of the source repository is a directory called CVSROOT. This directory contains the basic settings information applicable to the projects in the CVS source tree.

The other directories listed in the source root directory will contain either project files or child directories with more projects. For instance, in Figure 5-1, there are two groups of projects at the root level, which both contain three subprojects. Inside each of the projects is a CVS administration directory that contains file attribute information applicable only to the project.

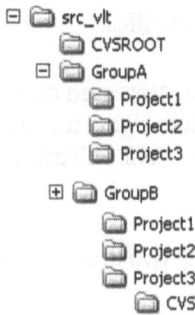

Figure 5-1. A possible CVS source tree in Windows

As each source file is added, CVS creates an equivalent file in its repository that's marked as read-only and ends with the extension ,V. For instance, FOO.TXT would be stored as FOO.TXT,V. These are RCS storage files that contain the original addition of the source plus any deltas that might have occurred since. These files should never be edited by hand.

If you choose to use a security model on the repository, you can make projects accessible to different sets of users by setting the operating system permissions on the project directories. In the Windows world, simply set permissions on the project directories as you would with any other directory. On Unix-flavored systems, create user groups and then use the chmod command to flip the "group permissions on execution" bit.

NOTE *Any permissions you set apply directly to the source repository. Users can bypass the CVS executable and delete or corrupt entire sections of the source unless the client/server model is put in place. Use care when giving write permissions to the repository.*

As a quick example, let's set permissions for a CVS repository stored at C:\SRC_VLT or /home/src_vlt:

1. First, create a system-wide group called *cvs* and add your team members to it. The cvs name is an arbitrary moniker—name your group however you want.

2. Next, you want to change the permissions on your root source directory so that anyone in the cvs group has the right to modify the files.

3. If you're using Windows,[4] right-click the C:\SRC_VLT directory and choose Properties. Under the Security tab, choose the appropriate rights for the users. Make sure that any directories underneath C:\SRC_VLT will inherit its parent's security.

    If you're using a Unix-flavored system, type the following two lines in the command window:

    ```
    chgrp -R cvs /home/src_vlt
    chmod -R 02770 /home/src_vlt
    ```

    The chgrp command recursively changes the primary group for the /home/src_vlt tree to *cvs*. The chmod statement indicates that all new files created in this directory (and its subdirectories) should inherit its group from its parent directory instead of being set by the current user.

You can further limit access to parts of the tree by adding more groups and assigning subprojects or files to those groups. If you're unsure about taking these steps, talk to your system administrator for more information before completing this step.

---

4. Windows 95, 98, Me, and XP Home may not support the security rights detailed in this section.

NOTE *There are known issues with using file permissions while using Samba. Consult the CVS README file for more information regarding this problem.*

Creating a Repository

Now that you have an understanding of how CVS stores files, let's go ahead and create a repository.

You probably have already designated the location for your source repository—for instance, I've chosen C:\SRC_VLT as the repository location on my Windows machine—but so far none of CVS's required parameter files have been created there yet. The repository is unusable until those files are properly situated. To do this, the first step you take is the initialization of the source repository.

The init command takes care of this for you. For instance, after making sure that your CVS executable is in the path, you might type the following:

```
cvs -d c:\src_vlt init
```

The -d parameter tells CVS where the repository will be located, and the init keyword tells CVS to create the necessary configuration files in that location. After you've hit the Return key, a directory called CVSROOT is created and populated in your C:\SRC_VLT directory.

Fulfilling the same task in the Unix-flavored operating systems would be just as easy—but you'd replace the C:\SRC_VLT location with one more suitable for the applicable file system. For instance:

```
cvs -d /home/src_vlt init
```

Yep, that's it. Your source repository is now ready to accept files.

NOTE *Running an init command on a created database is harmless. CVS is smart enough to know that a configuration currently exists and will simply exit without making any changes.*

Identifying the CVS Source Repository to Clients

Because you accomplish almost all of the administrative functions for CVS through command-line or GUI clients, your next step is to configure one or more of them for use.

CVS started out and remains in core a command-line utility, so let's start by talking about the CVS executable. In fact, most of the GUI tools simply call this tool in the background to fulfill their functionality. As mentioned in the installation section of this chapter, the command-line client uses only one executable called *cvs* (or CVS.EXE in the Windows world) and can be placed or called from anywhere on the file system.

 TIP *Copy the CVS executable into a directory that's listed in the Path environment variable (such as the Windows or /usr/bin directories). This makes calling the executable much easier because a complete path isn't required to be typed every time you call the executable.*

The `init` command you just used didn't save the repository location in such a way that your clients know to use it. The reasoning for this is that you might want to access more than one repository from this machine—it would be problematic if you had to "hard code" the client machine with only one repository location. Instead, you tell the client where your chosen source repository is in one of two ways.

The first is to specify the location on the command line using the `-d` parameter as you did when you called the `init` command. This is convenient when there's more than one source repository to which you need to connect.

A second method of identifying the repository is to set the CVSROOT environment variable. In Windows, this might be called a *system variable*. You can create it on a Windows machine by typing the following into a command shell:

```
set CVSROOT=c:\src_vlt\cvsroot
```

Using the bash command shell in Unix or Linux, you can type the equivalent command:

```
export CVSROOT=/home/src_vlt/CVSROOT
```

Once set, you no longer need to specify the -d parameter as you work. In fact, had the CVSROOT environment variable been set before you initialized your repository, you could have simply typed the following:

```
cvs init
```

Keep in mind that creating the CVSROOT environment variable in this way is only a temporary solution—as soon as you close the shell window or restart the machine, the variable and its contents are erased. If you plan to access this source repository frequently, you may want to set the CVSROOT variable in a more permanent way.

To do so on Unix-flavored systems, add the CVSROOT variable to applicable startup scripts. For instance, if you're using the bash shell, copy the export line listed previously to the .bashrc or .bash_profile files located in your home directory.

Setting the CVSROOT environment variable in the Windows GUI is a little trickier. First, you right-click My Computer, choose Properties, and click the Advanced tab. Choose the Environment Variables button and click the New button either for the current user or for all users. Then fill the text boxes in the environment variable setup dialog box, as displayed in Figure 5-2.

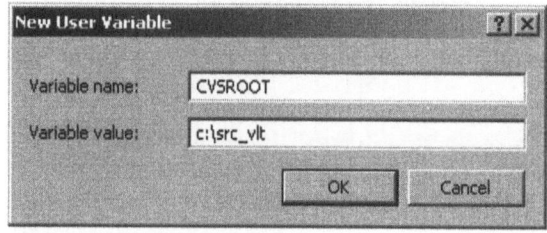

Figure 5-2. The Windows New User Variable dialog box

If you plan on accessing multiple repositories, you can still use the CVS -d parameter—it will always override the CVSROOT environment variable.

Using the CVS GUI Clients

There are many freeware CVS clients that can be downloaded and quickly installed. The two most popular tools are similarly named—WinCVS (also known as *CVSGUI*) and LinCVS. But don't let the names fool you—contrary to the implications of their names, the tools are available in both Windows and Unix flavors. WinCVS is also available for the Macintosh with the MacCVS moniker.

Both tools support most if not all of CVS's basic features by presenting them in an Explorer-like GUI application. Although both tools are a far cry from the simplicity of SourceSafe's user interface, I find that they're easier than using the command line in a shell.

WinCVS was started as an open-source effort in 1998, and you can download it at http://www.wincvs.org. Saying that the WinCVS user interface, as displayed in the following figure, isn't very intuitive is an understatement. It's difficult to use at first, but it comes with a generous user guide and is fairly easy to pick up if you already know the command-line tool, as shown in the following figure.

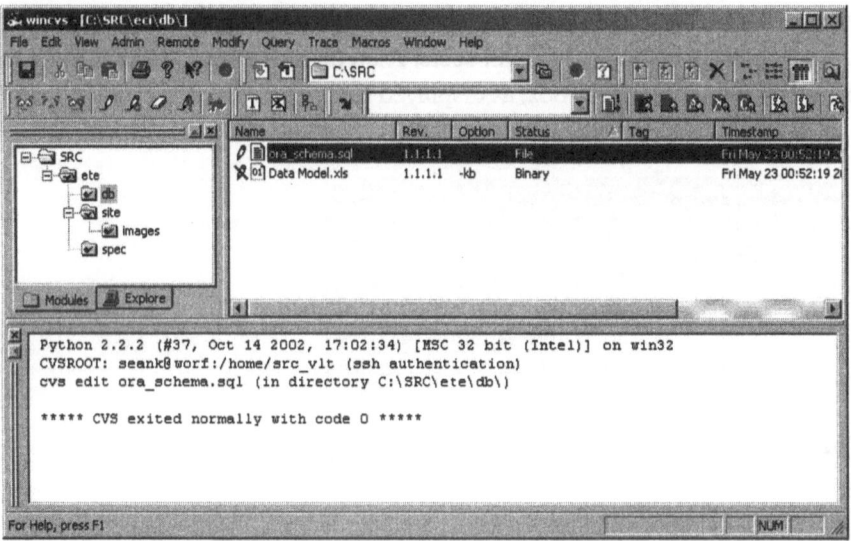

WinCVS, for its problems, does have a feature that differentiates it from the other CVS GUIs. For those who prefer typing to mouse clicking, WinCVS integrates two command-style languages (Python and TCL) for the creation of powerful macros that can save you steps when completing repetitive tasks. About 35 common-task macros are included with the current distribution, and you can find more on the Web.

Even though LinCVS has a superior user interface, it's still playing market share catch-up to WinCVS—in part because of its pitiful lack of documentation and a reliance on a cross-platform development tool that doesn't allow for such niceties as nested menus. What LinCVS does have is a cleaner look and feel, as displayed in the following figure, which is more intuitive for the user.

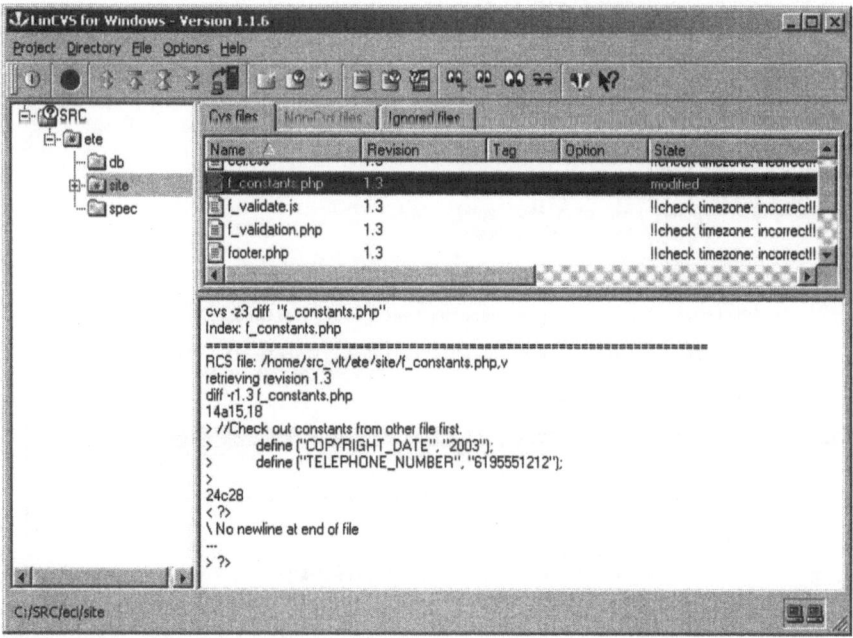

Both editors support most of CVS's command-line functionality as well as the ability to assign external editors and differentiation programs. Lastly, the CVS client/server model and the secure shell protocol are supported by both tools for accessing source repositories over the Internet.

 NOTE *See the sections "Working with CVS and Remote Locations" and "Network and Security" for more information on securing your CVS client-to-repository connections.*

If you're not thrilled with either of these choices, don't get depressed. One of the beauties of using a shared development solution such as CVS is the vigorous support that comes from the open-source community. There are a number of free tools and integrations for CVS—including a Visual Studio plug-in. For your consideration, explore the CVS integration written by Robert Hiestand for the VIM editor. As displayed in the following figure, VIM is the savvy update to the VI text editor paradigm and is popular with keyboard enthusiasts and programmers. After the integration installation, most of the basic CVS functionality, including checking in changes and differentiating versions of files, can be completed inside the text editor itself. Vim is available at http://www.vim.org, and you can find the plug-in by searching Google for the terms *vim*, *cvs*, and *integration*.

Continued

```
signup.php (c:\SRC\eci\site) - GVIM                              _ □ x
File Edit Tools Syntax Buffers Window Plugin Help

Index: signup.php
=================================================================
RCS file: /home/src_vlt/ete/site/signup.php,v
retrieving revision 1.4
diff -w -b -8 -c -r1.4 signup.php
*** signup.php   23 May 2003 01:15:25 -0000   1.4
--- signup.php   2  May 2003 22:25:54 -0000
**************
*** 359,364 ****
--- 359,365 ----
        if (strcmp($s_tmpstr = fixTelephoneNumber($_POST["telephone"]), RETURN_ERROR
        {
            $as_table["Company Information"]["telephone"]["color"] = "1";
            //Added new phone error code
            if ($phoneerror == 0)
            {
[Scratch]                                               12,5-9          Top
        if (strcmp($s_tmpstr = fixTelephoneNumber($_POST["telephone"]), RETURN_ERR
        {
            $as_table["Company Information"]["telephone"]["color"] = "1";
            //Added new phone error code
            if ($phoneerror == 0)
            {
                array_push($as_errors, ERROR_BADTELEPHONE);
                $phoneerror++;
            }
        }
        else
\SRC\eci\site\signup.php                                365,1-4         5 №
```

Importing Files

The import command is the easiest way to add files and directories to your source
repository. This command isn't as straightforward as it may seem, so you may
want to read this entire section before attempting its use.

NOTE *Binary files are treated differently from text files when using CVS, and
it's possible to corrupt them if they aren't handled correctly. Please see the section called "Binary Files in the Repository" before adding nontext files to the
CVS repository.*

The `import` command recursively imports every file and directory in the current folder. To use it on the command line, you utilize the following syntax:

```
cvs import -m "text" project_name vendor_tag release_tag
```

NOTE *You're no longer specifying the -d parameter because the rest of this chapter assumes that the CVSROOT variable is set.*

The `-m` parameter tells CVS that you're adding the comment specified in text via this command—otherwise, CVS would bring up your default editor and prompt you to comment.[5]

The `project_name` parameter specifies in which repository directory CVS should store the files being imported.

The `vendor_tag` parameter is a way to track third-party software dependencies of your products. I'll talk a little more about this later; however, the `import` command always requires its use. Because you're theoretically importing your own source code, feel free to use a short version of your company name as the vendor tag.

The `release_tag` parameter is equivalent to the labels discussed in earlier chapters. If your code has already been released to the public, you might use a tag such as *rel_1_0*. If this is the first time the code has ever been checked in, you might use the word *start*.

NOTE *Vendor and release tags can't contain any of the following characters: ampersand ($), period (.), colon (:), semicolon (;), and the at sign (@).*

The following is an example of how you might use the `import` command for source related to a music application called *MP3 Now*. The company responsible for the source is named *MusicMan*:

```
cvs import -m "First time check-in of code." mp3now musicman start
```

---

5.   The default editor is set by the operating system and not by an option within CVS.

Watch out for this newbie gotcha…. Let's say you want to import just the MP3NOW directory displayed in Figure 5-3 to the root of your source repository.

Figure 5-3. A possible source import scenario

You might think that you simply follow this set of shell commands:

```
cd c:\source
cvs import -m "First time check-in of code." mp3now cmready start
```

Makes sense, doesn't it? You want to import the MP3NOW directory and everything in it. Unfortunately, you're not going to get the results you wanted. When the command finishes, the tree in CVS would look like the one displayed in Figure 5-4.

Figure 5-4. The wrong result!

Why is that? Because the MP3NOW parameter you dictated in the import command doesn't dictate to CVS which directory to import. It's actually telling CVS what to call the repository directory being created in the database. Remember— the import command adds every file and directory in the current folder…so the MP3CONVERT and MP3GAIN source are also imported. Worse, the MP3NOW directory is repeated in the CVS tree, much to the annoyance of everyone on the staff.

To get around this problem, make sure you navigate into the directory you want to import before calling the command. The following set of commands will lead to the expected results:

```
cd c:\source\mp3now
cvs import -m "First time check-in of code." mp3now musicman start
```

This creates a directory in the source repository called MP3NOW and populates it with all the files and directories in the current folder.

NOTE *The* import *command ignores empty directories. Use the* add *command discussed later in this chapter to create an empty directory structure in a CVS source repository.*

ANOTHER NOTE *You should always try the functionality of any unfamiliar tool with nonproduction data on a test machine before using it in a real-world environment.*

Getting Source Code from the Repository

As the software configuration manager, you've created a source tree on your computer and imported it to the source repository. The developers, on the other hand, don't yet have the source on their machines. They can use the checkout and edit commands to get the files to their systems and begin to work on them.

First, the developer should create a directory on his or her hard drive where the downloaded copies of the source will be stored. There's no limitation as to where this directory may be located, but many people put it in their home directory or the root of the C:\ drive for convenience. Although the terminology is a bit outdated, this download directory is often referred to as a *sandbox*.

NOTE *Chapter 7, "In the SCM Lab," discusses best practices as to how developers might place source on their computers.*

After the directory has been created, the developer should ensure that the CVSROOT environment variable has been set on the machine as described in "Identifying the CVS Source Repository to Clients." The developer should also make sure that the CVS tool is in the path.

 NOTE *CVS comes standard on most Unix-flavored operating systems. The executable is usually located in either the /bin or /usr/bin directories and will therefore probably already be in the system path. Windows, on the other hand, doesn't install the CVS executable as part of its standard installation. Please see the "Installing CVS" section for more information.*

Once the configuration of the tool is complete, users can download code by using the checkout command. For instance, if you want to check out the entire MP3NOW project as discussed in the previous section, you might type the following in a shell window:

```
cvs checkout mp3now
```

 TIP *You can abbreviate the* checkout *command to* co *on the command line.*

You can also check out a single file in the MP3NOW project by specifying its name with the path listed previously. The path is always relative to the root of the source tree. For instance:

```
cvs checkout mp3now/mp3now.cpp
```

In this case, the MP3NOW parent directory is created on the local machine before the CPP file is checked out of the repository.

 NOTE *CVS understands Unix-style forward slashes as directory structure delimiters when referring to files inside folders on the repository. This is true even on the Windows operating system.*

In addition to checking out files from the tip of source, you can also use the -D and -r parameters to get previous revisions of the source. Be aware that CVS is case-sensitive with its parameters. They can be used with references to a particular date or to the tags (labels) assigned to the source. I'll discuss tags later in this chapter.

Unlike when checking out a file in SourceSafe and many other tools, a checkout in CVS is merely a way to do a "get" of the source. It's possible to lock files in CVS as you would in SourceSafe; however, most experts agree that locking source is a thing of the past. Instead, more-advanced tools allow multiple developers to check out the same files and check in each of their changes individually. The first developer to check in source gets a free ride—all of the others are prompted by the system to merge their changes before a checkin of the source is allowed. I agree with the experts, but use locks if your team prefers to work that way. And by no means should you make this decision on your own—rely on your development leaders to advise you on whether you should use the lock functionality. You can visit the CVS site at http://www.cvshome.com for more information on how to use locks.

Although keeping source unlocked has its benefits, one of its downsides is that developers won't know if there are other people working on the same file. This will be pretty annoying at checkin time if ten people have checked in changes to the same source files.[6] To address this problem, CVS allows other developers to see who's working on code with the edit and editors commands. After a file has been checked out to the local machine, the developer might use the edit command to publicize that he or she is working on a particular file. Anyone can then call the editors command to see who else might be working on a particular file. Here's an example of how these commands might be used—my comments describing each command start with the pound sign (#):

```
# First I check out the mp3now.cpp file.
C:\SRC> cvs co mp3now/mp3now.cpp
U mp3now/mp3now.cpp
# I then tell CVS that I plan on changing the file.
C:\SRC> cvs edit mp3now/mp3now.cpp
# I can then check and see who else might be working on the same file. The
# result is that Jeff is also modifying the same file.
C:\SRC> cvs editors mp3now/mp3now.cpp
mp3now/mp3now.cpp      sean    Sun May 25 01:22:19 2003 GMT    worf   c:\SRC\mp3now
mp3now/mp3now.cpp      jeffp   Thu May 22 10:17:56 2003 GMT    lama   c:\mp3now
```

---

6. Of course, if ten other people have checked in changes to the code without anyone knowing it, your team may have some serious process problems that need to be addressed.

Of course, the problem with this scenario is that it relies on developers remembering to use the edit command whenever they begin to work on source. The watch command can help to remind them:

```
cvs watch on mp3now
```

This command tells CVS to check out all files as read-only to client machines. Text editors will then display an error whenever developers try to open the file. Using the edit command flips the read-only bit of the file and makes it writable so the developer can again change the source. As you may have already figured out, this process is based on the honor system—anyone can easily get around this methodology and change source code without appropriately informing the other developers. Later, if you want to turn off the watch functionality, simply use the off keyword:

```
cvs watch off mp3now
```

CVS can also notify developers as files are marked for edit or committed to the repository. Refer to the CVS documentation at http://www.cvshome.org for more information on this functionality.

Checking in Code and Adding Source to the Repository

You've checked out your code and you've modified it. Now it's time to check the file back into the repository. You use the commit command to fulfill this:

```
cvs commit -m "Added ability to parse filenames" mp3now/mp3now.cpp
```

 NOTE *Binary files are treated differently than text files when using CVS, and it's possible to corrupt them if they aren't handled correctly. Please see the section called "Binary Files in the Repository" before adding nontext files to the CVS repository.*

Again, you use the -m parameter to specify a comment for this revision. If you didn't specify the parameter, CVS automatically starts your default editor and prompts you to add a comment.

NOTE *If the CVS command being called is acting on files on the local system (such as a checkin), the path and filenames can be relatively stated when using that command. For instance, you can refer to a file simply by BOB.TXT if you're currently in the directory that contains the file. Otherwise, you must use full module paths.*

TIP *You can abbreviate the* commit *to* ci *on the command line.*

If you've created new files in your local directory that don't yet exist in the source repository, you use the add command to insert them now into the repository. For instance, if you want to add a new file called MP3NOW_MAIN.CPP, you might do so by typing the following in a command shell:

```
cvs add mp3now/mp3now_main.cpp
```

After files have been added to the repository, other developers can't see them until these changes have been committed. The server reminds you of this by responding:

```
cvs server: scheduling file 'mp3now_main.cpp ' for addition
cvs server: use 'cvs commit' to add this file permanently
```

To finish your add, you'd type the following:

```
cvs commit -m " Added new main dialog box." mp3now/mp3now_main.cpp
```

Binary Files in the Repository

Let's take a couple of moments to discuss CVS's treatment of binary files. Unlike some of the other tools on the market, CVS wasn't well architected for use with binary files. Source code was comprised mostly of blocks of text back when CVS got its start.

Binary files face several challenges in the CVS repository:

You can't merge binary files: They can't be differentiated in the same way as text files and therefore can't be merged together when branches come together or two programmers work on and commit source at the same time.

Binaries are checked in full size: Only the delta of text files are committed as changes in CVS. Binary files, on the other hand, aren't saved as deltas, but instead each revision contains the latest full version of the file. This means they take up more storage space and also take longer to download.

Keyword expansion can break binaries: A function in CVS called *keyword expansion* allows users to automatically comment their code as they commit it by using specific variables that start and end with a dollar sign. Although unlikely, it's possible that binary files might coincidentally contain one of these variables and thus be corrupted when checked into the repository.

Added or removed line feeds can corrupt files: In the Unix world, the end of a line in a text file is designated by a special escape character called a *line feed*. The developers of DOS, however, decided to combine the line feed character with a carriage return character to create an end-of-line escape sequence. Because folks code on both of these different platforms, the programmers at CVS decided to add an automated end-of-line detection scheme to the executable. When a text file is committed to the repository, CVS translates the text file so that it uses Unix-style end-of-line characters—regardless of the end-of-line characters that were actually in the committed file. When the user checks out a file, the reverse takes place—the CVS executable changes the end-of-line style to match the operating system on which the user is working. Binary files also contain line feed and carriage return characters, but they're used in different ways. If a binary file is committed to CVS using the same methodology as a text file, they'll become corrupted as carriage returns are stripped and/or added to the file.

For these reasons, CVS must treat binary files differently than it does text files. End-of-line characters must be ignored and any coincidental keywords found in the file must not be expanded. You can identify binary files to CVS by using special command-line parameters—but this can be clumsy because you'd then have to check them in using different batches than your text files. Worse, it's easy to forget that you might be checking in a binary file.

NOTE *Some of the CVS GUI programs will advise you when it thinks you're checking in a binary file.*

CVS provides an ability to specify name patterns for files that will always be binary. When these identified files are added to the source repository, CVS knows not to change the end-of-line characters or expand the keyword variables.

To add name patterns, you need to modify the CVSWRAPPERS file located in the CVSROOT directory. First, you check it out to your local source directory and then, if necessary, mark it for editing:

```
cvs co CVSROOT/cvswrappers
cvs edit CVSROOT/cvswrappers
```

Next, you open the CVSWRAPPERS file in a text editor. The file will appear much like that in Listing 5-1.

Listing 5-1. The CVSWRAPPERS File

```
# This file affects handling of files based on their names.
#
# The -m option specifies whether CVS attempts to merge files.
#
# The -k option specifies keyword expansion (e.g. -kb for binary).
#
# Format of wrapper file ($CVSROOT/CVSROOT/cvswrappers or .cvswrappers)
#
#  wildcard      [option value][option value]...
#
#  where option is one of
#  -m            update methodology      value: MERGE or COPY
#  -k            expansion mode          value: b, o, kkv, &c
#
#  and value is a single-quote delimited value.
# For example:
#*.gif -k 'b'
```

The pound sign at the beginning of each sentence indicates comments that are ignored by CVS. By default, the file actually does nothing—every line in it is a comment. You now add the name patterns for file types that you want CVS to treat as binary. For instance, you can use the *.GIF pattern to indicate that any file that ends with the extension GIF is a binary file. Or you can command that any file that contains the word *SPEC* is a binary file by using the *SPEC* pattern.

Name patterns listed in the CVSWRAPPERS file must be labeled as one of four types. The -m parameter followed by the word copy indicates that any files matching the name pattern are text files but that they must not be merged for one reason or another. A good example of this type of file might be a Visual Studio project file that becomes corrupted if edited by hand. The -k parameter stands for "keyword expansion"—this is the parameter you use to indicate binary files when you use it with the letter b.

Here are some examples of name patterns you might add to the CVSWRAPPERS file:

```
#Image files
*.GIF -k 'b'
*.JPG -k 'b'
#Executables
*.EXE -k 'b'
*.DLL -k 'b'
#Postscript Files
*.PDF -m COPY
#Visual Studio Files
*.DSP -m COPY
*.VBP -m COPY
```

Once you finish updating the CVSWRAPPERS file, you commit it back to the database. CVS indicates whether the commit was successful in the lines following your command:

```
C:\SRC> cvs ci -m "Added basic binary file types." CVSROOT/cvswrappers
Checking in cvswrappers;
/home/src_vlt/CVSROOT/cvswrappers,v  <--  cvswrappers
new revision: 1.4; previous revision: 1.3
done
cvs commit: Rebuilding administrative file database
```

Of course there are times when pattern matching might not be appropriate. For instance, many Unix files don't have extensions and are difficult for which to determine a name pattern. In these cases, you simply use the -kb parameter on the command line as you fulfill tasks. For instance, to add a new binary file to the repository, you might type the following:

```
cvs add -kb mp3now/testsong.mp3
cvs server: scheduling file 'testsong.mp3' for addition
cvs server: use 'cvs commit' to add this file permanently
```

NOTE *Once you've added the file to the repository as a binary file, you don't need to indicate the -kb on following operations such as checkout or commit. CVS remembers that the file is binary.*

Creating Modules

So far in this chapter, you've known the exact path and name of all the files you've wanted to check out of the repository. As your source tree grows, this is going to get more difficult. Unfortunately, you can't simply type an ls or dir command to get CVS to list your files and directories like you could in a command shell. Your only option so far would be to get the entire source tree from the root—a task that could be inconvenient with large code bases.

To deal with this issue, CVS allows you to specify modules for specific branches of your tree. You can make these modules mimic your source tree exactly, or you can choose to lump directories together in a way that's more intuitive to your developers. Either way, you can use these modules with commands in the same way you specify files.

Let's take a look at an example. The following is an example source tree that you might have in your CVS database:

```
\mp3
    \mp3\mp3now
    \mp3\mp3gain
    \mp3\mp3convert
\jpg
    \mp3\jpgnow
```

Note that the repository location reflects the Unix-style forward slashes when delimiting the directory structure. You have two major projects named MP3 and JPG. MP3 has three subprojects: MP3NOW, MP3GAIN, and MP3CONVERT. JPG has only one subproject: JPGNOW. Now let's organize these sets of source into modules—such as the six listed in Table 5-2.

Table 5-2. An Example of Module Creation

Module	Repository Location
mp3	/mp3
mp3now	/mp3/mp3now
gain	/mp3/mp3gain
convert	/mp3/3convert
jpg	/jpg
jprnow	/jpg/jpgnow

So what exactly does this give you? First, you now have the ability to "query" the source repository by using the checkout command with the -c parameter. This command displays a list of all modules and what values they represent inside the repository. For instance, if you were to set up the modules as displayed in Table 5-2, you might use the checkout command to display the results:

```
cvs co -c
```

CVS returns to you the following information:

```
mp3        mp3
mp3now     mp3/mp3now
gain       mp3/mp3gain
convert    mp3/mp3convert
jpg        jpg
jprnow     jpg/jpgnow
```

In addition to listing modules, you can now also fulfill any of your regular CVS commands on them. For instance, to check out only the MP3GAIN code, you might type the following:

```
cvs co gain
```

You no longer need to append a directory structure or use filenames. The previous command will get all the files located in the MP3/MP3GAIN directory as if you had typed the following:

```
cvs co mp3/mp3gain
```

NOTE *The directory structure on your local machine will reflect module names and not necessarily the source's true structure as it exists in the repository. By getting the GAIN module, a directory called GAIN is created locally, and all the files and directories in the repository's MP3/MP3GAIN location are copied to it. If you were to also download the MP3 directory, the MP3GAIN source would be duplicated under it.*

You can see why using modules makes sense. To use them, you must update the MODULES file located in the CVSROOT directory as you did the CVSWRAPPERS file in the previous section. First, you check the file out to your local directory and, if necessary, mark it for editing:

```
cvs co CVSROOT/modules
cvs edit CVSROOT/modules
```

Next, you open the MODULES file in a text editor. The file will appear much like that in Listing 5-2.

Listing 5-2. The MODULES File

```
# Three different line formats are valid:
#       key      -a    aliases...
#       key [options] directory
#       key [options] directory files...
#
# Where "options" are composed of:
#       -i prog         Run "prog" on "cvs commit" from top-level of module.
#       -o prog         Run "prog" on "cvs checkout" of module.
#       -e prog         Run "prog" on "cvs export" of module.
#       -t prog         Run "prog" on "cvs rtag" of module.
#       -u prog         Run "prog" on "cvs update" of module.
#       -d dir          Place module in directory "dir" instead of module name.
#       -l              Top-level directory only -- do not recurse.
#
# NOTE: If you change any of the "Run" options above, you'll have to
# release and re-checkout any working directories of these modules.
#
# And "directory" is a path to a directory relative to $CVSROOT.
#
# The "-a" option specifies an alias.  An alias is interpreted as if
# everything on the right of the "-a" had been typed on the command line.
#
# You can encode a module within a module by using the special '&'
# character to interpose another module into the current module.  This
# can be useful for creating a module that consists of many directories
# spread out over the entire source repository.
```

The pound sign at the beginning of each sentence indicates a comment that will be ignored by CVS. By default, the file actually does nothing and contains only comments. You're going to add the six modules you defined earlier to the end of the file:

```
mp3              mp3
mp3now           mp3/mp3now
gain             mp3/mp3gain
convert          mp3/mp3convert
jpg              jpg
jprnow           jpg/jpgnow
```

Once you've finished updating the MODULES file, you need to commit it back to the database and you're told that CVS has been updated with your changes:

```
C:\SRC> cvs ci -m "Added basic modules." CVSROOT/modules
Checking in modules;
/home/src_vlt/CVSROOT/modules,v  <--  modules
new revision: 1.4; previous revision: 1.3
done
cvs commit: Rebuilding administrative file database
```

Once you've committed the files, you can treat the newly listed modules as you would files.

Labeling Revisions in the Source Repository

The ability to group revisions of source files together into reusable "objects" is one of the most important functions of a source control tool. You're already familiar with these Label "objects" because I discussed them in Chapter 3, "All About the Source."

> **NOTE** *I discussed labeling with detail in Chapter 3, "All About the Source." If you need a refresher on what constitutes a label, you may want to reread that chapter's "What's in a Label?" section.*

You can use the `tag` command to label revisions of source in this manner with CVS. I briefly touched on tags when I discussed the `import` command, but you can do much more than use them in that context. You can also use tags for the following:

- You can designate milestones, such as the releases of product. For instance, you might label the tip of your source tree as *Rel_1_0* when Release 1.0 is sent to customers.

- You can use tags in a promotion scenario. You might label one set of code revisions *QA* while another set is labeled *Beta*. This allows the beta coordinator to send out copies of an older, more stable line of code without affecting the quality team's schedule.

- Developers can use tags to inform the build engineer of which file revisions should be included in builds. This allows developers to back up their work by checking in unstable versions of code during build cycles—without having to create a branch.

You can apply tags to modules or sets of one or more files—though it's unlikely that you'll have a use for tagging a single file. They can contain upper- and lower-case alphanumeric characters, but you must avoid all other special characters, including spaces. The only exceptions to this rule are that the underscore (_) and dash (-) characters may be used. You can also delete or move tags to different versions of files should the need arise.

Listing 5-3 displays the `tag` command and the possible CVS response should you choose to label the GAIN module with the `rel_1_0` tag.

Listing 5-3. Tagging the GAIN Module

```
C:\SRC> cvs tag rel_1_0 gain
cvs server: Tagging gain
T gain/MainFrm.cpp
T gain/MainFrm.h
T gain/ModelessDlg.cpp
T gain/ModelessDlg.h
T gain/mp3gain.cpp
T gain/mp3gainView.cpp
T gain/StdAfx.cpp
T gain/StdAfx.h
T gain/resource.h
T gain/thread.cpp
```

CVS uses a T character during its output to indicate which files were actually tagged. There may be times when tagging can fail—such as when a local file hasn't been synced with the repository—so you'll want to pay attention to the command's output to ensure that it worked appropriately.

You can now refer to this tag in several different ways. The most obvious utilization of tags is that you can check out groups of files as they were at a certain point in time. You use the checkout -r parameter to specify a tag:

```
cvs co -r rel_1_0 gain
```

There are other commands that use tags as parameters, such as when you update your local directory or create branches. This functionality is discussed later in the chapter. In addition, you can also use sticky tags, which allow you to glue your working directory to certain revisions or change tags to different revisions—such as moving the stable tag from an older revision of a file to a newer one. Find out more about these options by visiting the CVS documentation located at http://www.cvshome.org.

Viewing History and Status About Files

CVS, like other source control tools, saves all the versions of files as they're committed to the repository and other applicable information such as comments and the date. To view the history of a particular file or module, you can use the log command:

```
cvs log gain/mp3gain.cpp
```

 NOTE *Regardless of whether a logged file is specified through its path or through a module path, the same historical information displays.*

In return, you get back the historical information regarding the queried file as displayed in Listing 5-4.

Listing 5-4. The History of MP3GAIN.CPP As Returned by log

```
RCS file: /home/src_vlt/mp3/mp3gain/mp3gain.cpp,v
Working file: gain/mp3gain.cpp
head: 1.3
branch:
locks: strict
access list:
symbolic names:
        init: 1.1.1.1
        gain: 1.1.1
keyword substitution: kv
total revisions: 3;     selected revisions: 3
description:
---------------------------
revision 1.2
date: 2003/05/23 01:12:22;  author: sean;  state: Exp;  lines: +35 -14
Added keyword expansion.
---------------------------
revision 1.1
date: 2003/05/23 00:37:34;  author: sean;  state: Exp;
branches:  1.1.1;
Initial revision
=================================================================
```

Every revision of the file is listed alongside the name of the committing developer, the date and time, and the developer's comments. This can be invaluable when attempting to debug what went wrong with a code update.

A second way to get information regarding a file is to use the status command. With it, you can determine the following:

- Whether a file is currently synced with the repository

- Which revision of the current file represents the tip

- Which tags (labels) are attached to source files

- Whether a file has been designated as binary—a sticky option of kb indicates this designation

Listing 5-5 displays an example of the status command. By default, tag information is omitted during a status check. You use the -v parameter to display it.

Listing 5-5. The History of MP3GAIN.CPP As Returned by log

```
C:\SRC> cvs status -v gain/mp3gain.cpp
===========================================
File: mp3gain.cpp        Status: Locally Modified
   Working revision:    1.1.1.1
   Repository revision: 1.1.1.1 /home/src_vlt/mp3/mp3gain/mp3gain.cpp,v
   Sticky Tag:          (none)
   Sticky Date:         (none)
   Sticky Options:      (none)
   Existing Tags:
      init                           (revision: 1.1.1.1)
      a_1                            (branch: 1.1.1)
```

The "status" of the file—which in this case is Locally Modified—indicates how your local file compares to that of the tip in the source repository. One of four statuses might be applicable:

- **Up-to-Date:** The files in the source repository and the local drive are the same.

- **Locally Modified:** The file on the local drive has been modified and doesn't require a merge if checked in to the repository.

- **Needs Patch:** Another developer has checked in a new revision of the file since it was checked out to the local drive. The file will need merging if any new changes are introduced on the local drive, so it's wise to "patch" the file from the source repository before making changes.

- **Needs Merge:** Another developer has checked in a new revision of the file since it was checked out to the local drive, and the local version has also been modified. A merge will need to take place before you can check in the file.

 NOTE *Running the log and status commands on a module results in the history listing of every file in the module's directory structure.*

Differencing Code

You use the `diff` command to see the differences between code on your local drive and that which is held in the repository. Listing 5-6 displays a sample use of the command.

Listing 5-6. Differentiating MP3GAINM.CPP Against the Repository Version

```
C:\SRC> cvs diff mp3gain.cpp
RCS file: /home/src_vlt/mp3gain.cpp,v
retrieving revision 1.7
diff -r1.7 mp3gain.cpp
10a12
> //New code added here
```

The output is a little cryptic. The `10a12` line in Listing 5-6 indicates that the change occurred at the twelfth line in the text file. It also lists the differences directly beneath the line number, and a greater-than or less-than symbol indicates which file holds the change. The tool provides the ability to see the differences side by side though it doesn't work very well using the standard output.

The following are some other important notes about the `diff` command:

- By default, `diff` will show the differences between the local working file and the *revision from which it was checked out*; changes made and committed by other programmers will not be displayed. To see the differences between your file and that which has been most recently committed, use the `-D` parameter with the `now` keyword:

  ```
  cvs diff -D now mp3gain.cpp
  ```

- Use the `-r` parameter to specify a particular revision or tag. For example:

  ```
  cvs diff -r rel_1_0 mp3gain.cpp
  ```

- The `diff` command is also applicable to modules; however, every modified file and its modifications are sent to standard output. Instead, you may want to `diff` modules using the `--brief` parameter. This will only display the filenames of differing files.

- Most people prefer to use an external differentiation program that allows GUI side-by-side comparisons of files. You can find a freeware differentiation program called *ExamDiff* at http://www.examdiff.com; a more fully featured professional version of the tool is also available.

- WinCVS and LinCVS both have GUI differentiation components and support using external tools.

- The diff command has almost 40 parameters available to it—refer to the documentation at http://www.cvshome.org for more information about the many things DIFF can do.

Bringing the Local Directory Up-to-Date

After you've used the status command to check whether your source files need to merged before checking in, you may want to update your local directory with the code others have committed since the original checkout took place. This can be especially important when developers work on a single piece of code for long periods of time—frequent small merges are much easier and safer to conduct than waiting until the last moment and trying to merge in a large amount of code.

You use update to fulfill this task. This command will query the source repository and do a "get" if it finds differences in the tree. If any of your files have been locally modified, update will attempt to merge the two files together automatically. Because both the local version of the file and the tip may have been modified since the original checkout took place, it's possible that there might be conflicts during the update. If so, update informs you and places bookmarks in the file so you know to manually merge the code.

TIP *Use the* -n *parameter to run the* update *tool without actually making changes to the local file system. This is a great way to do a quick check without having to run the* status *command on every file. The* -n *is a global parameter (versus a command parameter) and must be used after the CVS call instead of following the command as you've done with other parameters—for example,* cvs -n update. *You can use global parameters with any CVS command.*

Let's use the GAIN module as an example. You've checked out all 15 files in the module and have begun to work on the code. Specifically, you modified the MP3GAIN.CPP and MP3GAINVIEW.CPP files. After a week or so, you may want to bring your local directories up-to-date with those located in the tip of the repository. You now run the update command, as displayed in Listing 5-7, to query the repository and attempt to sync your local directory.

Listing 5-7. Updating the GAIN Module

```
C:\SRC>cvs update -P gain
cvs server: Updating gain
U gain/gain.rc
U gain/gain/gain.bmp
retrieving revision 1.6
retrieving revision 1.7
Merging differences between 1.6 and 1.7 into mp3gain.cpp
M gain/mp3gain.cpp
retrieving revision 1.3
retrieving revision 1.4
Merging differences between 1.3 and 1.4 into mp3gainview.cpp
rcsmerge: warning: conflicts during merge
cvs server: conflicts found in gain/ mp3gainview
C gain/mp3gainview.cpp
```

After typing the command, update indicates the action it has taken on each file to update the local directory. The U symbol next to a filename indicates that the local directory file was replaced by an updated version in the source repository. An M symbol indicates that a new version of the file had been checked into the source repository and was merged into your locally modified version of the file. C means the same thing—however, it also indicates that one or more *conflicts*, places where the tool can't automatically merge code, were found when the files were merged together.

Should a conflict be found, you must resolve it by opening the file in a text editor and deciding which change is appropriate in the new context. For instance, Listing 5-8 displays a snippet from a file that was merged by CVS and presented to you with conflicts.

Listing 5-8. The MP3GAINVIEW.CPP Conflict

```
int iNumFiles=0;
int iOldFiles=0;
iNumFiles =GetNumFiles();
iOldFiles =GetNumOldFiles();
if (iOldFiles>iNumFiles)
{
<<<<<<< mp3gainview.cpp
    CheckSystem(iNumFiles);
=======
    CheckSystem();
>>>>>>> 1.4
}
```

The conflicted section of code is in bold. The set of seven < characters indicates the start of the conflict, and the changes listed until the seven = characters demarcate the other changes from the merging file. Seven > characters, followed by the number of the version in which the change was made, close the conflict.

 NOTE *There may be more than one conflict in a file. Be sure to search for seven < characters until you've resolved all conflicts.*

In this example, you'll look at the differences and reassure yourself that your code is correct while the code being merged is out-of-date. You'll also remove the excess information that CVS inserted in order to point out the conflict. The resolved file might look like that listed in Listing 5-9.

Listing 5-9. The Resolved MP3GAINVIEW.CPP Conflict

```
int iNumFiles=0;
int iOldFiles=0;
iNumFiles =GetNumFiles();
iOldFiles =GetNumOldFiles();
if (iOldFiles>iNumFiles)
{
    CheckSystem(iNumFiles);
}
```

Once you've updated the file, you commit the changes to the source repository.

> **NOTE** *CVS will not allow the commit of a file with unresolved conflicts in it.*

It's important to note that update is a one-way tool—it will never update the repository with the changes you've made on the local drive. User-modified, merged, and conflicted merged files must be committed to the source repository before others can ever share the code.

> **NOTE** *You can update from more than just the tip—there are many update options that allow you to merge from certain dates, tags, or revisions. Refer to the documentation at* http://www.cvshome.org *for more information about the* update *command.*

Branching and Merging

Release 1.0 of the MP3GAIN software has gone out the door and now the development team is working furiously on Release 2.0. But a terrible bug is found in the 1.0 version months before 2.0 will be ready for the outside world. Because customers need this fix now, you have to create a branch for the patch. When the patch is released, you'll go ahead and merge the changes back into the main line so Release 2.0 will also be fixed.

> **NOTE** *I discussed branching with detail in Chapter 3, "All About the Source." If you need a refresher on what constitutes a branch, you may want to reread that chapter's "Understanding Branches" section.*

CVS's branching mechanism is handled through the tag (or rtag in different contexts) command almost as if you were creating a label. It's important, however, to note that branches are an entirely different species than labels. Even though the same command is used for the two different tasks, it doesn't mean that labels and branches are interchangeable and shouldn't be treated as such.

The tag command works in relation to the files that already exist in your working directory, so you want to make sure you've already checked out the source you plan to branch before you use it:

```
cvs co gain
```

You can assume that the software configuration manager would be sure to have labeled the source as released before it went out the door.[7] Let's go ahead and simulate that now by labeling the source as *rel_1_0*. If the source is properly labeled, it won't matter whether you create a maintenance branch now or three months from now—any changes made to the trunk of GAIN after the tag will be ignored when the branch is created:

```
cvs tag "rel_1_0" gain
```

Now that you've made sure that the source has been labeled, you go ahead and branch the code by using the tag command again—but this time with the -b parameter. You branch the GAIN code in relation to the rel_1_0 tag so that you don't place any Release 2.0 code into the branch. You'll call the new tag *maint_1_1*:

```
cvs tag -b -r rel_1_0 maint_1_1 gain
```

CVS outputs to the screen that the files have been branched. But even though you just branched the code, the CVS client still reflects that your working local directory is "attached" to the main branch of the source—not the one you just created. If you were to check in files, for example, the main branch, not maint_1_1, would be updated. There are two ways to tell CVS that you want to work on the maintenance line of code. The first way is to delete the code you have on your local system and then check it out again using the -r maint_1_1 parameter and tag. Before you do so, of course, you want to be sure that you've checked in or otherwise saved everything that's currently in your GAIN folder:

```
del /s gain
cvs co -r maint_1_1 gain
```

The second way to attach to the maintenance branch is to use the update command with the -r parameter. This tells CVS to "merge" the maintenance branch into your existing GAIN directory:

```
cvs update -r maint_1_1 gain
```

---

7.   If you forget to tag the code properly, you could still access and tag the source by specifying a valid date and time.

You can confirm the action you just took by viewing the output of the status command. Whenever you attach to a branch, the working file's "sticky tag" is set to reflect it. The code on your local system is "stuck" to the branch instead of the tip. For example, the sticky tag for the MP3GAIN.CPP file has now been set to *maint_1_1*, as displayed in Listing 5-10.

Listing 5-10. The status *Command on MP3GAIN.CPP*

```
File: mp3gain.cpp       Status: Up-to-date
   Working revision:    1.8.2.2
   Repository revision: 1.8.2.2 /home/src_vlt/mp3/mp3gain/mp3gain.cpp,v
   Sticky Tag:          maint_1_1 (branch: 1.8.2)
   Sticky Date:         (none)
   Sticky Options:      (none)
```

NOTE *If you were working on the main branch of the tree, your sticky tag would be set to* (none).

Now that you've branched and ensured that your working directory is ready to go, you can make whatever source modifications are necessary to fix the bug. In this case, you'll say that the bug was fixed both by adding a new file called NEWGAIN.CPP and by modifying MP3GAIN.CPP. When you're finished, you check them in as usual:

```
C:\SRC> cvs ci -m "Fixed sound bug #56434" gain/mp3gain.cpp
C:\SRC> cvs add newgain.cpp
cvs server: scheduling file 'newgain.cpp for addition
cvs server: use 'cvs commit' to add this file permanently
C:\SRC> cvs ci -m "Fixed sound bug #56434" gain/newgain.cpp
```

NOTE *You could have completed the checkin of both files after NEWGAIN.CPP's addition had you simply referred to the module instead of the individual filenames.*

Let's now merge the updated code back into the main branch. Just before, however, let's prepare for a future "gotcha." You're going to tag the maintenance branch with a label before the merge takes place. You'll see the benefit of this in a few moments:

```
cvs tag "bug_56434_merge"
```

Once tagged, you merge the maintenance branch back into the main line of source. In order to complete this step, you need to check out the main line's code. You check to ensure that you've checked in or otherwise saved everything in your GAIN folder and then you type the following:

```
del /s gain
cvs co gain
```

> **NOTE** *The "sticky tag" setting under* status *will be empty after fulfilling this command—check it out on one of your files to be sure that you're now working on the main branch.*

The release code has been placed in your local source directory. You merge the maintenance branch changes into this code by using the update command with the -j parameter, which indicates to CVS that the merging of a branch is taking place:

```
cvs update -j maint_1_1 gain
```

Just as if you had used the update command regularly, CVS merges your files together and tells you of any possible conflicts. For more information about how to resolve conflicts or the update tool itself, refer to the "Bringing the Local Directory Up-to-Date" section earlier in this chapter.

Note that the update command has also automatically added the new file, NEWGAIN.CPP, to the main branch. Now you resolve any conflicts that might exist and then do a cursory check to ensure that all files merged as expected. Once you're ready, you check the merged files back to the main branch:

```
cvs ci -m "Merged changes from maintenance branch." gain
```

Voila! The merge is complete!

But there is one more scenario of which you need to be aware. What if the bug fix needed revising again in the future? You'd need to fix the bug in the maintenance branch and then merge that change back to the main branch once more. But now you run into a problem. If you use the update command as previously stated, CVS complains about imaginary conflicts. This is because update can't tell the difference between the changes you just made and the changes that were made before the last merge.

To get around this problem, you have to tell the update command which file revisions were current before you made the latest change. For instance, let's say that the revision number for the maintenance version of MP3GAIN.CPP was 1.4.1 the last time it was merged into the main branch. You just fixed it again, and now you're at version 1.4.2. You can indicate to the update tool to merge the delta of these two revisions by typing the following:

```
cvs update -j 1.4.1 -j maint_1_1 gain/mp3gain.cpp
```

The order of the -j parameters is very important. In the previous command, you've told CVS to merge the changes that were made to MP3GAIN.CPP after revision 1.4.1 into the code in your local source directory. The second -j parameter indicates that the delta between the tip and 1.4.1 contains the changes to be merged. It's not pretty—but that's the way it works.

Now imagine having to merge just ten files in this way. What a nightmare! Ah—but remember when you created that premerge label on the GAIN module? This is where it comes in handy! Because you created it, you can now use it with the module instead of merging every file separately:

```
cvs update -j bug_56434_merge -j maint_1_1 gain
```

Whew—that saved you some time. Now be sure to label the maintenance branch again so you don't run into the same problem the next time around!

Understanding Keyword Expansion

Ever opened a source file and wondered why the last guy made the change he did? If you're a developer, you're sure to have run into this. Of course, it's possible to check the version comments for each revision by using the log command, but that can be time-consuming if you're checking for more than just a few files.

CVS has provided a mechanism for tracking checkin comments and other pertinent information in the source files themselves. It's called *keyword expansion*.

Placing keywords surrounded by dollar signs in the comments of source files, it's possible to automatically append historical comments, revision numbers, authors, dates, and any number of other information to source files at checkin time.

For instance, you might type the following bolded information at the beginning of a C++ source file:

```
/*
 * $log$
*/
#include "msdos.h"
void main(int iNum)
... more code ...
```

The /* and */ indicate to the C++ compiler that everything between them is a comment and should be disregarded. CVS, on the other hand, sees the log keyword and adds specific historical information to the file each time that it's checked in. After checking in a bug fix with the comment "Bug 5645: Create user failure," the file might now look like this:

```
/*
 * $History: base64.c $
 *
 #    $Log: main.cpp,v $
 #    Revision 1.5  2003/05/23 01:15:25  sean
 #    Bug 5645: Create user failure.
 *
*/
#include "msdos.h"
void main(int iNum)
...  more code ...
```

The `log` keyword was filled by CVS with the appropriate checkin information including filename, revision number, date, user, and comment. This occurs every time this file is checked in, regardless of the user or comment.

The following are some things to keep in mind while using keyword expansion:

Only text files can use this feature: Binary files can become corrupted if this feature isn't used correctly—see the "Binary Files in the Repository" section of this chapter for more information.

Keywords are flexible: You can place keywords anywhere in a file.

Keep keywords in comments: You should specify keywords within comments for your programming language. Otherwise, the files will not compile properly.

Put keywords at the end of files: Every time a file is checked in and gets "stamped," it gets that much larger and difficult to navigate. You may consider putting the keywords at the end of the file to make it easier for developers. Many experts believe that the use of keyword expansion and general checkin comments by developers should be required as a general practice.

Ignore keywords when merging: When keywords are used, merging branches can display unnecessary conflicts. Be sure to use the -kk parameter with the update command so it knows to ignore expanded keywords when merging files. Keep in mind that this parameter will "stick" to all the files to which you apply this command. In other words, you won't need to use it more than once unless the sticky option is toggled. The status command can tell you if a file has the -kk sticky option attached to it.

Use $$ in HTML: HTML files must use double dollar signs ($$) because their singular value is a language escape character.

There are many keywords that can expand: You can use many keywords in addition to log. You can find them in the CVS documentation at http://www.cvshome.org for more information.

Working with CVS and Remote Locations

CVS has several models for allowing source access over a network—whether two developers are sitting side by side or whether they work on different continents.

To set up an internal network for use with CVS, you simply create a shared file system for the developers to access. On the other hand, things get a bit trickier when you need to distribute source over the Internet. File shares are notorious for their security flaws, and the server/client model of CVS has been known to have its problems.

A fairly easy solution to the remote access challenge is to use CVS in the remote protocol model. Both RSH and SSH capabilities have been built into the CVS executable. Because SSH is both encrypted and trusted by the networking community, I'll talk about its use in a distributed CVS environment.

NOTE *Windows machines aren't installed by default with an SSH client or server. For a CVS repository that will be made available to other locations, you must install the SSH daemon through either the Unix emulator Cygwin (http://www.cygwin.org) or an open-source OPENSSH distribution. For client machines, you must install the PLINK SSH command-line client from the Putty group or use the Cygwin version of SSH. Keep in mind that PLINK will only allow for a single command-line call—any UI that might display, such as a password prompt, may cause the command to fail. To download PLINK, search Google for the word* putty *and follow the first listed link. For exact instructions on how to hook up Windows with CVS and PLINK (and get around the password problem), search for CVS and PLINK.*

It might sound scary, but using SSH with CVS is actually not so bad.[8] Let's take a look at an example: Perhaps there's a CVS source repository server in Bulgaria that you'd like to access from California. The server's name is exposed on the Internet as cvs.bob1234.com[9]—you need to know this or the machine's Internet Protocol (IP) address in order to attach to the server. The directory on the remote machine containing the repository is /bin/cvs/vault. In addition, the system administrator for the machine has opened port 22 for SSH connections.

To create your access, the system administrator for the machine must create a login account for you. Some systems use a shared accounts for CVS access—especially with large groups of developers—however, this type of setup can lead to a loss of accountability both from a system and a source perspective. Better that you're each given your own account on the machine. For instance, my account might be sean. Before moving on, you should ensure that your access to the machine is ready for you. In Unix-flavored environments, you can type the following on the command line to test this:

```
ssh cvs.bob1234.com -l sean
```

At this point, you'll be prompted for a password. If your shell opens in the remote machine after entering the password, you've successfully used the secure shell protocol to access the machine.

Once you've ensured that you have access to the remote machine, you now make two small changes to your local system. The first is to let CVS know what executable to use for the remote protocol access. You do this by setting the

---

8. As stated earlier, it's more challenging on Windows machines.

9. Apologies to whomever might purchase the BOB1234 domain name—as of this writing, it hasn't yet been acquired.

CVS_RSH environment variable to SSH. For example, in Unix-flavored systems using bash, you might type the following:

```
export CVS_RSH=/bin/ssh
```

If you'd like to make the change permanent, refer to the "Identifying the CVS Source Repository to Clients" section presented earlier in this chapter. Once you've set the CVS_RSH variable, it's time to change your CVSROOT variable so the CVS client can access the BOB1234 machine.

NOTE *Only change the CVSROOT environment variable if the remote machine will be your most frequently used source repository. Otherwise, use the -d parameter to specify the server on the command line. Regardless, the CVS_RSH variable must be set or the RSH protocol is assumed.*

You use the ext keyword along with your account and server names to indicate that a remote protocol is being used. For instance, you might change you CVSROOT variable as follows:

```
export CVSROOT=:ext:sean@cvs.bob1234.com:/bin/cvs/vault
```

Note the colons surrounding the ext keywords and following the server name. The connection errors out if they aren't included. In addition, you use the familiar at sign (@) to designate your account on the machine.

That's it! The client is now set up to access the repository on cvs.bob1234.com. No other special CVS considerations must take place on the server—however, your system administrator may have some other firewall or network changes that must be put in place.

TIP *If you use this connection frequently and get tired of being asked for a password, ask your system administrator about using SSH's authorized users ability. By setting this up, you'll no longer be prompted for passwords when running CVS commands. Keep in mind, however, that some system administrators find this to be an insecure method of access.*

Backing Up and Restoring

Because CVS source repositories are just directories containing flat files, they're fairly easy to back up and restore. You simply copy the files contained in the source repository root directory—in addition to the CVSROOT directory—to tape or archive them as you would any other file on the file system. For instance, if your repository were located at C:\SRC_VLT, you'd back up everything in that directory.

NOTE *It's not enough to back up only the CVSROOT directory in the source repository root. For a full backup, you must include the entire source repository root directory.*

Keep in mind that there exists a slight chance that parts of the source files can corrupt if a backup takes place while users access the repository for commits. For this reason, it's best to lock the repository before the backup takes place. Unfortunately, this isn't as easy as it sounds—every directory in the repository must have a CVS lock added to it, or a system administrator must turn off access to the machine. Should corruption occur, it's normally localized to the historical information of a revision and not the file itself. However, this is still a problem that must be considered when planning a backup strategy.

Summary

This chapter discussed the basic administration and use of the CVS source tool.

Because it's a low-end tool, CVS does have some serious limitations that you should consider before you choose it as your primary source control database. Based on the information in chapter, you should be much closer to an informed decision.

In this chapter, you learned the following:

- How to obtain and install the product

- How to initialize a CVS repository

- How to set up clients to attach to the repository

- How to use the CVS command-line client to add, check out, and commit files

- How to use the client to label source with tags

- How to obtain alternative GUI clients such as WinCVS and LinCVS

- How to differentiate files against those in the repository

- How to view file history and status

- How CVS handles binary files

- How to create and manage branches

- How to use CVS with the SSH protocol

- How to back up your source control database

CHAPTER 6

SourceSafe

THIS CHAPTER DESCRIBES both the benefits and shortcomings of Microsoft Visual SourceSafe,[1] the bundled software configuration management tool available with the Microsoft Visual Studio .NET package. A tool for the cost-conscious, Microsoft's Visual SourceSafe is the low-end leader for Software Configuration Management (SCM) for the Windows operating system. Lacking many of the bells and whistles of the other tools, it can still do the job for small projects and teams working exclusively in the Windows environment.

Most of the basic functionality required of a software configuration management product—versioning files, viewing the delta between revisions, labeling the source—comes in the package. Although the lack of a robust branching mechanism is the weak point of the product, SourceSafe can still be heartily considered for use with Windows applications that don't require strong parallel development abilities.

Chutes and Ladders

Every product has its strengths and weaknesses—and SourceSafe is no exception. The following are a few notes to keep in mind when deciding upon its use in your shop.

The upside is as follows:

It's mostly free: SourceSafe is a relatively inexpensive tool. A license for its use is provided with almost every purchased version of Visual Studio. You can also purchase it in a shrink-wrapped package for a semireasonable fee from many retail outlets.

It's easy to use and intuitive: Because it's been used in the software industry for nearly ten years, there are few experienced Windows programmers who don't already know how to use it.

It's built into Visual Studio: Because it's bundled with Visual Studio 6.0 and Visual Studio .NET, great pains have been taken to ensure its seamless integration into Microsoft development environments. Almost all of SourceSafe's client functionality can be fulfilled through the Visual Studio tool interface.

---

1. The current version of SourceSafe at the time of this writing is 6.0d.

It's extensible: Hey—it's Microsoft. Many third-party vendors have created tools to increase SourceSafe's functionality.

It authenticates through the operating system: The SourceSafe client uses the "one-step" login functionality of the Windows operating system instead of badgering users for passwords each time its starts. It prompts for a user name only if the currently logged-in user doesn't exist as an administrator-created SourceSafe user.

It's getting more and more efficient: The latest version of the tool uses a reverse delta process on binary files in addition to text files—a feature not previously available. This helps keep the source database compact and efficient.

It's somewhat portable: Versions of the SourceSafe client are available for other operating system through third-party Microsoft partners. However, a third-party Network File System (NFS) product such as Samba or Maestro is necessary for mounting SourceSafe shares between operating systems.

It's been localized into several different languages: It's been localized into French, German, Italian, Japanese, and Spanish.

The downside is as follows:

It still doesn't branch well: SourceSafe isn't well reputed for its branching mechanisms. The honest truth is that the tool just isn't designed for large parallel development projects. It's possible for smaller shops, however, to suitably simulate a parallel development environment if necessary.

It can't deal with large databases: SourceSafe will not perform well when its database gets too large.

It has several security issues: A Windows share with read-write security rights must be exposed to users in order for the SourceSafe client to connect to its database. Thus, anyone with rights to the database can easily alter or delete files in the share outside of the tool's interface. This is a serious security flaw.

Administration can be a pain: Because security is based upon both Source-Safe's internal methodology and the operating system's share, all security changes must be updated in two places.

It has limited abilities with binaries: It's not possible to use the merging or multiple checkout features with binary files.

SourceSafe databases can corrupt themselves: SourceSafe databases are known to corrupt from time to time. Strict administrative and recovery strategies must exist to ensure source integrity.

It allows for permanent deletion of files: It's possible to permanently delete files from the SourceSafe database—a feature absent from more sophisticated tools. When files are permanently deleted, they can't be retrieved and previous labels can no longer reflect the true nature of the database at time the label was created.

WORD OF THE DAY

his·to·ry, *n*

"History is more or less bunk."—Henry Ford.

From its inception in 1975, Microsoft has put its spin on such standardized languages as Fortran, Basic, C++, Java, and Assembly. Some of these languages even mutated into proprietary beings—Visual Basic, C#, and J++ being notable examples.

Never one to be left out, Microsoft has no problems acquiring companies to fill a market niche that it hasn't yet tapped. It has purchased a staggering number of unrelated development houses over the years and, in the process, picked up tools such as FoxPro, FrontPage, Visio, and SourceSafe.

One Tree Software was the original company that first published SourceSafe in 1992. The product was developed as the poor man's alternative to Rational ClearCase and a Windows alternative to CVS. Microsoft acquired the company in 1994 and introduced the tool with the release of its Visual Basic 4.0 product. In 1997, the product found its final home when it was wrapped into a suite of programming tools called *Visual Studio*.

Visual Studio has certainly thrived—and so has SourceSafe. It's the low-end leader for source control in the Windows programming world. It has its share of limitations, but it should be seriously considered for small software development houses without high-end resources. SourceSafe has been used successfully by many companies—even with large source trees.

Getting and Installing SourceSafe

As mentioned in a previous chapter, SourceSafe isn't *actually* freeware—even though it may seem that way.

Although the SourceSafe server requires no license, all clients that attach to it must each have their own purchased license. Licenses are per-user-based rather than per-seat-based. This means that users can legally have more than one copy of SourceSafe on different machines as long as there's only a single person who uses the product.

It's possible to purchase licenses for SourceSafe in one of three ways:

- There's a shrink-wrapped version of the product (containing only one end user license) that can be purchased from a retailer for a few hundred dollars. Those who owned a previous license of either SourceSafe or a competing product can purchase the upgrade version of the software at a lower cost.

- Bulk licenses for the product are available from Microsoft-authorized retailers.

- Each version of Visual Studio 6.0 or earlier is bundled with a single license of the SourceSafe product. Visual Studio .NET includes licenses with its Enterprise Architect and Enterprise Developer bundles, but you're out of luck with Visual Studio .NET Professional.

Contrary to popular belief, it's not legal to use the Microsoft Development Network (MSDN) version of the tool for real-life software development—that version is licensed only for integration testing. See the MSDN End User License Agreement (EULA) provided with the product for more information.

Implementing Smart Practices Before You Begin

Although the SourceSafe software may be inexpensive, ensuring the integrity of source can be expensive when it comes to hardware. Some of the following recommendations might be overkill for smaller shops, but always remember that the source is your company's most valuable asset. If in doubt, ask for recommendations from your Information Technology (IT) department or other knowledgeable software configuration managers:

Dedicate a machine to your database: It's wise to keep source databases on their own dedicated machines. This makes them easier to secure and at less risk from accidental corruption by well-meaning users. Never keep source databases on machines where testing or development takes place—this always leads to disaster.

Get a fast hard drive: Because SourceSafe itself is really just a database, the power of the machine hosting it isn't nearly as important as the speed of disk access.

Use high-end operating systems: Though it's possible to create a SourceSafe server on a Windows 95/98 family machine, it's not a smart way to care for the source. Always use an industry-standard server that supports strong and stable security models, such as Windows 2000, XP Enterprise servers, and Windows Server 2003. At the least, use Professional versions of operating systems whenever possible.

Get an Uninterruptible Power Supply (UPS): Make sure the machine chosen for the database has a consistent power supply. Purchase a UPS and ensure that it's properly attached to the machine's power cord. It's a good idea to buy a UPS with a serial connection that will gracefully shut down the machine automatically in the event of an elongated power outage. As the huge East Coast blackout of 2003 taught us, the power grid can be fickle.

Plan for the future: Think about the size of the source and how it might grow over the next year. Then ensure that there's enough disk space available for triple that number. SourceSafe has administrative tools that use additional space equal to the size of the database itself.

Get RAID: Consider a fault-tolerant disk management system such as RAID 5. If a hard drive fails for some reason, a RAID mechanism can re-create it without data loss. Be sure to keep an extra disk or two around in case of emergencies. The ability to *hot swap* hard disks—meaning to change disks without shutting down the computer or RAID—means that developers can continue to work as bad drives are replaced.

Invest in a system monitoring tool: Use system monitoring tools that send email or page your cell phone to be immediately notified of problems that might suddenly appear.

Installing SourceSafe

Microsoft has provided several ways to install SourceSafe using a rather standardized wizard.

Installing the SourceSafe 6.0d Client or Server from the Stand-Alone Media

The SourceSafe server installation must take place on the machine that will hold the database. To install it, follow these steps:

1. You begin by loading the setup disk into your CD-ROM drive. The autorun feature begins the installation.

2. The first three dialog boxes spell out the usual legal mumbo-jumbo. When asked, confirm that you'll adhere to the licensing agreement and then you fill in your name, company, and product license key.

3. After navigating through a couple more screens informing you (once again) of the product license and the product identification, you see the dialog box displayed in Figure 6-1.

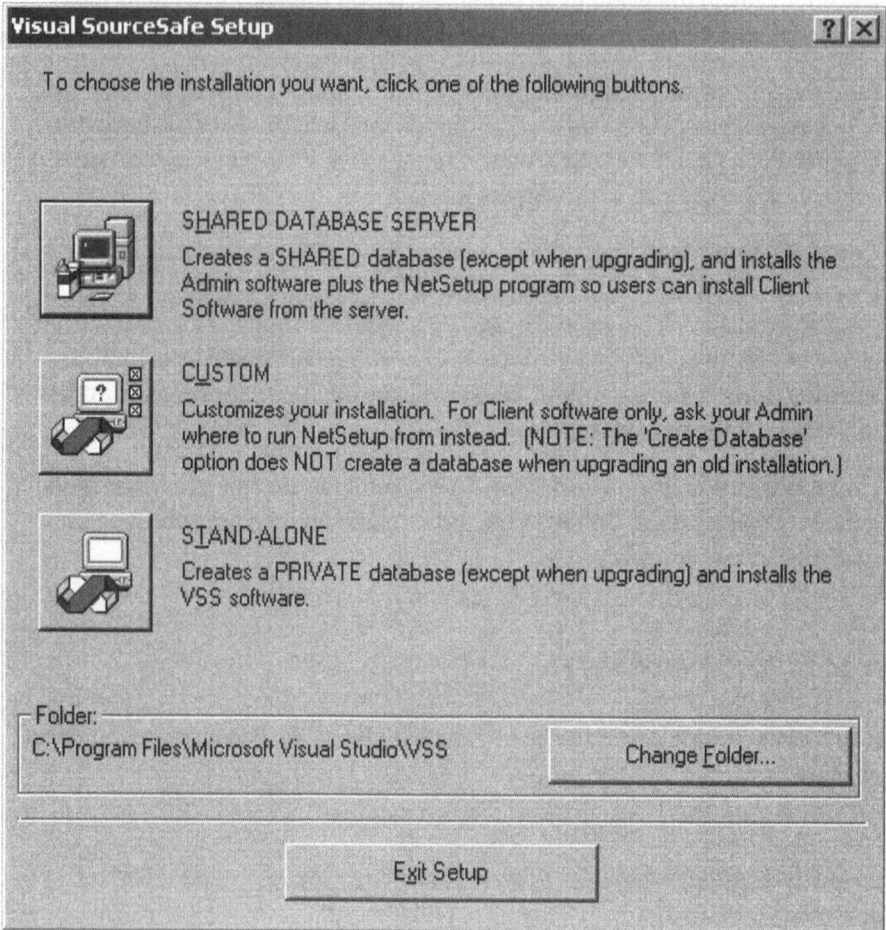

Figure 6-1. The Visual SourceSafe Setup Wizard

4. You must choose the type of installation you'd like to perform. The first choice, Shared Database Server, is the most common installation choice. You click it if you'd like to have a database that will be shared among your developers. The second choice, Custom, allows you to save disk space by removing unnecessary tools such as the help and network setup files. You should choose the last choice, Stand-Alone, only if this will be a personal database that will not be shared among developers.

NOTE *The network setup files are provided as a convenience to your users. Not installing them by clicking the Custom button means that your users will need to use a CD in order to install the SourceSafe client.*

5. The next dialog box, as displayed in Figure 6-2, asks you if you'd like to use the latest version of the database technology. Microsoft totally revamped the SourceSafe database model between versions 5.0 and 6.0. The version 6.0 database is much faster and more stable. However, it's incompatible with any version 5.0 clients that might be hanging around. If there are any version 5.0 clients (or earlier) that might attach to your new database, you choose No at this time.

NOTE *There are several features available only if the 6.0 database is installed. To take advantage of these, I recommend that all clients upgrade to the 6.0 version.*

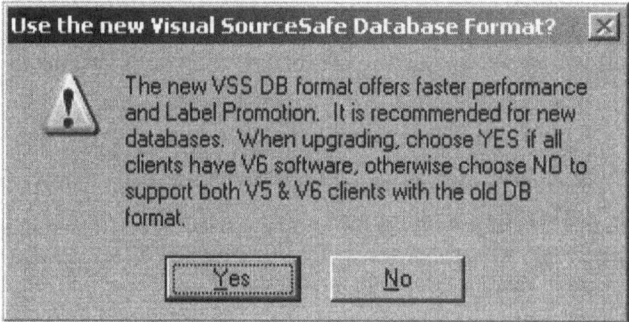

Figure 6-2. The Visual SourceSafe Setup Wizard, client choice

6. The setup then copies files to the machine and informs you that the installation is complete. You're given an opportunity to register the product with Microsoft—be sure to refer to Microsoft privacy policies (as you should do with any product and company) before registering the product.

Installing the SourceSafe 6.0d Client from an Existing Network Database

The SourceSafe network installation provides a convenient way for your developers to install the client without the need of a CD or other removable media. This version of the setup, however, doesn't install the administration tool or create a local database. If, for some reason, developers need this functionality, they'll need to install the product from the SourceSafe 6.0 stand-alone media as detailed in the previous section.

NOTE *The network setup can also be run on the Internet using a Virtual Private Network (VPN).*

To run the network installation, follow these steps:

1. First, you navigate to the SourceSafe database share location and then run the NETSETUP.EXE executable located at the root. Alternatively, you can type the Universal Naming Convention (UNC) path for the executable by using the Start ➤ Run menu item. For instance:

   ```
   \\worf\vss\netsetup.exe
   ```

2. Much as in the stand-alone installation, several dialog boxes appear asking you to adhere to Microsoft's licensing agreement. When asked, you should confirm that you agree and fill in your name, company, and product license key.

NOTE *Make sure that every copy of the client is properly licensed before allowing your developers to install the product. See the "Getting and Installing SourceSafe" section in this chapter for more information.*

3. Microsoft asks you where to install the product and offers its proposal for the location. If this location works, you simply click the OK button; otherwise, you change the directory as necessary.

4. A final confirmation screen appears. To continue the installation, you click the large command button with the computer graphic on it.

5. This copies the files to your local computer, and the wizard informs you that the installation is complete.

Detailing the installation instructions for previous versions of Visual Studio is out of scope for this book—please refer to the instructions that came with the product for more information.

Let's face it—it's usually best to use the latest versions of Microsoft software.[2] Luckily, SourceSafe 6.0d has virtually the same interface as the previous incarnations of the product. The program has become much more stable as the years have gone by, and some operations, such as getting source, are much improved.

Multiple Databases

After installing SourceSafe from the stand-alone media, your first database is created automatically.

NOTE *The network client setup doesn't automatically create a database.*

Developers can create their own SourceSafe databases locally on their machines. This might be useful for private development documents that they want to version. Keep in mind that these databases don't exist on the source server and need to be individually backed up.

Administering SourceSafe, Part 1

The SourceSafe administration tool is installed by default by the stand-alone setup media. This tool allows you to complete a variety of database administration tasks such as adding users, creating new databases, or archiving old source.

Access the administration tool by clicking the Start menu and choosing Programs ➤ Microsoft Visual SourceSafe ➤ Visual SourceSafe 6.0 Admin.[3] If administering a database that has just been installed, log in as the Admin user. By default, the Admin account has no password, but you can (and should) set one by choosing Users ➤ Change Password.

When first opened, the tool displays the users who are currently allowed to use the database, as displayed in Figure 6-3. The rights of the users and their login status display in table format relative to each user's login.

---

2. Sure, we've all been burned by new versions of software—who else remembers Visual Basic 4.0?—but I've found burns to be the exception, not the rule.

3. SourceSafe is a Windows product so this chapter is written from the perspective of that operating system.

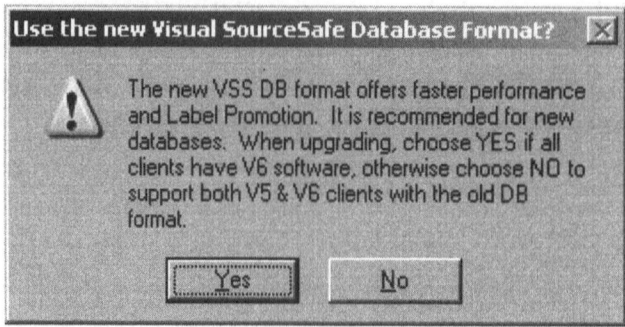

Figure 6-3. The Visual SourceSafe Administrator tool, users

To administer a different database, choose the Users ➤ Open SourceSafe Database menu item. You can open any database to which you have operating system rights by typing the UNC path that identifies the database share. Choose the Browse button to search for a database either on the local computer or on the network. To use the UNC convention, type two backslashes followed by the computer's name followed by a backslash and the share location. For example, to access the VSData share on a computer named *Worf*, you might type the following:

```
\\worf\vsdata\srcsafe.ini
```

When opening the Open SourceSafe Database dialog box, locate the database's SRCSAFE.INI file and highlight it before choosing the Open button. By default, only SRCSAFE.INI files display in the Find Database dialog box. To find out more about the SRCSAFE.INI file, see the "A Ini Cnt Txt Dat B" sidebar near the end of the chapter.

Every opened SourceSafe database is added to the Open SourceSafe Database dialog box, as displayed in Figure 6-4. Should you want to delete a reference to a database, you can simply highlight the database to be deleted and click the Remove button. Note that this doesn't actually delete the SourceSafe database— it only removes the ability to access it through the administration tool (and client!) on this computer. If a reference is deleted in error, add it again simply by opening the database once again using the Users ➤ Open SourceSafe Database menu item. If the Open This Database Next Time I Run Visual SourceSafe checkbox is checked, the currently opened database becomes the default for the administration tool *and* the client on the current machine.

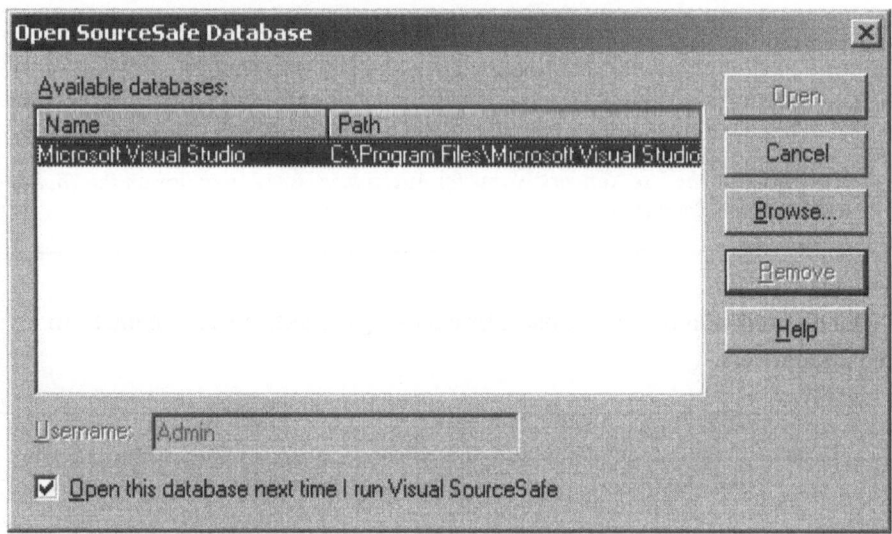

Figure 6-4. The Visual SourceSafe Administrator tool, the Open SourceSafe Database dialog box

Adding Users to the Database

Generally, once a database is created, the first thing you want to do is to create users who will access the source. If you have more than one SourceSafe database, you must take this step for each. For this reason, it's definitely in your best interest to keep as few databases as possible.

The administration tool makes this step fairly simple. Simply choose Users ➤ Add User. Add the user's name and, if desirable, a password for the account. If a password isn't set, anyone can access the source database using this account.

SourceSafe has a convenient feature called *one-step login* that allows developers to use their operating system credentials when logging into the SourceSafe database instead of typing a user name and password. To use the one-step login feature, user names must match individual user's Windows network access account. If passwords are assigned in SourceSafe, they're required only on systems where the user isn't logged into the Windows network.

NOTE *Your developers will definitely prefer to use the one-step login feature. If you worry, however, about nefarious coworkers who might check in code from your machine while you're in the kitchen getting a soda, I recommend you see your human resources department about those employees—or, better yet, lay off the caffeine and sugar. If you do decide to turn off this wonderful feature, uncheck the Use Network Name for Automatic User Log In box on the Tools ➤ Options General tab.*

Once added, edit or remove users by choosing the appropriate menu item listed under Users.

NOTE *Renaming or removing an established user can cause problems if they currently have files checked out (discussed later in this chapter). Be sure to uncheck out or check in all files before deleting or renaming users. In addition, historical information will not reflect name changes. For instance, if I were to change my account name, history for every action I took previous to the change would still reflect the old name.*

Make sure that every user who is added to the SourceSafe database has the equivalent rights to the network share that I talked about in the "Getting and Installing SourceSafe" section. All users, including those who only have read-only permissions in SourceSafe, must still be able to create, modify, add, and delete at both the share and folder levels. See your IT administrator if you have questions regarding this step.

Creating Additional Databases

There isn't any limit to the number of SourceSafe databases that you can create. Using the administration tool, simply choose User ➤ Create Database and specify the location of the new database. Just remember that all the same rules apply— you must create a share with the proper security in order for multiple users to access it.

For large amounts or extremely diverse sets of source, consider using more than one SourceSafe database. Just remember that there's administrative overhead that comes with each one:

- If creating source databases on different machines, each machine needs to have fault-tolerant mechanisms. Can they both be backed up and restored properly? Is the power supply adequate for more than one machine?

- Every time a new employee starts work, the change must be propagated through both the share and project security for every database to which they need access.

- There are tools, such as the one detailed in the "Using the Analyze Tool" section at the end of this chapter, that must be run against the SourceSafe database in order to keep it healthy. Each database must be maintained separately.

Isn't There More to the Admin Tool Than That?

There is, indeed—but it's important to understand some of SourceSafe's basic functionality before you take a look at the administration tool's advanced features. You'll revisit the tool later in the chapter.

Using the SourceSafe Client

The SourceSafe client is the tool that you (and your developers) use to maintain and change your source tree. As displayed in Figure 6-5, it consists of three window panes, a toolbar for the common commands, and a typical menu bar. It appears and acts much like the Windows Explorer.

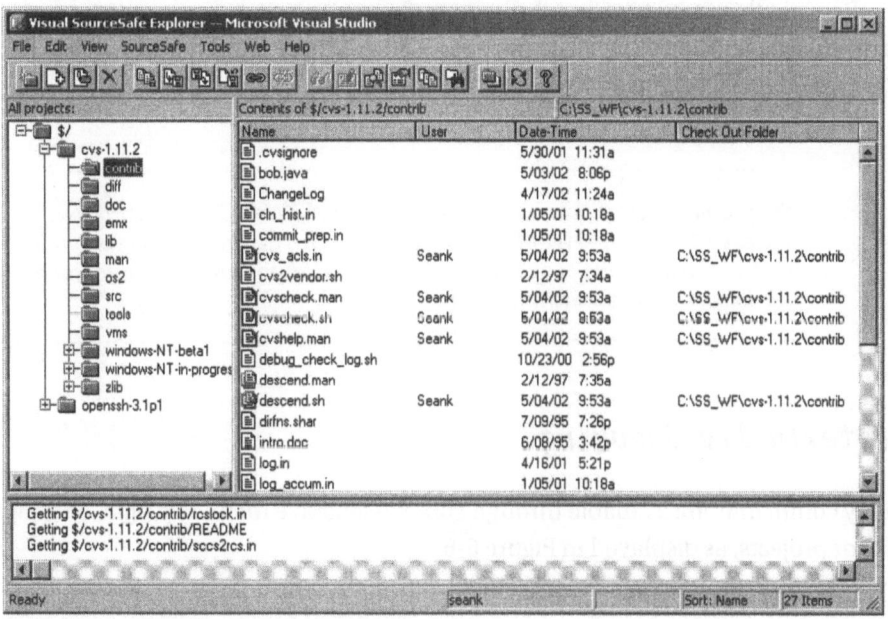

Figure 6-5. The Visual SourceSafe client

The top-left window is the project pane. Inside is a tree listing of *projects*, analogous to folders in Windows Explorer. Every item listed in this tree is called a *project*, no matter how deeply it might be buried in the tree. The right-side window is called the file pane. All of the files listed in this pane belong to the highlighted object in the project pane.

> **NOTE** *Though the client emulates Windows Explorer, it doesn't have the same set of functionality or follow the same rules. For example, child folders are listed in the file pane for Windows Explorer, but the equivalent isn't true for child projects in SourceSafe.*

The bottom window is called the *results pane*. As various tasks are completed, the results pane displays the output for the requests. For instance, in Figure 6-5, a variety of files have just been downloaded to the local computer. The results pane updates as the task is completed for each file.

In the project pane, there's no typical root directory (for example, C:\ or D:\). This is because the SourceSafe environment is *virtual*. Even though the data is stored safely on the SourceSafe server, the structure you see in the project and files panes don't actually exist in that format in your database. See the "A Ini Cnt Txt Dat B" sidebar near the end of the chapter to understand how SourceSafe actually stores your code in the database.

Because there's no true "root" directory, SourceSafe can't display the typical path which you've become accustomed to with Windows Explorer. The root project is therefore displayed as a virtual dollar sign ($).

> **NOTE** *SourceSafe displays project paths using the Unix-like forward slash (/) instead of the typical Windows backslash (\). This distinction allows you to easily recognize when you're living in SourceSafe's virtual world and not on the local drive of a machine.*

Contextually Speaking...

Many commands are available through context-sensitive menus by right-clicking files or projects, as displayed in Figure 6-6.

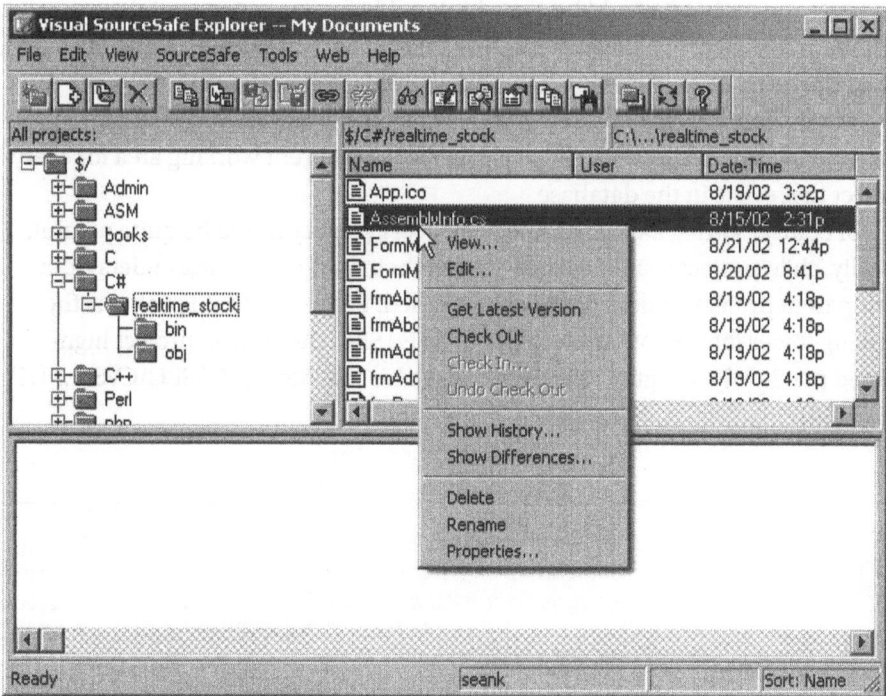

Figure 6-6. The Visual SourceSafe client with contextual menu

Working Folders

Enter the concept of working folders. When source is downloaded to working folders, projects and their contents appear as simple folders and files. Working folders are necessary because every developer has a different environment in which they work. For instance:

- Bill's C:\ drive is filled, so he does all of his development work on his D:\ drive.

- Frank's C:\ drive is also pretty full, and his D:\ is actually his CD drive—so he uses his E:\ drive instead. In fact, he likes to keep his source in a directory called SRC.

- Brenda uses her C:\ drive for code in a folder called My Source; however, she works only in one project that's buried pretty deeply in the tree structure. She has no interest in downloading all of the projects—she wants only to get the source with which she actually works.

You can see that it would be quite impossible for SourceSafe to follow the same source directory paradigm for everyone in the company, let alone the world. Working folders allow developers to work with the virtual project tree in any way they see fit. Frank can tell SourceSafe to always get source to his E:\SRC directory—but even better, if desired, he can specify a different working area for every project that exists in the database.

Of course, setting a working folder for every project would be quite painful. Luckily, child projects automatically inherit their relative working folders from their parent projects unless otherwise specified. For example, if Frank sets the working folder for the root project ($/) to be E:\SRC, the contrib project highlighted previously in Figure 6-5 downloads to his machine as E:\SRC\CVS-1.11.2\CONTRIB.

TIP *Consider providing working folders through a network share. This allows workspaces to be backed up on a nightly basis and provides easy administrative access to "in-progress" source should a developer go AWOL for one reason or another. Depending on the speed of your network, this scenario can also be more efficient for the developers as they compile.*

As source is downloaded from the database, one or more files may appear in the working folder unexpectedly. These files, ending with the extension .SCC, are used by SourceSafe to track changes to working folders and to aid with the Visual Studio integration. You can ignore them during development, but you shouldn't deploy them to customers.

TIP *Never share working folders between users. By creating a common working folder where two or more individuals can check in source, you defeat the purpose of tracking changes and keeping developers accountable.*

The working folder defaults to a position relative to its parent project—however, there's no limitation as to where you can set the working folder. Use the File ➤ Set Working Folder menu item to set it for the currently selected project.

> **NOTE** *Every time you use the Set Working Folder command, SourceSafe saves this information in its configuration files. It will remember these settings even if the parent project's working folder changes in the future.*

Adding Files to SourceSafe for the First Time and Other File Management Tasks

To add new files to a newly created source database, open the SourceSafe client on a machine that has access to the database's share. Use the File ➤ Open SourceSafe Database menu item if necessary to navigate to the proper network location.

Create new projects in SourceSafe by using the File ➤ Create Project menu item. Newly created projects appear as children to the project that was highlighted when this menu item is chosen. Once created, add files to the project using the File ➤ Add Files menu command. This command displays all of the files in the current working directory that haven't yet been added to the source database. Choose one or more files and click Add. You can choose multiple files by holding down the Control key as you click the filenames. Regardless of where you might have navigated on your file system to find files to add, all selected files are added to the currently highlighted project.

> **TIP** *SourceSafe supports the drag-and-drop functionality of the Windows operating system. Using drag and drop, you can save steps by dropping in a tree of working folders instead of adding projects one by one. All folders turn into projects when dragged and dropped.*

Once you've added files and projects to the source database, use the File ➤ Delete menu item if you ever need to remove from the database. When the Destroy Permanently option isn't checked, the file or project is simply hidden from view to users. This is the safest way to remove files or projects because they can be recovered at a later time, much like retrieving files from the Recycle Bin in the Windows operating system. If the Destroy Permanently option is checked, the file or project is purged forever from the SourceSafe database and isn't recoverable.

Use the File ➤ Properties menu item while a project is highlighted and choose the Deleted Items tab to recover any files or child projects that might have been deleted. As displayed in Figure 6-7, simply highlight the file in the dialog box to be restored and then click the Recover button. Using this tab, it's also possible to permanently purge any previously deleted files. Again, this will forever purge the chosen file from the SourceSafe database.

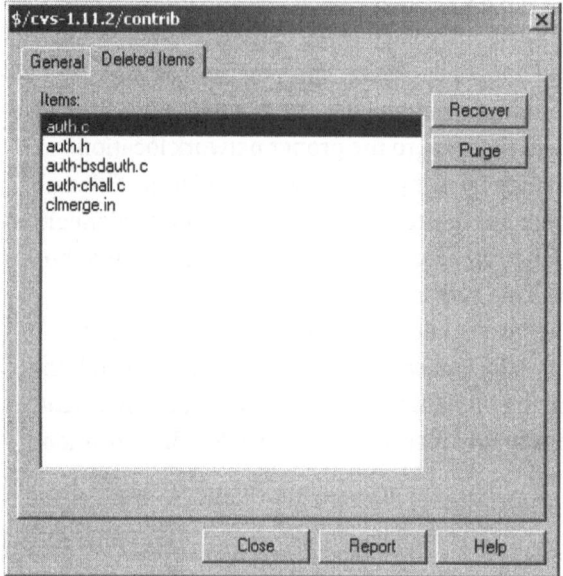

Figure 6-7. The Visual SourceSafe client, the Deleted Items tab

> **NOTE** *If you delete a file that has been shared with another project, file icons will continue to indicate that it's shared until the deleted one is purged/destroyed from the database. Because destroying isn't recommended in most cases, these files may always appear to be shared.*

In addition to recovering and purging deleted items, the properties dialog box can display quite a bit of information regarding the selected projects or files. If the selected object is a project, the dialog box shows the most recent label comment attached to the project and indicates whether the current project is cloaked. The cloaking feature allows you to specify a project that shouldn't be included when its parent is chosen for a recursive operation. In other words, cloaked projects don't respond to the Get, Check Out, Check In, Undo Check Out, or Show Difference commands as described in future sections. If the highlighted object is a file, the properties dialog box displays the file's checkout status and whether the file has been shared or branched.

Moving projects or files used to be a major pain in previous versions of SourceSafe. First, you were forced to share the files to the new location and then delete the original files from the first project. SourceSafe now allows you to complete these tasks in one step by using the File ➤ Move menu item. However, the program still doesn't purge/destroy the original files from the database, and newly moved files appear to the user as shared items. To get around this, purge the file from the original project's properties dialog box.

Getting Source and Committing It Back to the Repository

SourceSafe provides two mechanisms to fulfill the task of downloading source to local machines. You can *check out* files, indicating that you plan to make changes to them. Alternatively, you can simply *get* the files, which copies the source to your hard drive.

Using the Get Command

The SourceSafe ➤ Get Latest Version menu item (also available contextually for both projects and files) downloads the selected object (and its child files if the selected item is a project) to the client machine. If you've selected a project and chosen the Recursive checkbox on the Get dialog box, all child projects and their files are also downloaded.

NOTE *When projects are recursively gotten, files are placed in the user set of working folders—and don't necessarily reflect the original file tree as presented by the SourceSafe interface.*

By default, SourceSafe downloads files to the local machine with the read-only attribute set. This is how SourceSafe informs you that the files haven't been checked out and shouldn't be edited. You can choose to make the files writable by indicating so on the Get dialog box that appears when you choose the Get Latest Version menu item.

TIP *If the Get dialog box offends and you always choose its default actions, try checking the Only Show This Dialog When the Shift Key Is Down option the next time it appears to get rid of it. From that point forward, the dialog box won't appear—unless you hold down the Shift key when you click the Get Latest Version menu item. Several other menu items—such as Check Out, Show Differences, and Show History—follow this same paradigm.*

Using the Check Out and Check In Commands

Copying files to the local drive is great, but as I discussed in previous chapters, the meat and potatoes of source control is the ability to track changes made to source. In SourceSafe, you achieve this ability by checking out files and then checking back changes into the database. Use the SourceSafe ➤ Check Out and SourceSafe ➤ Check In menu items to fulfill this task. In SourceSafe, the checkout and checkin commands are applicable to both projects and files.

TIP *Many SourceSafe commands allow users to add comments when completing tasks. Developers should add checkin comments on their source detailing the changes they made. This can help in later debugging. If you choose to compel users to use checkout comments as well, you may add this ability using the Tools ➤ Options menu item.*

When a file is checked out, its icon becomes outlined in red and a large check-mark is placed on it. The Check Out Folder attribute of the files pane also refers to the location where the file exists on the user's local machine. While a user has a file checked out, no one else is allowed to check it out or in. This prevents developers from overwriting each other's changes.

NOTE *You can also allow for multiple checkouts of files. In this case, the first user to check in the file gets a free ride, but everyone else has to merge their changes into the database afterward. This function is turned off by default but can be activated by using the Tools ➤ Options menu item. Although the multiple checkout feature can sometimes be a headache, most SCM experts agree that its usage can make a shop more efficient.*

Choosing the Check Out menu item when a project is highlighted causes every file within the project to be checked out to you. If the Recursive option is also checked, every file in every child project is checked out at the same time. Both of these same ideas are applicable in reverse for the Check In menu item. Projects themselves can't be checked out or marked as exclusive in any way. Other users are always able to add files to the project.

TIP *Your developers should be advised to check out only the files needed to complete tasks—checking out more than what's necessary will hamper other developers from getting their work completed in a timely fashion. You can get around this by allowing multiple checkouts on files. See the previous note for more information.*

Using the Undo Check Out Command

There are times when a developer checks out a file and then decides later that he or she won't need to change it after all. Instead of checking in the copy of the file that lives on his hard drive—which may have changed—the developer can choose the SourceSafe ➤ Undo Check Out menu item. By default, SourceSafe replaces the file on the local system with the tip version of the file in the database. Users can only undo checkouts for files that they themselves have checked out. The Admin account has rights to undo the checkout of any file in the system.

Using the Share Command

A feature that Microsoft hypes but is feared by software configuration managers, the sharing mechanism allows a file to exist in more than one location within the database. This is analogous to a "link" in the Unix operating system. When the file is checked in with changes to one location, the change is propagated to all of the other shared versions of the file. Working folders, however, aren't updated with these changes until the next get or checkout.

NOTE *You should use shared files with caution. Developers may make changes to one copy of the file without understanding the consequences the change has in the other locations where it's shared.*

When a file is shared, its icon changes from the standard document icon to one that appears to be a stack of paper. A checked-out shared file will appear checked out to the same user in all locations.

TIP *For the most part, functionality that needs to be "shared" among projects should be formed into their own components. See Chapter 3, "All About the Source," for more information regarding sharing code among projects.*

ANOTHER TIP *Although sharing is generally be frowned upon, it can be a helpful tool for numbering your build's versions. See Chapter 9, "Builds for Windows .NET," for more information.*

Labeling Revisions in the Source Repository

As discussed with detail in Chapter 3, "All About the Source," it's important to attach labels to the tree or specific projects when certain milestones are met or during the build process. This helps to guarantee the ability to re-create the source as it was when the label was created.

As a quick refresher, you use labels to tie together different versions of source files at a moment in time. For instance, when you release your product to the quality team, a file named ENTRY.H might be at version 1.2, and another file named ENTRY.CPP might be at version 1.7. By using a label, perhaps called *Quality Release 1*, you "package" these files together for future use. Alternatively (and much more tediously), you'd have to keep track of every revision for releases in a document.

Use the File ➤ Label menu item to add a label to a project or set of files. Although it's possible to label a single file, there's rarely a case where it's necessary. When added to a project, labels propagate recursively to all child projects. For instance, fulfilling the command on the root of the SourceSafe database ($/) would label all objects in the database.

It's possible to move a previously created label from an older revision of a file to the most current one. Microsoft calls this *label promotion*. To do so, select the file and choose File ➤ Label. When the Label dialog box appears, re-enter the label name as you first typed it. SourceSafe may ask to confirm the change, and then it updates the label in the user interface and history. This type of label promotion can be performed either on a single file or in bulk.

Should you want to move a label to a revision that's not currently the tip, you can use the Tools ➤ Show History command. See the "Viewing History About Files" section for more information.

It's also possible to get all the source attached to a previously created label. See the "Viewing History About Files" section later in the chapter for more information.

Searching for Files

As databases get larger and larger, it's often handy to be able to search for a specific file in the source tree. SourceSafe fulfills this functionality in a couple of ways.

First, you can use the View ➤ Search menu item to completely "mask" the file pane relative to your search choice. For instance, you might choose to search for all files that match the *.CPP wildcard specification. After using the View ➤ Search menu item, the file pane only displays files in your projects (and child projects should the Search in Current Project and All Subprojects option be checked) that end with the .CPP extension. This masking stays in effect—even in other projects—until you choose the View ➤ Cancel Search menu item. Using this method, you can also search based on checkout status—for instance, you might find all of the files that are currently checked out to seank.

It's also possible to use the View ➤ Search menu item to search the entire database for certain filenames or wildcard specifications. To do so, choose the Search in All Projects option before searching. After the entire database is searched, all files that match the specification display in the file pane with their full paths. The search area changes automatically to Search in Current Project and All Subprojects should another project be clicked. Again, you can cancel this search with the View ➤ Cancel Search menu item.

The second way to search for files is to use the Tools ➤ Find in Files menu item to look for specific strings in a set of files. You can also run this command recursively—so take care when running the command on large projects. The results appear in a new dialog box that also displays the context of the found search string.

Viewing History About Files

The ability to view historical information is one of SourceSafe's most valuable tools. To do so, choose the Tools ➤ Show History menu item on any project or file. Figure 6-8 displays an example of the project history dialog box. The file and project versions of this dialog box differ slightly, but the crux of the functionality is the same. Note that displaying history on a project displays all labels and a list of every revision for every file within the project.

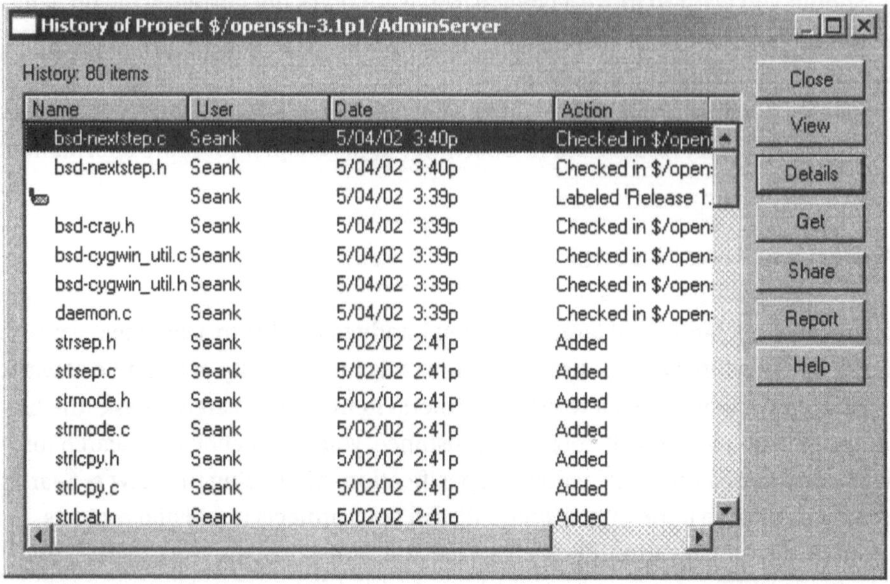

Figure 6-8. The Visual SourceSafe client, the History of Project dialog box

The following is a quick list of the command buttons available in the History of Project dialog box and their respective functions (some of the commands are only available depending on type of object you've highlighted and therefore may not be reflected in Figure 6-8):

View: Click View to display the revision of a file at any point in its lifetime.

Details: Click Details to look at the comments that were made as revisions of a file were checked in to the database. You can also use this button to promote or change the label for a particular file as previously detailed in the "Labeling Revisions in the Source Repository" section of this chapter.

Get: The get command allows you to download any previous revision of a single file—or even re-create an entire project based upon a previously created label. For a file, you simply highlight the revision and then click Get. For a project, highlight the label—identified with a yellow icon to the left of the list box—and again choose Get.

Diff: Use the diff command to see the difference between two versions of the same file. See the "Differencing Code" section for more information on this functionality. This command is available only to file objects.

Pin: The pin command is used for branching source code. See the "Branching and Merging" section of this chapter for more information. This command is only available to file objects.

Share: The Share button allows you to create copies of the project/files for sharing and branching. See the "Branching and Merging" section of this chapter for more information.

Report: Use the Report button to take the contents of the list box and output it to a printer, file, or the Clipboard.

Rollback: Use Rollback to purge newer revisions of a file. This can be handy should a new bug destabilize the tree or if a change is no longer necessary. To do so, select the previous revision of a file that should now be the tip and choose the Rollback button. Use the Rollback command with caution—it can't be undone and the later revisions are lost forever. This command is available only to file objects.

NOTE *If you use the archive tool or the purge commands to destroy previous revisions of files, they'll no longer appear in the History of Project dialog box.*

Differencing Code

Use the Tools ➤ Show Differences menu item to compare the files between the local directory and the database—or even to compare different revisions of files in the database itself.

After highlighting a file and choosing the menu item, a dialog box asks which files to compare. By default, the Compare and To edit boxes contain the file that was currently in context and its working folder equivalent. You can modify these edit boxes in order to compare any two files you'd like—compare a database file to another database file, two files on the local drive, or a file on the hard drive to a file in the database. Use the Browse buttons to make these changes or simply type them in manually. Remember that project paths in SourceSafe must begin with the dollar sign ($) so the tool knows to use the database version of the files.

NOTE *If you choose to show the differences between binary files, you will only receive a message indicating whether they're different. You can't graphically view the differences between binary files.*

Once the files are chosen, choose the OK button and the differencing window opens, as displayed in Figure 6-9. The window is divvied up into two panes—each holding one of the files selected for compare. When possible, SourceSafe glues the two windows together so they "stick together" when the scroll is clicked. The toolbar for this window provides buttons to find text in the files, jump to the next or previous difference, or bookmark sections of the files for later perusal.

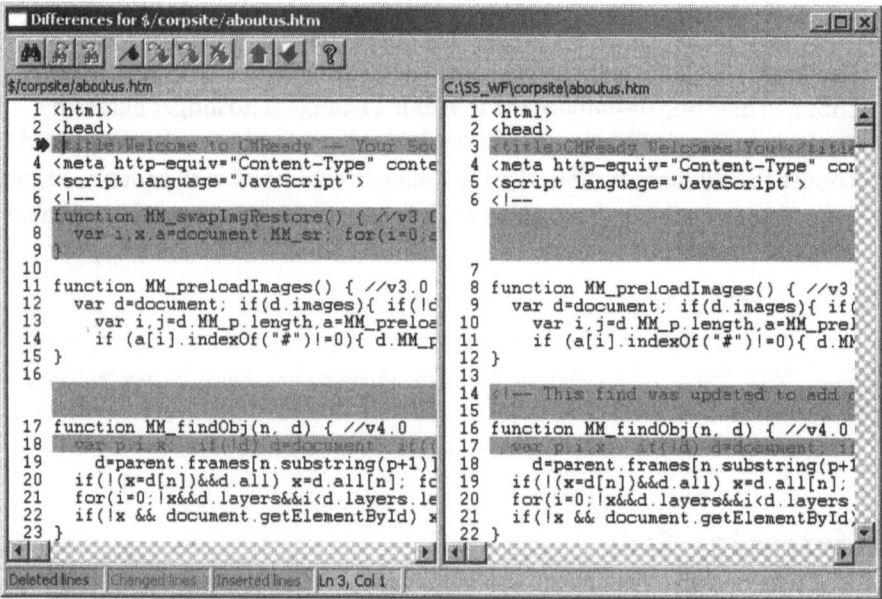

Figure 6-9. The Visual SourceSafe client, file show differences

A color-coded legend appears at the bottom of the screen:

- Lines of code that exist in the file in the left window but not in the file on the right side are blue.

- Lines of code that exist in the right window but not in the left window are green.

- Lines of code that exist in both places but have differences are red.

- Lines of code that exist in both places but haven't been changed in either location will not have color highlighting.

In addition to comparing files singularly, it's also possible to compare the local directory against the equivalent project in the database. To do so, highlight a project in SourceSafe and choose the Tools ➤ Show Differences menu item. The dialog box displayed in Figure 6-10 appears.

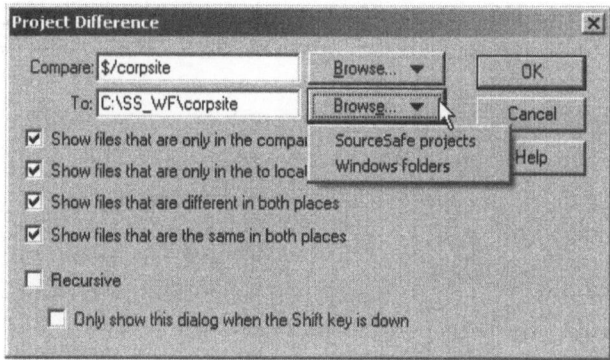

Figure 6-10. The Visual SourceSafe client, the Project Difference dialog box

You can choose four options to filter what results should be displayed. For instance, if you were only interested in files that need to be added to the database, you might turn off the three other choices by unchecking their respective options. You can also choose to search recursively—but this can take some time on large amounts of source.

After clicking OK, the Show Differences window appears. Near the top of the window are two labels indicating the two paths being compared. In the current example, you're comparing $/corpsite on the database (remember that the $ tells you where it's originating) and the C:\SS_WF\corpsite folder on your local drive. The two panes beneath these labels display the differences for the project and the local directory.

There's a color legend at the bottom of the window, and it pretty closely matches that of the file compare tool:

- Files that exist in the project or directory listed in the left window but not the project or directory listed in the right window are blue.

- Files that exist in the right window but not in the left window are green.

- File that exist in both places but are different are red.

- Files that exist in both places but haven't changed in either location don't have color highlighting.

After taking a look at the differences, such as the ones displayed in Figure 6-11, you can take one of several steps. Add any green items to the database by right-clicking them and choosing Add Files. Right-click the different red file to compare, check out, and then check in differences. You can delete any file in either pane—but remember that if a file is deleted in a working folder, it's permanently destroyed.

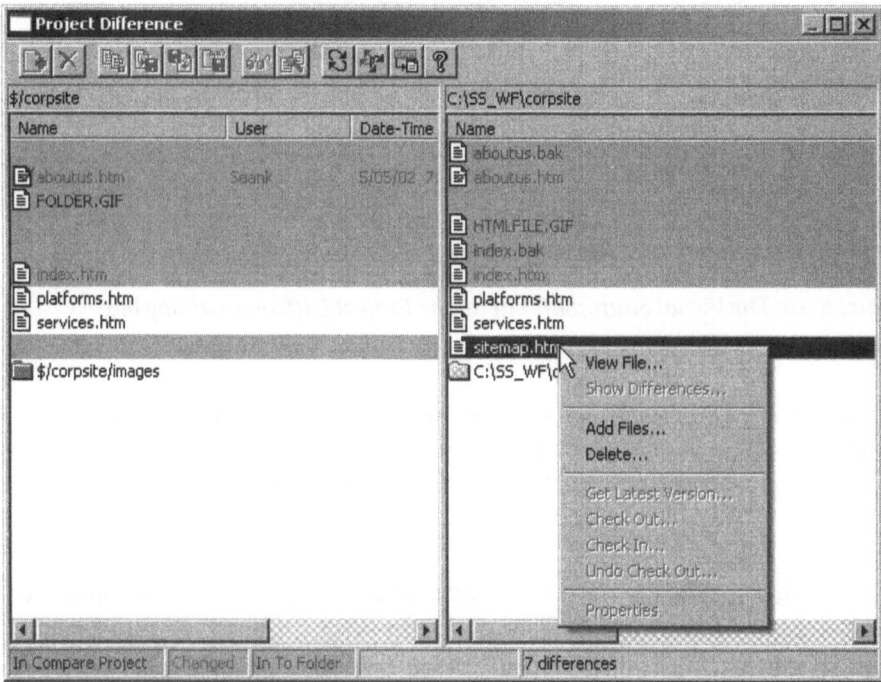

Figure 6-11. The Visual SourceSafe client with contextual menu

Branching and Merging

SourceSafe provides a simple branching mechanism for the parallel development models discussed in Chapter 3, "All About the Source."

 NOTE *SourceSafe can be a powerful tool. Unfortunately, branching is its weakest link. Branching using the following method should be limited to patches and small releases. Although following the same model for large branch releases is theoretically possible, its use isn't recommend. You may want to look at alternatives to SourceSafe if you need strong branching functionality.*

Let's discuss a possible example how you might use branching in SourceSafe:

1. You have released the first version of your software and labeled the source as *Release 1.0*. Because the entire source base is dedicated to this release, you've placed the label on the root project ($/), and it has trickled down automatically to all of your child projects. The developers begin to work on the second release of the product.

2. A bug is suddenly found in the Release 1.0 product, and a patch must be created from several files located in a project called *AdminServer*.

3. First, you highlight the AdminServer project in the source tree and choose the Tools ➤ Show History menu item, making sure you choose to display labels before clicking OK. This displays the History of Project dialog box described earlier in the "Viewing History About Files" section of this chapter.

4. Now you select the Release 1.0 label and click the Share button to display the Share From dialog box. This allows you to "copy" the revisions of files that makes up the Release 1.0 label into a newly created project elsewhere in the source tree. In the Share From dialog box, you select the project *that should be the parent* of what will be a newly created project. You don't check the Branch After Share option unless you plan on changing every file within the project.

TIP *When dealing with patches and service releases, you may want to create a tree structure that matches the release tree and store it at the root of the project database. This allows you to keep your patch releases completely separate from the main tree and makes creating a full maintenance release of your product much easier. For example, in the scenario mentioned previously, if you were patching a component located at $/openssh/AdminServer, you might want to create an empty project called $/ openssh_r1.0 and share the Admin-Server project there. Note the addition of _r1.0 to the project name—this designates it as the Release 1.0 maintenance branch. All other patches for Release 1.0 are then also placed here in the same relative project path as the trunk. To build a new maintenance release, you simply get the main branch source from the Release 1.0 label and then copy the source from the maintenance branch on top of it.*

5. After you click OK and display the Share dialog box, enter the new name for the shared project you're about to create. If you followed the advice in the previous tip, you'd have chosen a maintenance tree parent location and can now keep the project name the same as it was.

6. Once created, all of the icons for the files in the newly created project appear to be push pins. This is because the files are now shared with those in the original AdminServer directory but reflect (or are "pinned to") the revisions of files as they were when the Release 1.0 label was created. The files in the original AdminServer directory display as the usual "share" icon.

7. Next you choose the files that you need to change to make your bug fix. In the example displayed in Figure 6-12, the two files necessary for the fix are BASE64.C and BASE64.H. SourceSafe doesn't let you check out the files while they're pinned—instead, you must branch the two files. You choose the SourceSafe ➤ Branch menu item to create new versions of the files that are no longer shared to the versions in the original AdminServer project. The icons for both the original version of the files and the new versions now again appear to be single sheets of paper.

NOTE *Even though the files in the original project appear to be shared (and they are), you can continue updating them for Release 2.0. As long as the files in the new project are pinned to Release 1.0, they'll always reflect the revision they were when they labeled Release 1.0. If you need to, you can unpin them using the Tools ➤ Show History menu item. Once unpinned, they'll again act as normal shared files.*

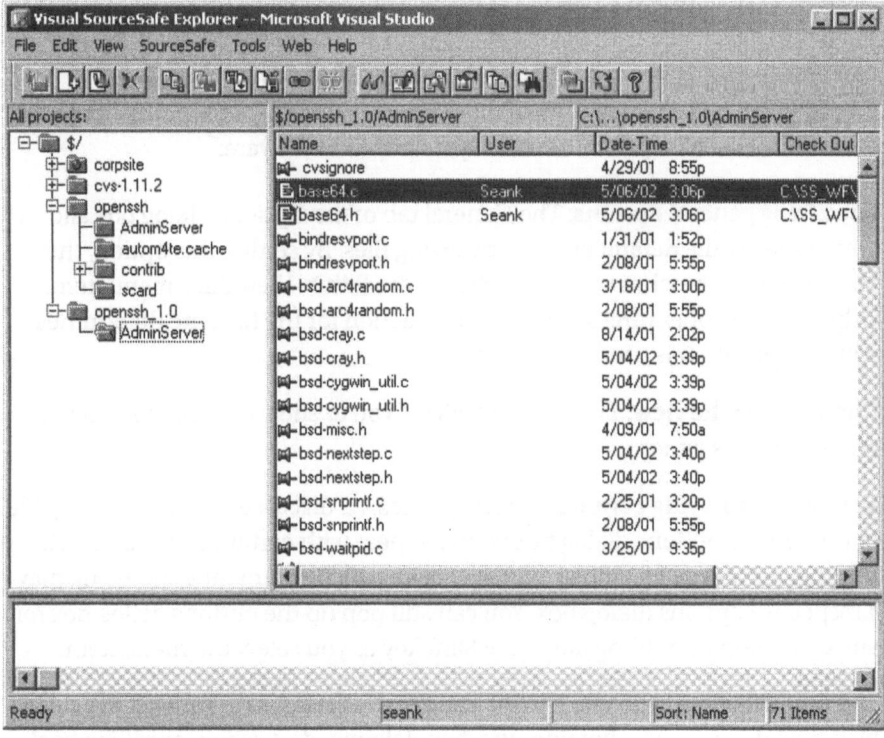

Figure 6-12. A branching example using Visual SourceSafe

8. Now your developers can check out, change, and check in the two files as necessary.

9. At some point after the patch is released, your developers need to merge the changes made in the maintenance branch to the main branch. You merge each file separately using the SourceSafe ➤ Merge Branches menu item. The Merge dialog box appears and displays the link between the branched files. Choose the maintenance version of the file and click Merge. SourceSafe attempts to automatically merge the two files, but if it can't do so without conflict, it opens the Merge Files window. This allows your developers to choose which changes should be copied to the main branch. Then you check in the newly modified file to the trunk as you normally would do.

NOTE *SourceSafe always tries to automatically merge files unless you instruct it not to using the Tools ➤ Option menu item.*

Options for the Client

You can personalize many of SourceSafe's default behaviors by choosing the Tools ➤ Options menu item. Many of these options are self-explanatory; however, there are some notable options of which you may not be aware:

Specifying general options: The General tab of the Options dialog box allows you to specify the default editor for viewing files. By setting this option, the chosen editor launches when you choose the Edit ➤ View Files menu item. Otherwise, the operating system's default action for the file type determines which application is used as the editor.

Customizing the view: The View tab allows you to show or hide the project, file, and results panes.

Removing annoying command dialog boxes: As discussed earlier, it's possible to turn off the options dialog boxes that appear with certain commands. The Command Dialogs tab allows you to choose which commands should display a respective options dialog box. You can still pop up the options dialog box for any command by holding down the Shift key as you select the menu item.

Turning off warning boxes: The Warnings tab allows you to turn off the confirmation dialog boxes that pop up when deleting, destroying, or rolling back files.

Customizing the toolbar: The main client toolbar is customizable. You can use the Tools ➤ Customize Toolbar menu to add icons for commands that you use frequently and remove those that you don't.

Changing your password: You change your account's password by choosing the Tools ➤ Change Password menu item. You must know the previous password to fulfill this task.

Administering SourceSafe, Revisited

Let's take a few minutes to revisit the administration tool once again now that you understand the basics of how SourceSafe works.

Setting Security for Projects and Users

It's highly recommended that you use project security for any SourceSafe database. This is an additional security feature that allows you to set different user permissions for each project folder in the database. These permissions trickle down to all child projects unless otherwise specified. This is an important feature to implement—especially for projects containing build scripts, certificates, or other SCM-related materials that shouldn't be accessed by other developers.

Before you can begin assigning rights, however, you must enable project security. To turn on this feature, you choose the Tools ➤ Options menu item in the Administration Tool and click the Project Security tab. A dialog box appears, as displayed in Figure 6-13, and you check the Enable Project Security option.

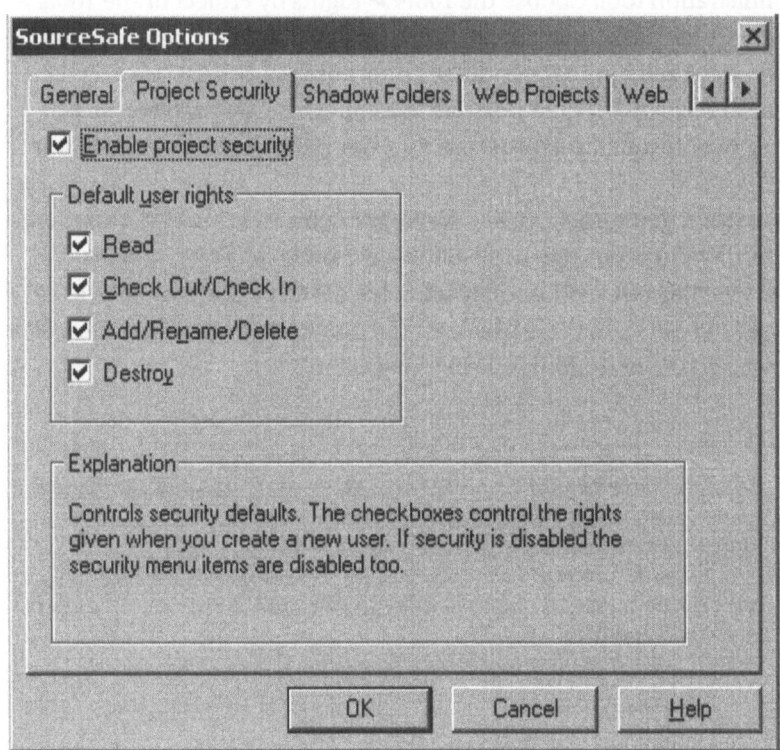

Figure 6-13. The Visual SourceSafe administrator tool, the Source Options dialog box's Project Security tab

After checking to enable project security, the Default User Rights options become enabled. Unless these are otherwise changed, all users can permanently destroy files within the database. This is an extremely powerful tool, and rights to destroy should be allotted only to the Admin account—you want to be sure to turn off the default destroy as soon as you've created your first database. Source-Safe doesn't permit you to change the rights of the Admin account—so instead you hold its password closely.

TIP *Because the SourceSafe Admin account is so powerful, consider creating a second account for you to use during your daily tasks that doesn't have destroy rights. This prevents you from accidentally destroying source. Only use the Admin account when absolutely necessary.*

Once project security is enabled, you grant security rights to projects again using the administration tool. Choose the Tools ➤ Rights by Project or the Tools ➤ Rights Assignments for Users menu items. Both methods provide the same end functionality though their approaches differ. Unfortunately, SourceSafe doesn't handle role-based security—it's not possible to template rights based on someone's job description. Instead, you must use the copy rights feature detailed later in this section.

For the most part, you assign certain developer rights to the root of the source where you want them to propagate to all of the child projects. There are times, however, when you may not want developers to have read or change rights to certain files and child projects. In these cases, set the rights for the parent project first and then change each unique child project as necessary.

TIP *The data folder in your SourceSafe database share contains all checked-in files in a nonencrypted format. Even if you choose to reserve read rights with project security, complete access to the share and its contents is still available to knowledgeable users. You can circumvent this hole by encrypting the data before you check it in. Even more simply, don't keep sensitive data in the SourceSafe database.*

The Project Rights dialog box, as displayed in Figure 6-14, allows you to navigate between projects and set rights for users. All child projects inherit the security unless specifically changed.

User rights appear in the bottom-right corner of the dialog box:

Read: The user is able to get and view files for this project. The initial R refers to "read" when rights abbreviations are used in the product.

Check Out/Check In: The user is able to revise and check in changes to files for this project. The initial C refers to "check in/check out" when rights abbreviations are used in the product.

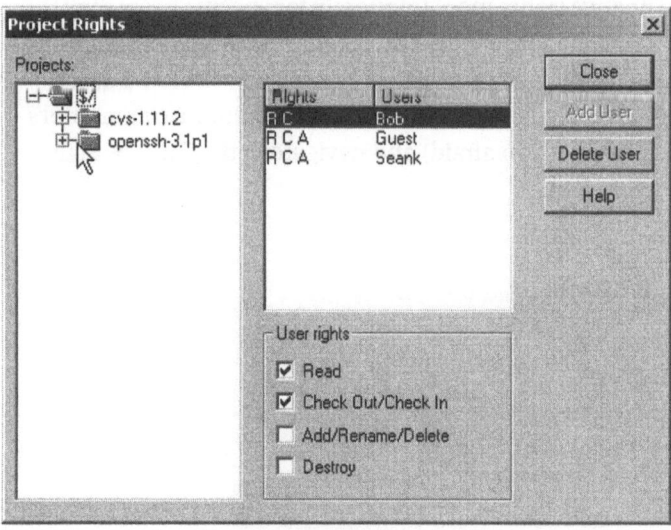

Figure 6-14. The Visual SourceSafe administrator tool, the Project Rights dialog box

Add/Rename/Delete: The user is able to add and rename files. The user is also able to mark files for deletion. If deleted, files no longer appear in the view; however, they aren't removed from the database, and previous labels will reflect that the file exists. The initial A refers to "add/rename/delete" when rights abbreviations are used in the product.

Destroy: The user is able to destroy files and projects (also known as *purging*), which removes them completely and permanently from the database. All aspects of the file, including its history, are forever lost. You should undertake destroying only in extreme cases—for instance, if a user accidentally added his Windows directory to the database. Source that has been built and distributed to customers should never be destroyed under any circumstances. The initial D refers to "destroy" when rights abbreviations are used in the product.

TIP *As previously mentioned, destroy rights are extremely powerful and should be granted on a limited basis. Directly after creating a database, it's wise to remove destroy rights for all users on the root directory ($/). This change will propagate to all child projects.*

If you find that you change rights more frequently for specific users than based upon project, you might choose to use the Assignments for *User* dialog box, displayed in Figure 6-15. This dialog box provides an easy way to view a user's rights at a glance and appears if you highlight a user in the administration tool's main window (only one at a time, I'm afraid) and navigate to the Tools ➤ Rights Assignments for Users menu item.

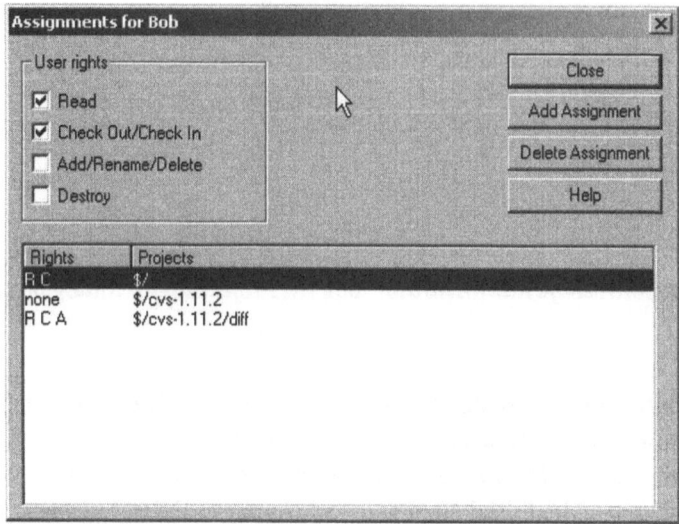

Figure 6-15. The Visual SourceSafe administrator tool, rights assignments for users

The Add Assignment button allows you to choose a project that isn't currently listed in the Rights/Projects list box. To delete the user's rights to a project, including read access, you click the Delete Assignment button. To change security for a certain project, you highlight it and then mark the appropriate rights in the top-left corner.

Luckily you're not stuck with manually changing rights for each new user if you have a security policy in place that you like. To copy rights to a new user, you highlight the user *to* which you want to copy rights in the administration tool's main window. Then you navigate to the Tools ➤ Copy User Rights menu item and choose the user whose rights you want to emulate.

Using SourceSafe to Push Simple Web Sites

SourceSafe provides a mechanism for deploying files via the File Transfer Protocol (FTP) to a simple Web site. You can also create a simple site map or do a quick check to make sure that your site's internal and external links are accurate. Before you can use this functionality, however, you must Web-enable your projects using the administration tool.

In the administration tool, you choose the Tools ➤ Options command and navigate to the Web Projects tab, as displayed in Figure 6-16.

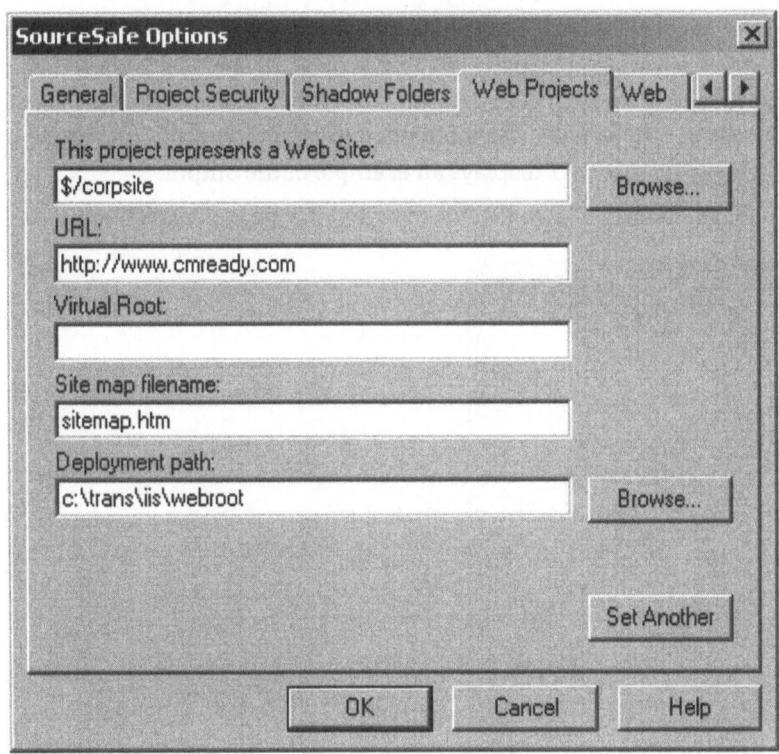

Figure 6-16. The Visual SourceSafe administration tool, the SourceSafe Options dialog box's Web Projects tab

Using the Browse button, you navigate to the project that you want to Web-enable and then type in the full Uniform Resource Locator (URL) of the Web site as it would appear if someone were navigating to the site from the Web. Some Web server software requires a virtual root to exist—if you're using such software, you enter the virtual root value; typically, however, you can leave it blank. Should you choose to use the site-mapping feature, you designate the name for the map in the Site Map Filename edit box. Lastly, you type in the path where the project's files should be deployed. This can be a local path, a UNC path, or an FTP path (for example, `ftp://bob12345@ftp.mysite.com/pub`).

Once your project has been Web-enabled, you use the Web ➤ Deploy menu item in the SourceSafe client to copy the project's tip to the deployment path. The Web ➤ Check Hyperlinks menu item checks the relative and external links in your files. This command must be run against every Web page for which you want the hyperlinks checked.

Lastly, you can use the Web ➤ Create Site Map menu item to create a simple site map for your site. Figure 6-17 displays an example of the output.

Figure 6-17. An example of the site map command output

Understanding Keyword Expansion

Ever opened a source file and wondered why the last guy made the change he did? You could use the SourceSafe client and check the checkin comments for each revision, but that's pretty inefficient.

SourceSafe, along with most other SCM tool vendors, has provided a mechanism for tracking comments (and pretty much any other pertinent SourceSafe information) in the source files themselves. Called *keyword expansion*, this feature means SourceSafe looks for certain variables shrewdly placed in special sections of source files. Using these variables, you can automatically append historical comments, revision numbers, authors, dates, and other information to your source files at checkin time.

For instance, you might type the following bold variable at the beginning of a C++ source file:

```
/*
 * $History: $
*/
#include "msdos.h"
void main(int iNum)
... more code ...
```

The /* and */ symbols indicate to the C++ compiler that all text between them should be disregarded at compile time. SourceSafe, on the other hand, sees the History keyword at checkin and adds historical information to the file. For instance, after you check in a bug fix with the comment "Bug 5645: Create user failure," the file might now look like this:

```
/*
 * $History: base64.c $
 *
 * ****************  Version 2  ****************
 * User: Sean          Date: 5/05/02    Time: 9:03a
 * Updated in $/openssh/AdminServer
 * Bug 5645:  Create user failure
 *
*/
#include "msdos.h"
void main(int iNum)
... more code ...
```

You must enable the use for keyword expansion using the administration tool. You choose the Tools ➤ Options menu item and navigate to the General tab. Under the Expand Keywords in Files of Type edit box, you enter a wildcard specification, separated by commas, for each type of file that should have keywords expanded. Examples might be *.CPP, *.C, and *.H.

See Chapter 7, "In the SCM Lab," for best practices and more information about keyword expansion.

Creating Shadow Folders

An understated feature that exists in SourceSafe is the ability to create *shadow folders*. These are folders that always display the source tip—as files are checked into the database, they automatically refresh in the shadow folder. Any number of shadow folders can exist, and any project can be shadowed.

You might use shadow folders for a number of reasons:

- Developers can immediately ensure that their changes work as designed when integrated with the main line of source.

- Builds and compilations can take place from shadow folders, thereby removing the need to do a time-consuming "get" of source before the build begins.

 NOTE *This isn't the best way to acquire the source for a build because it's impossible to label a shadow folder. See Chapter 8, "Basic Builds," for more information regarding retrieving source for builds.*

- Shadow folders can exist on any machine.

- Shadow folders exist outside of the database, so non-SourceSafe users can view the latest versions of source at any time.

To use the shadow folder feature, you must choose the Tools ➤ Options menu item from the administration tool and click the Shadow Folders tab so it displays as in Figure 6-18.

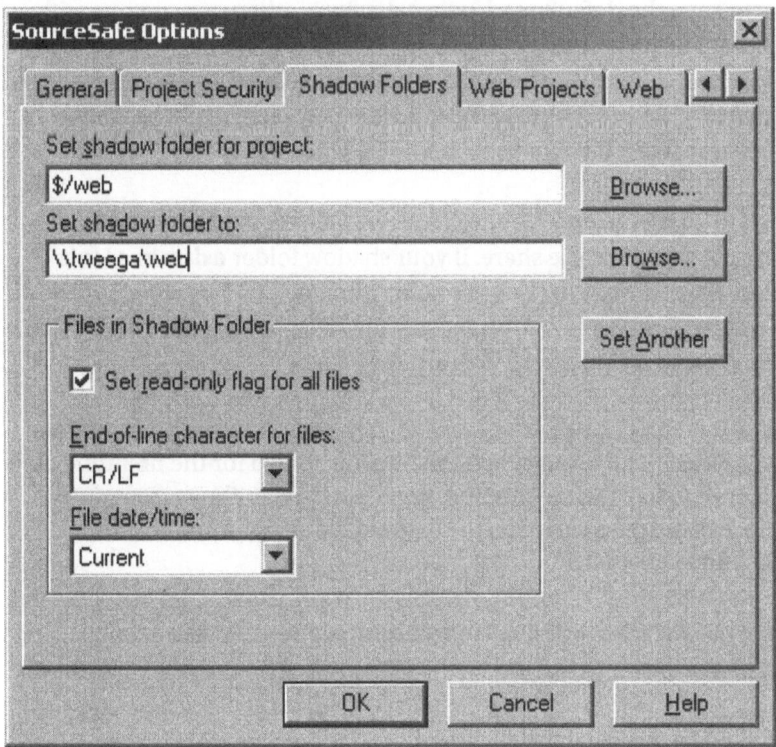

Figure 6-18. The Visual SourceSafe administrator tool, the SourceSafe Options dialog box's Shadow Folders tab

To create a shadow folder, follow these steps:

1. You type a project name in the Set Shadow Folder for Project edit box or search for it using the Browse button. The project I've chosen to shadow in Figure 6-18 is called $/web.

2. You choose a file system location for the shadow folder by typing a path or browsing to it. Because each SourceSafe client is responsible for copying checked-in files to the shadow folder, you'll use a UNC path to a central share with appropriately liberal security rights. If you choose to specify a mapped drive for the path, all clients need to have the same mapping. The UNC path I've chosen for the shadow folder is \\worf\web.

3. It's wise to keep the default read-only behavior—otherwise, anyone with write access to the directory can accidentally or maliciously change files that reside there. Because all database users must have write access to the share, they're able to set or remove any file's read-only attribute. This is a well-known security flaw for the shadow folders feature.

4. You need to verify the end-of-line character that should be used when your files are copied to the share. If your shadow folder exists in a Unix environment, you want to choose a simple linefeed (LF) as your end-of-line character. For Windows, the end-of-line escape sequence needs to be a linefeed followed by a carriage return (LF-CR).

5. The File Date/Time option is relevant to you only at the time the shadow folder is created. By default, when the files are copied for the first time to the shadow folder, the files' modification date is set to the current date and time. Instead, you can have the date set to the last modification or checkin date as desired.

This is a nifty feature, but there are some considerations to make before choosing to utilize it:

- Only the tip of a project can be shadowed, and it's constantly updated. This makes it impossible to properly label the source code at build time.

- The client actually takes care of the "get" to the shadow folder, and there are times when, for one reason or another, the source doesn't update properly.

- Because all clients must have write access to the share, there's an inherent security risk to using the shadow folder. Any user can enter the share and change a file at will. The file doesn't update again until someone checks in a new revision.

Locking the Database

There are times when you need to lock the database—most notably during maintenance or when you choose to build from a shadow directory. Although SourceSafe clients automatically close any open-source files after 15 minutes of inactivity, they reopen when users again begin to use their client. To force a lockout, you can choose the Tools ➤ Lock SourceSafe database option. The Lock Visual SourceSafe Database dialog box appears, as displayed in Figure 6-19, and you check the Lock All Users Out of Visual SourceSafe option.

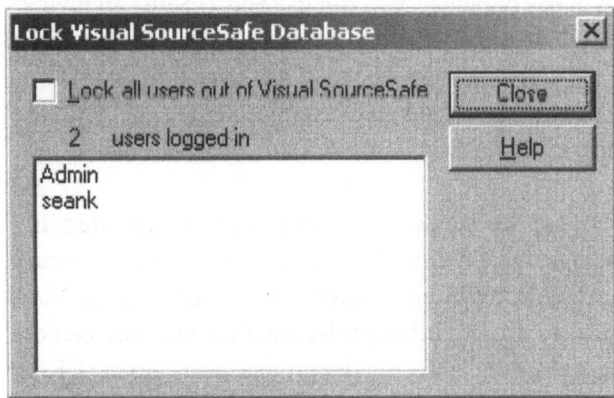

Figure 6-19. The Visual SourceSafe administrator tool, the Lock Visual SourceSafe Database dialog box

Unfortunately, users who are currently logged into the database aren't automatically booted out by this command. The dialog box therefore displays a listing of all users currently logged in so you can go to each individual user and ask them to shut down their SourceSafe client. Because you're logged into the administration tool to fulfill this command, the Admin account is always listed in this window.

Cleaning the SourceSafe Temporary Directory

Every now and again, when a SourceSafe client doesn't close cleanly, some temporary files are left in the server's temporary use folder. Over time, this can lead to a large amount of wasted disk space. Periodically, perhaps once a month or so, it's a good idea to clean out these files by choosing Tools ➤ Clean Up Temp Directory from the administration tool.

Moving, Archiving, and Restoring Projects

SourceSafe databases are stand-alone sets of files that have no running executables. This makes them easy to move to new directories or machines. To move or copy a database, you simply use a Windows Explorer window to drag the source tree's parent folder to a new location. Once completed, you have to create a new share for this location, and all users have to browse their SourceSafe clients to the new location by using the File ➤ Open SourceSafe Database menu item.

NOTE *It's best to lock the database before attempting to move, archive, or restore projects.*

To move or copy portions of the database, you can use SourceSafe's archiving tool. Additionally, the tool is useful for saving and removing obsolete projects from the database to regain disk space. By archiving, you save database objects and their history to a special file that can be copied off to another SourceSafe database or onto backup media. You restore the project with all of its history should you ever need to refer to it again.

To archive projects, you choose the Archive ➤ Archive Projects menu item in the administration tool, and the Archive Wizard appears asking you to add a project. Once you've chosen your project, it's listed in a new window, entitled *Archive Wizard, Step 1 of 3*. If you choose to archive other projects at this time, you can do so by clicking the Add command button, choosing the project, and clicking OK. It, too, is then listed in the Archive Wizard window.

Once you've specified all of the project you want to archive, you click Next to get to step 2 of the Archive Wizard, as displayed in Figure 6-20.

By default, archive files are associated with the .SSA extension—so it's smart to follow this convention so the operating system properly recognizes the file. There are three choices you can make:

- **Save data to file**: This command creates an archive file for the listed projects but leaves the original files unchanged in the database. This command is handy for copying source with all its history between two different Source-Safe databases.

- **Save data to file, then delete from database to save space**: You use this command to archive obsolete projects from view to a secure media and thereby free up disk space.

- **Delete data permanently**: This command is synonymous with the destroy command—the source and its history is *not* archived and is irretrievably purged.

Step 3 of the wizard allows you to specify specific revisions of files to archive. For example, you might want to remove only revisions prior to a specific label. If so, you can do so by choosing the Archive This Version and Older radio button and manually typing the letter L followed by the label name. For instance, removing all revisions up to and including the REL_1_0 label, you might type *LREL_1_0* into the edit box. Otherwise, choose the Archive All of the Data radio button to archive all revisions of files in a project, as displayed in Figure 6-21.

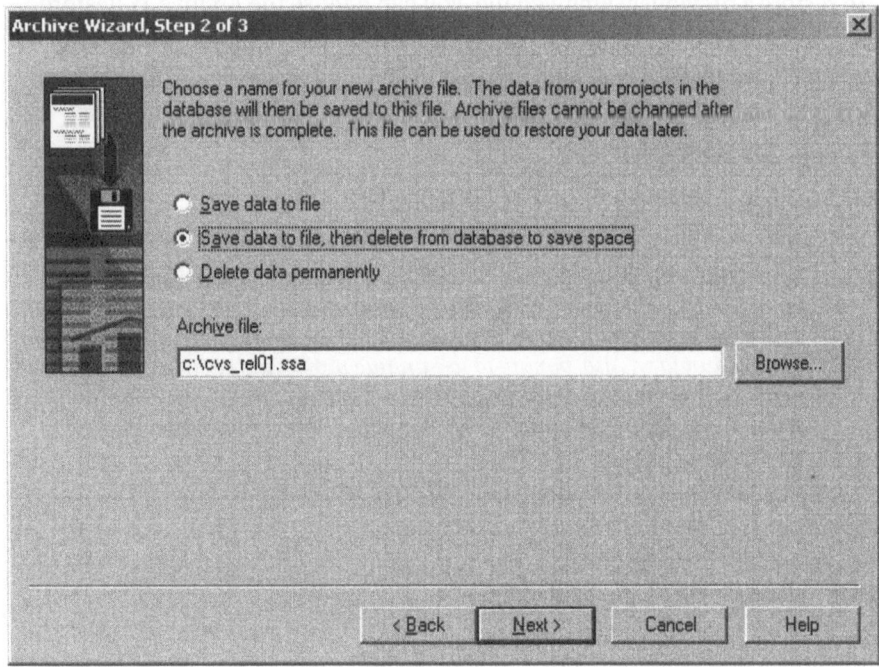

Figure 6-20. The Visual SourceSafe administrator tool—the Archive Wizard, Step 2 of 3 page

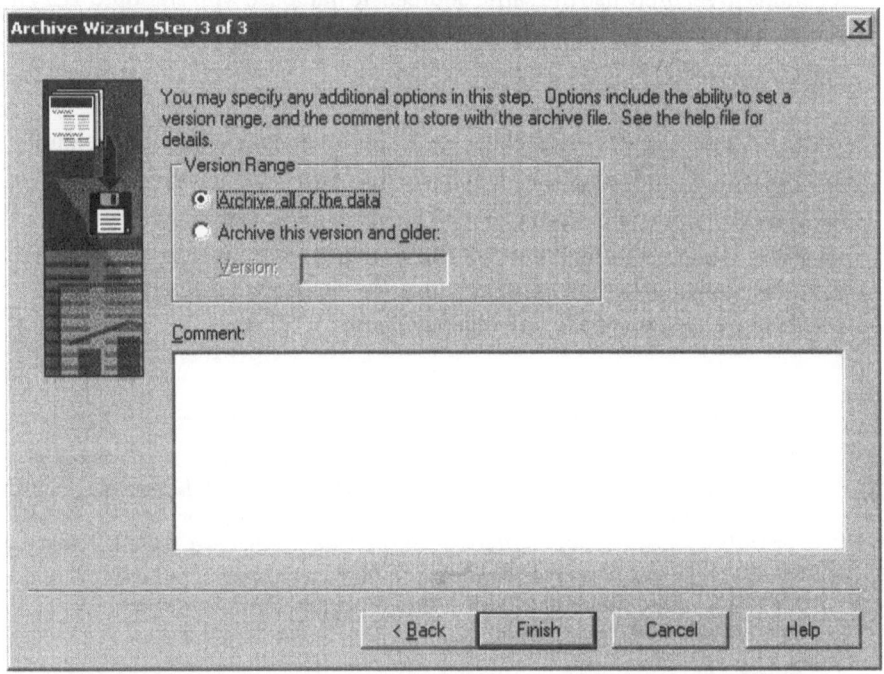

Figure 6-21. The Visual SourceSafe administrator tool—the Archive Wizard, Step 3 of 3 page

To restore a previously archived file, you can choose the Archive ➤ Restore Projects menu item. You browse to or type in the archive filename—by default SourceSafe looks for files with the .SSA extension—and click Next. The Restore Wizard asks whether you'd like to restore the files to the original location or somewhere else in the database.

NOTE *The Archive and Restore Wizards can be a little flakey, and they don't always work as designed. It's advised that you get source to a local working folder before creating an archive and do a file system backup of that location to be redundant. Also, be sure to use unique project names when creating new projects in SourceSafe—the Restore Wizard will not be able to complete its job if you've created a new project that shares the same name with a project in an archive.*

Using Third Party Add-Ons

There's quite a bit of functionality that you can add to your SourceSafe database through third-party vendors and freeware products:

- SourceOffSite provides you with a mechanism to allow developers in varied locations to securely use the same SourceSafe database with standard TCP/IP Internet connections. Visit parent company SourceGear's Web site at http://www.sourceoffsite.com.

- If you have developers using Unix, they can use the same SourceSafe database as your Windows folks by installing the Mainsoft's Visual SourceSafe for Unix products (http://www.mainsoft.com). Source databases can exist on either Unix or Windows and are usable with clients on either platform; unfortunately, at the time of this writing, the similar Macintosh program provided by Metrowerks is no longer available.

NOTE *If you're attempting to use SourceSafe on two different platforms such as Unix and Windows, you need an appropriate Network File System (NFS) software that allows both operating systems to see each other's shares. Samba for Unix is freeware and available at* http://www.samba.org. *It allows Unix mounts to be visible on Windows. Hummingbird's Maestro conversely allows Windows shares to be visible on Unix systems. Visit them at* http://www.hummingbird.com.

- Many development tools have SourceSafe integration built into them. Look for tools that say that they're SCC-compliant and SourceSafe-compliant.

- Visual Studio itself is integrated with SourceSafe. Refer to its help files for more information.

Using the Command Line

You can complete many of SourceSafe's commands on the command line—this is necessary for builds and other tasks that require some sort of scripting automation. This ability is available to any application that uses DOS-style commands including:

- The Windows command prompt

- The Windows Start ➤ Run menu item

- Makefiles

- Perl scripts

- Batch files

NOTE *The SS.EXE executable used for command-line calls is located in the win32 folder of your SourceSafe client installation. For ease of use, you might add this folder to your system path by right-clicking My Computer on your desktop, choosing Properties, and clicking the Environment Variables button on the Advanced tab. If you choose not to use a Path environment variable, you must type the full path to the SS.EXE executable every time you choose to use SourceSafe's command-line functionality. All the examples in this section assume that this executable can be found in the system path. See your Windows documentation for more information about setting the system path.*

The syntax for command-line use is as follows:

```
ss.exe command [file specification] [options]
```

where *command* is the SourceSafe task you want to run, [*file specification*] is the set of files on which you want the command to run, and [*options*] are specific options available to the command. Options for SourceSafe will always begin with a hyphen (-).

NOTE *Brackets ([and]) are used as a standard when describing commands and are used to denote parameters that may not be necessary depending on the command's specific function.*

As an example, if you choose to retrieve all of the files in the $/corpsite project to the C:\test directory on the local file system file system, you might type the following bolded text:

```
C:\> cd c:\test
C:\Test> ss get $/corpsite/*.*
```

NOTE *Command-line calls are made relative to projects in SourceSafe's database and not your working folder versions. Don't forget to use dollar signs and forward slashes when referring to database projects on the command line.*

To get the $/corpsite project recursively as it was when it was labeled Release 3.0 and then make the files writable, you simply add the -V, -R, and -W options. As a convenience (or inconvenience depending on your view of things), SourceSafe asks you if you want to permanently change the working directory for the $/corpsite project to C:\TEST every time the command is called. You can give SourceSafe a default "no" by adding the -I- ("never ask me questions") option. Don't forget the extra dash! The final call might look something like this:

```
C:\test>ss get $/corpsite/*.* -V"Release 3.0" -W -R -I-
Set C:\Trans\bob as the default folder for project $/corpsite?(Y/N)N
$/corpsite:
aboutus.htm
FOLDER.GIF
index.htm
platforms.htm
services.htm

$/corpsite/images:
bottom_home.jpg
home_menu_aboutus.jpg

C:\test>
```

Notice that there's no space between the -V and the Release 3.0 label. You never use spaces between options and the values that accompany them.

NOTE *Most SourceSafe commands carry out their tasks in whatever is the current directory. Because the command prompt opens to the Windows system directory, be sure to change the directory to an appropriate working folder before making any calls to ensure that files are copied to the correct location.*

Table 6-1 represents a list of some of the more popular SourceSafe functionality available through the command line. This isn't a comprehensive list.

Table 6-1. Some of the SourceSafe Functionality Available at the Command Line

Command	Action
Add	Adds a file to the database
Checkin	Checks a file into the database
Checkout	Checks out a file to the current directory
Create	Creates a new subproject of the current or specified project
Directory	Lists the contents of the current or specified project
Filetype	Displays whether a file is text or binary
Get	Gets a copy of the specified file(s)
Help	Displays the SourceSafe command-line help
Label	Assigns a label to the specified version of a file or project
Physical	Displays the SourceSafe logical name for the given file or project
Project	Displays the current project path
View	Displays a file in a textual view
Whoami	Indicates the currently logged-in user
WorkFold	Sets the current working folder

Describing each of these commands and their options is outside the scope of this chapter; be sure to visit the Microsoft MSDN Web site at http://msdn.microsoft.com and search the Knowledge Base for *SourceSafe command line*.

> **NOTE** *By default, the command-line tool uses the database located in the DATA directory located relatively to the SS.EXE executable being called. You may find this problematic if you have more than one database on the same machine or if you're using another located on a network share. In those cases, use the SSDIR environment variable to specify the database location before calling the SS.EXE command-line executable.*

A Ini Cnt Txt Dat B

On the server, the SourceSafe database creates two files in its DATA directory for every file and project. These two files are given names that SourceSafe understands but that look awfully odd. For instance, the ABOUTUS.HTM file in my $/corpsite project might actually exist as two files in the SourceSafe's DATA directory called LKBAAAAA and LKBAAAAA.A. One file, called the *log file* by Microsoft, has no extension; the other file always reflects the latest version of the source and has an added .A or .B extension.

The log file stores all of the version deltas that have taken place on the file since its addition to the database. It also keeps information regarding who added the file and where it exists in the project tree. Every time a file is checked in, the log file is updated and the latest version of the file is saved with an .A or .B extension. The extensions alternate with every check in—there are few circumstances where both an .A and a .B file exist for a single file. When a file is shared, the file's log is updated, but a second pair of files isn't created.

In addition to the files in the DATA directory, the SourceSafe database and client have a number of textual configuration files, as displayed in Table 6-2. You can make changes as necessary to some of these files—notably the SRCSAFE.INI file—but not all of them. Only ever make changes to these files if you know what you're doing.

Table 6-2. SourceSafe Configuration Files

File/folder	Description
SrcSafe.ini	Visual SourceSafe database global settings and database configuration information relative to users.
Users.txt	List of the users in the database.
Data\Aaaaaaaa.cnt	Physical name of last file added to the database.
Data\Names.dat	Long filename mappings.
Data\Rights.dat	User and project security information. This file can be rebuilt using the Analyze tool.
Data\Status.dat	SourceSafe client cache file. This file can be rebuilt using the Analyze tool.
Data\Um.dat	Name, password, and database identifiers.
Data\Version.dat	SourceSafe database version.
Data\A...Z (folders)	Actual data files as explained at the beginning of this section.
Data\Backup (folder)	Analyze log file (ANALYZE.LOG), list of bad files (ANALYZE.BAD), and backups of files changed by Analyze are placed in this folder when the tool is run.
Data\Labels (folder)	Information used for label promotion.
Data\Locks (folder)	Used if Visual SourceSafe locking is enabled.
Data\Loggedin (folder)	User logon files and an Admin.lck file if the database is locked.
Users (folder)/*.INI	Default settings and specific user settings kept in named user folders. Each folder contains an SS.INI file that holds specific user information. The Admin folder contains the SSADMIN.INI folder that defines administration settings. These files are limited to being 64KB in size and can keep settings for only ten local machines for each user. Microsoft suggests deleting the unnecessary entries in the SS.INI file should you encounter user-specific errors.

Using the Analyze Tool

It's a sad truth—SourceSafe databases corrupt every now and again. Most of the time, these corruptions occur in small doses and are easily corrected. If left unchecked, however, a good part of the source can mistakenly be destroyed.

The Analyze tool provided with the SourceSafe Administrator can help to detect small problems before they become unmanageable. Depending on the size of the database and the amount of users, Microsoft recommends that you run the tool weekly. For smaller databases with few users, this task can be completed less frequently. Users can continue to work within the database when the Analyze tool is used to check its health, but you must lock out all users if you want to have the tool automatically fix the problems it finds. This makes completing this maintenance on a scheduled basis a little bit challenging.

TIP *Always run the Analyze tool from the server that holds the database. Attempting to run the tool from a client machine can take much longer and cause indeterminate problems.*

The Analyze tool fulfills several obligations when it's run against the database:

- It checks that each file hasn't become corrupted.

- It ensures that the project structure is valid—for instance, that child projects still map to their proper parent projects. It also ensures that branch files and shares are mapped properly.

- It makes certain that the main database security and naming files aren't corrupted.

If any of these problems are found, the tool reports the error and, if instructed, attempts to correct the error.

NOTE *The Analyze tool must be allowed to complete its run, or serious problems can arise. Always make sure you have at least enough space for a full additional copy of the database files so the tool doesn't error out in the middle of its work.*

SourceSafe doesn't save files on the server based upon either project name or filename. Instead, because source deltas are saved with every checkin, SourceSafe uses its own naming methodology that allows it to save historical information about files. Unfortunately, this means that the Analyze tool will report file errors based entirely upon SourceSafe's native naming convention. These filenames are completely unrelated to what you might see in the client—for instance, a file checked into the database as GETLINE.CPP might be really named ABCAAAAA.A. See the sidebar entitled "A Ini Cnt Txt Dat B" for more information.

In order to save some grief, you can use the Physical command-line tool to map project and filenames to their SourceSafe odd-named equivalents. For instance, if you wanted to redirect this map into a file called C:\FILENAME.TXT, you might type the following in a Command Prompt window:

```
ss physical $/ -r > c:\filename.txt
```

NOTE *You must specify the full path of the SS.EXE executable unless you added SourceSafe's command directory to the system path as described in the "Using the Command Line" section.*

The Physical tool then creates a text document called C:\FILENAME.TXT, which maps out all of SourceSafe's internal filenames to the filename you see in the client tool. An example of the output might look like this:

```
$/:
cvs-1.11.2      BAAAAAAA
$/cvs-1.11.2:
.cvsignore      DAAAAAAA
acconfig.h      EAAAAAAA
acinclude.m4    FAAAAAAA
aclocal.m4      GAAAAAAA
```

When you run into a corrupted file, you can use this map to determine to which file the error refers. In some cases, you may need to delete the file and re-add it to the database. Of course, you lose the file's history and label information when this happens.

You run the Analyze tool from the command line, and Microsoft recommends that you run the tool several times to ensure that all problems are corrected. The following steps assume that you've placed the SourceSafe command directory in the system path as described in the "Using the Command Line" section:

1. The first pass is simply to identify problems and not to fix anything. You don't have to lock the database for this step. You do this to avoid inconveniencing your developers if no errors are found. You can use the -X parameter so Analyze doesn't attempt to lock the database. You can also use the -V4 parameter so the tool will report errors in its most verbose way:

   ```
   analyze -x -v4 <database path>
   ```

2. If errors are found, you run the tool again using the -F option. This instructs Analyze to try to correct any problems that it finds. Users should be locked out of the database during this step:

   ```
   analyze -f -v4 <database path>
   ```

3. After it has completed, you continue to run the tool until it no longer reports any errors:

   ```
   analyze -f -v4 <database path>
   ```

The Analyze tool places a full report and copies of the files it changes into a backup directory. By default, this directory is called BACKUP and exists in the server's DATA folder. The tool can't run if the backup directory exists, so you must rename or delete the current BACKUP folder if it exists before you can call the tool. If you want to specify a different directory to be used for backup, you can specify the -B option with a new path when running the tool.

If the STATUS.DAT, NAMES.DAT, or RIGHTS.DAT files have become corrupted, they can be rebuilt by removing the original from the DATA directory and then running the Analyze tool with the -F option.

 NOTE *The NAMES.DAT file doesn't get re-created to its proper name. Rename the new version of the file to NAMES.DAT after the Analyze tool has finished.*

Be aware there are some errors that the tool simply can't fix on its own. Microsoft provides detailed information on these kinds of analyze errors and their possible solutions at http://support.microsoft.com. Search for article ID Q152807 in the Microsoft knowledge base.

Food for Thought

As with any tool that requires administrative support, there are several tasks and scenarios of which to be aware when working with SourceSafe. Read the following sections carefully—SourceSafe has a few not-so-obvious "gotchas."

Setting System Clocks

Because clients on local machines date-stamp files as they're checked in and out to the server database, computer clocks that are out of sync can make server operations appear out of sequence. Consider using a Windows Domain Time Source server or, alternatively, the Network Time Protocol (NTP) to ensure all machines accessing the database are synced.

Backing Up and Restoring

As described in Chapters 3 and 7 ("All About the Source" and "In the SCM Lab," respectively), backing up the source is an extremely important part of the software configuration manager's responsibility. There are some considerations for SourceSafe when contemplating the backup/restore schema:

Lock out users: Files that are opened by for use by clients can't be backed up, so it's wise to lock out users before beginning a backup. There's no command-line executable that can be run to lock out users, which makes it difficult to schedule this task nightly. SourceSafe automatically closes files after 15 minutes of inactivity, but keep in mind that the RIGHTS.DAT and STATUS.DAT files are never backed up properly if the database isn't locked. Because the Analyze tool can rebuild those two files in a pinch, late-night backups are usually safe for backing up the source. Unless, that is, you have night owls working with you.

Don't back up during an analyze session: Backups should *never* be performed when an analyze is taking place. This can cause Analyze to shut down in the middle of an operation and destroy the database.

Don't restore databases over the previous version: When restoring a database, *don't* do so over an existing one. This can cause irregularities because of SourceSafe's file naming and structure architecture.

Working folders must be separately backed up: Unlike some other source tools, working folders don't exist on the server—thus, they aren't usually a part of the standard backup and restore plan for SourceSafe. If you choose to back up working folders—which some might call an unnecessary redundancy—do so from the individual development machines. As mentioned earlier, you may want to try to keep workspaces on a shared network drive to help solve this problem.

Utilizing the Automation Capabilities

You can enrich the feature set of SourceSafe by writing custom tools using its automation objects. Find out more about this by navigating to `http://msdn.microsoft.com` and searching the Knowledge Base for *SourceSafe automation*.

Summary

This chapter discussed the basic administration and use of Microsoft SourceSafe.

Because it's a low-end tool, SourceSafe does have some serious limitations that you should consider before you choose it as your primary source control database. You should now be able to make an informed decision.

In this chapter you learned the following:

- How to obtain, license, and install the product

- How to use the administration tool to add users and create databases

- About the use of working folders on users' hard drives

- How to use the SourceSafe client to add, check out, and check in files

- How to use the SourceSafe client to label and get source

- About the SourceSafe client's basic user interface

- How to lock the database during maintenance periods

- How to back up and restore your source control database

- How to use the tool's command-line interface

- How to use the Analyze tool to protect your database's health

In addition to these topics, this chapter also provided tips that should make using SourceSafe a little easier. If you decide to use SourceSafe as your source control database, be sure to refer to this chapter when you get to Chapter 8, "Basic Builds."

Part Three

The Tasks

In the SCM Lab

Many Software Configuration Managers (SCMs) have a commonly accessible area outside of their cubical or office where builds take place. This area, oftentimes dubbed the *SCM lab*, might also be the place where developers test their code, burn media, and have meetings.

But most importantly, it's the place where builds take place. You want to create builds in a common area because they often break and require the attention of other developers. There might also be times when people other than yourself need to create a build for one reason or another. Do you really want to have those people trudging through your cube all of the time?

Although having a lab will definitely increase the quality of your SCM life, you might still want to make a few changes to your everyday practices. In addition to talking about how to create the lab itself, this chapter also describes some of the better practices that an SCM can follow to ensure that the source stays secure, builds get built, and everyone is generally happy.

Stocking the Lab

What's in a lab, anyway? In the case of the SCM lab, it's you. You'll probably spend half of your time in your lab creating and testing builds, so you want it to be somewhat spacious and comfortable. Getting space for a lab might be difficult if your company is already settled and fairly full. On the other hand, one of the only bright aspects of a sluggish economy is the space that generally opens up as employees leave.

If your location has a lot of open space or if you're changing locations, be sure to talk to your management about creating an SCM lab. Even if there isn't a lot of space available, you might want to try to create some room somewhere—otherwise, people will start treating your cube or office more and more like common space. That can be pretty irritating when you're trying to get some work done.

Scope out your needs before you actually ask for space. After all, do you even know how much space you'll need? The following are some tips as you begin to plan it:

You'll need room for build machines: You'll probably want space for at least one build machine—see Chapter 8, "Basic Builds," for more information about creating build machines. If you plan on having multiple build machines for different streams of code, consider buying a Keyboard-Video-Mouse (KVM) switch that allows several computers to share a common keyboard, monitor, and pointing device. This will save you a great deal of space (though you'll still need room for the processor boxes). You may find this scenario limiting in that people will have to share the common keyboard when using different machines.

You'll need room for test machines: Test machines are valuable in an SCM lab. It's likely that you'll want to make several of them available. As described more thoroughly in Chapter 2, "The SCM and the Software Development Process," your test machines' primary purpose is conducting smoke tests on builds when they've completed. In addition, your developers can test their code additions and integrations after the build has completed. Requiring that code works on an SCM test machine is the best weapon you'll have against the "it works on my machine" refrain. But the benefits don't stop there—these machines can be used by other interested parties, such as the documentation team members, who may not want to install volatile products on their own machines. Keep in mind that using KVM switches for test machines saves some space but also severely limits the developers' ability to efficiently test their work because they'll have to take turns. Each test machine has its own keyboard, monitor, and pointing device.

Find utilities that help you "start from scratch": If you're using Microsoft Windows, the best test machines are the ones that can quickly be "burnt down" and reinstalled with the operating system and other prerequisites. There are several utilities, such as Symantec's Ghost, which allow you to take a snapshot of a hard drive and save it to a network location or write it to CD. Using this type of software, you can burn down and rebuild a test machine in just 15 or 20 minutes. Just remember not to install a version of your product before saving your hard drive image! Having any of your product installed onto the image destroys your ability to have a controlled test environment.

Leave room for the people: In addition to a monitor and keyboard, every "seat" in the lab should have an appropriate amount of desk space for manuals, notebooks, paper, and pens. What's the use of a work area if there's no place to check off lists or to document how the product works? If you choose to use a racking mechanism for your lab, make sure there's plenty of desk space nearby or incorporated into the rack itself.

Rent it out for meetings: Consider using your SCM lab as an alternative meeting room. This may not sound attractive at first—but decision-wavering managers might be more amenable to giving you lab space if your argument is that the space will be multifunctional.

Check the "juice": Ensure that your electrical and network wiring schemes can support the number of computers you plan on using in the space. Your facilities and Local Area Network (LAN) managers can normally confirm your space's wiring status.

Creating an SCM Guide for Developers

Life in your lab can be a nightmare if your developers fulfill tasks in a haphazard method. They might create directory structures in the source tree that break your builds. Or they might check in large, unnecessary binary files into the source database—causing it to bloat to an unhealthy size.

It's wise to have a set of written directions for developers to use when testing the source database and developing code. You should update this document frequently as new issues arise or standards are set. Distribute this guide to each developer as they're hired so they fully understand their sourcing responsibilities. Managers should also hold the developers accountable should they not follow the directions properly.

> **TIP** *Although you may choose to dictate these rules to the developers, you'll find that they'll be much more amenable to following directions that they had a part in creating. You may want to create a draft document and pass it around for comments and criticisms before setting the regulations in stone.*

Although every shop has different processes it follows, the following are some items you may want to include in your SCM guide:

Installing and using the source database tool client: The source won't do anyone any good if it isn't accessible to the developers. The SCM guide should clearly state how to install any client tools necessary to access the source. If addition, it should also explain how to fulfill common tasks such as getting and committing code, displaying file history, and showing differences between versions.

Navigating the source tree: Most likely, your source tree is going to contain several complicated projects. Consider adding a section to the SCM guide that describes the source tree and how it's divvied up. Try to imagine being a new developer at your location—if you were to sit next to them as they navigated the tree, how might you describe it to them?

Adding new components to the tree: Instruct the developers on the proper way to add new components to the source tree. How should components be named? Should one form of directory structure be dictated? Are there other directions that should be followed before a component is added? Refer to Chapter 8, "Basic Builds," to get an idea of why component names and directory structure might matter to you.

Adding components to the build and the installation: Developers should instruct the build and installation script writers with instructions on how to build and install the component. Consider creating template documents that developers can easily fill in using Microsoft Word or other common word processors. Examples of what you might need to know include the name of the component, where it's located in the source tree, and special tools that might be necessary for the component to build or be installed.

Specifying files types that should excluded from source: Binary object files should never be added to the source because they're consistently generated directly from source and are often large in size. Depending on your operating system and compilation tool, you may want to specify which file types shouldn't be added to the source tree. Some source database and compilation environment tools can automatically detect these file types and help you block the user from committing these bloated objects—refer to your tool's documentation to see if it can fulfill this functionality.

Consolidating common code into common components: Instead of sharing code between different components, consider creating a single common component library that can be called by any number of other components. If you can't create this component yourself, speak to the lead developer about it— it's generally agreed that having common code in different components is dangerous.

Creating a software installation policy: Even small inconsequential programs can change system files on your developers' machines. And you'll see it in action the first time one of their installed shareware products changes a Global Unique Identifier (GUID) that causes the build to break. Although this tends to be more of a threat in the Windows world—and Microsoft is improving this as the versions go by—you may want to work with the development management to create a software installation policy.

Creating a source locking policy: Your source database tool may allow you to choose whether files can be exclusively locked for editing. Although locking files can ease merging confusion later, it also tends to slow down other development—especially in larger environments where many developers work on the same source files. Whichever method you choose, make sure to put it in writing in the SCM guide so that there's no confusion.

Watching out for the bus: Employees quit, go on vacation, and get fired. What happens to the unchecked-in source on their machines when that happens? Consider making it a policy that supervisors must be able to get on developers' machines when they're away.

If a component is part of the build, it must be able to build: Developers should be discouraged from checking in code that doesn't build—especially for code that previously did. They can ensure that they fulfill this responsibility by copying the current component directory to a different location, getting the code they just checked in from the source database, and trying to rebuild it.

Synchronizing with the source tree (as long as it doesn't break): A by-product of the previous tip, developers should be encouraged to check in their code as often as possible without breaking the build. Going too long without syncing and checking in code can lead to large, unmanageable merges. If a developer plans to take a while to work on a component, consider coming up with another way to back up code without having to check it into the main source branch.

Avoiding user intervention during builds: There's nothing more frustrating than starting a build and then coming back a couple of hours later to see a modal "Do you want to continue?" input box waiting on the screen. The *auto* in *automated build* means that no user interaction should be required to build your product. Work with your developers to get around any possible user interface interruptions.

Considering which compilation warnings are legal: Most compilers have the capability to echo out warnings when they see questionable code. Your compiler can even be set to error out when it runs into certain levels of warnings. Work with your lead developer to determine which warning levels are dangerous and should be considered errors. When chosen, publish that certain warning levels aren't acceptable. You may also want to provide instructions to the developers on how to error out on certain warnings.

Using a common source tree structure with relative paths: Because every machine is set up differently, using absolute paths can slow the build down to a crawl. Most shops enforce the use of a common source tree structure and relative paths. In other words, the source's root directory and how it relates to its child directories should be standard on each developer's machine. As long as the developers use relative paths, they can still place the source's root wherever they want on their machine—for instance, C:\SRC or C:\My Documents\SRC—as long as the child directory's tree reflects the original source tree.

WORD OF THE DAY

shāme, *n. v.*

Living with dishonor.

Hey, we're all adults here…so we should be responsible for our actions, right?

It's a nice dream. Unfortunately, time and time again, there are those people who simply can't seem to follow simple rules for one reason or another. Here's some of the excuses you might hear:

"It works on my machine."

"There just wasn't time to test it."

"It wasn't just me who merged. What about Joe's code?"

"Dude—just deal with it. I'm busy."

Regardless of the excuse, it means the same thing: a broken build. Because builds are time consuming to create and valuable to other team members, you must pay special attention to those who don't follow the rules and cause them to break.

Consider using a toy or paper certificate to "mark" a developer when he or she breaks the build through a disregard of policy or laziness. For instance, at one of my previous jobs, I had a troll doll that would sit on the top of a blatant build breaker's cube plainly visible to all who visited the department.

Of course, this mark shouldn't be permanent. Only one developer at a time should ever have it and only then until someone else deserves the mark of nonachievement. Remember to keep the situation lighthearted and full of humor. The idea isn't to necessarily punish the developers—it's to remind them to be cautious. Involve a development manager when someone consistently receives the dishonor—this type of behavior should be noted at review time.

You'll find that as time goes by, the notorious build breakers won't break the build quite as often. In fact, you may find that one developer has had the mark for so long that it's just not befitting anymore. I always removed the troll after a week or two of solid builds.

If you do choose to use this method to decrease the number of broken builds, be sure to document how the whole thing will work so there isn't any grumbling when it's awarded. You may find that you won't ever need to award it. And be charitable—only give out the mark for true acts of negligence. People shouldn't be marked if they break the build through no fault of their own—in fact, doing so will lessen the tool's effectiveness because people won't consider it a fair deal.

Most importantly, pass the idea by management and the leading developers to gain their support before putting it in motion. You may even want to document how often the build is breaking before even approaching anyone with the idea. If the development leaders don't buy into the plan, it's not worth even trying to put it in motion. You're not looking for a morale buster or a fight. You just don't want broken builds.

Merging code: Developers should be told how to merge branched code back into the main code stream. See the "Best Practices for the SCM" section of this chapter for more information on the best ways to merge code.

The build and source database machines should be off-limits to everyone but SCMs: One seemingly innocuous change to a build or source machine can lead to disaster—so it pays to err on the side of safety. In addition to publishing an "off-limits" rule, consider using automated screensavers that lock the machines after ten minutes of nonuse. SCMs should be trained to lock the machines after using them.

Encouraging the use of keyword expansion and checkin comments: Keyword expansion allows users to automatically comment their code as they check it into the source. These comments are easily read from within the source code itself and can save the user a trip to the file's history log. Check with your source database tool's documentation for more information.

Everything that's considered "source" should be added to the source database: If it's source, it belongs in the database. Only files that are generated by the compiler should be excluded from addition.

Encouraging the use of the test machines: Inform the developers that test machines are available for everyone's use. Point out that they must be used to test the integrity of merged code before a developer's job is considered complete.

In addition to the previously described SCM guide, your development group should also consider creating a programming guide for its members. This type of document details how source code should be written. For instance, it might dictate how many characters equal a tab space, how lines of code should be laid out, and how programmers must comment their work. Some groups consolidate the SCM and development regulations into one guide so all information can live in one easily accessible document.

Best Practices for the SCM

In every aspect of life, there are opinions as to the best way to do things. I bet you haven't ever made a large purchase without a neighbor or friend informing you that you could've saved a bunch of money by going to a different store. Everyone always has an opinion—and the good ones are based upon experience.

SCM best practices are no different. They're the opinions of people who have done this sort of thing before and—in some cases—have done it for many years.

The best practices I write about in this chapter are generally accepted through the SCM community.

I strongly advise you to safeguard your source and builds by following the practices in the following sections.

Workspaces

The workspace is the place where developers change code. In most cases, these workspaces are private—only one person uses them at a time. Some source control database tools may provide workspaces as part of their functionality, or they may simply exist as a directory on the developer's hard drive. The following are some workspace pointers:

Don't share workspaces: I can't think of a need to share workspaces between developers—even for integration testing. Instead, each developer should have his or her own workspace, and integration testing should take place on test machines. By allowing developers to share workspaces, your source control database tool can no longer keep track of who made individual changes— leading to reasonable doubt when something goes wrong.

Developers shouldn't go stale—but don't force them to update: Workspaces allow developers to isolate themselves from the changes being made by other developers. If they isolate themselves too long, they'll have a nasty merge to do (see the upcoming "Branching and Merging" section for more information). But the opposite is dangerous as well—automatic propagation of changes into developers' workspaces can and will compromise their ability to test their work in a controlled environment. And anyone who remembers Mr. Duvall's eighth grade science class will tell you that a test in an uncontrolled environment is no test at all. Instead, developers should be empowered to completely manage when and how they update their workspaces with the latest and greatest code.

Branching and Merging

Branching and merging is one of the most difficult aspects of trying to manage a large source tree. I talked about the basic processes of creating branches in Chapter 3, "All About the Source," so refer to that chapter if you need a refresher. All the SCM tools handle branching and merging somewhat differently—so it's difficult to give you a straight answer as to the "how" of the task. What I can talk about, however, are some general thoughts on how you can avoid problems:

Use monikers for branches instead of release numbers: The time and order of when your product versions ship can change. As described in more detail in Chapter 3, "All About the Source," using internal names for releases and branches can ease a lot of headache when things change in a hurry.

Use the trunk as the current version: For reasons explained with more detail in Chapter 3, "All About the Source," the trunk should always contain the latest and greatest source. Creating new branches for every new release will quickly become overwhelming. Instead, branch for maintenance versions or for product spin-offs.

Only branch when necessary and do it as late as possible: Getting huge, painful shots in the belly are required when you've been exposed to rabies—so you don't want to get the shots before you're exposed, do you? Think of branches as huge, painful rabies shots—you only want to deal with them when you absolutely must. Sure, you may know that a maintenance branch is going to be necessary further down the road—just don't create it until the first developer needs to start work on it. Why? Well, let's say that a bug that has been fixed in the trunk, and it may need, at some point, to be given to customers as a maintenance patch. If you branch late, you can solidify the bug fix in the trunk before it's ever propagated to a new maintenance branch. On the other hand, if you branch early, every change to the bug fix will require changes or merges to both branches. And don't fret...any source control tool worth its salt can branch based on a label or a date—so there's no impetus to branch early.

Always make large changes early in the schedule: See the previous pointer. The earlier a change is made, the more likely it won't need to be merged to multiple branches.

If you know you're making a change in two branches, make the change first in the one with the fewest modifications since the branch occurred: The fewer the changes the better—otherwise, you'll later be spending precious time trying to sort through which changes need to be merged for the patch and which instead are parts of new features. Believe me, there are many wonderful things to do in life instead of spending time doing unnecessary merges.

Don't share files between branches: When a file is shared in multiple places in the source tree, all shares of it get automatically updated when someone makes a change to one copy of it. There should never be a reason to share files between branches—it defeats the purpose of a branch. You just spent thousands of dollars for a tool to get around this sort of thing!

Have a recurring merge timetable: If you let too much time go between merges, you'll find yourself with a huge integration mess. Instead, consider trying to automatically merge once a week (or more) to ensure that branches always stay close in sync. But remember to follow whatever merge rules you came up with when the branch was created: You want to merge the maintenance branch changes into the main line—and probably not the other way around.

Track changes in addition to files: The easiest way to handle merges is to know what files need to be merged. By encapsulating a set of source files into a "change" object, you'll always know what makes up a particular bug fix. Many source control tools provide this functionality by allowing you to specify what files make up a "change" in the defect tracking tool.

Developers should merge their own work: An automatic merge is one thing…but pesky manual merge changes are another. SCMs can be relied upon to run automatic merges, but the developer who wrote the code should be the one who manually merges. After all, who knows the code better? Only in rare cases should an SCM manually merge other developers' code.

Developers should merge out before they merge in: Scared of a big integration mess? One way to ensure a smoother path is for developers to merge out of the source control database into their private workspaces before they merge their changes back in. This allows the developer fully test the integrated changes before he or she commits the changes to the main branch. Alternatively, many organizations create a branch just for the integration of changes—but beware: Too many branches can be just as ugly as not having any. Depending on your tool, it's probably better that the developers merge out into their own workspaces before merging back.

Builds

Building may be the most important job you have after protecting the source. The following are some guidelines to help you keep those builds flowing:

Ensure builds can be re-created if necessary: The Holy Grail for every build should be the ability to re-create it 100 percent of the time. Why? In order to debug problems, it's often important to understand the process of how a build was constructed or be able to reproduce it in its entirety. You can facilitate this goal easily by simply combining the same source, tools, and build steps. If done correctly, the same output will get created every single time.

Automate whenever possible: All procedures required to create a build should be automated whenever possible. This will ensure that the same procedures are always followed every time—without the possibility of human error.

Build scripts should be treated as source: Every change to a build script needs to be tracked as if it were source. What if you cut out a large chunk of automation and realize two days later that you need it after all? Add a directory in the source control database just for your build scripts and associated objects.

Document everything: Every action that takes place during a build that can't be automated should be recorded in a process document. It should be a living document—every time you alter a procedure, be sure to update the process in the document. Print multiple copies of this document so you can use it as a checklist during builds.

And document the build machine itself: What good is the process if you don't know what belongs on the build machine? The build machine and every step you take to set it up should be documented as you're creating it. Otherwise, you'll forget steps when you try to record it later. And don't cut any corners—start by documenting the type of machine it is, which operating system has been installed, and any system patches that might have been added. Then, one by one, document each build tool used and write down any options that must be set when they're installed.

Imagine that someone else will be doing all of your tasks when you're documenting: This is because someone else may have to rebuild the build machine a year from now. By creating strong documentation now, you'll save yourself hours of unnecessary work later.

Allow for the ability to build from scratch: An automated build should be able to run on a clean system after all the object and old source files have been deleted from the machine. After the deletion, the script should then obtain the code once again from the source database. Failure to follow this rule will lead to builds that don't re-create later (thereby breaking the first and most important rule in this section). See Chapter 8, "Basic Builds," for more information on creating build scripts.

All developers should be able to build the product: As mentioned earlier, if the developers download the source, install the tools, and have the right automation scripts, they should, in theory *and* in practice, be able to build the entire product on the machine of their choice at the time of their choosing. Try using one of your test machines to see if you've achieved this goal.

Keep significant builds forever: A significant build and its binary files—meaning a build that has been distributed outside of the company—should be kept forever in a secure location. Even though you plan to be able to re-create builds from source whenever possible, there's a chance that a forgotten step or tool will cause differences. To ensure the ability to fix bugs—and to protect your company from liability—be sure to always keep copies of every build that goes out the door. And, of course, make sure the source was labeled properly. Many companies also consider builds that go to other departments (for example, to the quality team) as significant.

Every build should have a respective label in the source control database tool: Did I mention that source needs to be labeled properly? How can you re-create a build if you don't know what versions of source files make it up? Be sure to label the source every time you do a build. See Chapter 8, "Basic Builds," for strategies on how to label the source during a build.

Use a build account to access the source when building: There should be a difference between you, as a developer, and the automated robot that runs the builds. This will allow you to debug problems should a file be deleted or changed in the source control database tool during a build. You don't really want your name attached to that kind of mistake anyway, do you?

When using automation, avoid changing code in the source database whenever possible: A typo in an automation script can be disastrous…so you want to be sure that the automated scripts don't touch permanent objects as they do their work. You may want to build using read-only security rights for the source control database. There may be exceptions to this rule—such as when incrementing version information during builds—but try to avoid changing code in the source database whenever possible in scripts. Most source control database tools have security policies that let accounts to access only certain directories—your build account should have this type of policy applied to it so it only has write access to the directories it needs to be able to change.

Don't allow long periods to go by without building: Even if it's not required by the organization, try to build often enough that you're up-to-date with the changes that developers make. Otherwise, you might find yourself spending a day or two fixing breaks in your scripts before builds can take place.

Labels and Versions

Have respect for the mighty labels and versions. Without them, you'd be stuck comparing your binary and source files by date, time, and size. The following are some tricks to make life a little easier:

All version information should be dynamic: When building, version numbers shouldn't rely on human intervention in order to increment. What happens when the step is forgotten and you suddenly have two different builds with the same version number on your hands? Find a way to automate the versioning process. Chapter 8, "Basic Builds," discusses this in more detail.

Use moveable labels: Most tools support moving a label from one version of a source file to another. This can be handy when a single file change is required to complete a build after the main script has run. Simply move the build label of the file from the old version to the new one that fixes the bug. But you should also beware of unexpected changes to the file that might have been made since the build machine created the original label!

Every component should have its own version number: In the Windows world, individual components can have their own version information. This is handy when users call technical support or when you need to identify the installed build number. Every component that's capable of embedding version information should reflect the build number from which it was created. See Chapter 9, "Builds for Windows .NET," for more information about version numbers.

Use promotion labels when possible: Many tools support promotion labels. These special markers allow you to designate sets of source with particular transition labels such as "In Development," "In Quality," or "Release Candidate 1." Chapter 4, "Source Control Tools," describes promotion labels in more detail.

Redistributing Binary Files and Third-Party Programs

One of the great headaches in the SCM world is trying to take care of other people's software. Unfortunately, at some point in your career, you're bound to run into this no-win carnival ride. Whether it's because you partner with another company, you use a third-party component in the code, or you require certain prerequisites before your software can install correctly, dealing with third-party programs can be a large challenge. The following tips will help you:

Watch the prerequisites: Does your software have any prerequisites that are required to be installed before it can work correctly? It's possible—be sure to check your build machine's tool list. Did you install a Windows service pack? Or a certain version of a compiler? Before you distribute your product, be sure to install the product on "naked" operating systems to ensure you're not missing anything. Otherwise, make sure that the quality group has this on its to-do list.

Fulfill your due diligence before adding third-party programs: Adding third-party binaries to your product can end up being a nightmare. Before you or your developers do it, consider asking some questions: Is the functionality truly necessary? Can you get by without it? How strong is it from a defect perspective? How flexible is it to match your needs? How secure and responsive is the company providing the product? Will the company still be around next year to provide updates when you need them? How often can you get updates? Is it possible to get customized versions of the product?

Get the source whenever possible: If it's all possible for you to do so, get, track, and build the source for the third-party tool yourself. This will allow your developers to fix small bugs when customers and the quality group complain about problems. Otherwise, you're stuck at the mercy of the company that provides it. You might get a new version of the binaries tomorrow or sometime next year—who knows? In the meantime, your team will still be responsible for supporting its software for your (possibly irate) customers.

Try to get separately installable prerequisites: If you can't get the source for the binaries (and let's face it—it's not likely to happen), consider asking customers to install the product as a stand-alone prerequisite instead of incorporating the binaries into your product. Then the support headache goes where it belongs—right to the company that makes the product.

Treat third-party binaries as source: If you can't get a package and you can't get the source, then you're stuck with distributing binaries that you didn't create. In this case, you should treat these binaries as a source package. Perhaps you might create another instance of your source database to version the components. As versions of the binaries go into builds, they should also be labeled with the build number so you can always know exactly what you distributed.

Always keep copies of the prerequisites for builds that have gone out the door: For the exact same reason that you label the source for builds that go out the door, you should always keep copies (and documentation) of anything that your customers were required to install before using your product. Otherwise, you might get stuck not knowing if a reported bug is your problem or that of the third-party binaries.

Watch out for updates: Nothing is worse than buggy binaries that you have to try to distribute seamlessly to your customers. Watch for updates and, if appropriate, update your versions in the source control database. Before you do anything, however, be sure the updates actually fix real problems or add functionality you need. Otherwise, you're forcing a complete retest of the binaries integration for no reason.

Tools

Whether you're using Visual Studio or the GCC compiler, keep the following tips in mind when working with any build tools:

Keep track of all your build tools and their versions: With limited exceptions, each developer should be writing code with the same version of the tools that are installed on the build machine. If the developers upgrade tools on their own, it can cause problems on the build machine later. Consider publishing the acceptable tools and their respective versions for your shop.

Debate development-driven upgrades: Sure, the new version of Visual Studio has some handy features to it. But the cost of upgrading the software involves more than just money. What will it do to the build of the product? Will it affect other tools that are always integrated? Do you have the correct operating system patches for it? The upgrade of tools should always be strongly debated. Although you don't want to deny anyone access to exciting new features, you still have to consider what will happen to the source and the build. Of course, don't think you have to make this decision by yourself—always engage the leaders of the development department in any conversation regarding the upgrade of tools.

Check your licensing: Remember that the use of new tools may require more licenses than just those needed for the development staff. You may have to install this software on build and test machines. Check licenses to see if they're based on seats or users. Though the trend seems to be changing, most licenses are based on a per-seat model—which means that any software on unmanned machines will still need to be paid for when new tools or upgrades are installed.

Breaking Down the SCM Task Schedule

Unlike many others in the development process, the SCM must complete several recurring maintenance tasks. It might be running a health check on the source database. Or maybe it's restoring the source from tape to a test machine to ensure that the backups are occurring properly.

As displayed in Figure 7-1, you can use a calendar tool such as Microsoft Outlook to assign yourself tasks that will actively pop up and remind you to do maintenance at allotted times. Alternatively, you can keep a diary indicating the jobs you completed and the date for upcoming tasks. Choosing to use such a passive tool, however, can lead to forgotten steps—be sure to check it frequently.

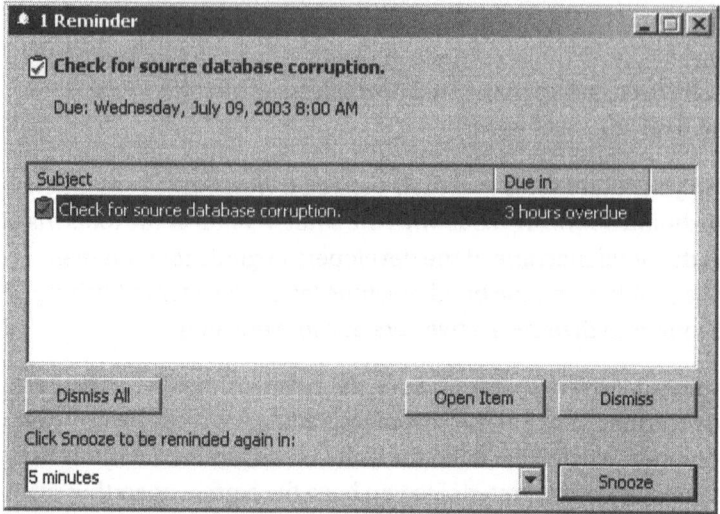

Figure 7-1. A task reminder from Microsoft Outlook

The following sections contain items that you might add to your task list. Keep in mind that this is by no means an exhaustive list.

Daily

You should perform the following tasks on a daily basis:

Ensure source availability: Make sure the source database is available to the team. There are times when computer, network, or source tool problems might bring down access to the source tree. You may want to create a script that automatically checks to see if the source is available in the early morning before other developers arrive. Then just have the script page you in case of emergencies.

Back up the source: The best way to circumnavigate a catastrophe is to have a strong backup policy in place. The policy itself will depend on the size of your organization and the source database itself—and many small shops can get by with a full backup taking place weekly while incremental backups happen daily. Be aware that you may need to shut off access to your source database while backups take place—be sure to refer to your tool's documentation to make sure you're backing it up properly. You should periodically restore your backups to ensure that it took place properly. See the "Quarterly" section of this chapter for more information on confirming your backups.

Create Builds: If your team is in the swing of things, you may need to provide daily builds. This is another task you can automate if you've written build scripts (see Chapter 8, "Basic Builds," for more information). Use the AT command in Windows or cron on Unix-flavored machines.

Source database specific tasks: Check your source database's documentation for daily tasks that might need to take place.

Weekly

You should perform the following tasks on a weekly basis:

Spot check projects for proper source usage by developers: Sometimes team members take shortcuts, or they might not understand the source policies you've published. Every now and again it's smart to spot check the source to make sure that agreed-upon policies are being followed properly. If you find that they aren't, send a gentle email reminder. If you find that the same policy is being ignored by many developers, you may need to re-evaluate its need or how it has been described in published procedure documents.

Check for source database corruption: Some tools, such as Microsoft Source-Safe or CVS, must be health checked weekly to ensure that corruption doesn't occur. Refer your tool's documentation to see if this step is needed.

Remove recent backup media to outside facility: What good are backup tapes if a fire sweeps your building and they go up with source database machine? Fire safes, even if they're good, will only last for an hour or so in a hot fire. Whether it's to your home or to a professional archive center, your source's backup media (tapes, CDs, and so on) should be removed from your facility to a different location either weekly or monthly. Your management might not be comfortable with you taking the tapes off-site; in that case, research outside media storage facilities in your area. If you're using a rotating media backup policy, send yourself email reminders when it's time to bring the tapes back to the office.

Source database specific tasks: Check your source database's documentation for daily tasks that might need to take place.

Monthly

You should perform the following tasks on a monthly basis:

Archive obsolete source as necessary: You may find that large groups of source in your source database are no longer included with the product and are difficult to maneuver around. Many source database tools provide mechanisms in which you can either hide or archive legacy source so your developers need not see it. Check with your source database documentation for more information on how to archive obsolete source.

Create backup of source onto permanent media: If you're using a rotating media model for backups, be sure to create a separate, permanent backup copy of the source at least once a month. Should you discover an accidentally deleted file a month or two after it occurred, you'll still be able to use your permanent backup media to retrieve it without loss.

Check for operating system and source database updates: Whether it's Windows, Linux, or Solaris, all of the operating systems require periodic monitoring and security patch updating. Many operating systems provide an easy interface to apply security patches—such as the Windows Update tool displayed in Figure 7-2. If your source machine is completely behind a firewall (which I recommend), this may not be as important to you—but if it's exposed in any way to the Internet (or even a large intranet), you'll want to make sure it's consistently updated with the latest security patches. In addition, check for patches to your source database tool. But, of course, you should never install patches all willy-nilly. Because patches to the operating system and source database tool can conceivably cause problems, always check that the patch solves a necessary problem before installing it. For example, if a patch simply adds a new feature that isn't necessarily desired by your team, you may want to skip it to avoid possible source outages. You'll also need to make sure that all the tools already installed on the machine support any new system patches before continuing. And don't forget that patches often require a system or tool restart—you may want to patch during off-hours.

Source database-specific tasks: Check your source database's documentation for daily tasks that might need to take place.

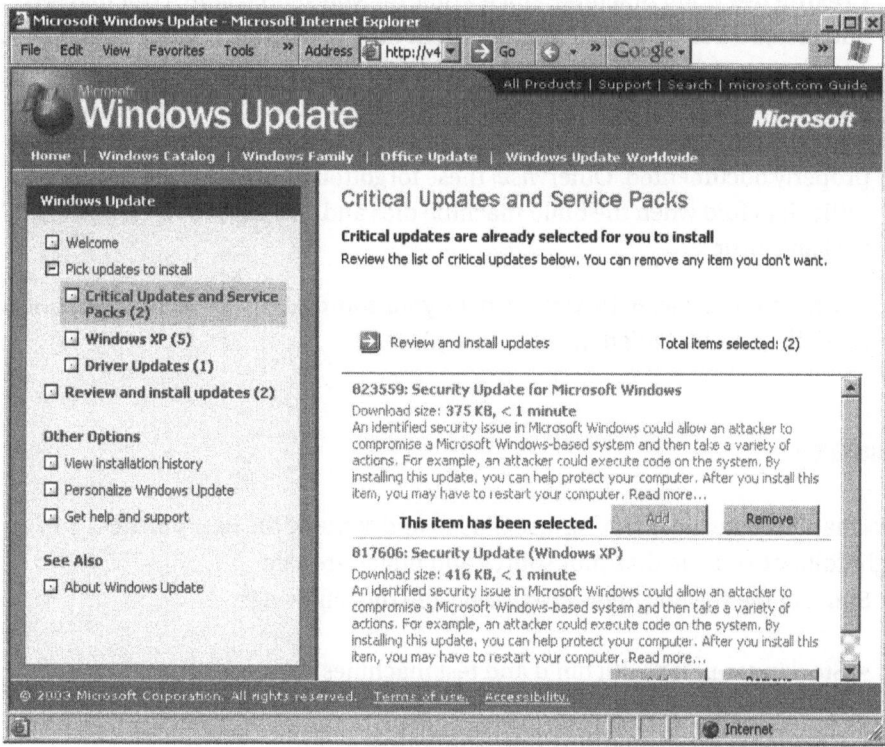

Figure 7-2. The Microsoft Windows Update tool provided through Internet Explorer

Quarterly

You should perform the following tasks on a quarterly basis:

Check your backups: It's important to restore from backup media *onto a test machine* at least once a quarter to ensure that the backups are occurring properly. You may even choose to do so monthly. It's wise to check both the last permanent backup drop and an arbitrary date from the last week. For instance, if you needed to roll back the source to last Tuesday, could you do so from the backup media as created by your policy? Always conduct this restore on a test machine that's somehow not connected to the true source machine. By default, many backup programs restore to the same location where the backup took place, and you don't want to take a chance of overwriting the real source. If the media drive is permanently connected to the source machine, be sure to do a full backup of the source immediately before conducting this test—then you can recover that copy should you accidentally write over the real source with last Tuesday's data. No, you'd never mean to make that kind of mistake. Yes, there's a chance you still might.

Create a test build machine: Once a quarter, you should grab a test machine and create a build machine from scratch. Chapter 8, "Basic Builds," describes how to document the creation of a build machine so it can be replaced in a pinch. Use that document every now and then to run a build. This ensures that recent tool or configuration additions to the build machine have been properly documented. Otherwise, these forgotten items can be much more difficult to find when the build machine dies and you have to re-create it by trial and error.

Source database specific tasks: Check your source database's documentation for daily tasks that might need to take place.

Summary

This chapter discussed creating an SCM lab and some of the best practices you might follow to ensure that your source and builds are safe.

Some of the specific items discussed were the following:

- Stocking your lab with build and test machines

- Creating an SCM guide for your developers

- Best practices you can follow for workspaces, branching/merging, builds, labels/versions, and redistributing third-party binaries and tools

- Tasks you might place on your recurring calendar

CHAPTER 8
Basic Builds

I RECENTLY DID SOME CONSULTING for a small Web shop in San Diego, California. Actually, it only felt small; the company created and maintained 12 large Web sites with various content. The Chief Technology Officer (CTO) was in despair—every time the sites were deployed or updated, some huge complication downed one or more of the production sites for long periods of time. The business folks were coming down hard on him—they calculated exactly how much money the company lost each time the sites went down. The CTO asked me to do a quick Software Configuration Management (SCM)–related evaluation of the development group.

One of the first observations I made was that the group was living without the security of an automated build. The lead developer argued that there was no need.

"Most of everything we write is ASP and therefore script," he said. "We only have two or three COM objects to build. Every time a developer changes code and says it's ready for the site, he updates a Web log we created. Then the QA guy cherry picks the changes onto the Web machines."

He laughed when I suggested an automated build.

"Why?" he asked. "If it isn't broken, why fix it?"

It was one of the most disconcerting things I'd ever heard. Has software come to this? I asked myself. Are we so habituated to debilitating bugs and shoddy installations that even developers and others in the technology industry can't distinguish what makes software "broken?" I was forced to explain to him that something is wrong when you break your site each time you deploy.

Once we started talking about the whole thing, he began to see the advantages to an automated build. Developers would no longer have to update a log with every changed file—a task periodically missed because of human error. There would be no need to build components at the beck and call of the build technician. And most importantly, instead of shouldering 100 percent of the responsibility for broken builds, he and the other developers would be accountable only for the source on which they worked.

The good stuff doesn't end there. With a centrally located build machine and automation, you can always be sure of the environment in which your software lives. You can easily document that environment and all of the prerequisites that might be needed from an end user perspective. Lastly, you can always be sure that what's in the source is reflected in the compiled objects. If you ever need to re-create a build for any reason, you'll be able to do so.

Javier, a wise quality expert, once told me the following:

I'm the laziest man alive. The first or second time that I'm approached with a task, I try to automate it. Then I never have to do it again.

I absolutely agree. But perhaps *laziest* isn't really the right word in the context of the previous quotation. Your goal is to be an *efficient* SCM. To do that, you need to automate as many tasks as possible. This frees you up to conquer other duties and lowers the risk of the ever-present human error. Better, it increases your ability to go on vacation, take sick days, or attend conferences. Without automation, you chain yourself to your desk—and rightly so.

The first thing you should automate is the *build* of your product. The build can be defined as the compilation and gathering of the developers' code into installable user packages. I'm not just talking about picking up executables and dropping them into an installation tool—instead, I mean starting from nothing but source and building a complete product. Creating an automated build can be time consuming. Depending on the sophistication of the product, maintaining it can be demanding.

Ah! But the payoff!

An automated build frees your developers from having to build their own components and from the more tedious task of instructing a builder how to create executables over and over again. You can schedule builds to run once a month, once a week, three times a day, or even twice on Sundays. Because the build requires no human intervention (other than for scheduling or pushing the Start button), developers can work during off-hours and still see the results of their labor on a Saturday. All the while, you can be sipping a mai-tai on a beach in Maui.

In addition to compiling and collecting objects, you may also be responsible for *deploying* a finished build to a user's machine. You might complete this task by building an installation package and burning it onto a CD or placing it on a Web site.

Oftentimes, the deployment of software to the end user is in the hands of another department, such as a manufacturing or Information Technology (IT) department. Before this occurs, however, there are still many conditions in which you might need to simulate the deployment for your own group. For instance, you might place the installation package on test machines so the quality department can perform testing. Or you may be responsible for updating an internal Web server with build changes. Of course, in a smaller development shop, the responsibility for the deployment might fall completely on your shoulders.

Getting Ready to Build

A build can be as simple as copying script files to a Web directory. Conversely, sometimes you may have to build and deliver hundreds of components.

In Windows, it's always a good idea to provide an installation program that completely sets up an end user's machine. On the Linux/Unix side, you achieve this same goal by providing packages created for the operating system, such as using the RPM Package Manager (RPM) for Linux, or by simply allowing users a chance to compile the binary objects themselves.

 NOTE *Chapter 10, "Installations," discusses installations and the tools to create them in much more detail.*

Regardless of the complexity of the build, all builds have some things in common:

- Every build should have a unique identity, which means you should use an incremented numbering scheme so that each build has a higher value than the last. Some compilation tools may provide this functionality.

- You should label the source that makes up the build, even if simply scripts, to reflect that unique identity. By doing so, you can re-create any previous build at a future time.

- You should gather the source that makes up the build from the source control tool's database using a label and not from the tip. Otherwise, you'll never be able to ensure that you can rebuild what's in the binaries.

- Use an automation tool and scripting when building.

- Schedule builds so that developers know the windows of time available for checking in fixes and functionality.

- Create builds on a well-documented machine that can easily be re-created should it become corrupted during automation.

- Make builds available to other groups in your company on a shared network device or internal Web site.

> **NOTE** *This chapter concentrates on builds for the Windows environment, and most of the examples will reflect that. Many of the concepts presented, however, are applicable to Unix-flavored operating systems.*

Creating the Build List

All right—let's start from scratch. You have source that has been written by developers, and, in theory, they've been building the components themselves periodically and then publishing them upon request. You now want to create a build that does this for you.

The first step to doing this is to determine the components that make up the product. This can be an overwhelming task—especially when developers are resistant to helping out because of workload or apathy. Apologize to the developers in advance for the numerous questions you are bound to ask.

When organizing, create a spreadsheet that lists each file you plan to include in your package. Oftentimes, you can get a head start on this list by looking at the current installation package or the product's source. As the list is created, add columns for other pertinent information regarding the objects. The following are some questions you might ask:

Is the object binary? Determine whether an object is binary by attempting to view it using a text editor. It's fairly obvious if it's a binary file—the text editor fills with empty squares and strange characters. Binary files may still have text and words in them, however. Don't assume it's a text file simply because words are recognizable.

Is the object internally created or provided by a third party? If your developers didn't create the object, you won't be able to build it—but you may still have to include it in the final package.

What tools are necessary for building the object? You may need to ask the developer for assistance with this step.

> **NOTE** *Be careful not to annoy the developers with repetitive or simple questions. The rule of thumb is to always try and figure things out yourself—and then set up appointments to discuss your questions. If you must ask questions outside of set times, try to do so using email. Failing to follow this model may cause management to deny you access to these people and the valuable information they can give you.*

In the source tree, where is the directory containing the object? Knowing the correct location of source files is one of biggest hurdles for creating a build.

Does the component depend on the existence of other objects? Java, C++, and Visual Basic executables often rely on other objects that must be built in order. If there are dependent objects, be sure to add them to this list so you can determine this order. Don't forget that every object that appears as a dependent on this list must also be added as its own line item!

Are there special creation considerations for the object? For instance, you must authenticate some Web components before you distribute them.

Are there special runtime considerations for the object? If you provide an installation package for the end user, it's especially important to keep track of any special steps that should be taken when the objects are installed. For instance, on the Windows side, does the object need to be registered? Are you required to place it in a certain directory?

NOTE   *There may be times where you run into directories consisting only of text files or third-party software. For the purposes of this spreadsheet, create a line item listing the directory rather than each item in the list. Of course, when you have completed the process, you should still list every file in build reports.*

Believe it or not, creating this list considerably lessens the headache of creating an automated build. More importantly, it places you in the enviable position of being the most knowledgeable person at your company regarding the creation of the product.

NOTE   *Don't fret if you have to tweak the list or add new components. Much like solving a mystery, working on the build list will lead to revelations and refugee objects. This is the purpose of the list, and you should be encouraged by these small successes.*

Getting to Know the Command Line

In the old days, there were no computer mice or desktops. Users did everything by typing directly on the command line—and if you're older than me, you may have had to pile punch cards into a reader. I started using my first Unix machine when I was 13 years old. I soon moved on to CP/M and then to DOS. I finally took the graphical world plunge by buying a Mac SE back in the late 80s. It took quite a bit of getting used to—I hated taking my fingers off the keyboard to move the mouse around.

Luckily, much of the keyboard functionality that was stripped with the advent of the mouse has returned in new iterations of graphical environments. Personally, I'm still drawn to the command line. I can type faster than the time it takes for me to lift my hand from the keyboard and move the mouse.

Regardless of ease of use, however, mice rear up as one of the SCM's worst enemies. It can be extremely difficult to automate mouse strokes while scripting. Of course, there are packages that allow you to script your mouse movements. I don't recommend their use, however. Many scripts break for simple reasons, such as the relocation of an icon or file additions. In addition, maintaining mouse movement scripts is exponentially more difficult than simply updating commands.

When I became an SCM, I moved back full circle to the command line and its flexibility. There are few programs in the Unix world that can't be manipulated by using the command line. And although this isn't quite as true for Windows, the situation is steadily improving. In addition to the standard DOS commands available using the Windows command shell, you can also use the Perl scripting language on the Windows platform. Microsoft even provides command-line usage for its own Visual Basic and Java-esque scripting languages. Finally, if you're an old Unix pro using Windows, consider installing the Cygwin Unix emulation package available at http://www.cygwin.com.

You may find that you don't need to use the command line for building. Some Integrated Development Environments (IDEs) allow you to create installation packages from within the tool itself. In this case, you simply open the IDE and choose the proper command with the mouse, and the package is created. This is convenient for small applications, but the ideal in build automation is no human intervention.

Your first decision to make is whether you plan to use the command line or another graphical automation tool. If you can manipulate all of your tools using the command line, I strongly advise its use via a script. The decision is easy if you're working in the Linux/Unix world. When working in the Windows world, check to see if the tools you plan to use support command-line invocation. Table 8-1 lists some tools and their command-line abilities.

Table 8-1. Windows Build Tools[1] and Command-Line Compatibility

Tool	Command-Line Functionality?	Can You Create an Installation Package Using the Tool?
Microsoft Visual Studio 6.0	Yes	Limited
Microsoft Visual Studio .NET	Yes	Limited[2]
Sun Java	Yes	Depends on tool
InstallShield	Yes	Yes
Wise	Yes	Yes
RoboHelp	Yes	No
GPG	Yes	No

In the Windows world, there may be unfriendly tools that don't have command-line ability and must be run graphically. In these cases, you'll be stuck trying to script your build graphically or building by hand. You'd be well-advised to upgrade the tool or choose a competitor's tool in its place.

Preparing the Build Machine

Once you've identified the objects that you'll be building or copying to your installation package, you should begin preparing your build machine.

As discussed earlier in this book, dedicate a machine for the single task of building and creating the installation package. It's tempting to actually write code or test on this machine, but you should avoid this for a number of reasons—some of which I'll discuss now.

When developing on a machine, it's often necessary to install tools or utilities that aid in writing code. And here's a universal truth: No matter how responsible and conscious you are of your actions, *you will forget to document changes you've made to the environment.* This is simply a fact of life and can't be ignored—believe me, it's no reflection upon your character...I don't even know you!

One of the advantages to having a dedicated machine is that builds are designed to fail when tools haven't been properly installed on the machine. This may seem more like a curse; on the contrary, it's a reminder to document these new changes.

---

1. Many Java development environments, such as Symantec Café, rely on Sun's Java package. In these cases, refer to Sun Java.

2. Both Visual Studio 6.0 and .NET have limited functionality installation programs built in. In addition, Visual Studio .NET supports the add-in of installation programs such as InstallShield and Wise. With these tools in place, an entire build and installation can be completed by a click of the mouse.

Documentation? Ugh! But I can't tell you how many times I've had to reinstall the build machine from scratch (also known as "burning down the machine") after making what seemed at the time like a trivial change to the system. It's absolutely unacceptable to spend two or three days trying to figure out what environment changes have been made since the last time the machine was burnt down. It means two or three days without a build! Documenting your build machine well means that burning down a machine will never take more than a few hours.

TIP *You can speed up that few hours to a few minutes by using the right tools. Several utilities, such as Symantec's Ghost, allow you to take a snapshot of a hard drive and save it to a network location or write it to CD. When you get your build machine to a point where you're satisfied with its performance, it's time to save a snapshot. Should anything happen to the drive or the machine, you'll be able to restore it quickly. Be sure to check the features of the tool carefully—it may limit your ability to restore the image to a machine with different hardware.*

Testing on the build machine can be even more damaging. Builds meant for testing are inherently buggy—there's no way around that—and pretty soon, you've accidentally deleted the root directory of the build machine. Untested code is notorious for destroying perfectly good build machines.

Save yourself some grief and dedicate a machine to the task of building. Document the installation of the operating system, all applicable patches and/or service packs, and build tools such as compilers. You may need to install tools in a certain order (especially if working in Windows!), so pay close attention and update the document as each tool is added. If you find that you missed a step, go back and update the proper order for the document.

Once you've installed the tools, add any third-party programs or files that components may reference during the build. These might include sets of libraries that your developers use or required security certificates for authenticating the product executable.

Lastly, create a directory where the builds takes place. It can be simply C:\BUILD or /HOME/BUILD. If you're working on a network, you may want to share this directory so you can monitor the build as it's occurring—this proves important when the build machine is located somewhere other than in your immediate cubicle or office.

To Skip the Build Script...

As the years go by, IDEs become more fully featured. If you're using Microsoft's Visual Studio .NET and your application is small enough, you may want to dispense with build scripts and use the IDE to create builds.

If this is your choice and you're pressed for time, go ahead and skip to Chapter 9, "Builds for Windows .NET." Keep in mind, however, that this chapter discusses the fundamentals of building software. If you choose to skip this chapter now, you may want to come back to it later to ensure that your methodology for creating builds is complete.

...Or Not to Skip the Build Script

On the other hand, you may not be using a fully featured compilation tool, or you may rightly decide that build scripts provide flexibility not available from an IDE. In either case, the rest of this chapter provides a strong foundation for creating builds—read on!

Creating a Pseudo-Build

Now that you've compiled your list of objects and you've readied the build machine, it's time to start contemplating the "how" of the build. Do this by creating a build pseudo-script: a storyboard of how the build should proceed. This doesn't actually build anything—it provides you with the outline you'll use while scripting.

Every build is different, so I'm going to use some generic examples throughout the rest of the chapter. Use your judgment and cut out unnecessary work whenever possible.

Using the text editor of choice, create an empty file called SCRIPT.TXT. Begin by adding markers that delineate the beginning and end of the file. Use a number sign (#) to indicate comments such as these to yourself. Your first entry might look like this:

```
#BEGIN SCRIPT.TXT-the storyboard for your build
#END SCRIPT.TXT
```

NOTE *If you're already a strong command-line user, feel free to combine the tasks in the following steps with those listed in the "Building Components for the First Time" section.*

Step 1: Create the Directories in Which You'll Work

In most circumstances, you'll work with three sets of directories while creating build scripts. The first directory contains the code as downloaded from the source database.

Depending on the programming language used by your developers, you may create intermediary objects during this process that are necessary for the build but shouldn't be distributed to customers. Create a second directory to house the temporary working area for these objects.

The third directory emulates the resulting installation package after the build has finished. For example, it might contain a Windows Microsoft Installer (MSI) file, a Java Archive (JAR) file containing Java classes, or a complete InstallShield package.

For the purposes of your build, your directory structure might look something like this:

```
c:\build\current
c:\build\current\dist
c:\build\current\media
c:\build\current\src
```

The SRC directory contains the downloaded source code. The DIST directory is the temporary working area. And the MEDIA directory contains the product package after the build has completed.

NOTE *There are some source control databases that allow you to virtualize labeled code so that it appears to exist in a directory. In that case, there would be no reason to create the SRC directory. Instead, go ahead and get the source directly from the source database as detailed in "Step 2: Get the Source."*

You can apply this same structure to the Linux/Unix platform. Starting in your home directory (or the directory where you want the build to take place), create the build directory and add its three children:

```
/home/builds/current
/home/builds/current/dist
/home/builds/current/media
/home/builds/current/src
```

It's likely that you'll use these same three directories every time you build. Because you don't want to build on top of a previous build, you should add another step that deletes previous builds before creating the directories.

Voila! The first step of your pseudo-build script is complete. Your SCRIPT.TXT file might reflect this step, as displayed in Listing 8-1.

Listing 8-1. The First Step of the Pseudo-Script

```
#SCRIPT.TXT-the storyboard for your build
#
1. Create directories
      a. Delete previous build.
      b. Create build
      c. Create build\src
      d. Create build\dist
      e. Create build\media
#END SCRIPT.TXT
```

Step 2: Get the Source

Don't fool yourself into thinking that getting the source is as easy as grabbing the tip. Unfortunately, life is never easy for the SCM.

To be sure that what you give to your customers can be rebuilt at any time— see earlier chapters for the numerous reasons why this is essential—you need to label the source and then get the source *from that label*. By doing so, you avert any problems that arise should a developer submit changes to files as you download the source to the build machine. If you later find that a single file needs to be updated to make the build complete, simply use the source control tool to manipulate the label on that one file to match the new revision,[3] recompile it, and then re-create the distribution package.

---

3. Only certain source control tools have this feature. See Chapters 4, 5, and 6 for more information.

If you're lucky (and well funded enough) to a have a tool that virtualizes source directories based on their labels, you won't need to copy the source to your local drive unless you find that a lack of network bandwidth causes the build to take more time than you can afford.[4] For the purposes of this book, I'm going to assume you're using either SourceSafe or CVS—tools that don't provide this feature.

Your first task in getting the source is to assign the build a unique identifier. I've done this through automation in a number of ways. One way is to use the date and time as an identifier of the build. An example of this might be "20020624_101103" where 20020624 (year/month/date) would indicate June 24, 2002, and 101103 would represent the eleventh minute and third second of the ten o'clock hour. This is a simple and effective way to label the build—however, it can lead to slipups. Builds often occur more than once a day, and this numbering sequence can lead to confusion when searching for specific builds labels. It becomes even more difficult after working a ten-hour day or a long weekend!

I've found it easier to label builds using the typical software versioning sequence: using major and minor versions with a third specific build number. For instance, if you're working on version 3.1 of your product and you've now created 143 builds of this version, your label might look more like 3.1.0143. Note the 0 in front of the 143— be sure to give yourself enough digits to accommodate future builds.

 NOTE   *You can configure some tools, such as Visual Studio .NET, to handle versioning without your intervention. See Chapter 9, "Builds for Windows .NET," for more information.*

Update the identifier during the build by either incrementing the build number or assigning a new date and time. From an automation standpoint, this isn't as tricky as it may sound—I'll discuss ways to handle this task later in the next chapter. For the time being, simply write down that the action will take place.

 NOTE   *Some tools allow you to rename a label after it has been created. If you're lucky enough to have one of these tools, you may want to designate a label called "Build in Process" and then rename the label to the unique identifier after the build has successfully completed. This allows you to avoid creating useless labels for builds that didn't complete and makes searching for previous versions easier.*

---

4.   Some might argue that creating the build on a well-engineered network is faster than creating the build on a local drive. Your results may vary!

Listing 8-2 reflects how your script might look after adding the tasks listed in this section.

Listing 8-2. The Second Step of the Pseudo-Script

```
#SCRIPT.TXT-the storyboard for your build
#
1. Create directories
    ...
2. Get the source in SRC directory
    a. Create/update unique identifer    # using  the format 1.1.0001
    b. Label the tip of the source database to this identifier
    c. Get the source from the label
#END SCRIPT.TXT
```

Step 3: Compile Binary Objects

You've labeled and gotten the source, and now you're ready for the meat and pota-toes of the build script. Find that spreadsheet you created at the beginning of this chapter and list each file ordered by the tool you used to create it. By sorting in this manner, you'll save steps later when you turn your pseudo-build script into the real build script.

NOTE *In some cases, certain objects have to build (for instance, server objects) before it's possible to build other objects. Refer to your developers for this information and be sure to reference these "dependents" in your build file spreadsheet.*

Let's say you're building five Visual Basic 6.0 client components and two Visual C++ 6.0 server components. Because the client components depend on the exis-tence of the server objects before they can be built, you'll want to make sure that the C++ compilation takes place first. Now list each of the files in the pseudo-script, as reflected in Listing 8-3.

TIP *Work with the developers as they add new components to the source so that file and directory names follow the same patterns. When your components are stored logically in the source control database using standard 8.3 filenames, setting up the automated build is exponentially easier. Be sure to read this entire chapter before exploring naming conventions so you understand what patterns the files should follow!*

Listing 8-3. The Third Step of the Pseudo-Script

```
#SCRIPT.TXT-the storyboard for your build
#
1. Create directories
    ...
2. Get the source in SRC directory
    ...
3. Compile Binary Objects into DIST directory
    a.  Server (located at $/office/server)
          i.  docsrvr.dll  (VC6)
         ii.  logsrvr.dll  (VC6)
        iii.  websrvr.dll  (VC6)
    b.  Client (depends on Server) (located at $/office/client)
          i.  office.exe  (VB6)  (depends on speller/spredsht/database/wordproc)
         ii.  speller.exe  (VB6)
        iii.  spredsht.exe  (VB6)
         iv:  database.exe  (VB6)
          v.  wordproc.exe  (VB6)
#END SCRIPT.TXT
```

Step 4: Fulfill Post-Creation Requirements

You may need to make changes to components after they're compiled but before they're put into an installation package. For instance, if you're creating a Web site that uses ActiveX components, you may need to digitally sign those components.

Now is the time to add these directives to your SCRIPT.TXT file, as displayed in Listing 8-4. In this example, you're going to authenticate an ActiveX component and change the date stamp for all newly created files so they're consistent with each other.

Listing 8-4. The Fourth Step of the Pseudo-Script

```
#SCRIPT.TXT-the storyboard for your build
#
1. Create directories

    ...
2. Get the source in SRC directory

    ...
3. Compile Binary Objects into DIST directory

    ...
4. Post-Creation Requirements
    a.  Sign logsrvr.dll (Verisign signing tool)
    b.  Date stamp all created components
#END SCRIPT.TXT
```

Step 5: Create an Installation Package

Once you've created and copied all of your objects into a common distribution directory, it's time to gather everything together into an installation package.

If you're distributing to a Web site, this may be as easy as creating a directory hierarchy and then copying the files from the distribution and source directories into their appropriate places. Later, in "Step 7: Add [Insert Task Here]," you might also package these files into a compressed file (such as a zip, a tar/gzip, or a self-installing executable).

On the other hand, when you provide enterprise application solutions to your customers, you'll have a horde of binary and text files. In this case, you might consider using a tool such as InstallShield or Wise to package your components. On the Linux platform, you might create an RPM package management file—a freeware installation tool that uses a common interface for your users. The RPM equivalent on Sun Solaris systems is a "package" file. I discuss these tools with more detail in Chapter 10, "Installations."

In some companies, the SCM is also responsible for providing installation packages. In other companies, a special department may handle this task. Regardless, simply indicate that the build will create an installation package, as displayed in Listing 8-5.

Listing 8-5. The Fifth Step of the Pseudo-Script

```
#SCRIPT.TXT-the storyboard for your build
#
1. Create directories

   ...
2. Get the source in SRC directory

   ...
3. Compile Binary Objects into DIST directory

   ...
4. Post-Creation Requirements

   ...
5. Create Package
   a.  Create installation (InstallShield) in MEDIA directory
#END SCRIPT.TXT
```

Step 6: Copy Media Files

You're not finished yet—documentation departments get mighty annoyed if you don't include the proper README.TXT file and other installation instructions. In addition, you may need to supply third-party add-on tools that must be installed on an end user's machine before your set up can run. This may include updates to the operating system (for instance, a Windows service pack or the .NET Framework) or a documentation rendering program (such as Adobe Acrobat Reader).

NOTE *Make sure you have the legal right to distribute third-party tools! Many larger companies have liberal rules about distributing their "freeware" applications, but they might ask you to fill out a form or sign a contract. Others want to completely control the distribution of their product from their Web site. Frankly, distributing any third-party tool without written permission may open your company to legal action, so be sure to take care.*

TIP *Sometimes it's easier to provide an Internet link to the provider of a third-party tool than to include it as part of an installation. Who wants to keep track of another company's software? Keep in mind, though, that Web links change frequently—you may want to refer to the company's main site instead of a more specific location. An example sentence in your README.TXT file might be as follows: "This product requires the use of Acrobat Reader. Download Acrobat Reader from the Adobe site at* http://www.adobe.com.*"*

Listing 8-6 displays what your script might look like as you add documentation files to your media directory.

Listing 8-6. The Sixth Step of the Pseudo-Script

```
#SCRIPT.TXT-the storyboard for your build
#
1. Create directories
     ...
2. Get the source in SRC directory
     ...
3. Compile Binary Objects into DIST directory
     ...
4. Post-Creation Requirements
     ...
5. Create Package
     ...
6. Copy Media Files
     a.  copy README.HTML ($/doc/html) to MEDIA directory.
     b.  copy INSTALL.HTML ($/doc/html) to MEDIA directory.
     c.  copy Adobe Reader (\\3rdparty\adobe\acrordr5.exe) to MEDIA directory.
#END SCRIPT.TXT
```

Step 7: Add [Insert Task Here!]

Every build is different, and there's always a little special something you need to complete before you can consider the build finished. For instance, it's a nice touch to date/time stamp installation files before your product goes out the door. Additionally, it's important to virus check your build to protect end users. Go ahead and add these types of additional steps, as displayed in Listing 8-7.

Listing 8-7. The Seventh Step of the Pseudo-Script

```
#SCRIPT.TXT-the storyboard for your build
#
1. Create directories
    ...
2. Get the source in SRC directory
    ...
3. Compile Binary Objects into DIST directory
    ...
4. Post-Creation Requirements
    ...
5. Create Package
    ...
6. Copy Media Files
    ...
7  Other
    a.  Change date stamp on MEDIA directory.
    b.  Virus check software.
#END SCRIPT.TXT
```

Step 8: Copy to a Public Directory on the Network

You're almost finished!

One last task remains—you need to move or copy your package to the holding directory that's accessible by other team members. The documentation team needs to write about the product, the quality team needs to test the product, and the marketing department needs to ensure that it meets the public's needs.

Be sure to protect the build by placing it in a read-only directory—only the build machine account should have write access to the drive. This ensures that others don't accidentally corrupt the build media by adding or deleting files to the directory. Contact a network administrator for instructions on how to implement this step. Listing 8-8 displays an example of this step.

TIP *I always keep my builds in the same directory, such as C:\BUILDS, which I then share on a read-only basis on my network. Every time I begin a new build, I place it in a directory called CURRENT. When the build is finished, I simply rename the build to the same identifier that I used to label the source. This happens again the next time around—a new directory called CURRENT is created and renamed for each build. After a certain time period (normally a month or so), I delete builds that I have deigned "insignificant": those that have never gone to the quality team or those that were used only for development testing. It's okay—remember, if you've followed all the right steps, you can always re-create any build from source. Of course, always keep the versions of your software that went to your customers—you never know when you might need them.*

 ANOTHER IP *There are times when you or someone on your team needs access to a single object in a build. Keep the DIST directory handy for "significant" builds. That way it's easy to find the object without installing the entire product.*

 AND ANOTHER TIP *Be sure to delete the SRC directory before renaming the parent CURRENT directory. There's no need to waste disk space, and you've got copies of the source labeled in the source control database.*

Listing 8-8. The Eighth Step of the Pseudo-Script

```
#SCRIPT.TXT-the storyboard for your build
#
1. Create directories
    ...
2. Get the source in SRC directory
    ...
3. Compile Binary Objects into DIST directory
    ...
4. Post-Creation Requirements
    ...
5. Create Package
    ...
6. Copy Media Files
    ...
7  Other
    ...
8 Copy to Directory
    a.  Delete current\src directory
    b.  Rename current directory to label
#END SCRIPT.TXT
```

Is That All?

Depending on your operating system, you may have a few additional tasks. For instance, in Windows, you may need to unregister Component Object Model (COM) objects before the build begins or increment version numbers of the individual components before they're compiled. Be sure to add these steps to the pseudo-script before continuing.

Your Complete Pseudo-Script

You now have a complete pseudo-script that spells out the steps you need to take to ensure a successful build of the product. Listing 8-9 displays a full version of the script.

Listing 8-9. Your Complete Pseudo-Script

```
#SCRIPT.TXT-the storyboard for your build
#
1. Create directories
        a.  Delete previous build.
        b. Create build
        c. Create build\src
        d. Create build\dist
        e. Create build\media
2. Get the source in SRC directory
        a. Create/update unique identifer    # using  the format 1.1.0001
        b. Label the tip of the source database to this identifier
        c. Get the source from the label
3. Compile Binary Objects into DIST directory
        a.  Server (located at $/office/server)
            i.  docsrvr.dll  (VC6)
            ii. logsrvr.dll  (VC6)
            iii. websrvr.dll  (VC6)
        b.  Client (depends on Server) (located at $/office/client)
            i.  office.exe  (VB6)  (depends on speller/spredsht/database/wordproc)
            ii. speller.exe  (VB6)
            iii. spredsht.exe  (VB6)
            iv: database.exe (VB6)
            v.  wordproc.exe (VB6)
```

4. Post-Creation Requirements
   a. Sign logsrvr.dll (Verisign signing tool)
   b. Date stamp all created components
5. Create Package
   a. Create installation (InstallShield) in MEDIA directory
6. Copy Media Files
   a. copy README.HTML ($/doc/html) to MEDIA directory.
   b. copy INSTALL.HTML ($/doc/html) to MEDIA directory.
   c. copy Adobe Reader (\\3rdparty\adobe\acrordr5.exe) to MEDIA directory.
7 Other
   a. Change date stamp on MEDIA directory.
   b. Virus check software.
8 Copy to Directory
   a. Delete current\src directory
   b. Rename current directory to label
#END SCRIPT.TXT

Refining Your Pseudo-Script

Believe it or not, you've reached the top of the hump. I won't say that it all gets easier from here. As I've said before, an SCM's life is never easy. But you now have a thorough plan for your build. You've won half the battle.

Building Components for the First Time

It's time to build your components manually one by one and keep track of the steps you take while doing so. This can be tricky because this is the time when you interface frequently with your engineers—and they're always in the middle of something! On the bright side, you really get to know the source and can start to recognize build patterns.

Many believe that building components is as trouble free as opening the appropriate IDE and running the Build command. That's true in a way—but only if you never want to go on vacation again! Instead, ensure an automated build by learning how to create components on the command line in a console window such as that displayed in Figure 8-1. As you build them, you find through trial and error where they might require user interaction (for example, asking questions such as "Are you sure?") or need specific information.

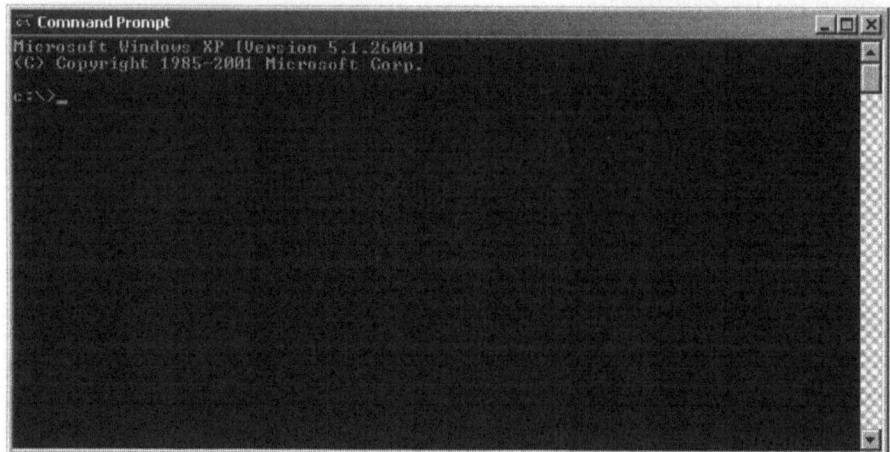

Figure 8-1. The Windows Command Prompt window

Luckily, you're fairly prepared. You have your pseudo-script in place, and you know the tools that you need to use. Save off a copy of your SCRIPT.TXT now—you're going to start making some serious changes to it. It's wise to keep copies of your early scripts someplace safe—mistakes happen.

 NOTE *There are times when using the command line to build components may not be necessary—in particular when using tools such as Visual Studio .NET and Visual Build. See Chapter 9, "Builds for Windows .NET," or the "Visual Build by Kinook Software" sidebar for more information about these tools.*

Creating Directories and Using Shell Commands

Let's revisit your list and substitute actual commands for the pseudo-steps you listed. Start with step 1, creating the directories. Your pseudo-script looks like this:

```
1. Create directories
       a.  Delete previous build.
       b. Create build
       c. Create build\src
       d. Create build\dist
```

After you're finished substituting commands, it might look something like this:

1. Create directories
   a. del /s /q /f c:\build\current*.*
   b. md c:\build\current
   c. md c:\build\current\src
   d. md c:\build\current\dist
   e. md c:\build\current\media

NOTE *If you're a Linux or Unix user, I assume you're familiar with shell commands—after all, they're an integral part of the Unix-flavored operating systems. The examples in the "Refining Your Pseudo-Script" section are Windows-based and may not be applicable to your operating system.*

TIP *Be sure to use full path names when adding commands. Otherwise, starting the script in the wrong directory can cause havoc!*

You use the del command on the Windows command line to delete a file. The /s option makes it recursive, meaning that the command will delete the file specification listed in every subdirectory. The /q means to do it quietly without asking for confirmation, and the /f tells the operating system to force the deletion even on read-only files. The *.* file specification means to delete every file it finds.

The del command is powerful—many command-line options are. Be sure that you understand each command before you use them. If you call this same command at C:*.* instead of at C:\BUILD\CURRENT, you'd delete everything on your hard drive!

For those unfamiliar with the Windows command-line executables (also known as *shell commands*), let's have a quick lesson. To open the command shell, choose the Start ➤ Programs ➤ Accessories ➤ Command Prompt menu item. A window opens with a prompt indicating the current drive and directory.

You can run any executable object, such as files with the .exe and .com extensions, simply by typing their appropriate directory and executable name at the prompt followed by a Return. You can also run programs whose directories are listed in the Path environment variable without indicating their directories at all. For instance, by typing *notepad.exe* and hitting Enter, the Windows Notepad application opens because the C:\WINDOWS directory is in the system path.

A special set of programs can be run at the command line that don't require the operating system to open any other windows—all action takes place in the

command window. These are called *shell commands*—get a list of them by typing
help at the command prompt and hitting Return. Examples of these special shell
commands are del and md. To get more information regarding a specific command,
type help followed by the command. For instance, the output you might see if you
typed help del appears in Listing 8-10.

Listing 8-10. The Output of help del

```
C:\> help del
Deletes one or more files.

DEL [/P] [/F] [/S] [/Q] [/A[[:]attributes]] names
ERASE [/P] [/F] [/S] [/Q] [/A[[:]attributes]] names

    names           Specifies a list of one or more files or directories.
                    Wildcards may be used to delete multiple files. If a
                    directory is specified, all files within the directory
                    will be deleted.

    /P              Prompts for confirmation before deleting each file.
    /F              Force deleting of read-only files.
    /S              Delete specified files from all subdirectories.
    /Q              Quiet mode, do not ask if ok to delete on global wildcard
    /A              Selects files to delete based on attributes
    attributes      R  Read-only files        S  System files
                    H  Hidden files           A  Files ready for archiving
                    -  Prefix meaning not

If Command Extensions are enabled DEL and ERASE change as follows:

The display semantics of the /S switch are reversed in that it shows
you only the files that are deleted, not the ones it could not find.
```

Note that many shell command executables expect certain parameters to be
listed as you run them. For instance, the md command expects to be given a directory name to create. Some commands (and even many regular Windows executables) also have optional parameters that can be specified. For instance, the /s
parameter for del tells delete to act recursively.

NOTE *Most Windows shell commands were created for the DOS operating system back in the 80s. If you used DOS at some time in the past, you'll probably recognize many of the existing commands.*

If you need more help, there are many references for Windows commands on the Internet. In addition, you can go to your local technical bookstore and ask for a Windows shell command reference.

Completing the Run-Through

After you've completed the substitution of commands, it's time to try them out in the command shell. As you do, you ensure that each command runs successfully.

If things don't work as expected, what's the reason? Is a step missing? Is there something, such as directory security rights, that prevents the command from finishing? Troubleshoot the problems and then take the appropriate action to fix the problem. If necessary, add new steps to the SCRIPT.TXT file.

Getting the Source and Finding Missing Steps

It's time to get the source as listed in your pseudo-script. For the purposes of this chapter, let's say you use Visual Studio 6.0 and SourceSafe, respectively, to create and store the source of your components.

NOTE *You may not be familiar the shell command features for SourceSafe and Visual Studio. Chapter 6, "SourceSafe," describes the SourceSafe command-line options. Chapter 9, "Builds for Windows .NET," details the Visual Studio .NET commands. Examples in this chapter are built using Visual Studio 6.0 commands.*

Download the source code from SourceSafe onto your hard drive using the command line and, once perfected, add the exact commands to your SCRIPT.TXT file. Once completed, you'll run through the steps in the command shell once again from scratch to ensure that you've written them down properly.

Take a look at the SourceSafe command-line substitutions in Listing 8-11.

 CAUTION   *Don't run through Listing 8-11 just yet—I've put a roadblock in this example, and you won't like the results!*

Listing 8-11. Getting the Source and Finding Missing Steps, Part 1

```
2. Get the source in SRC directory
     a. Create/update unique identifer-1.1.0001
     b. ss label $/ -L1.1.0001 -I-
            #-L used for the label, -I- used for no interaction
     c. ss get $/ -I- -VL"1.1.0001" -R -W
            # Gets all the source from the root of Sourcesafe into the current
            directory.
            # -I- used for no interaction, -VL used to specify version 1.1.0001, -R
            for
# recursive and -W  to make downloaded source writable
```

If you were to try each of these commands, you might notice that the source probably wasn't downloaded to the SRC directory where you wanted it to go. That's because the get command downloads to the command shell's current directory—and you weren't prepared for that! Before you get the source, be sure to change the current directory for the command shell to C:\BUILD\CURRENT\SRC.

Finding missing steps such as this isn't only natural, it's exactly what you want to happen. Once found, simply add the new step to the pseudo-build script in the appropriate location. The bulk of missing steps are found during the first run-through of the script.

Unfortunately, there are times when these missing steps can cause disaster on the build machine. For instance, what if you had been in your Windows directory when you had gotten the source? What if you didn't use the del command properly and deleted your Program Files directory? If you followed the rules, you've documented everything that you've done so far—and you've got an easy roadmap should you have to burn down the machine and start from scratch.

You got lucky in this case. I warned you about the get command's stumbling block before you ran into it. You can see what your updated step might look like in Listing 8-12.

Listing 8-12. Finding Missing Steps, Part 2

```
2. Get the source in SRC directory
     a. Create/update unique identifer--1.1.0001
     b. ss label $/ -L1.1.0001 -I-
            #-L used for the label, -I- used for no interaction
     c. cd C:\BUILD\CURRENT\SRC
            # Change directory so source is downloaded to proper location
     c. ss get $/ -I- -VL"1.1.0001" -R -W
            # Gets all the source from the root of Sourcesafe into the current
            directory
            # -I- used for no interaction, -VL used to specify version 1.1.0001, -R
            for
            # recursive and -W  to make downloaded source writable
```

Compiling Objects and Determining Patterns

Let's now move on to the compilation of objects. This time, watch for steps that you seem to take more than once. When you determine patterns in the build, you can avoid repeating steps by combining several steps in one. By stripping out repetitive lines in your script, you'll find debugging and updating it to be much easier.

If you've developed a good naming strategy for your components, this section is a piece of cake. In my naming strategy, each component lives in its own project/directory whose name matches that of the compiled executable's name. I also group similar objects together in a parent directory named after their general purpose.

Let's look at the server objects you need to build:

```
3. Compile Binary Objects into DIST directory
     a.  Server ($/office/server)
           i.   docsrvr.dll  (VC6)
           ii.  logsrvr.dll  (VC6)
           iii. websrvr.dll  (VC6)
```

Because these objects follow my source code naming rules, you know that whatever steps you need to take to build DOCSRVR.DLL will be the same for both LOGSRVR.DLL and WEBSRVR.DLL. That means you only have to plot out these steps once!

Before you do this, however, you should know a little bit about how the Visual Studio tool works. When developers create code in Visual Studio, the relationship between all the source files that make up an application are kept in what's called a *project* file. This file keeps track of the different source files and the special compiling options that should be used with each of them. Visual Studio allows you to build all the source in a project file with a single command. This is great—without it, you'd have to find a way to build each source file in the project individually. In Visual Studio 6.0, project files have file extensions of .DSP for Visual C++ and .VBP for Visual Basic. Visual Studio .NET handles things slightly differently—see Chapter 9, "Builds for Windows .NET," for more details.

The following is what the command-line compilation of the DOCSRVR.DLL object might look like for Visual Studio 6.0:

```
"C:\Program Files\Microsoft Visual Studio\Common\Msdev.exe" ↵
c:\build\current\src\office\server\docsrvr.dll\docsrvr.dsp ↵
  /MAKE "docsrvr - Win32 Release" /USEENV
```

 NOTE   *Your tool's directories may vary from mine. If your system doesn't appear to match mine, search in the Program Files directory for executables such as MSDEV.EXE.*

This command tells Visual Studio to make the DOCSRVR object by following the instructions in the DOCSRVR.DSP project file. The MAKE directive tells Visual Studio to create the application based on the Win32 release configuration set up by the developer. See Chapter 9, "Builds for Windows .NET," for more information on configurations. The USEENV directive tells Visual Studio to use standard system environment variables to locate directories for included source or libraries.

So what will your pattern look like? If you follow my source code naming rules, you can simply substitute the word DOCSRVR with any other server object's name. For instance, by substituting DOCSRVR with the word WEBSRVR, you can compile the second component with pretty much the same command:

```
"C:\Program Files\Microsoft Visual Studio\Common\Msdev.exe" ↵
    c:\build\current\src\office\server\websrvr.dll\websrvr.dsp /MAKE ↵
    "websrvr - Win32 Release" /USEENV
```

This isn't luck—not by any means. The ability to follow the same convention for building components depends on following the source code naming rules previously mentioned. For instance, the WEBSRVR folder must live in the same parent directory (SERVER) as the DOCSRVR folder. The projects must also be named in a similar fashion and both have a "Win32 Release" configuration.[5] If you followed those rules, you can abstract this task to look like Listing 8-13.

Listing 8-13. Step 3 Command Substitution, Part 1

```
3. Compile Binary Objects into DIST directory
    a.  Server ($/office/server)
        "C:\Program Files\Microsoft Visual Studio\Common\Msdev.exe" ↵
            c:\build\current\src\office\server\OBJECT.dll\OBJECT.dsp  ↵
            /MAKE "OBJECT- Win32 Release"  ↵
            /USEENV
                i.   docsrvr.dll  (VC6)
                ii.  logsrvr.dll  (VC6)
                iii. websrvr.dll  (VC6)
```

Now when you run through this step, you simply substitute out the word OBJECT with the names of the three components by cutting and pasting the words on the command line.

But wait! Another missing step shows up! You create the objects using this step—this doesn't copy them to the DIST directory. The inability to name an output directory is a limitation of Visual C++ 6.0—instead, the built objects are placed in the SRC directory rather than in the DIST directory. This is based on options set in the project file. Because your developers use these project files much more often than you do, you shouldn't reset the option and check it into source. Instead, you'll use automation to copy the objects yourself to the DIST directory. Add that command now to your script, as displayed in Listing 8-14.

---

5. The Win32 Release configuration is provided by default by Visual Studio.

Listing 8-14. Step 3 Command Substitution, Part 2

```
3. Compile Binary Objects into DIST directory
     a.  Server ($/office/server)
          "C:\Program Files\Microsoft Visual Studio\Common\Msdev.exe"  ↵
               c:\build\src\office\server\OBJECT.dll\OBJECT.dsp  ↵
               /MAKE "OBJECT- Win32 Release"  ↵
               /USEENV
          copy "c:\build\src\office\server\OBJECT.DLL\Release\OBJECT.DLL"  ↵
               "c:\build\current\dist"
                    i.   docsrvr.dll  (VC6)
                    ii.  logsrvr.dll  (VC6)
                    iii. websrvr.dll  (VC6)
```

Visual Basic components follow a similar pattern, as displayed in Listing 8-15. But leave out the copy step—Visual Basic 6.0 allows you to specify an output directory for the executable.

Listing 8-15. Step 3 Command Substitution, Part 3

```
b.  Client (depends on Server) ($/office/client)
        "C:\Program Files\Microsoft Visual Studio\VB98\vb6.exe"  ↵
            /m c:\build\current\src\office\OBJECT.exe\OBJECT.vbp  ↵
            /outdir c:\build\current\dist /out " c:\build\current\dist \OBJECT.txt"
                 i.   office.exe
                        #depends on speller, spredsht, database and wordproc
                 ii.  speller.exe  (VB6)
                 iii. spredsht.exe  (VB6)
                 iv:  database.exe (VB6)
                 v.   wordproc.exe (VB6)
```

Finishing the Pseudo-Script

Now you have a good idea on how to complete the rest of this task. Following the lead outlined in the first three steps, go ahead and fill in the command-line equivalents for every step in the pseudo-script.

Your script is going to vary from the one I used as an example in this chapter. I'm sure your product doesn't have components named WORDPROC.EXE and DOCSRVR.DLL. And you may not have any idea how to compile the installation script or date stamp the DIST directory. But you do know what the steps are—use other resources to determine how to complete them. For instance, if your install developer is using InstallShield, search the tool's Web site knowledge base for information on how to build at the command line. If you want to date stamp your files, search the Web for a tool that does the job—or better yet, write one yourself. Because every build is unique, it's impossible for this book to give you all of the specific commands you might need to call.

After you've run through each portion of the script, you have a finished product that you can use. You are 85-percent finished creating an automatic build! All that you have to do now is change your text file into a true script.

Introducing MAKE

An automated build requires a scripting mechanism that runs the commands you wrote down in SCRIPT.TXT. Any scripting program will do—you could use any of the Batch, Visual Basic, or Perl scripting languages to accomplish this task. Luckily for you, however, a utility has been created just for this task. I'm going to tell you now about the granddaddy of all build tools: MAKE.

What differentiates a build utility from a regular scripting tool is its ability to "componentize" builds and, more important, understand the dependencies between the objects you're building. Sure, you could write this functionality yourself in Perl or some other scripting language. But why reinvent the wheel?

 NOTE *Visual Studio in Windows uses a variation of MAKE called* NMAKE, *which has a slightly enhanced feature set. For the purposes of this chapter, however, all functionality listed is available for use in both MAKE and NMAKE.*

Targets and Dependents

MAKE is an excellent SCM tool. It looks at the objects that make up your project and builds them—automatically—starting with the smallest possible part. For instance, your pseudo-script mentions that the OFFICE.EXE program requires a variety of Visual Basic programs to be built first. The Visual Basic objects require the C++ server objects to be built first. And you can take this a step further—you could say that the C++ server objects require the source to be gotten and the initial directories created.

The MAKE utility allows you to prioritize builds in this manner. You provide it with a *target* step and then tell it what *dependent* steps must be taken before that target step can start to build.

Let's look at a real-world example of the MAKE tool.

NOTE *For the ease of this example, I've decided to write this sample applica-tion using the Linux operating system and the C programming language. Visual Studio certainly supports the ANSI industry standard for C, so you can build this same code in the Windows environment.*

This program consists of one source file called HELLO.C. Listing 8-16 displays its contents.

Listing 8-16. The Source for HELLO.C

```c
#include <studio.h>

int main()
{
    printf("Hello World!\n");
}
```

It's a pretty simple program. Its only task is to type "Hello World!" to the moni-tor. Now I'm going to take this code and turn it into an executable that an end user can use. I do this by using the standard C compiler provided through the Linux operating system. The following are the commands I might type on the command line to build my program:

```
/usr/bin/cc -c hello.c
/usr/bin/cc -o hello.exe hello.o
```

The first line compiles the HELLO.C file into object code. The second line takes that object code and turns it into the HELLO.EXE executable.

Working backward, perhaps you'll see that HELLO.EXE would make an excel-lent final target for this code. To create HELLO.EXE, HELLO.O must exist. In MAKE, you can express this dependency in the following way:

```
hello.exe : hello.o
    /usr/bin/cc -o hello.exe hello.o
```

In this example, the first line, or "rules" line, states that HELLO.O must exist before HELLO.EXE can be built. A colon separates the target from its dependen-cies. The second line, or "command" line, is the action that's taken once all of the dependencies have been created. To comply with MAKE syntax, the rules line can't be indented. On the flip side, the command line must always be indented with a tab.

You can apply this same logic to build HELLO.O. Its only dependency is the existence of HELLO.C. But HELLO.C is a text file that isn't built per se, so you can leave the dependency portion of that rule blank. Note, however, that the colon must still be placed after the target name:

```
hello.o :
    /usr/bin/cc -c hello.c
```

A single rule line can have several commands following it. For instance, I could also throw in a line informing the user of the build's current step by using the operating system's @echo command:

```
hello.o :
    @echo Now building:  hello.c
    /usr/bin/cc -c hello.c
```

This is now an official *makefile*, the term used for MAKE scripts. Once I've written the script, I can save it with the name MAKEFILE on my hard drive and then run MAKE to create my executable. To run MAKE or NMAKE, make sure that the executable's parent directory is in the system path and that MAKEFILE exists in the current directory.

The output might look like Listing 8-17.

Listing 8-17. MAKE Output

```
(bob1234@worf) /home/bob1234>>> make
Now building: hello.o
/usr/bin/cc -c hello.c
/usr/bin/cc -o hello.exe hello.o
(bob1234@worf) /home/bob1234>>>
```

By default, MAKE searches for a file called MAKEFILE in the directory from which it's run. This naming convention can be an obstacle when you want to "componentize" your builds into separate makefiles. Get around this by renaming MAKEFILE to HELLO.MAK and then use MAKE's -f command-line parameter. The makefile name is separated by a space immediately following the -f parameter. For instance:

```
make -f hello.mak
```

After renaming the makefile, you may find that MAKE tells you that the HELLO.EXE object is up-to-date. That's because MAKE builds only components that it believes need an update or that don't exist. MAKE first looks to see if the HELLO.EXE exists. If it does exist, MAKE looks at the file's date/time stamp and compares it to the stamp of its dependencies. MAKE will only build objects if, somewhere down the line, a dependency has changed since the last time of the build.

This is an important distinction from a regular scripting tool. Using MAKE can save you time because it only builds components that need building.

NOTE *If you use Visual Studio for building in Windows, MAKE can't always determine if the dependencies for an object are newer and may always build. Even in this case, MAKE still has several advantages over using a regular scripting tool.*

Creating Macros

At this point, you might think it would be easier to create a simple Batch or shell script to create this component. For this one small program, that's probably true. The beauty of MAKE, though, is that things get easier to use as the project gets bigger. For example, what if there were five C files to build for this project instead of just one? With MAKE, you can easily *scale*, or enlarge, your application.

MAKE scales well because of its use of *macros*. You may be familiar with the term *macro* from Microsoft Word or other applications. The term isn't really used in the same sense here—in MAKE, a macro acts more like a variable. Most macros are made up by the script writer, but there are also several internal macros that are defined by the MAKE utility itself.

Use macros for any action that you might take more than once. For instance, look at the HELLO.MAK script displayed in Listing 8-18, and you see that the compiler (/usr/bin/cc) is called more than once.

Listing 8-18. HELLO.MAK Without Macros

```
hello.exe : hello.o
    /usr/bin/cc -o hello.exe hello.o
hello.o :
    @echo Now building:  hello.c
    /usr/bin/cc-c hello.c
```

Let's use a macro to simplify the compilation command. First, define the macro on its own line at the top of the file. Like the rules line, macro definitions aren't indented:

```
CC = /usr/bin/cc
```

Now you can substitute the CC macro wherever you called the /usr/bin/cc command. Use a dollar sign ($) and parentheses[6] to tell MAKE you're calling a macro, as displayed in Listing 8-19.

Listing 8-19. HELLO.MAK with Macros

```
CC = /usr/bin/cc
hello.exe : hello.o
    $(CC) -o hello.exe hello.o
hello.o :
    @echo Now building:  hello.c
    $(CC) -c hello.c
```

This may seem like a ridiculous thing to do. Why change out the compiler like that? You build your makefile in this manner so you can easily switch out the compilation tool should the need occur. For instance, let's say you wanted to change to the GCC open-source compiler instead of using CC. Instead of having to change every single line that builds an object, instead you simply indicate the change by updating the macro definition:

```
CC = /usr/bin/gcc
```

Another advantage is that operating system environment variables are macros to MAKE. If MAKE doesn't find a macro declaration inside the makefile, it queries the operating system to see if there's an environment variable of the same name. You could use this if you need to query the system for the name of the machine or the logged-in user in order to build. Or better yet, this allows you to build on two separate machines using the same build script—simply use environment variables to specify tool and source locations.

---

6.   You can use braces {} instead of parentheses.

> **NOTE** *If you don't explicitly declare the value of a macro and it hasn't been set as an environment variable, MAKE will consider it blank or empty. MAKE doesn't see this as an error—but you may get unexpected results. For instance, if you choose to use a command such as del with an empty macro, you can accidentally delete all the files on your C drive! Take care and make sure that all macros will have values. See the "Debugging Your Builds" section for information on how to correct this problem.*

To demonstrate the usefulness of macros, I'm going to add another source file called DEBUG.C to the makefile, as displayed in Listing 8-20.

Listing 8-20. HELLO.MAK with Multiple Dependencies

```
CC = /usr/bin/cc
hello.exe : hello.o debug.o
     $(CC) -o hello.exe hello.o
hello.o :
     @echo Now building:  hello.c
     $(CC) -c hello.c
debug.o :
     @echo Now building:  debug.c
     $(CC) -c debug.c
```

Note that I added the DEBUG.O object code to the right of the colon on the HELLO.EXE rules line. This tells MAKE that both of the .O objects must exist before HELLO.EXE can be created.

You can see that there are two components that follow the same *pattern*. Take a look: You follow pretty much the same steps to build DEBUG.O that you do when you build HELLO.O. MAKE has an internal variable that you can use to combine these steps. By using the $* internal variable[7] in a command line, you indicate to MAKE that it should substitute the macro with the current target minus its extension. For example, you compile the HELLO.O object in the following manner:

```
hello.o :
     $(CC) -c $*.c
```

---

7. Macros with a single character following the dollar sign ($) don't require parentheses (though it's okay to use them).

In the previous example, the $* internal macro evaluates to HELLO, and the $*.C value evaluates to HELLO.C. Now take this one step further. Build both HELLO.O and DEBUG.O using the same command rules displayed in Listing 8-21. In the echo line, use a $@ macro to indicate the full target name.

Listing 8-21. HELLO.MAK with Targets Sharing Command Rules

```
CC = /usr/bin/cc
hello.exe : hello.o debug.o
    $(CC) -o hello.exe hello.o
hello.o debug.o :
    @echo Now building:  $@
    $(CC) -c $*.c
```

When MAKE runs this makefile, it takes the following steps:

1. MAKE sees HELLO.EXE as the first component and checks to see if it currently exists. If the file doesn't exist, MAKE looks at the HELLO.EXE rules line and determines that HELLO.O must be built before HELLO.EXE. If HELLO.EXE does exist, MAKE checks the file's date/time stamp and that of all of its dependencies. If any of the dependencies don't exist or if their stamps are later than that of HELLO.EXE, it will be rebuilt now.

2. MAKE checks to see if HELLO.O exists. Again, if the file exists, all the dependency date/time stamps are checked to see if an update is necessary. If the file doesn't exist, MAKE searches the rest of the makefile for a target called HELLO.O. Once found, it looks for any dependencies that HELLO.O might have. Seeing none, it runs the command line below the HELLO.O rules line. When running, it replaces the $@ macro with the phrase HELLO.O and the $* macro with the word HELLO.

3. Having built HELLO.O, MAKE tries again to build HELLO.EXE. It sees that there is another dependency called DEBUG.O. Once again, it searches for the DEBUG.O target, creates its dependencies, and then runs the commands following the rules line.

4. Having completed building all of dependencies, MAKE links the object files together into the HELLO.EXE executable.

Now you can easily use these same rules to add any number of C files to your project—as long as they follow the same compilation pattern. If you take a look at Listing 8-22, the addition of five new C files doesn't seem so scary anymore.

Listing 8-22. Adding More Dependencies to HELLO.MAK

```
CC = /usr/bin/cc
hello.exe : hello.o debug.o input.o output.o user.o
    $(CC) -o hello.exe hello.o debug.o input.o output.o user.o
hello.o debug.o input.o output.o user.o :
    @echo Now building:  $@
    $(CC) -c $*.c
```

The output for this makefile might look like that displayed in Listing 8-23.

Listing 8-23. Your Console's Output When Running MAKE

```
(bob1234@worf) /home/bob1234>>> make -f hello.mak
Now building: hello.o
/usr/bin/cc -c hello.c
Now building: debug.o
/usr/bin/cc -c debug.c
Now building: input.o
/usr/bin/cc -c input.c
Now building: output.o
/usr/bin/cc -c output.c
Now building: user.o
/usr/bin/cc -c user.c
/usr/bin/cc -o hello.exe hello.o debug.o input.o output.o user.o
(bob1234@worf) /home/bob1234>>>
```

Another scripting tool would have required many more lines of code to achieve the same goals. By using MAKE, the script stays compact and manageable. Even better, a single change to a configuration aspect of the script (such as a compiler change) only needs to be made once.

Visual Build by Kinook Software

So you want to build using a GUI frontend. Frankly, I don't blame you. Scripting is tough, and sometimes a tool that makes life easier is a good investment.

Kinook Software, a privately held Colorado company, created a Windows tool back in the late 90s to help you out. Visual Build Pro, now in its fifth version, is available for free evaluation on the Kinook website at http://www.kinook.com. The following figure displays its current interface.

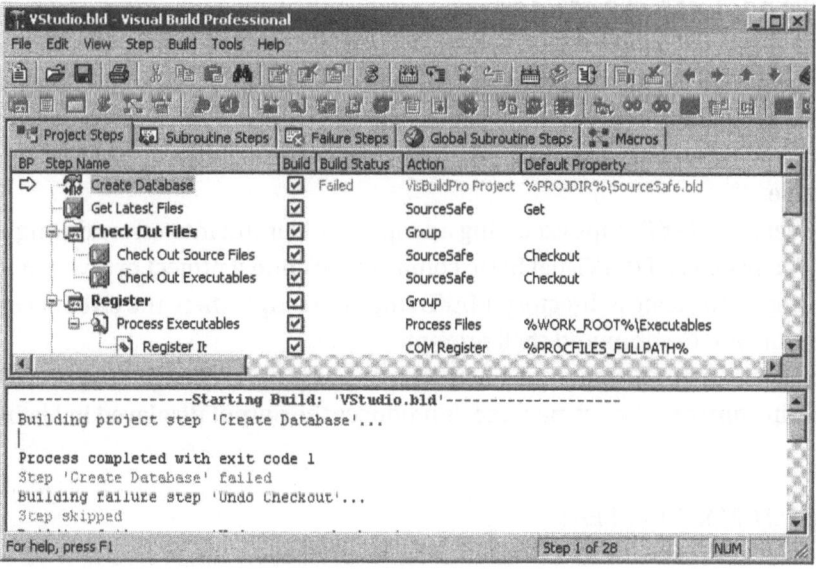

With features such as single-step debugging and the integration of both VBScript and JScript, Visual Build Pro is capable of building an enterprise application. It has built-in support for both Visual Studio 6.0 and .NET projects, as well as the ability to interface with Visual SourceSafe, CVS, and Perforce. Pretty much any source control tool can also be used with Visual Build Pro—though the end user must manually enter each individual command.

One of the highlights of the software is its out-of-the-box capability to increment version numbers and then brand components with them for both Visual Studio 6.0 and .NET components. This functionality alone is almost worth the few hundred dollar purchase price. Another strong feature is that the program scans projects as they're built for dependencies that might need to be created beforehand. Most importantly, the tool comes with a console interface so automatic scheduled builds can take place without opening the IDE.

Although it's a Microsoft-centric program, support has recently been added for some Borland products, such as JBuilder and Delphi. In the end, you can integrate any tool that has a command-line or scripting interface into the environment.

Several prebuilt scripts come with the product. How they work isn't obvious at first, but a strong help collection features an overview and many samples. The scripts themselves are Extensible Markup Language (XML) text files, so quick changes don't necessarily require you to open the tool. They aren't the easiest scripts to read, however, so keep the hard stuff for inside Visual Build itself.

This product doesn't negate the need to architect your build. You still have to "program" the tool for your particular build. But Visual Build can certainly help to hide many of the more tedious tasks associated with a build's creation. If you're a GUI fan, this might be your favorite new toy.

Checking Exit Statuses

Most operating systems allow programmers to generate exit codes when programs end. The programmer can use these codes to communicate when an error has occurred. To the operating system, an error code is normally designated as a non-zero value.

By default, MAKE stops executing a script should it run into errors during the build. For instance, if the Visual Basic compiler can't find a project or if you failed in an attempt to create a directory, MAKE stops the script where the error occurs and returns you to command shell prompt.

As an example, I'll create a deliberate error by trying to change to the C:\WIN-DOWS directory on a Linux machine. It produces the output displayed in Listing 8-24.

Listing 8-24. MAKE Fatal Error

```
/home/bob1234>> make -f bob.mak
cd c:\windows
/bin/sh: cd: c:windows: No such file or directory
make: *** [cd] Error 1
(bob1234@worf) /home/bob1234>>>
```

At first glance, this seems an irritating flaw. On the contrary, it's quite an important feature. If the MAKE script didn't stop, the build continues without properly creating all the component and directory objects necessary.

Of course, there are times when you know that your script can't run completely in its existing condition—for instance, in a testing situation. For troubleshooting purposes, you might want the script to continue all the way to its end. In this case, you run the MAKE script with the -i parameter. With this, you instruct MAKE to ignore any error exit codes it may receive from the operating system during the build.

Alternatively, you can also use the .IGNORE target within the makefile. Treat it as if it were a target by following the keyword it with a colon. This provides the same functionality as the parameter—but without the need to specify -i every time MAKE is run. You can also use the .IGNORE keyword to be selective about which scripts should halt with an error. Ensure that the keyword is completely flushed left in the script because MAKE assumes that indented text is a command.

Listing 8-25 displays what a MAKE script with the .IGNORE target might look like.

Listing 8-25. The .IGNORE Target

```
.IGNORE :
CC = /usr/bin/cc
hello.exe : hello.o debug.o input.o output.o user.o
    $(CC) -o hello.exe hello.o debug.o input.o output.o user.o
hello.o debug.o input.o output.o user.o :
    @echo Now building:  $@
        $(CC) -c $*.c
```

There is a third way to ignore exit codes, which is especially helpful for pinpointing only certain commands that should ignore error codes instead of doing so for the entire file. Accomplish this by putting a hyphen (-) in front of the command line to be ignored, as displayed in Listing 8-26.

Listing 8-26. Ignoring Errors with a Hyphen

```
hello.exe : hello.o debug.c input.c output.c user.c
    - $(CC) -o hello.exe hello.o
```

In this case, all other commands listed in the makefile cause the build to break as usual.

Building Specific Command Targets

Building an entire MAKE script when you only want to test a specific section can be a real time waster. MAKE allows you to build specific targets simply by specifying the target name when you run the script. For example, if your makefile is named HELLO.MAK, you specify that you only want to build HELLO.O by typing the following:

```
make -f hello.mak hello.o
```

Apply this same technique to files named MAKEFILE by specifying the target directly after the MAKE command. For example:

```
make hello.o
```

In this case, all dependencies listed for HELLO.O (if there were any) are also built before the object is created.

You can build any number of targets at the same time in this manner. For example:

```
make -f hello.mak hello.o debug.o
```

Unless you use this method to specify a target as a parameter on the command line, MAKE only builds the first target (and its dependencies) listed in the script.

Adding Comments to Makefiles

Add notes to your make scripts by starting lines that shouldn't be interpreted as a rule or command with a pound sign (#). These notes are called *comments* in the programming world. Liberally use comments to add context when the logic you use may not be obvious to other people (or to you six months from now).

TIP *As a last step, I always copy my build log to the distribution directory for the build it's creating. Because directories may not exist when I start a build or because I may not be able to copy the log while the makefile is running, I originally save the log in a temporary location and then copy it to the DIST directory when the build has completed.*

ANOTHER TIP *By naming your log with an underscore as the first character, it will always show up first in directory listings.*

WORD OF THE DAY

in·for·māʹtion, *n.*

As the hub of the development team wheel, it's your job to provide other team members with as much useful documentation as possible.

Because of company regulations, or just for your own purposes, you may want to document your build. This sidebar focuses on several pieces of documentation that I've created in the past that others have found helpful. Your needs may vary—if you're working on a product that might affect public safety, your documentation requirements might be more stringent. Be sure to check the regulations for your company, state, and country to make sure you're providing all the documentation necessary for your builds. An important guideline to follow when creating documentation is to make sure that it's valuable to somebody. Documentation for documentation's sake is difficult to wade through and can cause a goodwill backlash.

CONTINUED

CONTINUED

As you start deciding what documentation you'll provide to other parties, you may think it's easier to create it manually rather than to automate it. At first, that may seem like a good idea, but as you do the same task everyday—and sometimes you'll forget to do it!—you'll begin to see the sense of automating all of your tasks whenever possible. Documentation tasks should also be automated unless there's a real reason not to do so. For the record, there aren't many reasons not to do so.

Build output: Luckily, there are several pieces of documentation that come for free. The first is the output of the MAKE script. By default, MAKE displays its activities in the standard output of the command window—the display. Change this behavior by using the greater-than symbol (>) to redirect MAKE's output to a file. For example:

```
make -f hello.mak > C:\logs\_build.log
```

In the previous statement, the redirect operator (>) saves the output that MAKE would normally display on the screen to a file located at C:\LOGS_BUILD.LOG.

Keep the build logs handy because they can be helpful when debugging problems. For instance, there may be times when you include a new target but forget to list it as a dependency for another target—if that happens, your new target will never build. Taking a look at the build log will tell you right away if and when the component was built.

Components list: Another easy report to create is the built components list. If you've followed the instructions in this chapter, your built components exist in a single distribution directory. Simply run a directory listing command (`dir` in Windows or `ls -la` in Linux/Unix) and then use the redirect operator (>) to write the output to a file. An example might look like one of the following depending on your operating system:

```
dir > c:\logs\component_list.log
ls -la > /home/bob1234/logs/component_list.log
```

These kinds of lists display the size and date/time stamp for the components in the current build—very helpful to the quality team. Consider creating this file and putting it in the same location as the _BUILD.LOG file.

Install listings and file locations: Your last documentation task isn't so simple. The quality team may find it convenient to know which files are meant to be installed on a user's drive and where they'll be located. They may also want to know operating system settings (such as Registry changes in Windows).

It may be your job to provide this list after every build. Although this can be a formidable task, there's no reason you can't automate it. Many install programs list installed objects and settings in text files and a few provide distribution manifests. Spend a little time getting to know your installation program, and you might be able to produce these kinds of lists fairly easily as part of the build.

Converting Your Pseudo-Script into a MAKE Script

Now that you understand the basics of MAKE, it's time to convert the steps in your SCRIPT.TXT to MAKE format. If you're following along, open the file and save it as SCRIPT.MAK—just make sure that you save a copy of the original script file in case you make a mistake!

Creating Dummy Targets

So far the targets that you've used have been tangible objects that you want to build. There are times, however, when you may want to assign dependencies to nontangible targets—also known as *dummy targets*.

The pseudo-script that you wrote earlier in the chapter contains an excellent example of why you might want to use a dummy target—the step that creates directories:

```
1. Create directories
      a. del /s /q /f c:\build\current\*.*
      b. md c:\build\current
      c. md c:\build\current\src
      d. md c:\build\current\dist
      e. md c:\build\current\media
```

This step doesn't contain an executable or object file to build. Instead, you only want to create directories. To use dummy targets, simply make up a name that describes the functionality of the command lines that follow. In this instance, you might choose to name the target make_directories. Then add command lines to it as you would with a normal target. For example, the previous step in MAKE format might look like the following:

```
make_directories :
      del /s /q /f c:\build\current\*.*
      md c:\build\current
      md c:\build\current\src
      md c:\build\current\dist
      md c:\build\current\media
```

Dummy targets follow these rules:

- A dummy target is built only if it's the first target listed in the script or if it's listed as a dependency for another target.

- Because the target isn't a file with a date/time stamp, MAKE always considers dummy targets as out-of-date. In other words, a dummy target is always "built"—even if some of its tangible dependencies aren't.

- MAKE always builds a tangible target (such as HELLO.EXE) if it has a dummy target as a dependency.

Now treat the make_directories target as a dependency for other objects. For instance, you might like to say that the directories must be made before getting the source. Again, getting the source isn't tangible, so I'll use a dummy target to get it done. Step 2 in its entirety might look like Listing 8-27.

Listing 8-27. MAKE Equivalent of Step 2 of the Pseudo-Script

```
get_source : make_directories
    # Don't forget to later get and increment the version!
    ss label $/ -L1.1.0001 -I-
    cd c:\build\current\src
    ss get $/ -I- -VL"1.1.0001" -R -W
```

Many developers choose to create a dummy target called *all* that will build every target listed in the script. The all dummy target should be the first nonkeyword target (such as .IGNORE) listed in the script. This iş handy; it means that you don't have to add every other target as a dependency of the last step—the installation, in this case. Instead, you place all of the build steps as dependents for the all target.

Listing 8-28 simulates using an all dummy target in your makefile. Notice that the make_directories target no longer needs to be listed as a dependency for get_source.

> **NOTE** *Don't forget that all dependencies are created in order. If you want to get the source after creating the directories, place them in the appropriate order when listing them as dependencies.*

Listing 8-28. Using Dummy Targets for Steps 1 and 2 of Your Pseudo-Script

```
all: make_directories get_source

make_directories :
     del /s /q /f c:\build\current\*.*
     md c:\build\current
     md c:\build\current\src
     md c:\build\current\dist
     md c:\build\current\media

get_source :
     # Don't forget to later get and increment the version!
     ss label $/ -L1.1.0001 -I-
     cd c:\build\current\src
     ss get $/ -I- -VL"1.1.0001" -R -W
```

Using What You've Learned to Tighten Your Script

Wait a minute—did you notice it? The C:\BUILD\CURRENT\SRC directory was repeated in both the make_directories and get_source targets. This is a great opportunity to tighten up your script by using a macro. Later, if you decide to change the location of the source directory, you'll have to make the change in only one place. You'll be glad you tightened things up when your scripts get larger, and you don't have to make the same change in 36 places.

 TIP *To create scripts that are portable to different machines, make sure you never specify hard paths and instead use macros. From there, create a simple batch or shell command script that sets those paths as environment variables. When the build begins, simply run the batch or shell script before you run the makefile.*

Take a look at the "tightened up" makefile in Listing 8-29. Remember to place macros early in the file to ensure that they're defined before they're used. As discussed in the "Creating Macros" section, don't precede the definition with a dollar sign and make sure they're all the way flush left in the file.

Listing 8-29. Using Macros to Tighten Your Makefile

```
TOP_DIR = c:\build\current
SRC_DIR = $(TOP_DIR)\src
DIST_DIR = $(TOP_DIR)\dist
MEDIA_DIR =  $(TOP_DIR)\media


all: make_directories get_source

make_directories :
    del /s /q /f $(TOP_DIR)\*.*
    md $(TOP_DIR)
    md $(SRC_DIR)
    md $(DIST_DIR)
    md $(MEDIA_DIR)


get_source :
    # Don't forget to later get and increment the version!
    ss label $/ -L1.1.0001 -I-
    cd $(SRC_DIR)
    ss get $/ -I- -VL"1.1.0001" -R -W
```

Note that the SRC_DIR macro has been defined using another macro: TOP_DIR. This is absolutely acceptable and actually makes the script more flexible—you can change the location of the entire build's output by changing only one line. There's no need to use a concatenation character or function as there is with other scripting languages.

Now add the compilation step of your pseudo-script to the makefile. Be sure to use macros for repeated code and especially for specific paths. Your completed script might look like Listing 8-30. Note that several dummy targets are added for the purpose of grouping the server and client objects. This allows you to build certain groups of executables by themselves. For example, if you only want to build the server portion of the build, you specify just the server_compile target to MAKE as a parameter on the command line.

Listing 8-30. Your Complete Makefile

```
BUILD_LABEL = 0001
TOP_DIR = c:\build\current
SRC_DIR = $(TOPDIR)\src
DIST_DIR = $(TOPDIR)\dist
MEDIA_DIR =  $(TOPDIR)\media
DOC_DIR = $(TOPDIR)\doc
3RD_PARTY_DIR = \\3rdparty
SS6 =  "C:\Program Files\Microsoft Visual Studio\VSS\win32\ss.exe"
VC6 = "C:\Program Files\Microsoft Visual Studio\Common\Msdev.exe"
VB6 = "C:\Program Files\Microsoft Visual Studio\VB98\vb6.exe"
SIGN_TOOL = "C:\Program Files\Signing\sign.exe"
FD_TOOL = "C:\Program Files\Utilities\fd.exe"
IS55 = "C:\Program Files\InstallShield\is55.exe"
VIRUS_CHECK = "C:\Program Files\Symantec\AntiVirus\av.exe"


all: make_directories get_source server_compile client_compile postcreate ↵
        package copy_media post_copy

make_directories :
    del /s /q /f $(TOP_DIR)\*.*
    md $(TOP_DIR)
    md $(SRC_DIR)
    md $(DIST_DIR)
    md $(MEDIA_DIR)


get_source :
    # Don't forget to later get and increment the version!
    $(SS6) label $/ -L1.1.$(BUILD_LABEL) -I-
    cd $(SRC_DIR)
    $(SS6) get $/ -I- -VL"1.1.$(BUILD_LABEL)" -R -W

server_compile : docsrvr.dll logsrvr.dll websrvr.dll

docsrvr.dll logsrvr.dll websrvr.dll :
    $(VC6) $(SRC_DIR)\office\server\$@\$*.dsp /MAKE "OBJECT- Win32 Release" ↵
        /USEENV
    copy $(SRC_DIR)\office\server\$@ $(DIST_DIR)

client_compile : office.exe
```

```
office.exe : speller.exe spredsht.exe database.exe wordproc.exe
    $(VB6) /m $(SRC_DIR)\office\client\$@\$*.vbp /outdir $(DIST_DIR) /out ↵
        "$(DIST_DIR)\$*.txt"

speller.exe spredsht.exe database.exe wordproc.exe :
    $(VB6) /m $(SRC_DIR)\office\client\$@\$*.vbp /outdir $(DIST_DIR) /out ↵
        "$(DIST_DIR)\$*.txt"

postcreate : logsrvr.dll
    $(SIGN_TOOL) $(DIST_DIR)\logsrvr.dll
    $(FD_TOOL) $(DIST_DIR)

package :
    $(IS55) -out $(MEDIA_DIR) $(SRC_DIR)\install\setup.rul

copy_media :
    copy $(DOC_DIR)\html\readme.html $(MEDIA_DIR)
    copy $(DOC_DIR)\html\install.html $(MEDIA_DIR)
    copy $(3RD_PARTY_DIR)\adobe\acrordr5.exe $(MEDIA_DIR)

post_copy :
    $(FD_TOOL) $(MEDIA_DIR)
    $(VIRUS_CHECK) $(MEDIA_DIR)
    del /s /q /f $(SRC_DIR)
    ren $(TOP_DIR) $(BUILD_LABEL)
```

Using Multiple Makefiles in a Single Build

Makefiles can get large—especially in enterprise projects—and you might find that they become difficult to maintain. To avoid this problem, divide your makefiles into separate MAKE scripts. For instance, you might remove the server objects from the build script you just created and place them instead in a file called SERVER.MAK. Because you can call any operating system command from MAKE, add a recursive call to the new script in the original SCRIPT.MAK file:

```
compile_server :
    nmake /f server.mak
```

But what about your macros? Thankfully, there's no reason to declare the same macros in each separate makefile. Instead, MAKE supports the `include` directive, which allows you to specify definition files that should be loaded before the script runs. MAKE then merges the two files and treats them as if they were one when the script runs.

To facilitate this, create a separate script where you put macro definitions. Call this file INCLUDE.MAK. At the beginning of the other makefile scripts, add the `include` preprocessing keyword to insert the definitions file at runtime. This might be written as follows:

```
include include.mak
```

Depending on the version of MAKE being used, you may be required to use the bang character (!) at the beginning of the line. Make sure you place the line at the top of the file—otherwise, only the macros used after its inclusion will fill properly. As with other keywords, the command must not be indented.

Debugging Your Builds

Just as in the programming world, you may need to spend some time testing your scripts and confirming that they work correctly—otherwise known as *debugging*.

The following are three command-line parameters for MAKE that you might find helpful when debugging:

-d: This parameter instructs MAKE to display extra information regarding this build. It displays every step taken in the build and the behind-the-scenes actions that MAKE uses to fulfill the task. Be warned, however, that this parameter can dump quite a bit of information to your screen. The HELLO.MAK makefile described earlier in the chapter caused MAKE to output hundreds of lines of debugging information when used with this parameter.

-n: This parameter tells MAKE to display commands but to not run them. While running, MAKE still stops for some basic problems, such as when paths don't exist. This parameter is handy for checking your makefile's syntax.

-p: This parameter tells MAKE to display extra MAKE information. This includes a listing of all of the macros for which it has found values (including operating system environment variables).

Finding More Information About Make...

There are many features of MAKE that, for sake of brevity, I can't address in this book. You can find lots of references for MAKE at your local technical bookstore or on the Internet.

If you're using Linux or Unix, you can also get more information about the MAKE utility by typing on the command line:

```
man make
```

Windows users should navigate to Microsoft's programmer's knowledge base at http://msdn.microsoft.com and search for *NMAKE Reference*.

....

Using Ant

MAKE was created to help ease the pain of building C, C++, and Assembly projects. As developers have moved toward programming languages that don't have the same complexity as those earlier languages, new building tools have emerged that are also easier to use.

One of these tools is Ant, a MAKE utility provided as freeware from the Apache project. Ant is a Java-based tool, which means it can be used in all environments that support Java. You still create build scripts, but they're written in a fairly straightforward XML format instead of the freely designed fashion of MAKE language. Like makefiles, these scripts can also be transferred across platforms with a minimal amount of fuss.

Ant scripts follow many of the same rules as MAKE, but some tasks, such as building Java objects or jarring groups of Java classes together, are built into the tool itself.

For instance, let's say you used Java to create a set of HELLO class files. An Ant script might look like that in Listing 8-31.

Listing 8-31. An Example of an Ant XML Script File

```xml
<project name="hello" default="all" basedir=".">

    <property name="src" value="."/>
    <property name="dist"  value="dist"/>

    <target name="init">
        <mkdir dir="${dist}"/>
    </target>

    <target name="hello" depends="init">
        <!-- Compile all of the java files in src to dist -->
```

(continued)

```
        <javac srcdir="${src}" destdir="${dist}"/>
    </target>

</project>
```

As with all tools, there's a tradeoff for some of this new functionality. Tools that are easier to use generally lose flexibility. And vice versa—more powerful tools are generally more difficult to use. Ant can make your life easier, but you lose much of the power available to you at the command line. Many people combine the use of shell scripts with Ant to get the best of both worlds.

Unfortunately, I can't spend as much time as I'd like discussing how to use Ant. If your team works primarily with Java and you're interested in the tool, you can find more information at http://www.apache.org. All of the non-MAKE-related steps in this chapter are still applicable to Ant and other MAKE tools.

Summary

This chapter's purpose was to get you started on creating an automatic build for your product.

You heard about the importance of automation and why you should create builds on a dedicated machine. Regardless of your operating system, you should now also have a working knowledge of the following:

- The components that make up your product

- The dependencies that those components might have

- How to build those components using the command shell interface

In addition to the previous topics, you created a base outline of your build (the pseudo-script) that describes how and when to build components with the result being a viable installation package.

In addition, I discussed the MAKE build utility and how you might use it to translate the outline into a build script for your product. You learned MAKE's rule syntax and some of its basic commands. You also determined patterns in your build script and used MAKE's inherent abilities to make it more efficient.

Lastly, I discussed the documentation you might be obligated to provide to other team members with your build.

After reading this chapter, you should now be able to build a full working version of your product. Your build may not have a lot of bells and whistles, but it can run with the touch of a button.

CHAPTER 9

Builds for Windows .NET

VISUAL STUDIO UNDERWENT a huge transformation when it moved from version 6.0 to .NET. Visual Studio .NET 2003 looks similar to previous versions and fulfills almost all of its previous functionality; however, the underlying foundation of the product has changed dramatically. The purpose of this chapter is to introduce you to these changes and display how a Software Configuration Manager (SCM) might work with the product.

Bear in mind that this isn't a comprehensive study of the product. Many books can teach you how to program in Visual Studio .NET's native languages. Instead, this chapter looks at it from an SCM's perspective—you'll learn how to use it in respect to builds and how to exploit its build features.

What Is .NET?

"What is .NET?" is an excellent question—one many marketers have sought to answer. Listen to Bill Gates talk about the .NET initiative sometime—frankly, it sounds like he himself isn't quite sure what makes up this new enterprise solution.

Truth be known, the .NET vision is much simpler than it might appear. Microsoft is attempting to present a way to create applications and services that can reside, in part or in whole, on the Internet. The grand theory is that someday applications will no longer deliver via tangible media such as CDs or other removable data storage media. Instead, functionality will be distributed by a seemingly central location (but in reality will probably be scores of different locations). .NET is the proposed first step in this direction. Imagine walking into a coffee house, sitting down at a public machine, and having everything that's on your home computer suddenly appear before you. In addition, all of the appliances in your house, your car, and your workplace can be wired to it—the inability to shut off a forgotten coffee pot will be a thing of the past. That's the vision anyway.

Setting Aside Programming Language Differences

Whether your developers use Basic, C++, Assembly, or one of myriad other programming languages, they're faced with the same dilemma: either program every application using the difficult and low-level Windows Application Programming

Interface (API) or learn a new set of less complicated operating system directives for each language they might use. Worse—when programmers want to release an application for more than one operating system, they're forced to compile two different executables that follow two different sets of coding rules.

In addition to the primary .NET vision of software distribution, Microsoft has attempted to address these other problems with its new set of programming tools.

All Visual Studio languages now use the same set of operating system directives. Don't underestimate the value of this particular feature—it's huge for programmers who work with several different languages. The message box functionality in Windows is a prime example. Instead of programmers being forced to learn both the MessageBox command for Visual C++ and the MsgBox command for Visual Basic, there's simply now the MessageBox.Show command for both languages.

This common runtime library is available to all .NET Framework languages. Third-party developers can exploit this runtime and create .NET-compatible versions of other languages. ActiveState, for example, has provided a .NET-compatible version of the Perl language that drops right into the existing Visual Studio .NET Integrated Development Environment (IDE).

This change can be credited to the introduction of the Microsoft Intermediate Language (MSIL), which now acts as a middle layer between individual programming languages and the operating system. This is in direct contrast to the way Visual Studio created applications in the past. In version 6.0 of Visual Studio, C++, and most other languages, code is compiled to *native* code—it's transformed into binary language for a specific microprocessing platform. Only J++ and Visual Basic relied on an interpreting middle layer—and with Visual Basic, it was an option.

Visual Studio .NET, on the other hand, translates applications into MSIL objects. Once these objects find their way to an end user's machine, the .NET Framework compiles the MSIL commands into native code the first time a user chooses to start the program.

This leads to the inevitable question: How is this different from Java? The truth is that it's similar, but has a subtle difference. Java uses a virtual machine/runtime to run what's known as *byte code*—the intermediate layer of a Java application that's created during compilation. On an end user's machine, a Java virtual machine interprets this code line by line each time the application runs. .NET is different in that it actually compiles small chunks of the application's MSIL to native machine language *before* the program runs. This allows .NET to optimize the code for the user's microprocessor. In theory, this makes the application run much faster and efficiently than Java code.

This new methodology can run on any platform (Windows, Macintosh, Unix, and so on) that has a .NET runtime installed. Therein, of course, lies the rub—as of this writing, the Framework exists only for Windows, but an open-source version of it for Linux and Unix is in the works.

Understanding Dependencies in .NET

SCMs in the Windows world used to live with the everyday horror of application delivery—trying to figure out, usually through trial and error, which Microsoft Dynamic Link Libraries (DLLs) must be distributed to support your applications. Worse yet, you were consistently forced to determine which builds of those DLLs should be installed depending on their version and appropriate operating systems. Frankly, it's amazing that previous versions of Windows ever worked properly after countless applications installed system DLLs willy-nilly.

Microsoft has tried to address this problem with Visual Studio .NET and the newer Windows operating systems. Windows 2000 and XP provide safety checks that prevent rogue applications from overwriting necessary system DLLs. And (finally!) Visual Studio .NET gives you the ability to see a list of dependent system objects before you build installations.

In addition to the previous features available through the Framework, you can now distance yourself from the Registry and its excruciatingly difficult method of handling Component Object Model (COM) objects. Much like in the Unix world, you can now encapsulate applications and their dependent DLLs into a single directory. Of course, developers can still utilize the Registry for user settings; however, you no longer have to register your objects or worry about what might happen should an end user decide to play with RegEdit.

NOTE *This isn't the end to objects that share common code—as I discuss later in the chapter, you just handle them differently. And COM isn't necessarily going away either—your developers can still exploit pre-existing COM objects in much the same way as before. It is, however, to your advantage (and to the developers' as well) to upgrade older COM objects to the new .NET format.*

Unlike with COM, .NET objects are now private by default. In the past, developers who didn't want their COM objects exploited by third parties used obscure naming conventions and tried to ensure that the objects were devoid of documentation. .NET no longer publishes interfaces to any program that might ask for them; however, you can still find this information if you know an assembly's location on the hard drive.

Another distinct advantage to using the .NET Framework is that you can install different versions of the same objects. Previously, COM provided this kind of backward compatibility with its "append, never delete" architecture. It's the responsibility of the COM developer, however, to maintain this compatibility, and it's often abused. In contrast, the .NET Framework allows you to run two different versions of the same object at the same time. In the true "do-no-harm" fashion, you can install newer versions of objects without having to overwrite a properly working previous one. Applications then choose which version of an object to run based upon how they were written.

Special Delivery

The delivery and deployment of Visual Studio applications has never been easier. Reminiscent of the DOS and Unix old days, you can now use a simple xcopy command to move your application in its entirety to wherever you choose. This depends, of course, upon whether your developers have followed the proper .NET guidelines.

SCMs will find this new method of application organization to be the Holy Grail of deployment. Simply pick up an application directory and place it wherever it needs to go. No Registry. No system files. No previous operating system nightmares.

Businesses are constantly searching for new cost-effective ways of delivering software. With the Internet becoming more ubiquitous, the .NET Framework is designed to meet this need. When properly architected, functionality can be delivered over the Internet in discreet units *based upon the user's need*. As a user clicks a menu item, the functionality downloads "on the fly" to the machine. In another scenario, an application can check for new versions of its objects at startup and then automatically install upgraded components as desired.

Does this portend the death of CD and box delivery? Probably not in the near future. At the Internet's current speeds, users are inconvenienced when they download enterprise-sized products. When architected correctly, however, it's certainly feasible to distribute small- or medium-sized applications in this manner. And for company intranets, you can exploit Active Directory to easily push .NET applications through the pipes for an enterprise-wide deployment.

"Parts Is Parts"

Although similar in nature to previous versions of Visual Studio, Microsoft has changed the terminology and functionality for the architecture of source code. The two most important objects in the .NET world are now the solution and the assembly—the much improved workspace and project, respectively.

Introducing the Solution

Microsoft addressed the need to work with multiple projects in tandem by introducing the *workspace* in Visual Studio 6.0. This pretty much summed up the workspace's
function—it was a personalized work area for developers and wasn't intended for
inclusion in the source control database. For small applications written in one language, SCMs could easily populate a workspace with several projects and then use
the batch build functionality for creation. This worked quite well in lieu of having a
build script.

The .NET version of Visual Studio takes this capability several steps further.
The project-gathering functionality of the workspace and the configuration ability
of the project have combined into what's now known as the *solution*. From an
SCM perspective, this is a great benefit.

Coding in Multiple Programming Languages

Because they share the same common runtime libraries, projects written in any
.NET language can now co-exist in the same solution. In addition to the obvious
advantage of having an entire application, regardless of the language used for
objects, available in one setting, developers can now build the complete version
of a product when testing code integrations. For instance, a C++ programmer can
modify a server component and, in the same "workspace," immediately test an
applicable Visual Basic client application to determine the robustness of the
change.

To make a good thing even better, .NET installations are now included as projects inside of solutions. Imagine that! In the time spent to click the mouse (and then
walk away to get some coffee), a developer can build all the projects contained in a
solution, regardless of the .NET language in which they were built, and encapsulate
the output into a single Microsoft Installer (MSI) package.

Uh-oh—starting to think Microsoft is trying to put you out of a job? Don't
sweat it too much—this type of automation frees you from the drudgery of menial
tasks and allows you to work on other more meaningful ones.

Setting Up Your Application Solutions

Depending on the scale of your application, Microsoft recommends three ways to
set up your solutions. An active discussion with your developers is in order before
making these choices—this equally affects them.

The "All-in-One" Approach

For small applications, it's definitely in your best interest to have only one solution that includes all the projects for your application. In one fell swoop, you can build the entire package—including an installation!—with a single mouse click or command-line call. Other advantages to the all-in-one approach include the ease of project referencing and software versioning (discussed later in the chapter).

As always, there's a flip side. Depending on how developers reference projects, a one-line change of code can force the rebuild of the entire solution—though this safety check isn't necessarily a bad thing. And if the solution contains many projects, your developers may need to proactively download the latest source to ensure that their code is properly integrated. Hard disk size limitations and the annoyance of navigating through many unrelated projects are other considerations to keep in mind when determining your application's architecture.

The "Partitioned" Solution

In many cases, partitioning your solutions into discrete parts makes a lot of sense. For instance, you may put your server application projects into one solution and your client application projects into another. In this fashion, developers work only with the code to which they're directly related.

In this scenario, you can ease the building task by creating a separate private solution that holds all of the projects. This second solution, not necessarily available to the developers, should also include the installation; however, you can use smaller-sized MSIs for each partitioned solution.

The downside to this approach is that you must add new projects to both solutions whenever they're introduced. This architecture also makes dependency checking more difficult.

The "Multi-Solution" Solution

Frankly, there aren't really any tangible benefits to keeping each project in its own solution—other than that there are always going to be some folks who are resistant to change. Developers will find in the long run that this architecture creates more work. Instead of using easy project references when they access code in other projects, they'll instead have to use file references—a much more tedious approach.

Many experts strongly recommend not using this as a standard solution model. I agree with them.

Lawful Assemblies

As discussed in the introduction to this chapter, Windows-based executables (such as .EXE and .DLL files) created by Visual Studio .NET no longer contain code that's native to the local computer processor. Instead, applications are compiled into MSIL and are compiled to native language (not interpreted!) at runtime. Applications are built piece by piece—the Framework compiles blocks of instruction the first time they're used.

These MSIL versions of applications are called *assemblies*. They still look like the same old applications—they have the familiar .EXE and .DLL extensions. And if you drop them into a text editor, you still see the old jumble of hex code and the admonishment that "this program cannot be run in DOS mode." Don't be fooled—this isn't your older brother's native code. Run this code on a version of Windows without the .NET Framework installed and start counting the runtime errors.

NOTE *There's an exception to the MSIL rule. It's still possible to create native machine code using the Visual C++ language. In fact, those projects build to native Win32 code by default. Developers can change this behavior so that Visual Studio creates MSIL assemblies instead. With its ability to exploit .NET features that aren't accessible to the other languages, Microsoft touts C++ MSIL code as the way to "produce the meanest, leanest .NET Framework applications."[1]*

Assemblies provide a way to expose data types to other executables without using COM. Furthermore, .NET Framework assemblies have an attached *manifest* that details the data types included in it. No more type libraries or annoying Registry settings! Instead, the assembly encapsulates this data into itself. The manifest also includes version information, security constraints, and assembly dependencies in addition to the data types. Though it may seem a little extraneous to you because SCMs have little need to know an assembly's data types, you can still explore an assembly's manifest just for interest's sake by using the ILDASM tool located in the BIN directory of the Microsoft Visual Studio .NET FRAMEWORKSDK directory. Figure 9-1 displays what might appear if you drag and drop an application onto ILDASM's open window.

---

1.   Microsoft's "Dr. GUI on Visual C++ .NET" article, February 2002

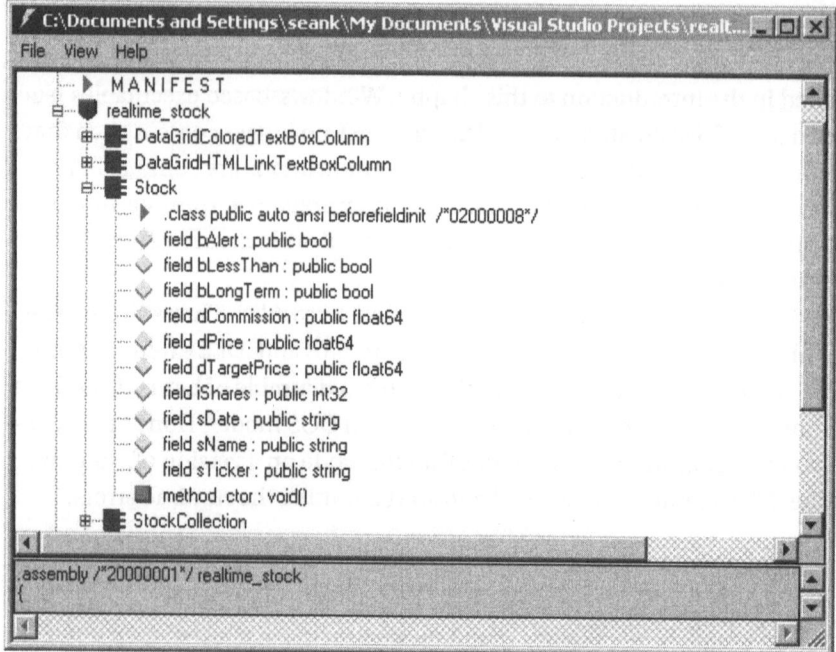

Figure 9-1. An assembly manifest displayed in the ILDASM tool

A single application can be a single assembly. However, there are times when it makes more sense to break up large applications into small discreet blocks of code. This can make distribution much easier—especially if you're distributing your application over the Internet. By breaking up the application, you can ensure that your users only download the portions of the software they currently need. For example, you might have your word processor's spell checker download upon first use instead of with the initial download of the application. By breaking the spell checker into its own encapsulated binary, you ensure that the word processor will work correctly with or without it.

In this case, you must somehow link your binaries together to let the word processor know that the spell checker exists and where to get it. This linking mechanism is known as creating a *multifile assembly*. The binaries that make up a multifile assembly are known as *modules*. All of the module's data types and other metadata are listed in a common manifest.

NOTE   *For the most part, creating single-file and multifile assemblies really falls into the responsibility realm of developers. However, because you must make developers aware of deployment restrictions, it remains important that you understand your product's architecture and terminology.*

Sharing Assemblies

By default, assemblies are considered private. This means that other assemblies can't access the data types of an assembly—otherwise known as *functions*, *subroutines*, and *variable members*—unless the assembly has been shared or its location on the hard drive is known.

If developers choose to make the members of assemblies public, or published to other assemblies for use, they must add the assemblies to the user machine's Global Assembly Cache (GAC). Using the GAC is analogous to registering COM objects; however, the difference is that all COM objects must be registered whereas only shared assemblies need be included in the GAC.

Shared assemblies must reside in a specific location in the Windows directory. This is in direct contrast to COM's "install anywhere" capability. Using a shared assembly thus diminishes the ability to install a product simply by using File Transfer Protocol (FTP) or copying a directory structure. From a development perspective, assemblies must expressly be designated as shared by setting several properties (such as creating unique identifiers) before they can be built and distributed.

Shared assemblies reside in the WINDOWS\ASSEMBLIES directory. Figure 9-2 displays an example of some of the objects you can find in the GAC.

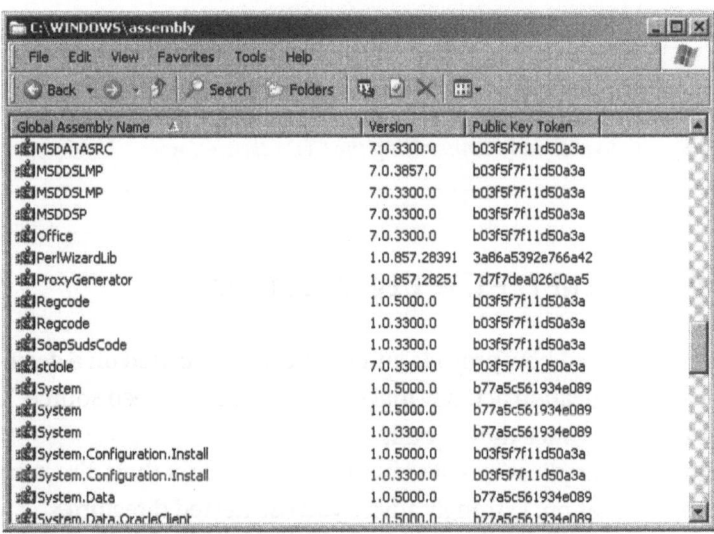

Figure 9-2. Assemblies in the Windows ASSEMBLIES directory

Side-by-Side Versions of Assemblies

One of the unique benefits you receive by using .NET assemblies is the ability to have more than one version of a shared component installed on the same machine. COM certainly handles this scenario somewhat less gracefully than the .NET Framework does.

For example, if you look back at Figure 9-2, you can see that two different versions of MSDDSUMP are installed on the machine. These two assemblies are both installed in full—meaning that they're distinct and complete application files. Any assembly that references the 7.0.3300.0 version of MSDDSUMP doesn't break when the new 7.0.3857.0 version of the component is installed. As you can see, properly versioning your shared assemblies is extremely important. I detail versioning more thoroughly later in this chapter.

Contrasting this behavior, COM components must be architected to be backward compatible and replace previous versions—a trick that's quite error-prone. You can see that the .NET formula seems preferable—but don't give up completely on COM just yet. Developers can still reference pre-existing COM objects as necessary. Although it's likely that developers will greatly desire to convert COM components into .NET assemblies, you may be forced to continue using COM objects considered lower in priority or provided by third-party vendors.

 NOTE *Most of the experts agree: When introducing .NET assemblies to your product, you should rearchitecture all COM components to the new format. Microsoft appears to be slowly deprecating the COM technology.*

Understanding the .NET File Organization

Visual Studio .NET has changed how projects and source are organized on a development machine. This organization actually makes it a bit easier to keep source separate and find executables once they're built.

When architecting your applications, it's important to consider their directory structures before project creation. I strongly advise you use nested directories when creating solutions with children projects—this makes navigating to projects more intuitive and also eases source control management. The top-level directory should contain the solution—created in one of the models (all-in-one, partitioned, or multi-solution) discussed earlier in the chapter.

TIP *All .NET projects are placed, by default, in a folder called VISUAL STUDIO PROJECTS in the MY DOCUMENTS directory. This not only makes it more difficult to keep developer source trees in sync, it also means that scripts must reference long filenames with dreaded space characters. I advise you to change this default directory to a friendlier location such as C:\SRC. To make this change, choose Tools ➤ Options and navigate to the Projects and Solutions tab where you'll be able to change the default location for Visual Studio projects.*

As an example, let's say your company has decided to build stock market tools for savvy business people. You'll include three tools in this application: a real-time stock ticker, an analysis tool for stocks, and a program that allows you to purchase or sell commodities at will.

If you were to create a directory tree for this application, it might look something like the one in Figure 9-3. The STOCKS directory holds your solution and its related data, and under it the REALTIMESTOCKS, STOCKANALYSIS, and STOCK-PURCHASE projects live in child directories. Note the inclusion of an MSI setup project that I've called INSTALL. Based upon the programming language chosen, each project has its own child directories, such as BIN and OBJ, that will hold object files and executables.

Figure 9-3. A proper solution directory structure displayed in Windows Explorer

 NOTE *The familiar DEBUG, RELEASE, and other configuration directories are now located in the BIN directory. Nonexecutable object code is now separated into the OBJ directory. This makes finding executables in a large assembly much easier.*

To build this solution, simply choose File ➤ New ➤ Blank Solution in the
Visual Studio IDE. Using the Location text box, navigate to the directory where the
solution should live. Make sure not to type the name of the solution in the Location text box—otherwise, you'll create a double folder. Instead, give it the name of
your source directory—for instance, C:\SRC. You should see the solution in the
Name text box, as displayed in Figure 9-4.

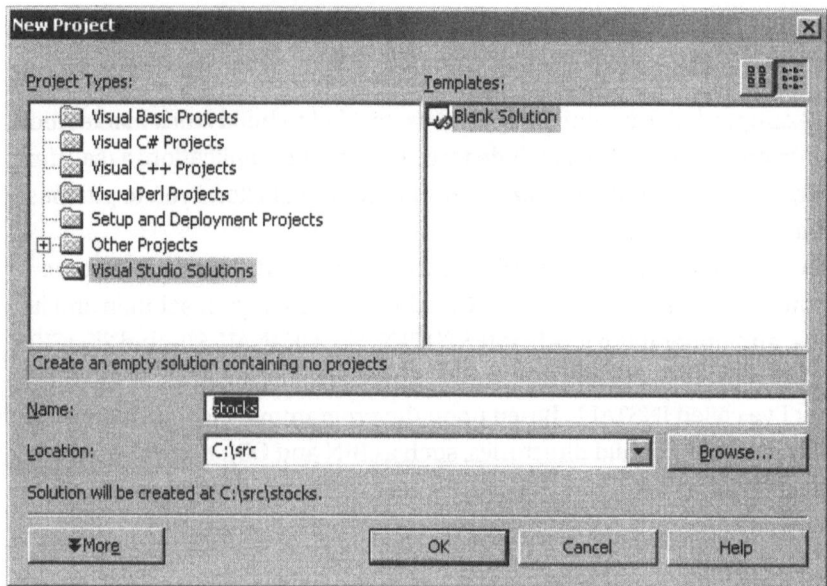

Figure 9-4. Giving the project a location of C:\SRC

If you're adding existing projects to the solution that haven't previously been
created in the source control, now is the time to drop them to the newly created
solution directory. Simply add the projects by right-clicking the solution in the
Solution Explorer window and choosing Add ➤ Existing Project. For new projects,
choose Add ➤ New Project. If there's a common installation for the application,
add that by choosing Add ➤ New Project and selecting Setup Project from the
Setup and Deployment Projects folder.

NOTE   *Chapter 10, "Installations," discusses creating .NET installations using
the IDE with much more detail.*

After adding the projects, the Solution Explorer might look like Figure 9-5.

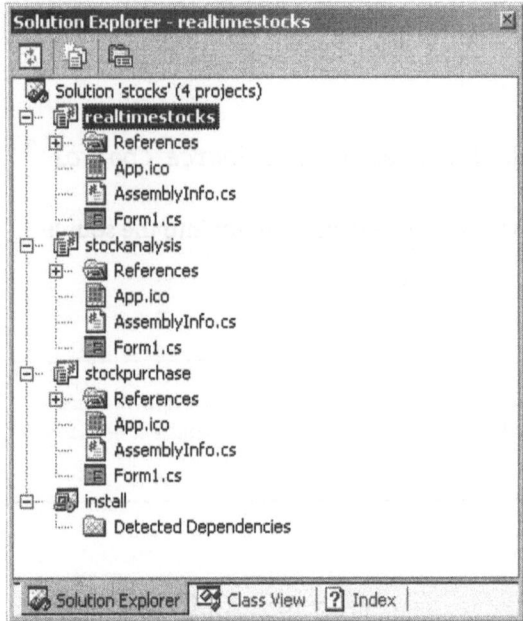

Figure 9-5. A proper solution hierarchy in Visual Studio's Solution Explorer

Now that the directory structure on your local drive and the solution hierarchy in Solution Explorer are synced, it's time to add your solution and projects to the source control database.

Source Control and Visual Studio .NET

Before you actually add your solution to the source control, you should be aware that Visual Studio creates several application-specific files that don't need and shouldn't be checked into your source control database. As I've mentioned before, the smaller the database, the healthier it is—for that reason, you should encourage developers to check in only those files that make up the "code" and leave out extraneous build and settings files.

NOTE *One of the benefits of using Visual Studio SourceSafe integration is that it automatically knows which files should and shouldn't be checked into the source control database. See the "Using the SourceSafe Solution/Project Integration" section for more information.*

Visual Studio .NET Files to Be Included in the Source Control

You should treat the following file types as code and check them into the source control database.

NOTE *SourceSafe is integrated into Visual Studio, and many of these files types will automatically be added to the source control database when added from the IDE.*

*.SLN: This file keeps track of projects and their interdependencies within the current solution.

*.CSPROG, *.VBPROJ, and so on: These files contain project information, such as build settings and the source files of the project.

*.CS, *.VB, *.ASP, *.CPP, *.VBS, *.JS, *.XML, *.HTM, and so on: These files contain the source code for the application. Keep in mind that it's possible to integrate Visual Studio with a number of different programming languages—so this is by no means an exhaustive list. Check with your developers as necessary about specific file extensions that may not be listed.

*.RESX, *.ASPX, and so on: These files contain information that define application resources. Again, this isn't a complete list. Check with your developers as necessary about specific file extensions that may not be listed.

*.ICO, *.BMP, *.JPG, *.CUR, and so on: These are individual resource files for bitmaps, icons, and cursors. Check with your developers as necessary about specific file extensions that may not be listed.

Visual Studio .NET Files to Be Excluded from the Source Control

You shouldn't check the following file types into the source control database:

*.SUO, *.USER, and *.WEBINFO: These are individual user settings files that can contain hard-coded paths to projects or solutions. Because many developers work on different drives or use different source paths, it's important that these files not be checked into the source control database.

*.EXE, *.OCX, *.DLL, and so on: Any executable file that's created during the build process shouldn't be checked into the source control database.

*.PDB and *.DBG: These files are automatically generated during the build process for debugging and can be discarded.

*.OBJ, *.PCH, *.NCB, *.OPT, and *.APS: When building native format applications using Visual C++, these output files are automatically generated by the build process and can be discarded.

Any files located in the BIN and OBJ directories: These output files are automatically generated by the build process and can be discarded.

Using the SourceSafe Solution/Project Integration

Visual Studio and SourceSafe are tightly integrated in the new version of the IDE. Almost all of the functionality provided by the SourceSafe Explorer has been added to Visual Studio. Microsoft recommends that developers *only* use the Visual Studio integration when adding new solutions or checking in code. Visual Studio is aware of which files should and shouldn't be checked into the source control database, and, more importantly, Visual Studio is only "source control aware" of solution files that it has added to the database itself.

 NOTE *Because the Visual Studio SourceSafe integration can get confused if you use more than one tool, your team should make an exclusive choice between it and the SourceSafe Explorer.*

If you've had the bad luck to check in a solution from the SourceSafe Explorer instead of the Visual Studio integration, there are two choices available to make amends. First, you can delete the project out of SourceSafe and re-add it properly through the Visual Studio integration. In this scenario, you lose all historical information and previous code versions. Second, you can use Visual Studio to "bind" the currently loaded solution to an existing one already added to SourceSafe. This is more complicated than the first option but preserves historical information. Choose File ➤ Source Control ➤ Change Source Control. Visual Studio opens a dialog box similar to Figure 9-6.

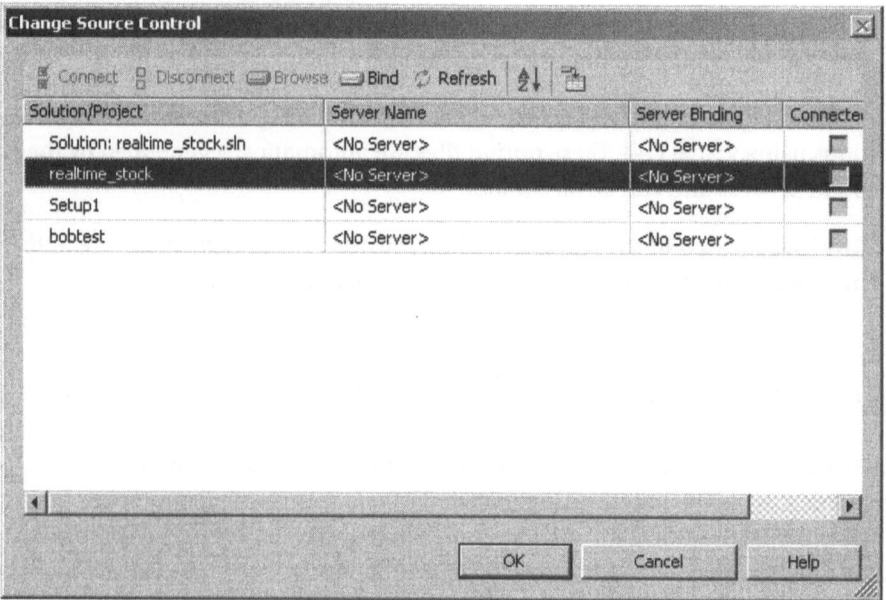

Figure 9-6. The Change Source Control dialog box

This dialog box allows you to bind existing solutions and projects in Source-Safe to those currently open in Visual Studio .NET. Simply highlight an object listed and choose the Bind toolbar item. Browse to the correct SourceSafe project directory and choose OK. You'll be offered the choice to check out the files in the project—in addition, you may be warned that the files on your hard drive don't match those listed in the source control database. Take care! If you do a standard Get command though the Visual Studio integration, you'll *write over any new code that hasn't yet been checked into SourceSafe*. Once this step is complete, Visual Studio is "aware" of that project, and the Solution Explorer changes to indicate file checkout status. Figure 9-7 displays an example of this. Note the new icons that indicate whether files are checked out or read-only.

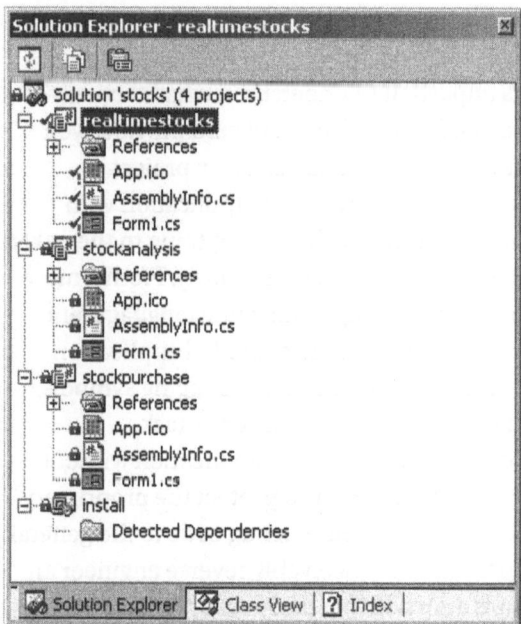

Figure 9-7. Checked-out files in Solution Explorer

Keep in mind that choosing the second option may mean that the directory structures on the hard drive and in Solution Explorer aren't synchronized. This can be confusing to everyone working on the code—it might be worth your while to move projects in SourceSafe so that they match the hierarchy setup in Visual Studio *before* binding the projects.

Building Applications

As before, there are two ways to build Visual Studio .NET applications:

- Using the Build command in the IDE

- Using a command line, Perl, or a Visual Basic Script (VBScript) build script

You should choose a method based upon the complexity of the application and the unique actions that might be required for a successful build. Now that MSI setup programs are integrated into the solution, it's actually quite easy to build the product completely from the IDE with just one mouse click—see Chapter 10, "Installations," for more information.

Using the Configuration Manager

Before starting the build, however, it's important to understand what's actually going to be built. By default, the Visual Studio New Project Wizard provides you with both "debug" and "release" solution configurations for every project.

Building the debug configuration of a project creates an application with debugging symbols attached to it. This doesn't really change anything to the naked eye—the application itself runs in the same way, albeit more slowly. From a more technical perspective, these debugging symbols map to machine language, and developers use it to debug code by stepping through the compiled application using the language with which they're familiar. Without the debugging symbols, developers are forced to step through machine code—an arduous task.

The release configuration of a project creates the same application without the overhead of providing debugging symbols. In order to protect the proprietary property of the company, it's important to never release debug code to the general public. Anyone with development expertise can conceivably reverse engineer an application that had debugging symbols attached to it fairly easily.

WORD OF THE DAY

ob·fus·cā'tion, *n.*

Keeping your source secret doesn't come out of the box.

By default, the .NET assemblies you create contain identifiers and algorithms that are easily identifiable should anyone choose to look. Malicious individuals can use simple tools to reverse engineer and, ultimately, steal your intellectual property as if you had handed them the source code yourself.

If you must protect your code through secrecy, you can better guard source by using an encryption tool that hides primary MSIL identifiers and metadata. This process is called *obfuscation*. The idea behind it is to create confusion by incomprehensibly changing as many identifiers within assemblies as possible without actually altering executable logic. And don't worry—obfuscation is a post-compilation step so your source code is completely unaffected should you decide to use the process.

If you're interested in a free obfuscation tool for personal use, try Dotfuscator by PreEmptive Solutions (http://www.preemptive.com). A professional edition is available for commercial use, but it can be a little pricey. Luckily, the plans for the next version of Visual Studio supposedly include a built-in "lite" version of PreEmptive Solution's obfuscation software.

Though some obfuscation tools have a Graphical User Interface (GUI) interface that can be "added in" to Visual Studio, I haven't at the time of this writing found one that can run inside the IDE between the time of object compilation and the generation of an install package. You won't find this to be as much of an issue if you're using scripts for building because most tools have a command-line interface. See Chapter 8, "Basic Builds," for more information on creating a build script for the command line.

This doesn't mean, however, that code produced by Visual Studio .NET in a release configuration is automatically protected from prying eyes. See the "Word of the Day" sidebar for more information on how to keep your code secret.

In addition to the debug and release configurations previously mentioned, it's possible to create any type of project configuration. Code can be optimized during compilation for many different situations. For instance, it's possible to build a product, such as a video driver, that's optimized for speed. Conversely, if building a downloadable application, developers may choose to optimize the build for file size.

Regardless of the optimization, Visual Studio allows these separate configurations to be created and saved with a unique name. The developers can edit these configurations by right-clicking the project in Solution Explorer, choosing Properties, and then navigating to the Configuration Properties folder. The default configuration loads, and its name displays in the Configuration drop-down combo box. In addition to the configurations already available, it's possible to make the same change to all available configurations by choosing the All Configurations option in the Configuration drop-down combo box.

To create a new project configuration, click the Configuration Manager button; alternatively, from the Visual Studio main menu, choose the Build ➤ Configuration Manager menu item. Once open, the Configuration Manager tool displays, as shown in Figure 9-8.

 NOTE *The Build menu appears only when a solution is loaded.*

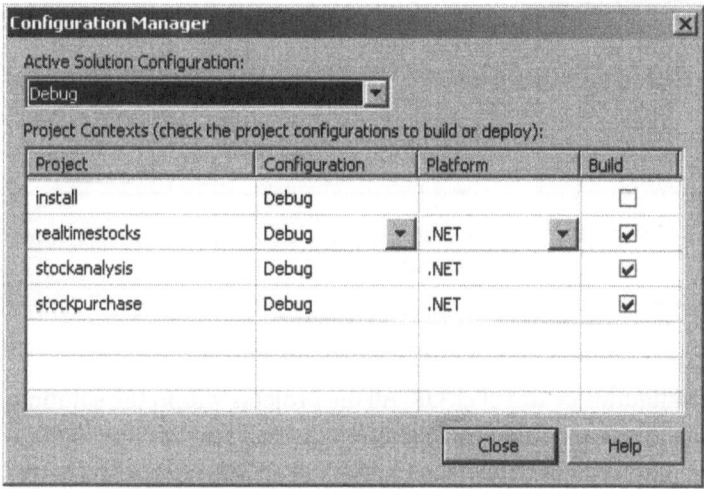

Figure 9-8. The Configuration Manager tool

A solution configuration is a combination set of all or some of the possible project configurations. The Active Solution Configuration drop-down combo box at the top of the Configuration Manager dialog box displays the configuration currently in use. The Project Contexts table shows you the project configurations that are created when this particular solution configuration is built.

The Project Contexts table lists all of the projects in the solution, their respective configurations for this solution configuration (there's a mouthful!), and a checkbox to determine whether each project should be built when you choose the Build Solution menu item. The currently displayed items relate only to the active build configuration item that's currently selected. Choose another active build configuration item, and all of the project configurations might (and probably will) change to new values.

NOTE *When you choose an active build configuration, it becomes the default build configuration until you choose a new one. This remains the case even if you close and reopen Visual Studio.*

To create a new configuration, choose the <New...> option from the Active Solution Configuration drop-down combo box, as displayed in Figure 9-9.

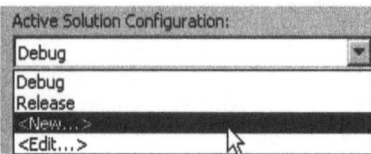

Figure 9-9. The Configuration Manager's Active Solution Configuration drop-down combo box

NOTE *You'll rarely need to create new configurations. The debug and release configurations are sufficient for most applications.*

Name the new configuration and click OK. All the projects within the solution appear, and each has the newly named configuration assigned to it in the Configuration column. At this time, you can close the Configuration Manager and change each project's configuration as necessary by right-clicking the project in the Solution Explorer and choosing Properties.

TIP *Don't personalize the default debug and release configurations. Instead, create new configurations to replace them when necessary. Doing otherwise causes confusion to developers who expect them to perform consistently.*

Oddly enough, the ability to change the order in which projects are built isn't included as an option in the Configuration Manager. Instead, you must right-click the solution in the Solution Explorer and choose the Build Order menu item. Figure 9-10 displays this dialog box.

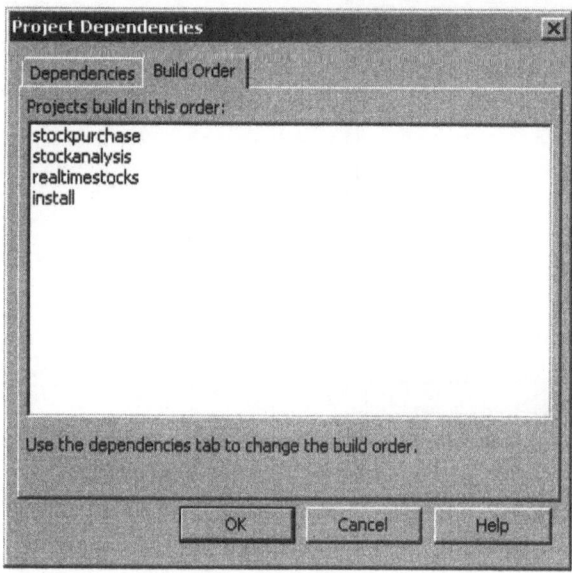

Figure 9-10. The Project Dependencies dialog box's Build Order tab

Don't bother trying to move the objects in this dialog box around—it's for display purposes only. Instead, choose the build order by creating dependencies in the Dependencies tab of this same dialog box, as displayed in Figure 9-11. For instance, if you want the REALTIMESTOCKS object to be built before STOCKPURCHASE, use the Dependencies tab to explicitly declare that the REALTIMESTOCKS object is a dependency of the STOCKPURCHASE object. Click back to the Build Order tab to see this change reflected.

TIP *If you have an installation as one of your projects, make it the startup object by right-clicking the solution and choosing it in the Startup Project property drop-down combo box. This makes the installation the default object to build when choosing to do so using the menus or shortcuts. In most cases, the projects included in the installation are considered its dependencies and will be automatically built.*

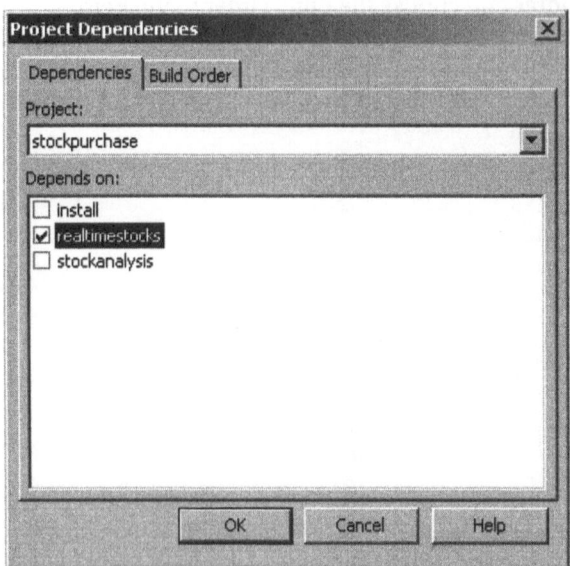

Figure 9-11. The Project Dependencies dialog box's Dependencies tab

Building Your Applications

Once your configurations are set, it's easy to build the complete solution from the IDE. Here's your checklist:

1. Update the version number and get the source as necessary. See the upcoming "Versioning Your Assemblies" section for more information regarding this step.

2. Open the Configuration Manager and choose the appropriate active solution configuration.

3. Choose the Build ➤ Build Solution menu item. Visual Studio builds all components and places them in their respective BIN directories.

It doesn't get much easier than that!

You may need to build several objects but not all of them. In this case, build each object by right-clicking the project in the Solution Explorer and choosing Build. Alternatively, it's possible to use the batch build functionality of Visual Studio. Choose Build ➤ Batch Build and click any combination of projects and configurations, as displayed in Figure 9-12. It's even possible to build every configuration of every project at the same time!

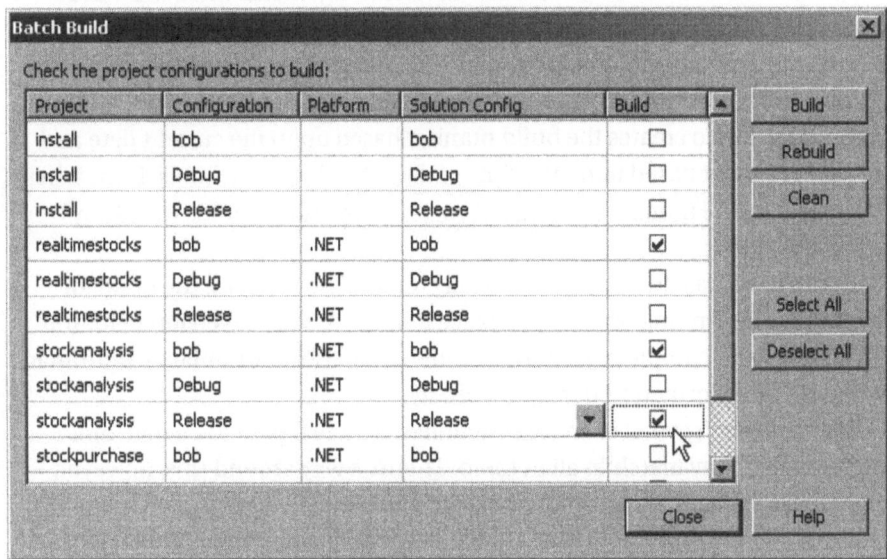

Figure 9-12. The Batch Build dialog box

Versioning Your Assemblies

Versioning components has always been extremely important, but with the advent of side-by-side components, it now takes on a more essential role when building your applications.

Visual Studio .NET makes this quite a bit easier to manage than with previous Microsoft IDEs. In Visual Studio 6.0, you placed version information in the .RC resource files for C++ and the .MAK project files for Visual Basic. Now all assemblies keep their version information in the same place. This file, by default, is called ASSEMBLYINFO.CS. Visual Studio places version, key signing, and other information into this file automatically on project creation.

Open the ASSEMBLYINFO.CS file and navigate down in the file until you see an example of an assembly's version information:

```
[assembly: AssemblyVersion("1.0.*")]
```

All new projects start at version 1.0, the first number reflecting the major application version number, followed by the minor. You can manually change this number to whatever versioning schematic you want to follow. Not so easily detected, Visual Studio also includes two other bits of versioning information: the build number and the revision number. The asterisk character (*) indicates to Visual Studio to automatically increment these two numbers. I might add that *increment* might not be the best word to describe what's happening...a better word might be *change*. Visual Studio creates the build number based upon the current date and the revision number based upon the time of day. This does two things: First, it helps to guarantee unique numbers. Second, it ensures that future builds will always have higher values.

You can use an asterisk to automatically update the revision, the build, or both numbers depending on how you place it in the AssemblyVersion field. You can even remove it completely, but this hinders Visual Studio's ability to automatically change the information during builds.

When you have several or more assemblies, it's a real pain to change build numbers so that they match in all of them. There's a way around this, however, that can make synchronizing build numbers much easier. You can follow along in this example by starting a new solution in Visual Studio and populating it with several projects. I'll use the STOCKS solution as an example, but the changes I make are applicable to any project.

 NOTE   *This example assumes that your solution and projects have already been added to a source control database and that the directory structure in the source matches the parent-child relationships in the solution.*

First, in Windows Explorer, you divvy out the common version information into a new file. Start by copying the ASSEMBLYINFO.CS file in one of the project's directories and saving it as ASSEMBLYVERSION.CS. Second, use Solution Explorer to add the new file to your project. Any file with the extension .CS in a project gets built when it's added to an assembly, so you don't have to change any of the project's properties. As a side note, you can place assembly directives in general, such as version information, in any file that ends with the .CS extension.

Before compiling, be sure to remove the original version information from
ASSEMBLYINFO.CS and any nonversion information from the new ASSEM-
BLYVERSION.CS file. Otherwise, the compiler balks at the repeated directives.

The revamped ASSEMBLYINFO.CS might look something like Listing 9-1.

Listing 9-1. ASSEMBLYINFO.CS

```
using System.Reflection;
using System.Runtime.CompilerServices;

//
// General information about an assembly is controlled through the following
// set of attributes. Change these attribute values to modify the information
// associated with an assembly.
//
[assembly: AssemblyTitle("RealTimeStocks")]
[assembly: AssemblyDescription("A real time stock ticker.")]
[assembly: AssemblyConfiguration("")]


//
// In order to sign your assembly you must specify a key to use. Refer to the
// Microsoft .NET Framework documentation for more information on assembly signing.
//
// Use the attributes below to control which key is used for signing.
//
// Notes:
//  (*) If no key is specified, the assembly is not signed.
//  (*) KeyName refers to a key that has been installed in the Crypto Service
//       Provider (CSP) on your machine. KeyFile refers to a file which contains
//       a key.
//  (*) If the KeyFile and the KeyName values are both specified, the
//       following processing occurs:
//       (1) If the KeyName can be found in the CSP, that key is used.
//       (2) If the KeyName does not exist and the KeyFile does exist, the key
//            in the KeyFile is installed into the CSP and used.
//  (*) In order to create a KeyFile, you can use the sn.exe (Strong Name) utility.
//       When specifying the KeyFile, the location of the KeyFile should be
//       relative to the project output directory which is
//       %Project Directory%\obj\<configuration>. For example, if your KeyFile is
//       located in the project directory, you would specify the AssemblyKeyFile
//       attribute as [assembly: AssemblyKeyFile("..\\..\\mykey.snk")]
//  (*) Delay Signing is an advanced option - see the Microsoft .NET Framework
//       documentation for more information on this.
```

```
//
[assembly: AssemblyDelaySign(false)]
[assembly: AssemblyKeyFile("")]
[assembly: AssemblyKeyName("")]
```

Notice the two lines in bold are specific only to the REALTIMESTOCKS assembly. In your projects, this should match the appropriate name. The three lines near the bottom of the file are for file-specific key signing information.

Copy ASSEMBLYINFO.CS to the other projects in the solution—in my case, I'll copy it to the STOCKPURCHASE and STOCKANALYSIS projects—and then update each of their unique attributes (the name, purpose, and signing information) as necessary. You're ready to check in the ASSEMBLYINFO.CS file for all projects!

Now let's take a look at the second file. ASSEMBLYVERSION.CS now contains information that I consider common to all the STOCKS projects. It might look like Listing 9-2.

Listing 9-2. ASSEMBLYVERSION.CS

```
using System.Reflection;
using System.Runtime.CompilerServices;

//
// General Information about an assembly is controlled through the following
// set of attributes. Change these attribute values to modify the information
// associated with an assembly.
//
[assembly: AssemblyCompany("cmReady Ssytems Incorporated")]
[assembly: AssemblyProduct("The Stock Program")]
[assembly: AssemblyCopyright("(c) 2003 cmReady Ssytems Incorporated ")]


//
// Version information for an assembly consists of the following four values:
//
//      Major Version
//      Minor Version
//      Build Number
//      Revision
//
// You can specify all the values or you can default the Revision and Build
// Numbers by using the '*' as shown below:

[assembly: AssemblyVersion("2.1.*")]
```

Notice that the lines in bold can now apply to any of the assemblies in the solution. Examples of these lines include the common umbrella name, company name, and copyright date. I also want each of them to have the same version number, 2.1. The asterisk indicates that the compiler should automatically create the build and revision numbers.

Now for the fun part…making the common ASSEMBLYVERSION.CS file available to all projects. Your goal should be that you check in the file only once—and have the new changes propagate to all the projects in the solution. Take the ASSEMBLYVERSION.CS file and check it into one (and only one!) relative project in your source control tool. Assuming you have a tool, such as SourceSafe, that allows you to share a file in multiple projects (see Chapter 6, "SourceSafe," for more information on this nifty feature), share the ASSEMBLYVERSION.CS file to the other projects in the solution. For example, I might add the file to the REALTIMESTOCKS project and then share it to the STOCKPURCHASE and STOCKANALYSIS projects. The same file now exists in three locations—and using this share feature ensures that I only ever have to change it once to effect the change in all locations.

CAUTION *Visual Studio's integration of SourceSafe doesn't handle checking out shared files well. For instance, let's say you have three projects in your solution that each use the same shared version information file. When you try to check out the complete solution, the SourceSafe integration checks out the first project correctly. However, when it reaches the second project, it'll see that the shared file is already checked out and cancels out without finishing the job. To get around this limitation, check out each project separately. The SourceSafe Explorer doesn't have this limitation.*

That's it! You've now created a single-version solution. When ready for a build, simply change the version number in one of the projects, check it into your source control tool, and then "re-get" the file in all the projects before building.

NOTE *Because Visual Studio's automatic versioning tool uses the time and date when updating versions, using the automatic asterisk tool will cause each project to have a different build and revision number. To ensure that the complete version number is synchronized for projects, use a four-digit version (for instance, 3.2.1234.1234) instead of using the asterisk operator.*

Using Scripting Tools in a Visual Studio .NET Build

Has the need for build scripts gone away? Not really. The following are several scenarios where you might find that a build script is necessary:

- When you must complete builds without human intervention. For instance, you might create a nightly build that takes place at 3 A.M. so it's finished when the developers walk in the door.

- When you work with a partitioned or multi-solution environment and it's not convenient to manage several solutions separately.

- When you want the version number to automatically change and synchronize in many projects.

- When you must use an obfuscation tool to mask binary objects.

- When an SCM replacement must complete builds during your vacations and dentist appointments.

Using Scripts or Commands Inside Visual Studio

If your need for automation includes a single step, such as updating a file or opening an application, you may want to use Visual Studio's "prebuild" or "post-build" steps. In the past, only C++ projects had this functionality. This remains somewhat true in Visual Studio .NET—but there's a good a trick to get around that limitation.

Let's say you have a solution with four C# language projects. Unfortunately, C# projects don't provide you with the ability to add prebuild steps. Knowing that C++ projects do, you can add one to your solution to fulfill this need. To do so, right-click the parent solution in the Solution Explorer and choose Add ➤ Add New Project. Don't choose the default C++ application listed—instead, choose a Visual Studio C++ Makefile Project, as displayed in Figure 9-13. Enter its name—you might call it VersionChange to synchronize project versions—and click OK.

Once you've created the new project, you must configure it to be a utility program. Do this by selecting the project in Solution Explorer, right-clicking it, and choosing Properties. Under the General tab, change the Configuration type from Makefile to Utility. This tells Visual Studio that you plan its use for only custom steps and that it won't create any output for this project during the build.

Now choose the Pre-Build Event tab from its parent, Build Events, as displayed in Figure 9-14. In the Command Line text box, add the syntax for the command that should run. This is equivalent to running a line in a command window...so be sure that the path is explicit! In this example, I've added a Perl script that increments build numbers.

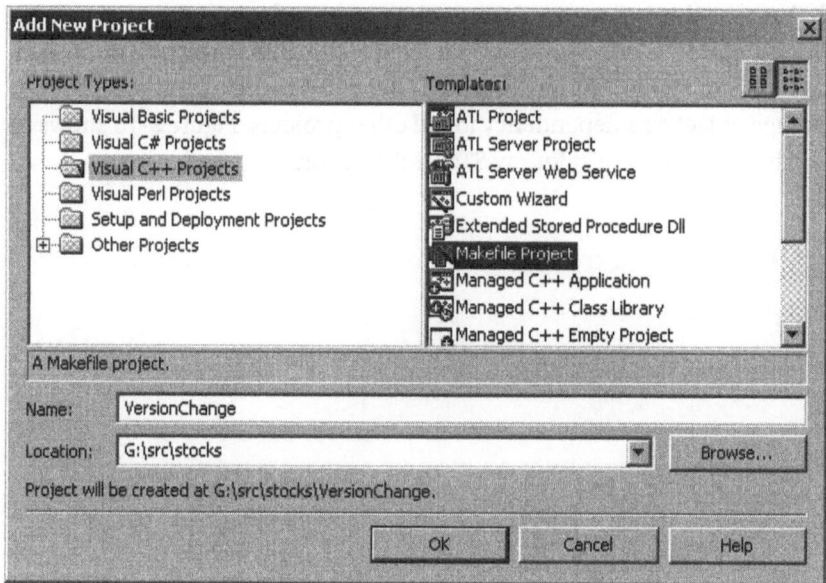

Figure 9-13. Creating a utility makefile in the Add New Project dialog box

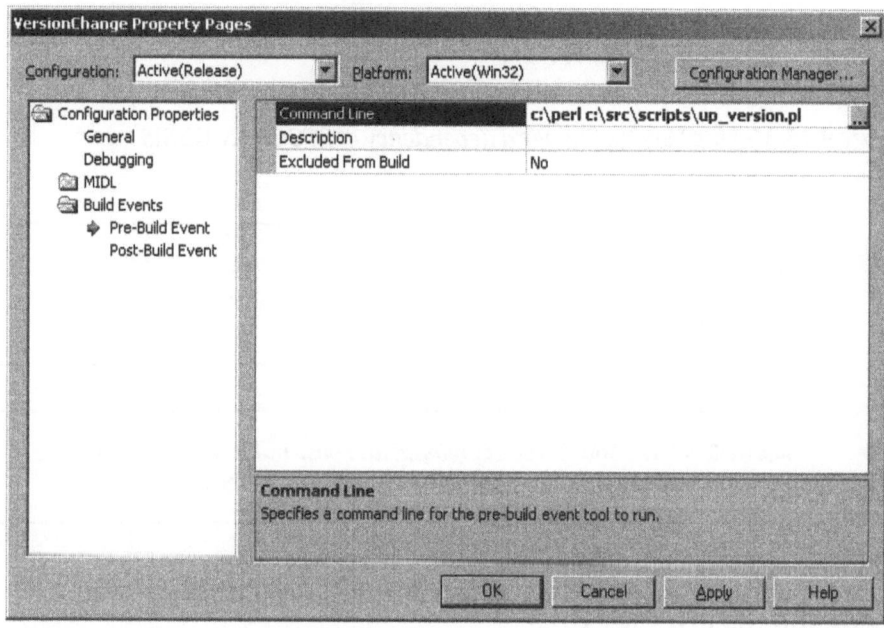

Figure 9-14. The utility makefile property pages

Lastly, because this is a prebuild step, you need to make sure that this object is always "built" before the other projects—much like the dummy targets discussed in Chapter 8, "Basic Builds." Go back to the Dependencies dialog box and list the VersionChange object as a dependency for all other projects. Figure 9-15 shows an example of the dependency list for my STOCKS solution.

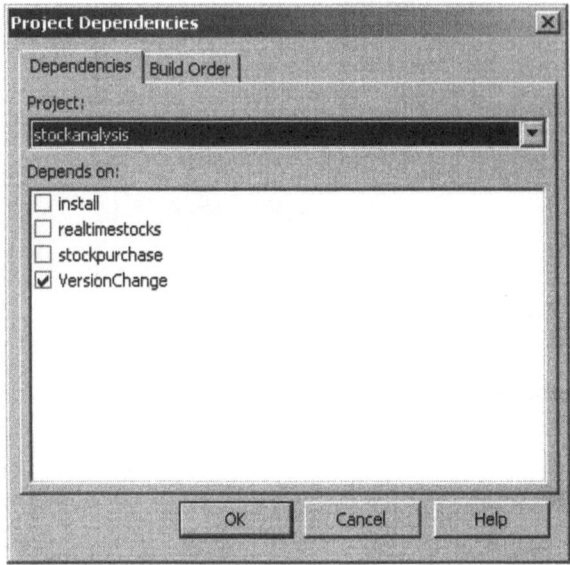

Figure 9-15. Making VersionChange a dependency of STOCKANALYSIS

 NOTE *If you were to create a post-build step, you must set all of the other projects as dependencies for the VersionChange object—thereby forcing it to be built last.*

 ANOTHER NOTE *You can't put prebuild and post-build steps into the same makefile utility object. You must create two different objects.*

Creating Build Scripts

You may want to build a complete build script as discussed in Chapter 8, "Basic Builds." If you do so, remember that it's important to map out the steps to create a functioning build before the script is written.

> **NOTE**   *You may have skipped Chapter 8, "Basic Builds," in your rush to get to .NET-specific information. That chapter holds a great deal of information about how to map out, create, and test build scripts. You may want to peruse that chapter now and then return to this section.*

In order to create a build script, you'll need to know the syntax for calling Visual Studio .NET from the command line. It's as follows:

```
"C:\PROGRAM FILES\MICROSOFT VISUAL STUDIO .NET\COMMON7\IDE\DEVENV.EXE" ↵
solutionfile.sln  /build solutionconfig [/command line switch]
```

> **NOTE**   *The path to DEVENV.EXE may vary depending on the choices you made during the Visual Studio installation process. The path listed previously is the typical default.*

For instance, if I were to build my STOCKS solution with debugging information attached, I might use the following command line:

```
c:\ >"C:\PROGRAM FILES\MICROSOFT VISUAL STUDIO .NET\COMMON7\IDE\DEVENV.EXE" ↵
G:\SRC\STOCKS\STOCKS.SLN  /build DEBUG
```

> **TIP** *You can use numerous switches with DEVENV.EXE—to review them, run the application on the command line with the /? switch.*

Using Automated Utilities

In Chapter 8, "Basic Builds," you used the MAKE script to build. You've exploited its strengths to determine dependencies and build your components in the proper order.

As you automate your Visual Studio .NET build, however, you may find that MAKE is too limited in its abilities to complete nonstandard operations. For tasks such as incrementing your build labels and date/time stamping your files, turn to other scripting tools better suited to those kinds of jobs.

There are many different kinds of scripting tools. I'll discuss three of the most popular in this chapter. It's out of the scope of this book to detail each of them—however, there will be enough information here for you to make an informed decision about which scripting tool you might like to use.

All of the script tools mentioned in this chapter use simple text files as scripts. These are the file types you can open in Windows Notepad. I suggest, however, using a hardier editor. Visual Studio itself is a great text editor—and it's already on the build machine! But if you need one with slightly less overhead, I've played with these in the past:

- **Borland CodeWright**: A fully featured editor that's integrated with Visual Studio. It's available for purchase at http://www.codewright.com.

- **Visual SlickEdit**: A fully featured cross-platform editor available for purchase at http://www.slickedit.com.

- **TextPad**: A small yet robust editor for less than $20. It's available at http://www.textpad.com.

- **Vim**: An off-shoot of the VI editor and the text editor I use. It's available for free at http://www.vim.org.

Using Batch and Shell Scripts

Microsoft built a scripting tool into its command window. It's called the BATCH language. These text file scripts, which end with the extension .BAT, run a "batch" of commands that would otherwise have to be typed individually at the command line. Because the BATCH scripting capability for Windows is mostly legacy driven from the old DOS days, it remains limited in its abilities. Looping and conditional usage in BATCH files is relatively difficult—much more reminiscent of the Assembly language than of languages used popularly nowadays. And much like MAKE scripts, shell script files can be difficult to debug. Many times, the only way to find errors in them is to print messages to the standard output.

Let's just say that the BATCH language is fine for simple scripts that require no real logic to complete. Otherwise, I suggest looking at Perl or VBScript.

TIP *BATCH isn't used very often anymore, and you might find it difficult to find references for it. If you're not able to find a reference on BATCH in your Windows books, try to locate DOS 5 books in used bookstores. Most DOS books carried adequate BATCH references.*

Using WMI and VBScript

If you plan to be a Windows-only shop and you already know Visual Basic, you may choose to use Windows Management Instrumentation (WMI) and VBScript as your tools of choice.

Microsoft created WMI in 1998 so Information Technology (IT) administrators could more easily configure and manage remote computers. An extra bonus included with the technology was the ability to automate repetitive tasks. Because of this, WMI can be an excellent tool for creating build tools.

You can access WMI functionality with any scripting language that supports COM automation. Many people choose to use VBScript because it's a subset of the Visual Basic language and is included for command-line use in the more recent versions of Windows (2000/XP). Don't try to use VBScript without WMI—for security reasons, VBScript by itself can't manipulate files or folders.

There's a major perk to using WMI and VBScript when working exclusively on the Windows platform. Developers in Windows shops are much more likely to know Visual Basic than other scripting languages. If you were to go on vacation or leave your job, there's a good chance someone else at your workplace could work on your scripts if necessary.

If you choose to use WMI with VBScript, you can get more information by going to `http://msdn.microsoft.com`, choosing the Knowledge Base option, and searching for *WMI scripting*.

Using Perl

Perl (which stands for *Practical Extraction and Reporting Language*) is an interpreted language that has many similarities to the C programming language. Because it also has several built-in text manipulation mechanisms, such as SED and awk, it's often the choice of IT administrators and SCMs. It's usually the choice for programming the Common Gateway Interface (CGI) on Unix-side Web servers.

Unlike BATCH and VBScript languages, Perl is a cross-platform tool that can be used in both the Linux/Unix and Windows worlds. It's an interpreted language, and the executables for running the scripts must be installed on your machine. On Unix and Linux machines, Perl usually comes with the operating system. If you're running Windows, however, Perl isn't installed on your machine by default, and you'll have to install a package to use the example scripts included with this book. ActiveState (`http://www.activestate.com`) puts out a fine open-source Perl interpreter. It also has a Perl plug-in that allows you to write and debug Perl scripts using the Microsoft Visual Studio .NET interface. Keep in mind that although the Perl interpreter is free, the Visual Studio plug-in and other nifty offerings aren't.

Once you've installed the Perl interpreter on your Windows machine, take care to put the Perl BIN directory into your system path. In order to call scripts from the command line or in makefiles, you'll need to reference the interpreter:

```
C:\>perl myscript.pl
```

Optionally, you can associate the .PL extension with the Perl interpreter by choosing Tools ➤ Folder Options from the Windows Explorer and navigating to the File Types tab.

Seeing a Complete Visual Studio .NET Build Script in Action

The following sections detail how you might create a complete automatic build script for your solutions. The script highlights include the following:

- Synchronizing the version information for projects and checking in the latest build number

- Labeling the source with the version number

- Getting the latest source before running the build

- Creating the application objects

Synchronizing the Version Information

One of the keys to maintaining sanity with your builds is to be able to identify them with a unique label. Unfortunately, the "unique" part makes this a difficult task to automate. Visual Studio takes care of much of that with the asterisk assembly version automation discussed earlier in this chapter.

If, however, you don't want to use the build and revision numbers that Visual Studio spits out—and let's face it, five- and six-digit numbers can be difficult to assimilate in your heads—there's another way.

Instead of letting Visual Studio projects keep track of the version numbers, put the unique version information into a separate file that you save in the source. Each time you build, you get this file from source, increment the version, and then check it back in. Call this file CM_VERSION.TXT and place it in a common location in your source tree. In the file itself, keep three build variables indicating the major, minor, and build version numbers, as displayed in Listing 9-3.

Listing 9-3. The CM_VERSION.TXT File

```
Major=1
Minor=1
Build=001
```

Once you create the CMVERSION.TXT file, it's time to create a script that builds the entire solution on the command line. I've included the script for my STOCKS solution in both Perl and VBScript/WMI.

CAUTION   *I've written these scripts for the Stock Suite product described in this chapter. If you're unfamiliar with these languages, pick up a book on Perl or VBScript before you attempt to modify these scripts for your own use. You must also run these scripts with a properly installed language interpreter. In other words, Perl must be installed to run the Perl version of the script, and WMI scripting must be installed for the VBScript version.*

Creating the Perl Version of dotNet_Build

To use this Perl script, create a new text file named DOTNET_BUILD.PL and copy the text in Listing 9-4 into it. Keep in mind that it's directly applicable to my STOCKS solution—you may need to personalize it for your use. Run the script in a command window and be sure to specify the perl keyword before calling the script. For example:

```
C:\> perl c:\trans\dotnet_build.pl
```

Listing 9-4. The Perl Version of the dotNet_Build Script

```perl
#!/usr/bin/perl


###########################################


$exename = "dotNet_Build.pl";
$friendly_title = "Build Script for Stocks Suite";
$version = "1.0";
$copyright_notice = "This script is (c)2003 by S. Kenefick";
$SS_path = "C:\\PROGRAM FILES\\MICROSOFT VISUAL STUDIO\\VSS\\win32";
$visual_studio = "C:\\PROGRAM FILES\\MICROSOFT ⤸
```

```
        VISUAL STUDIO .NET\\COMMON7\\IDE\\DEVENV.EXE";
$source_path = "C:\\SRC\\STOCKS";
$source_path_VSS = "\$/src/stocks";
$cmversion_filename = "CM_VERSION.TXT";
$temp_file = "$SOURCE_PATH" . "\\TMP.TMP";
$csprogfile_path = "C:\\SRC\\STOCKS\\REALTIMESTOCKS";
$csprogfile_VSS = "\$/src/stocks/realtimestocks";
$csprogfile = "AssemblyVersion.cs";
$build_type = "RELEASE";

MAIN:
{
    #Determine command line arguments.
    foreach $command (@ARGV)
    {
        if ($command eq '-h')
        {
            HelpOut();
            exit;
        }
        elsif ($command eq '-t')
        {
            $test = 1;
            print ("\n\nTEST ONLY MODE\n\n");
        }
        elsif ($command eq '-maj')
        {
            $do_major = -1;
        }
        elsif ($command eq '-min')
        {
            $do_minor = -1;
        }
        elsif ($command eq '-debug')
        {
            $build_type = "DEBUG";
        }
        $i++;
    }

    Salutation();

    #Check to see if source directory exists -- if not, create it.
```

```
if (not -e "$source_path")
{
    print "Creating directory: $source_path\n";
    if ($test ne 1)
    {
        mkdir($source_path);
    }
}


#Get full path of cmversion file for future use and then check it out.
$cm_filename = "$source_path" . "\\$cmversion_filename";
CheckOut($cmversion_filename, $source_path, $source_path_VSS);


#Get previous version numbers.
open (IN, "$cm_filename");
while (<IN>)
{
    if (/Major/)
    {
        if (/\d+/)
        {
            $major = $&;
        }
    }
    if (/Minor/)
    {
        if (/\d+/)
        {
            $minor = $&;
        }
    }
    if (/Build/)
    {
        if (/\d+/)
        {
            $build = $&;
        }
    }
}
close(IN);


#Display old version number.
if ($test == 1)
```

```perl
{
    print "Old build number = $major.$minor.$build.0\n";
    print "CMVERSION.TXT file = $cm_filename\n";
    print "TEMP file = $temp_file\n";
    print "CSPROG file = $csprogfile\n";
}

#Increment versions as necessary.
if ($do_major eq -1)
{
    $major++;
}
elsif ($do_minor eq -1)
{
    $minor++;
}
else
{
    $build++;
}

print "\nUpdating version numbers in $temp_file...\n";
if ($test != 1)
{
    #Write cmversion file out.
    open (OUT, "> $temp_file") or die("There was an error writing to ↵
        $temp_file  (1).  Do you have rights to the drive?  ENDING...");
    print OUT "Major=$major\nMinor=$minor\nBuild=$build" or ↵
        die("There was an error writing to $temp_file (2).  ↵
        Is the file read-only?  ENDING...");
    close(OUT);

    #Save the previous version as a "bak" file and rename the tmp version.
    rename ("$cm_filename", "$cm_filename" . ".bak") ↵
        or die("There was an error renaming $cm_filename.  ↵
        Is it read-only?  ENDING...");
    rename ("$temp_file", "$cm_filename") ↵
        or die("There was an error renaming $temp_file.  ↵
        Is it read-only?  ENDING...");
}

#Print status information.
$build_label = "$major.$minor.$build.0";
print "New build number = $build_label\n";
```

```
#Check in CMVERSION.
CheckIn($cmversion_filename, $source_path, $source_path_VSS);

#Check out the CSPROG file.
CheckOut($csprogfile, $csprogfile_path, $csprogfile_VSS);

#Update CSPROG file.
print "\nUpdating CSPROG file with new versions...\n";
if ($test != 1)
{
    open (IN, "$csprogfile_path" ."\\$csprogfile");
    open (OUT, "> $temp_file") ↵
        or die("There was an error writing to $temp_file (1). ↵
        Do you have rights to the drive?  ENDING...");
    while (<IN>)
    {
        if (/AssemblyVersion/)
        {
            print OUT "[assembly: AssemblyVersion(\"$build_label\")]"
        }
        else
        {
            print OUT $_;
        }
    }
    close(OUT);
    close(IN);

    #Save the previous version as a "bak" file and rename the tmp version.
    rename ("$csprogfile_path\\$csprogfile", ↵
        "$csprogfile_path\\$csprogfile" . ".bak") ↵
        or die("There was an error renaming $csprogfile. ↵
        Is it read-only?  ENDING...");
    rename ("$temp_file", "$csprogfile_path\\$csprogfile") ↵
        or die("There was an error renaming $temp_file. ↵
        Is it read-only?  ENDING...");
}

#Check in new CSPROG file.
FullFillCommand("\"$SS_path\\ss.exe\" CheckIn ↵
    \"$csprogfile_VSS\\$csprogfile\" -I- -W");

#Label source.
```

```perl
    FullFillCommand("\"$SS_path\\ss.exe\" Label \$/src -L\"$build_label\" -I-");

    #Get source from label.
    chdir($source_path);
    FullFillCommand("\"$SS_path\\ss.exe\" Get \"$source_path_VSS\" ↵
        -I- -W - -VL\"$build_label\" -R");

    #Build
    FullFillCommand("\"$visual_studio\" \"$source_path\\STOCKS.SLN\" ↵
        /build $build_type");

    #End Script.
    print "***************************************************************\n";
    print "END SCRIPT\n";
    print "***************************************************************\n";
}


sub CheckOut
{
    my($checkout_file) = $_[0];
    my($source_path) = $_[1];
    my($source_path_VSS) = $_[2];

    #Make sure your directory exists.
    if (not -e "$source_path")
    {
        print "Creating directory: $source_path\n";
        if ($test ne 1)
        {
            mkdir($source_path);
        }
    }

    #SourceSafe will only check out to the current directory unless -GL
    #parameter is set.  But sometimes SourceSafe is flakey even with -GL
    #so let's set the path manually
    chdir($source_path);

    #Check out the file, -I- for no interaction, -GRW to overwrite if it exists
    FullFillCommand("\"$SS_path\\ss.exe\" CheckOut ↵
        \"$source_path_VSS\\$checkout_file\" -I- -GWR ↵
        -GL\"$source_path\"" ↵
        or die("Error checking out checkout_file file."));
```

```perl
    #Ensure file exists.  If the file was already checked out, VSS will not
    #have allowed it to get copied out to the filesystem so you may have to GET it.
    If ($test ne 1)
    {
        if (not -e "$source_path\\$checkout_file")
        {
            FullFillCommand("\"$SS_path\\ss.exe\" Get ↵
                \"$source_path_VSS\\$checkout_file\" -I- -W ↵
                -GL\"$source_path\"");
        }
    }
}


sub CheckIn
{
    my($checkout_file) = $_[0];
    my($source_path) = $_[1];
    my($source_path_VSS) = $_[2];

    #SourceSafe will only check in from the current directory unless -GL
    #parameter is set.  But sometimes SourceSafe is flakey even with -GL
    #so let's set the path manually
    chdir($source_path);

    #Check in file.
    FullFillCommand("\"$SS_path\\ss.exe\" CheckIn ↵
        \"$source_path_VSS\\$checkout_file\" -I- -W");
}


sub FullFillCommand
{
    my($command) = $_[0];
    print "Fulfilling command:  $command\n";
    if ($test ne 1)
    {
        system("$command");
    }
}


sub HelpOut
{
    #Help.
    $msg_Param[0] = "\nUsage:  $exename [-t] [-h] [-maj|-min] cm_filename";
```

```
$msg_Param[1] = "        -t              Test mode only.";
$msg_Param[2] = "        -h              Show help screen.";
$msg_Param[3] = "        -maj            This will increment the major number";
$msg_Param[4] = "                        if listed.";
$msg_Param[5] = "        -min            This will increment the minor number";
$msg_Param[6] = "                        if listed.";
$msg_Param[7] = "        -debug          This will create a debug version ";
$msg_Param[8] = "                        of the software. default is a ";
$msg_Param[9] = "                        release version.";

    Salutation();
    foreach $msg (@msg_Param)
    {
        $sHelpMessage = $sHelpMessage . $msg . "\n";
    }
    $sHelpMessage = $sHelpMessage;
    print $sHelpMessage;
}


sub Salutation
{
    #Salutation.
    print "\n***************************************************************\n";
    print "$friendly_title $version\n";
    print "$copyright_notice\n";
    print "***************************************************************\n";
}
```

Creating the VBScript Version of dotNet_Build

To use this script, create a file called DOTNET_BUILD.VBS and copy the text in
Listing 9-5 into it. Again, this script is applicable to my STOCKS solution—you
may need to personalize it for your use. Run the script in a command window and
be sure to specify the cscript keyword before calling the script. Otherwise, the
script will echo all standard output through message boxes instead of in the console window—trust me, it gets annoying quickly. Use cscript as follows:

```
C:\> cscript c:\trans\dotnet_build.vbs
```

Listing 9-5. The VBScript Version of the dotNet_Build Script

```
sExename - "dotNet_Build.vbs"
sFriendlyTitle = "Build Script for Stocks Suite"
sVersion = "1.0"
sCopyrightNotice = "This script is (c)2003 by S. Kenefick"
sSSPath = "C:\\VSS\win32"
sVisualStudio = ↵
    "C:\PROGRAM FILES\MICROSOFT VISUAL STUDIO .NET\COMMON7\IDE\DEVENV.EXE"
sSourceDrive = "C:\"
sSourcePath = "SRC\STOCKS"
sSourcePathVSS = "$/src/stocks"
sCMVersionFilename = "CM_VERSION.TXT"
sTempFile = sSourceDrive + sSourcePath + "\TMP.TMP"
sCSProgfilePath = "SRC\STOCKS\REALTIMESTOCKS"
sCSProgfileVSS = "$/src/stocks/realtimestocks"
sCSProgfile = "AssemblyVersion.cs"
sBuildType = "Release"


bTest = false
For Each arg In WScript.Arguments
    if arg = "-h" then
        HelpOut()
        WScript.Quit(1)
    elseif arg = "-t" then
        bTest = true
        WScript.Echo
        WScript.Echo "TEST ONLY MODE"
        WScript.Echo
    elseif arg = "-maj" then
        bDoMajor = true
    elseif arg = "-min" then
        bDoMinor = true
    elseif arg = "-debug" then
        sBuildType = "DEBUG"
    end if
Next


Salutation

'Check to see if source directory exists -- if not, create it.
dim fso
set fso = CreateObject("Scripting.FileSystemObject")
CheckForFolderExistence sSourcePath
```

```
'Get full path of cmversion file for future use and then check it out.
sCMFilename = sSourceDrive + "\" + sSourcePath + "\" + sCMVersionFilename
CheckOut sCMVersionFilename, sSourceDrive + sSourcePath, sSourcePathVSS


'Get previous version numbers.
Dim bMajor
Dim bMinor
Dim iBuild
set objFile = fso.GetFile(sCMFilename)
if objFile.Size > 0 then
    set objReadFile = fso.OpenTextFile(sCMFilename, 1)
    do Until objReadFile.AtEndOfStream
        strLine = objReadFile.ReadLine
        if Instr(strLine, "Major") then
            iMajor = CInt(Right(strLine, len(StrLine) - 6))
        end if
        if Instr(strLine, "Minor") then
            iMinor = CInt(Right(strLine, len(StrLine) - 6))
        end if
        if Instr(strLine, "Build") then
            iBuild = CInt(Right(strLine, len(StrLine) - 6))
        end if
    loop
    objReadFile.Close
else
    WScript.Echo "ERROR:  The CMVERSION file is empty.  Exiting!"
    WScript.Quit(1)
end if


'Display current versions
Wscript.Echo "Old version:  Major = " + CStr(iMajor)
Wscript.Echo "Old version:  Minor = " + CStr(iMinor)
Wscript.Echo "Old version:  Build = " + CStr(iBuild)


'Increment versions as necessary.
if bDoMajor = true then
    iMajor = iMajor + 1
elseif bDoMinor  = true then
    iMinor = iMinor + 1
else
    iBuild = iBuild + 1
end if
```

```
'Display current versions
Wscript.Echo "New version:  Major = " + CStr(iMajor)
Wscript.Echo "New version:  Minor = " + CStr(iMinor)
Wscript.Echo "New version:  Build = " + CStr(iBuild)

Wscript.Echo  "Updating version numbers in " + sTempFile + "..."
if bTest = false then
    'Write cmversion file out to temp
    if not fso.FileExists(sTempFile) then
        fso.CreateTextFile(sTempFile)
    end if
    Set objWriteFile = fso.OpenTextFile(sTempFile, 2)
    objWriteFile.WriteLine("Major=" + CStr(iMajor))
    objWriteFile.WriteLine("Minor=" + CStr(iMinor))
    objWriteFile.WriteLine("Build=" + CStr(iBuild))
    objWriteFile.Close

    'Save the previous version as a "bak" file and rename the tmp version.
    if fso.FileExists(sCMFilename + ".bak") then
        fso.DeleteFile(sCMFilename + ".bak")
    end if
    fso.MoveFile sCMFilename , sCMFilename + ".bak"
    fso.MoveFile sTempFile, sCMFilename
end if

'Print status information.
sBuildLabel = CStr(iMajor) + "." + CStr(iMinor) + "." + CStr(iBuild) + ".0"
WScript.Echo "New build number = " + sBuildLabel

'Check in CMVERSION.
CheckIn sCMVersionFilename, sSourceDrive + sSourcePath, sSourcePathVSS

'Update CSPROG file.  First check to make sure the CSProg's directory
'exists!
CheckForFolderExistence sCSProgfilePath

'Check out the CSPROG file.
sCSProgFullPath = sSourceDrive + "\" + sCSProgfilePath
CheckOut sCSProgfile, sCSProgFullPath, sCSProgfileVSS

'Update the CSPROG file with the new build number

if bTest = false then
```

```
            WScript.Echo "Updating CSPROG file with new versions..."
            if bTest = false then
                set objFile = fso.GetFile(sCSProgFullPath + "\" + sCSProgfile)
                if objFile.Size > 0 then
                    set objReadFile = fso.OpenTextFile(sCSProgFullPath + "\" + ⤵
                        sCSProgfile, 1)
                    if not fso.FileExists(sTempFile) then
                        fso.CreateTextFile(sTempFile)
                    end if
                    set objWriteFile = fso.OpenTextFile(sTempFile, 2)
                    do Until objReadFile.AtEndOfStream
                        strLine = objReadFile.ReadLine
                        if Instr(strLine, "AssemblyVersion") then
                            objWriteFile.WriteLine("[assembly: AssemblyVersion(" + ⤵
                                Chr(34) + sBuildLabel + Chr(34) + ")]")
                        else
                            objWriteFile.WriteLine(strLine)
                        end if
                    loop
                    objReadFile.Close
                    objWriteFile.Close
                else
                    WScript.Echo "ERROR:  ⤵
                        The CSPROG file is empty or doesn't exist.  Exiting!"
                    WScript.Quit(1)
                end if
            end if

            'Copy the temp file to the orig
            'Save the previous version as a "bak" file and rename the tmp version.
            if fso.FileExists(sCSProgFullPath + "\" + sCSProgfile + ".bak") then
                fso.DeleteFile(sCSProgFullPath + "\" + sCSProgfile + ".bak")
            end if
            fso.MoveFile sCSProgFullPath + "\" + sCSProgfile, ⤵
                sCSProgFullPath + "\" + sCSProgfile + ".bak"
            fso.MoveFile sTempFile, sCSProgFullPath + "\" + sCSProgfile

        end if

        'Check in the CSPROG file.
        CheckIn sCSProgfile, sCSProgFullPath, sCSProgfileVSS

        'Label source.
```

```
FullFillCommand(Chr(34) + sSSPath + "\ss.exe" + Chr(34) + " Label " + ⤶
    Chr(34) + sSourcePathVSS + Chr(34) + " -L" + Chr(34) + ⤶
    sBuildLabel + Chr(34) + " -T-")


'Get source from label.
if bTest = false then
    Set objShell = WScript.CreateObject("WScript.Shell")
    objShell.CurrentDirectory = sSourceDrive + "\" + sSourcePath
end if
FullFillCommand(Chr(34) + sSSPath + "\ss.exe" + Chr(34) + " Get " + ⤶
    Chr(34) + sSourcePathVSS + Chr(34) + " -I- -W - -VL" + Chr(34) + ⤶
    sBuildLabel + Chr(34)+ " -R")


'Build
FullFillCommand(Chr(34) + sVisualStudio + Chr(34) + " " + Chr(34) + ⤶
    sSourceDrive + sSourcePath + "\" + "STOCKS.SLN" + Chr(34) + " /build " + ⤶
    sBuildType)


'End Script.
WScript.Echo "*********************************************************************"
WScript.Echo "END SCRIPT"
WScript.Echo "*********************************************************************"



sub HelpOut
    'Help.
    Salutation
    WScript.Echo "Usage: " & s_exename & " (-t) (-h) (-maj|-min)"
    WScript.Echo "       -t          Test mode only."
    WScript.Echo "       -h          Show help screen."
    WScript.Echo "       -maj        This will increment the major number if"
    WScript.Echo "                   listed."
    WScript.Echo "       -min        This will increment the minor number if"
    WScript.Echo "                   listed."
    WScript.Echo "       -debug      This will create a debug version of the"
    WScript.Echo "                   software. The default is release."
end sub


sub Salutation
    'Salutation.
    WScript.Echo "****************************************************************"
    WScript.Echo sFriendlyTitle & " " & sVersion
    WScript.Echo sCopyrightNotice
    WScript.Echo "****************************************************************\n"
end sub
```

```
sub CheckOut(sCheckoutFile, sSourcePath, sSourcePathVSS)
    'SourceSafe will only check out from the current directory unless -GL
    'parameter is set.  But sometimes SourceSafe is flakey even with -GL
    'so let's set the path manually
    Set objShell = WScript.CreateObject("WScript.Shell")
    objShell.CurrentDirectory = sSourcePath
    if bTest = false then
        'Check out the file, -I- for no interaction, -GRW to overwrite if it exists
        FullFillCommand(Chr(34) + sSSPath + "\ss.exe" + Chr(34) + ⤸
            " CheckOut " + sSourcePathVSS + "/" + sCheckoutFile + ⤸
            " -I- -GWR -GL" + Chr(34) + sSourcePath + Chr(34))
        'Ensure file exists.  If the file was already checked out, VSS will not
        'have allowed it to get copied out to the filesystem so you may have
        'to GET it.
        set fso = CreateObject("Scripting.FileSystemObject")
        if (not fso.FolderExists(sSourceDrive + "\" + sSourcePath)) then
            FullFillCommand(Chr(34) + sSSPath + "\ss.exe" + Chr(34) + ⤸
                " Get " + sSourcePathVSS + "/" + sCheckoutFile + " -I- -W -GL" + ⤸
                    Chr(34) + sSourcePath + Chr(34))
        end if
    end if
end sub

sub CheckIn(sCheckoutFile, sSourcePath, sSourcePathVSS)
    'SourceSafe will only check in from the current directory unless -GL
    'parameter is set.  But sometimes SourceSafe is flakey even with -GL
    'so let's set the path manually
    Set objShell = WScript.CreateObject("WScript.Shell")
    objShell.CurrentDirectory = sSourcePath
    if bTest = false then
        'Check in file.
        FullFillCommand(Chr(34) + sSSPath + "\ss.exe" + Chr(34) + " CheckIn " + ⤸
            sSourcePathVSS + "/" + sCheckoutFile + " -I- -W")
    end if
end sub

sub FullFillCommand(sCommand)
    WScript.Echo "Fulfilling command: " + sCommand
    if bTest = false then
        Set objShell = WScript.CreateObject("WScript.Shell")
        Set objExecObject = objShell.Exec(sCommand)
        Do While Not objExecObject.StdOut.AtEndOfStream
            strText = objExecObject.StdOut.ReadLine()
```

```
        Wscript.Echo strText
        Loop
    end if
end sub


'This function assumes the folder will be created on the "source drive"
sub CheckForFolderExistence(sFolder)
    WScript.Echo sFolder
    WScript.Echo sParentFolder
    dim fso
    set fso = CreateObject("Scripting.FileSystemObject")
    if (not fso.FolderExists(sParentFolder + "\" + sFolder)) then
        WScript.Echo "Now creating the " + sFolder + " directory folder..."
        if bTest = false then
            set objShell = CreateObject("Shell.Application")
            set objFolder = objShell.NameSpace(sSourceDrive)
            objFolder.NewFolder sFolder
        end if
    else
        WScript.Echo sFolder + " directory already exists..."
    end if
end sub
```

Summary

In this chapter, you learned how to use the features of Visual Studio .NET to build robust applications. In addition, I talked about the new objects specific to this version of Visual Studio and how to automate the build process.

Specifically, this chapter covered the following:

- How Visual Studio .NET differentiates from previous versions of the tool

- Solutions and assemblies and how they fit into the development model

- How source code files are organized in Visual Studio, on hard drives, and in source control

- How to build and create configurations for projects and solutions

- How to manually change the version numbers of applications and how Visual Studio automates version number updating

- How to create prebuild and post-build steps during a solution build

- How to automate a Visual Studio solution build

CHAPTER 10

Installations

ONCE YOUR DEVELOPERS CREATE a product, the resulting software must somehow end up on a customer's machine. Larger corporations used to divvy out these tasks to install teams—but this luxury is disappearing in these lean days. Many organizations today, especially small shops, choose to task the Software Configuration Manager (SCM) with installing and deploying the goods.

Creating installations for end users has many issues. Of course, instruction manuals for using the tools discussed in this chapter can (and do!) fill up entire books, so this chapter instead briefly describes some of the installation tools on the market and then presents a quick use case for each of them so you can make informed purchase decisions.

Installations are tricky—don't let anyone tell you differently. They seem like they should be simple—you merely ask your customers where they want the software installed and then copy the files over, right? And then come the other questions.... How is the product uninstalled? What if a previous version of the software exists on the machine? Will there be future enhancements to the product that will affect installing the product now? What about allowing the user to customize the application during the installation? You get the picture. Believe it or not, installations can be overwhelmingly complicated.

Worse, many installations are created by people who have never written code before. This can be a problem because a lot of logic is required when writing installations—and programming logic is often learned through experience. Unfortunately, as it is with the SCM, installation developers often get no respect. Other developers may thumb their noses at the install—and be ready, the install is *always* the first "fall guy" when bugs are found—but those same developers are at the mercy of the installation developer. Always remind the programming snobs that there's only one way for the end user to get the code—and that's through the install.

Thinking It Through

Before I discuss the tools used to create installations, let's first spend some time plotting them out. Why? Frankly, most of the large problems you'll run into when writing the installation come from poor preparation. Like any piece of code, an installation should be well architected with scalability in mind before any code is written.

NOTE *Building an installation is a team effort—even if you end up being the only one writing any code. Feel free to have the developers try to install their components to a common location early in the development cycle—even if it means simply copying them to a shared directory—so you have a good starting point from which to work. In addition to helping you out, this sort of exercise can weed out architectural issues and flaws without having to wait for the first draft of the installation project.*

Step 1: Break It Down

Depending on the type of product you support, you may need to provide separately installable features. To ensure that your customers receive the features complete with all of the proper components—regardless of whatever install choices the user may have made—it's important to break down your product into well-documented parts—much like I discussed in Chapter 1, "Getting to Know the SCM Role." Use a spreadsheet program to list all the separate features of the product and what they contain.

TIP *If supporting a large enterprise product, it might be worth your while to instead use a friendly database program such as Microsoft Access.*

When coming up with your list, don't be afraid to break it down into the smallest possible parts. Start by creating a column in your spreadsheet for each large feature of your product. Underneath the appropriate column heading, list the files to be copied and any database or system changes (for instance, the Registry in Windows) that might need to be performed for each feature. The first column should list the "default"—the shared objects that are always installed regardless of the options presented to the end user.

TIP *Don't fall into the shared features trap! It's tempting to group a shared set of features into every column. For instance, if you were to write an installation for an Office-style program, the spell checker might seem like it needs to be part of both the word processor and spreadsheet programs. Instead of simply adding the checker to both columns, try to imagine the spell checker as a separate and worthy feature in its own respect. Once it's been mapped out, you can group the features together as separate installable parts. This allows a great deal of flexibility should the requirements of your product change in the future.*

In Chapter 9, "Builds for Windows .NET," I used a stock market tool as an example. I'll use that same example for the installation preparation. Look at the product that was created, and you'll probably come up with six features:

- Shared objects and settings that are always installed.

- The real-time stock ticker. It's optionally installed at the request of the user.

- The stock analysis tool. It's optionally installed at the request of the user.

- The stock purchaser program. It's optionally installed at the request of the user.

- Help. It's a shared set of components that's always installed.

- The calculator. It's a shared set of components that's installed with both the stock analysis and the stock purchaser features.

TIP *Even though you'll always install the Help objects, you may come across a time when you want to optionally install it or split it into smaller Help objects. To facilitate this possibility and to ensure future scalability, separate Help objects into their own components. Think about the other components—a little consideration now can save you from huge headaches later.*

When you're finished, your spreadsheet might look something like Figure 10-1. Keep in mind that this is a simple example—the spreadsheet for your real-life product will probably be much more detailed (and you're the lucky one if it isn't).

TIP *List Windows Registry and initialization file (.INI file) changes in your spreadsheet as if they were files. By treating them as installation "objects," you ensure that they're only changed as necessary.*

Shared	Ticker	Analysis	Purchase	Help	Calculator
stockshared.dll	realtimestocks.exe	stockanalysis.exe	stockpurchase.exe	stocks.html	stockcalc.exe
stockcount.dll	Reg: d/l method		stockprice.dll		
Reg: version					
Reg: installed directory					
Reg: user name					

Figure 10-1. Divvying up the Stock Suite features

Step 2: Map the Features Together into Installable Parts

Once you create your feature chart, "map" the features together into installable parts. This allows users to decide which features they might want to put on their computers. Why install an entire office suite if you only need the word processor?

NOTE *Your product might be small with limited functionality. In this case, there may be no need to provide conditional installations of features. Feel free to skip this section.*

For instance, in the previous example, the Stock Suite has four installable parts:

- Shared objects, their settings, and Help

- The real-time stock ticker

- The stock analysis tool and calculator

- The stock purchasing tool and calculator

Create a new spreadsheet that details the relationship of these features. Most installable parts will repeat features—for instance, all of the parts will include the shared objects feature. However, only add features from the first spreadsheet to any installable part.

As you do this, think about how the features are packaged from a customer perspective. If a user wants to install just the real-time ticker portion, which objects would need to be installed? Most of the installable parts, though probably not all of them, should have a "conditional" aspect to their installation—they're only installed if the end user so chooses.

Look at the Stock Suite example—again, it's a simple one—displayed in Figure 10-2.

Always Installed	Stock Ticker Tool	Stock Analysis Tool	Stock Purchase Tool
Shared	Ticker	Analysis	Purchase
Help		Calculator	Calculator

Figure 10- 2. Listing installable components

Step 3: Architect the User Interface

Once you've determined the different parts in which you'll divvy up your product, now you must design how you'll graphically present these choices to the end users. When designing this interface, keep in mind that you want to make the installation experience as pleasant and easy as possible. Remember that a computer is a personal item, such as a house or a car, and you should balance the convenience of automation with the customers' desire to choose what's installed on their respective machines.

Ask yourself questions about the choices you might like to have when installing another company's software on your computer. In the case of the Stock Suite product, some of these questions might be as follows:

- In which directory would you choose to install the product?

- Which portions of the product would you like to install? The entire product made up of the ticker, analyzer, and purchaser? A combination of two of the components? One of the components?

- Should a program group be created? If so, should it be shared between all users on the machine or available to just the person installing the product?

- Should a desktop shortcut icon be created? Should a quick-launch shortcut icon be created?

- If this product is a client for an enterprise server product, what is the name or Internet Protocol (IP) address of the server?

Although this is by no means a comprehensive list of the questions you might come up with, it's a good starting point. Keep trying for the "Goldilocks" of installation User Interfaces (UIs): Ask only the questions necessary to ensure both flexibility and a correctly installed product. Too many questions will annoy the end user and create more work for yourself. Too few questions, and the complaints will roll in. In other words, try to be "just right."

 TIP *Consider a UI approach that presents both an express installation of your product's most common configuration and a customizable installation that allows power users to make detailed choices.*

Exploring the Windows Tools

Windows has a variety of tools designed for installation—some of which are now built into the operating system. The following sections explore the three most popular methods:

- The Microsoft Windows Installer (MSI) and Visual Studio's included MSI plug-in

- InstallShield and its line of tools, a third-party alternative to MSI

- Wise Systems and its line of tools, a third-party alternative to MSI

Using the Windows Installer

When Microsoft introduced Windows 2000, it included a new installation tool, the Windows Installer. In theory, this tool fixed many of the perceived problems presented by third-party installation engines and is still supported in all post–Windows 95 Microsoft operating systems.

Instead of using procedural scripts like previous installation tools, MSI is database driven. Installation writers create an MSI database object that details to the operating system how to install files, Registry settings, and other settings. Using this methodology, MSI mitigated the largest problem known to both developers and end users—system "DLL hell"—and ensured the easy, complete removal of products.

 NOTE   *To use MSI installations, the installer must be installed on your user's system. By default, it's included in all versions of Windows created after 1999.*

Surprisingly enough, the development community didn't open its arms to MSI when it was released. Much of this was because Microsoft insisted that developers use the new installation tool before they could receive the much-coveted "Designed to Work with Windows 2000" logo that gets pasted on software boxes. Developers found the new MSI Application Programming Interface (API) difficult to learn and complained about having to completely rewrite older legacy installations. Microsoft listened and summarily dropped the requirement.

There's truth that using MSI in its native state is an arduous task. Microsoft didn't provide a feature-rich graphical interface for the API—perhaps in fear that installation tool manufacturers would cry foul in the way Netscape did when Internet navigation was built into Windows. But with the release of Visual Studio .NET, Microsoft now provides a simple graphical version of MSI and leaves the "hard stuff" for the third-party installation tool developers.

The MSI tool provided by Visual Studio may not be feature rich enough for you. One of its largest limitations is that it can't automatically install the .NET Framework—a must for .NET applications. On the other hand, the default Visual Studio MSI integration is quick and easy for one-trick-pony software applications.

Creating an MSI Installation Using Visual Studio .NET

Let's build an MSI installation for the Stock Suite of products using Visual Studio .NET. If your team already has a solution containing your product's applications, you can easily create an installation project for Stock Suite in the same solution. On the other hand, you may want to create the installation in a different location, but as you'll see later in this chapter, it's much more convenient to have the installation in the same solution. Any number of MSI installation projects can co-exist in the same solution, and, if you chose to do so, you could create a separate installation for each product in the Stock Suite.

> **TIP** *If the developers are wary about having the installation in the same solution, create a copy of the solution for yourself and then rename it. Because solutions simply point to included projects, any changes your developers might make will still be accessible to you when you use your solution.*

The first step to creating your installation project is to right-click the solution in the Solution Explorer window and choose the Add ➤ New Project menu item. The Add New Project dialog box appears. By choosing the Setup and Deployment Projects folder in the Project Types window, you'll see the five installation/setup project templates available for use, as displayed in Figure 10-3. The five types are described with detail in the "Determining Which Setup Template to Use" sidebar. Regardless of whether you install other third-party installation tools on the same machine, only MSI projects appear in the Setup and Deployment Projects folder.

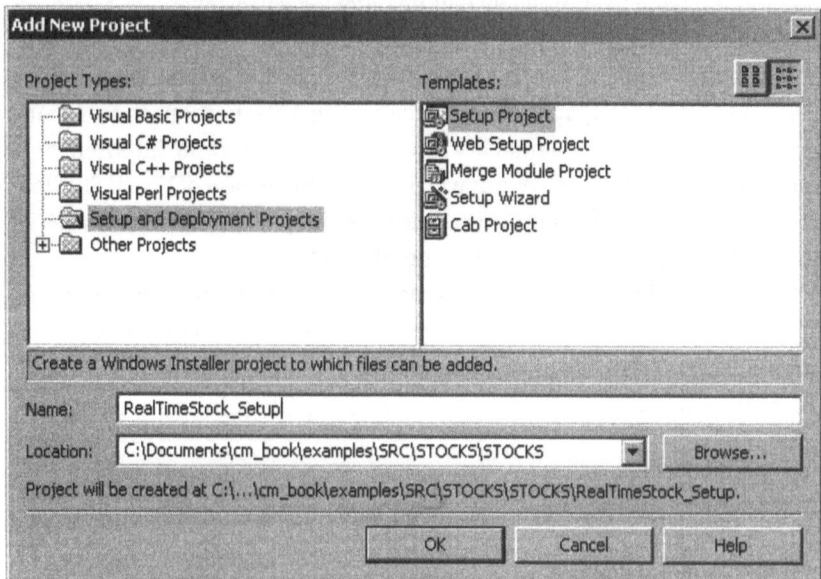

Figure 10-3. Adding a new MSI project

Determining Which Setup Template to Use

Five setup and deployment project templates are available through Visual Studio's default MSI offering.

Setup Project template: The Setup Project template is the standard installation project used for Windows applications. It has all of the standard installation features:

- **The ability to install and uninstall the application**: The application's icon is added to the Control Panel's Add/Remove Programs feature, and the user can, in most cases, uninstall it without any extra logic provided by the installation creator. It should be noted, however, that any custom actions provided by Dynamic Link Libraries (DLLs) or other scripts must have an action provided for both rollbacks and uninstalls to complete.

- **The ability to repair an existing installed application**: Should parts of the application become corrupted or deleted, the application can be reinstalled without the loss of user customization.

- **The ability to roll back all changes should any part of the installation fail or if the user chooses to cancel before it has completed**: Again, it should be noted, however, that any custom actions provided by DLLs or other scripts must have an action provided for both rollbacks and uninstalls to complete.

- **The ability to add or change the Windows Registry and product file associations**: If an application has a specific file type on which it can perform, these file associations can easily be made.

- **The ability to add shared assemblies to the Global Assembly Cache (GAC)**: As referenced in the previous chapters, any .NET assemblies that are shared must be added to the GAC.

- **The ability to confirm the existence of prerequisite software and to cancel gracefully should it not be found**: This is especially important with .NET installations because earlier Windows systems may not have the Framework installed.

Web Setup Project template: A Web Setup Project template has similar functionality to the Setup Project template but differs in that it installs itself into an Internet Information Services (IIS) virtual Web directory instead of the Program Files directory.

Merge Module Project template: You use merge modules for deploying separate "installation parts" instead of complete applications. An example of the proper use of a merge module is the installation of a shared utility. Merge modules have their own extension—.MSM—that can be added to a standard setup project.

(continued)

CAB Project template: Microsoft cabinet projects—often shortened to *CAB projects*—allow for the deployment of redistributable ActiveX controls. Once controls are added to these CAB files, they can then be signed as "authenticated" by a representative of the development house and placed on a Web site. When users access the page, browsers display a dialog box informing them of the ActiveX installation.

Setup Wizard: The Setup Wizard isn't actually a project template so much as a tool—it simply provides a friendlier face to the four installation templates mentioned previously in this sidebar.

NOTE *Discussing the entire feature sets of MSI, InstallShield, and Wise would be a book unto itself. This chapter provides only examples of basic installations.*

The Stock Suite is a simple application, so choose the Setup Project option. Solution Explorer uses the name you designate now for saving the installation project files; however, regardless of what name you choose, the default name for the installation output will be Setup. After typing a descriptive name and clicking OK, the system displays a window that looks similar to Figure 10-4. Keep in mind that Visual Studio is extremely customizable—the appearance of your environment may vary. Solution Explorer now highlights your new setup project, and the work area of Visual Studio lists three folders in an Explorer-like view.

The Properties window in the Visual Studio environment, as displayed in Figure 10-5, allows you to "personalize" the setup program with information about your company and the current project. If the Properties window isn't currently displayed, choose View ➤ Properties Window to bring it to the forefront.

NOTE *Unless you're working with a huge monitor, you'll quickly find that your screen doesn't have enough real estate for all the windows you want to open! In these cases, simply open and close the windows you need by using the View menu.*

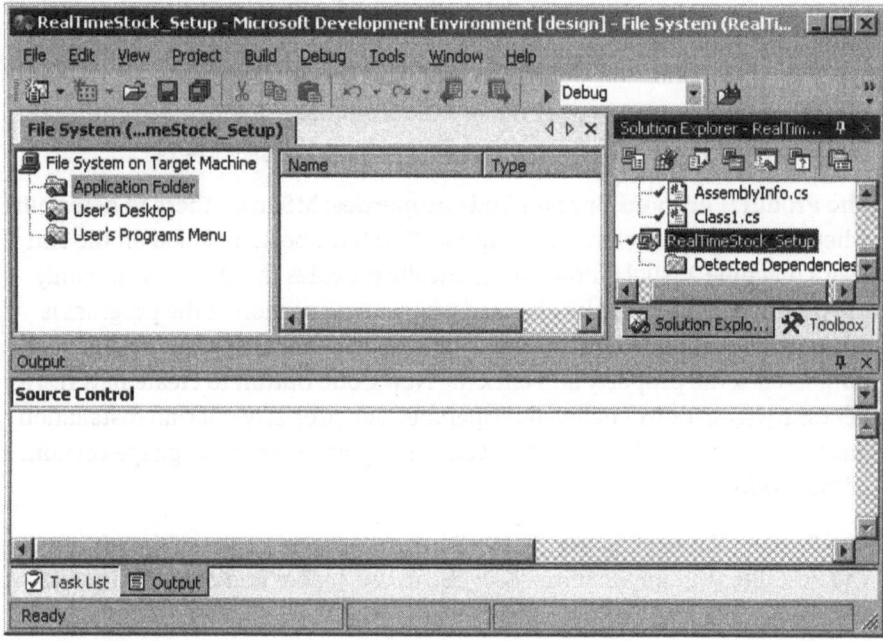

Figure 10-4. The newly created RealTimeStock setup project in Visual Studio

Figure 10-5. The setup's Properties window

The following are a couple of quick notes regarding the important properties for installation projects:

The Manufacturer property: This sets the "company" name used for the creation of the application's installation directory and Registry keys.

The ProductCode and UpgradeCode properties: MSI uses these to determine whether previous versions of the application have been installed on the end user's machine. Visual Studio automatically provides these values, and only the product code should be changed when a new version of the program is created. Don't try to come up with your own value for this property—instead, double-click the property and click the New Code button to create new IDs as necessary. Also, don't change the UpgradeCode property once an installation has been created and deployed—even to support different language versions of the product.

The ProductName property: This reflects how the title pane of the installation will describe your application—feel free to use spaces and capitalization as desired.

The Version property: This reflects the version of the resulting MSI or CAB file—it's in no way connected with the version of the separate executables included in the installation. For consistency, you may want to set this version number to match your product's release number.

Adding Files and Other Objects to the Installation

Once you've set the properties for your setup project, it's time to add files and Registry items. You may want to architect the user interface first, but that isn't advisable. Even with your detailed spreadsheet, you might have changes as you build your project that affect the user interface.

To add files, navigate to the File System window for your setup project in Visual Studio. If it's not already displayed, open it by right-clicking the setup project in the Solution Explorer and choosing View ➤ File System, as displayed in Figure 10-6. You can open all setup project windows in this manner.

The left side of the Explorer window lists three folders: the Application folder, the User's Desktop folder, and the User's Program Menu folder. These three folders simulate where you might place application files and shortcuts on your user's hard drive.

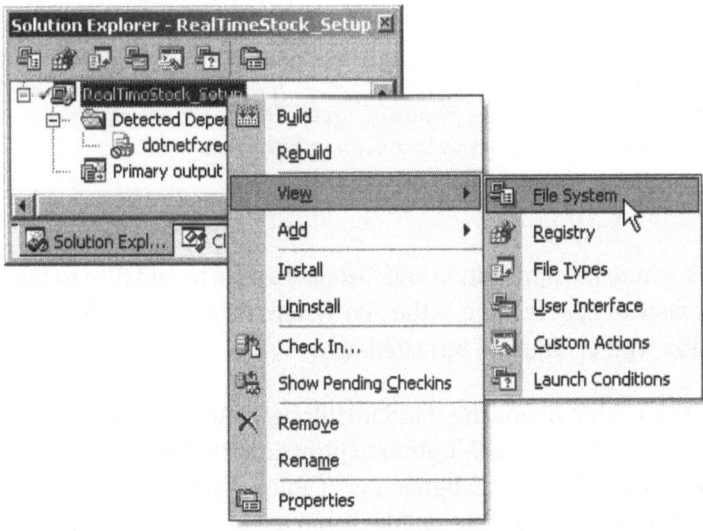

Figure 10-6. Viewing other setup options

Use the Application folder for the files that belong in the default directory of your application. The Setup Project Wizard creates this directory string automatically if you've set the Manufacturer and ProductName properties as previously instructed. Change the default installation location of the application by right-clicking the Application folder and choosing Properties Window.

NOTE *Some properties can use variable names for common directories or other project properties. For instance, the value for the DefaultLocation property of the Application folder object is [ProgramFilesFolder][Manufacturer] \[ProductName]. [ProgramFilesFolder] is a variable that stands for the user's default Program Files directory. You set the [Manufacturer] and [Product-Name] variables manually in the project's properties. Other variables that can be used for the DefaultLocation property include [CommonFilesFolder], [FontsFolder], [GAC], [SystemFolder], [WindowsFolder], and [TargetDir]. Only [TargetDir] isn't self-explanatory—this variable is used with merge modules to indicate the directory of the parent MSI file that installs it.*

TIP *If installing to a directory other than Program Files, such as a user's Favorites or Windows directory, don't try to guess the path. Instead, right-click in the left window to add the appropriate "special folder." There are 20 or so special folders into which you can install an application.*

Once you've set where the application will install, it's time to add files to the project. First, right-click in the file pane of the File System window and choose Add. Then choose the type of object to be installed:

File: Choosing this option opens the standard Windows Add File dialog box. For instance, you might choose this option to provide a README file by navigating to the file on the development machine. Though listed first, this isn't the choice you make for the application files listed in your solution—see the upcoming Project Output option.

Folder: Create a directory structure inside your default folder by using this command. For example, use this command if you want to keep your help and program files in separate child directories beneath the main application folder. Once created, navigate to the new folders and then use the Add menu to populate them.

Assembly: Use this command to install Windows system assemblies. This item displays the shared assemblies installed on the current machine. Use this only for third-party components—and not for shared assemblies you plan to put in the GAC. Add your own assemblies by using the Add ➤ Project Output or Add ➤ File command.

Project Output: This is the best way to add the applications you build. Choose a product in the solution using this option, and the installation automatically includes its output executables in the created MSI file. Visual Studio automatically checks the project's output files for dependencies and includes them in the installation. On the off-chance that a dependency can't be included for some reason—for instance, because of a licensing conflict—Visual Studio's Output window tells you as you build the installation. After choosing this command, the Add Project Output Group dialog box appears, as displayed in Figure 10-7. By using the Project drop-down list, choose the project whose output you want to include in the installation. Once the project is displayed, use the mouse to click any desired combination of project or source output. Choose multiple items by holding down the Control key during a mouse click. Lastly, choose from which configuration the items should come. Pick Active, and Visual Studio dynamically chooses which output to include based upon the current setup configuration. You can use the Project Output command only for projects included in the solution. Otherwise, use the Add ➤ File command.

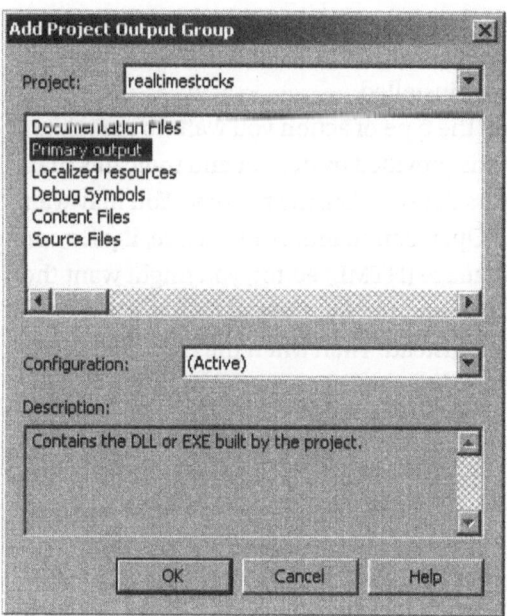

Figure 10-7. Adding executables to be installed by MSI

Once you've added all the application's files to the installation, it's time to include Registry items. Choose View ➤ Registry in the Solution Explorer to open a window that allows you to add Registry items in much the same way you did files. Simply navigate to the proper key in the left pane and add or edit Registry items as necessary. The [Manufacturer] variable indicates a default Registry key based upon the application's name and manufacturer—in most cases, it's what you'll use.

Add file type associations to the installation by choosing View ➤ File Types in the Solution Explorer. Once the window opens, right-click in the left pane and choose Add Type to add a new object entitled New Document Type. Use the Properties window to change the (Name) and Extensions property of the object to reflect the proper file type.

NOTE *Be careful when changing the default actions for common extensions such as .DOC, .HTML, and .JPG. Users may not appreciate your installation changing these default associations.*

Fill in the Extensions property with at least one file type; otherwise, you'll get a build error when trying to compile. Type extensions without the preceding period and add more of them by using a semicolon as a separator. For instance, setting the Extensions property to *YTG;EER* means that BOB.YTG and BOB.EER are both associated with your application once it's installed.

After adding the extensions, dictate the type of action you want to associate with your application. The Open action is provided by default and indicates that your application should start when users double-click the file type. You may want to add an action other than the default Open command. For instance, if your company provides a Hypertext Markup Language (HTML) editor, you might want the Open action to remain with the user's chosen browser. Instead, you might associate the Edit action with your application instead. Then when the user right-clicks an HTML file, he or she can choose either Open or Edit depending on the desired action. If you choose to use another action, be sure to remove Open.

NOTE   *Every file type grouped together in the Extensions property setting must have the same action. To have two different Open actions for two different extensions, you must create two different file type objects.*

Changing the User Interface

Now that you've got a good idea of how your setup will change the end user's system, it's time to create the user interface. Surprisingly, the default Visual Studio MSI integration provides a fairly robust tool for creating this interface.

The default interface that's created for new installations includes the following screens:

- The Welcome screen introduces the user to the installation and supplies the usual copyright notices.

- The Installation Folder screen asks the user to confirm the directory into which the application will be installed.

- The Confirm Install screen allows the user to cancel the installation before any changes have been made to the system.

- The Progress screen displays the progress of file copies and system changes.

- The Finished screen indicates to the user that the setup has completed the installation successfully.

NOTE *If for some reason the user cancels the installation, MSI displays what appears to be a different Finished dialog box and rolls back all changes made to the system. The new Finished screen is simply a different view of the regular one. Several screens in the user interface have double duty when installations are canceled, repaired, or removed. Be sure to test the installation thoroughly to ensure that the customizations you've added to dialog boxes are appropriate for all uses.*

To change the user interface, right-click the setup project and choose View ➤ User Interface. Your main work area then contains a user interface tree similar to the one displayed in Figure 10-8. The Properties window also reflects the currently highlighted dialog box.

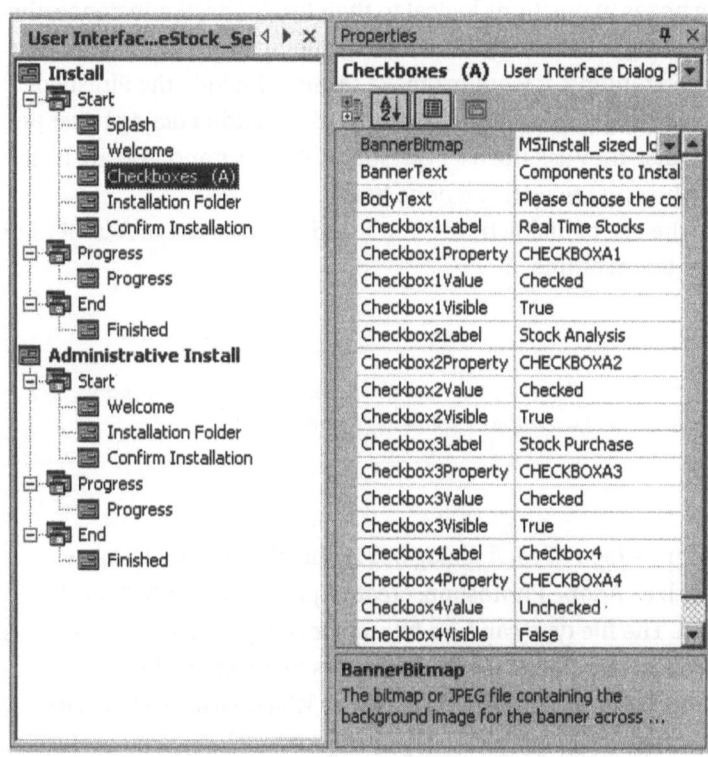

Figure 10-8. Listing the properties of your setup's user interface

NOTE *There's no way from within Visual Studio itself to preview customized user interface dialog boxes before adding them to the installation. To preview all the available MSI dialog boxes, hit F1 in the User Interface window and click the Deployment Dialog Boxes hyperlink.*

The User Interface window hierarchy is broken down into two sections—Install and Administrative Install. To keep things basic, this chapter only discusses the Install section—the part of the tree applicable to end users. The Administrative Install section is used when network administrators might distribute the product in bulk from network locations.

Each separate install type has three action nodes that reflect positions within the installation—Start, Progress, and End. You can drop about 20 nondefault dialog boxes into the installation in almost any position or order. It's important, however, to place dialog boxes in positions logical to their functions. For instance, the Start node is for gathering information from the user before the installation proceeds. With that understanding, it wouldn't make sense to include the Finished dialog box in that node. But no worries—99 percent of the added dialog boxes go in the Start node because they ask the user questions. Progress and End are likely to only have a dialog box that reflects the node itself.

To demonstrate the use of dialog boxes, you'll add and customize four of them in the installation for this example.

NOTE *Throughout this chapter, I use the name of my own company, cmReady, whenever a company name is required.*

First, add a corporate logo to each dialog box in the installation. Using a graphics program such as Adobe Photoshop, create a picture that is 500 pixels long by 70 pixels high. The file type can be a bitmap or compressed JPEG file. When designing the logo, remember that MSI displays text over the left three-quarters of the picture. For example, MSI displays the *Welcome to the Real Time Stock Ticker Setup Wizard* text displayed in Figure 10-9. There's no need (nor is it desirable) to write the text on the logo yourself.

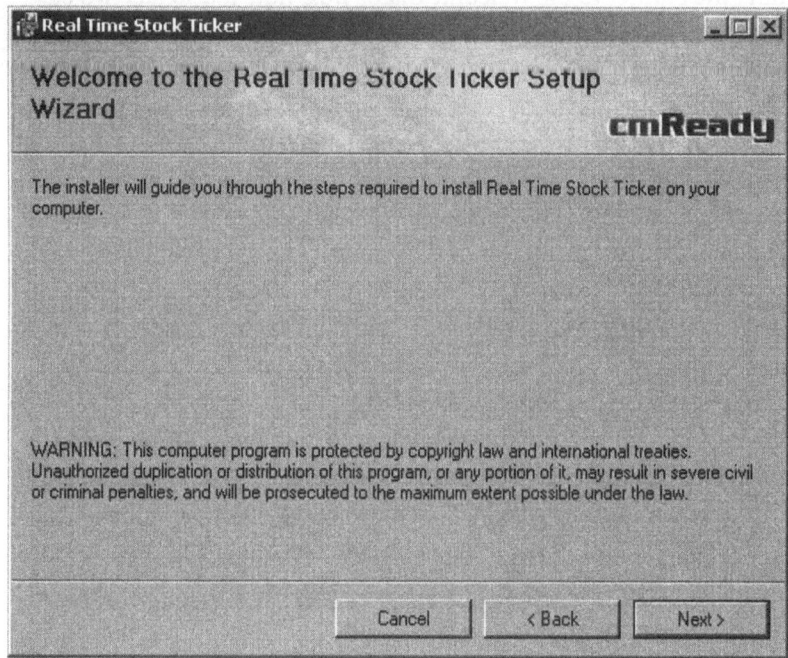

Figure 10-9. How a logo might appear in an MSI installation

Once created, add the bitmap to one of the install folders by right-clicking it and choosing the Add ➤ File menu option. Afterward, highlight each dialog box that should display the banner and set the BannerBitmap property as necessary. Unfortunately, you must add the banner to every dialog box. This does allow you, however, to use different logos on all of the dialog boxes if desired. You might want to use banners in such a manner to denote the user's current position in the installation—for instance, you may label the first dialog box as *Step 1*.

TIP *Using the Add ➤ File command to add banners causes the setup to copy them to the end user's file system. To get around this issue, set the logo's Condition property to zero (0). It will still display during installation but will not be copied to the end user's machine.*

After adding the banner to the Welcome dialog box, note it also has two customizable text properties. Customize the text as desired. Although you can customize all MSI dialog boxes in such a manner, it's likely that you'll accept the default settings. Multiple language installations require you to use separate setup projects so that you can customize these text settings for each language.

To add other dialog boxes, right-click the appropriate node and choose Add Dialog. MSI displays a list of available dialog boxes—choose to add one, some, or all of them. The names pretty much designate their functionality—but refer to the Help if you have further questions. Now, go ahead and add the Splash, License Agreement, and Customer Information dialog boxes to the installation and customize them appropriately. Splash logos must be bitmaps or JPEG pictures that are sized exactly 480 pixels long and 320 pixels high.

The last dialog box you'll add to the installation allows users to conditionally install your three main features. To do this, use one of the several "choice" dialog boxes. These allow you to display checkbox or radio button group choices to the end users. For instance, you might present a checkbox dialog box as displayed in Figure 10-10 to allow users to install any or all of the Stock Suite.

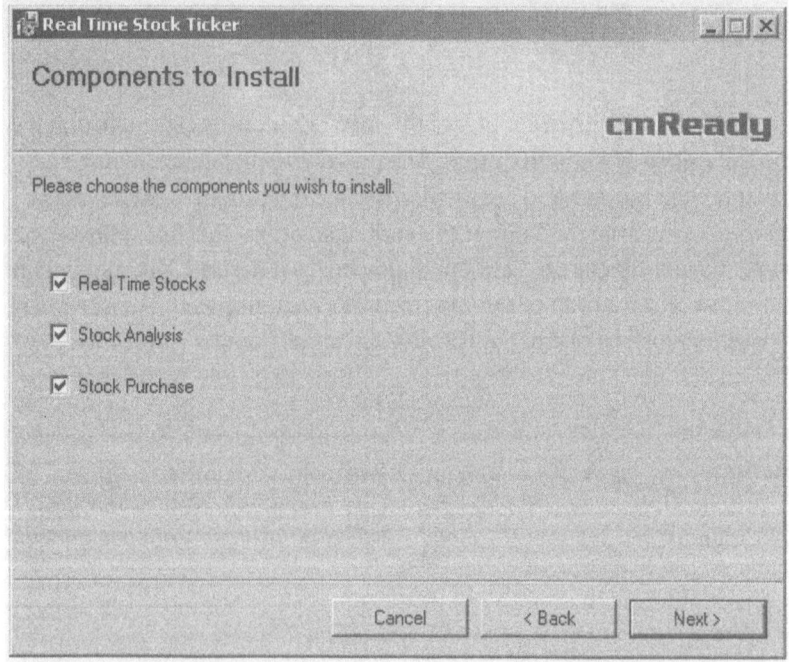

Figure 10-10. Allowing the end user to install all or part of the Stock Suite product

Because the "choice" dialog boxes are generic by default, create text for both the BannerText and BodyText properties that indicates to the user just what they're choosing. In this case, for instance, you might set the BannerText property to be *Components to Install* and the BodyText property to *Please choose the components you wish to install.*

To use choice dialog boxes, you set variables that indicate to the installer which choice the user made. As displayed in Figure 10-11, each checkbox on the dialog box has four properties attached to it.

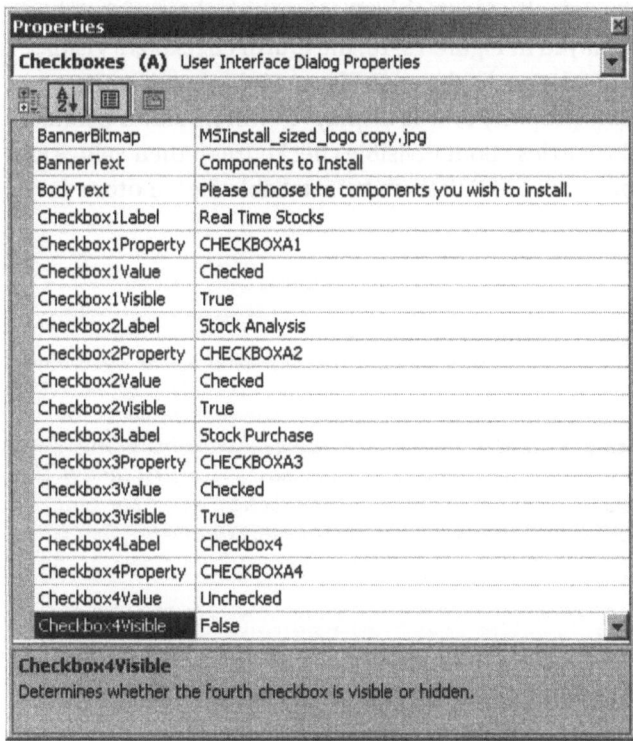

Figure 10-11. The Properties window reflecting the checkbox properties

The properties are as follows:

The Label property: This contains the phrase that indicates choices to the end user. For instance, the screen previously displayed in Figure 10-10 allows the end user to choose to install any or all of the three main Stock Suite features.

The Property property: This holds the variable that links to installable files and objects. This variable is a boolean value—if the user checks it, the variable value during file installation is true. If the user removes the check, the value is false. I'll discuss this property with more detail in a moment.

The Value property: This allows you to designate whether the checkbox is checked or unchecked by default when the dialog box first displays.

The Visible property: This indicates to MSI that the checkbox should be visible to the end user when the dialog box is displayed. You might ask: Shouldn't they always be visible? Not necessarily! The Checkbox dialog box always has four checkboxes on it by default—if you choose to use only three of the checkboxes, as previously displayed in Figure 10-10, the fourth checkbox's Visible property should be set to false as displayed in Figure 10-11. Leaving an unused checkbox's Visible property to true displays it with whatever default values it might have. No worries about invisible checkboxes—their values are unimportant unless you choose to link them to installable files or other objects.

 NOTE *You may notice that there are several checkbox dialog boxes available when adding to your installation's user interface. This is because MSI is limited in that each dialog box can only be used once. Microsoft provides the ability to retrieve information from multiple dialog boxes by including several of them. It doesn't matter which dialog box you choose to use first though the anal-retentive folks will want to use them in alphabetical order. The radio button and textbox dialog boxes both work in the same manner.*

After setting the values for each of the checkboxes, navigate to the File System window by right-clicking the setup project and choosing View ➤ File System. In the application folder, choose a file that's conditionally installed and set its Condition property to the same variable as the one set for the applicable checkbox. For instance, the Stock Analysis checkbox's property is CHECKBOXA2. Therefore, set the Condition property for every file object that should be installed when this checkbox is selected to CHECKBOXA2.

This is where the product spreadsheets you created at the beginning of this chapter come in handy. Use the mappings you created to determine what makes up each of the three features. For instance, the Stock Analysis feature consists of the Analysis objects and the Calculator objects. You must set the Condition property for every object listed under either the Analysis or Calculator headings to CHECKBOXA2.

Follow this same methodology for Registry objects. Simply navigate to the Registry window and set conditions for any objects as applicable.

 NOTE *Only files and Registry objects can be installed conditionally.*

What about objects that must be installed in more than one conditional feature? In this case, use bitwise operators in the Condition property. For instance, the Calculator feature should be installed with both the Stock Analysis and Stock Purchase tools. To ensure that this occurs, use the OR keyword in the Condition property for all Calculator objects to indicate that they should be installed if either the CHECKBOXA2 or CHECKBOXA3 variable is set to true when a file transfer occurs. In this case, the condition reads as follows:

```
CHECKBOXA3 OR CHECKBOXA2
```

You can also use the AND keyword in your conditions. If you used the AND keyword instead of OR in the previous statement, it would mean that the Calculator object should be installed only if both the Stock Purchase *and* the Stock Analysis checkmarks are ticked. Now that would be an unusual scenario!

···

Conditional Love

Using conditions in MSI occurs in more than just user interface dialog boxes. For instance, you might want to install files only on certain versions of Windows or based upon the end user's language settings. The MSI installer gives you a nifty way of making some of these checks.

In the choice dialog box example used earlier in this chapter, ticking a checkbox installs the items linked to the same variable in its Property property. With other available conditions, however, you have to give MSI a full phrase to evaluate. Table 10-1 displays several comparison operators that you can use to create those phrases.

(continued)

Table 10-1. MSI Comparison Operators

Operator	Description
>	The value on the left side *is more than* the value on the right side of the equation in order for the phrase to evaluate to true.
<	The value on the left side *is less than* the value on the right side of the equation in order for the phrase to evaluate to true.
>=	The value on the left side *is more than or equal to* the value on the right side of the equation in order for the phrase to evaluate to true.
<=	The value on the left side *is less than or equal to* the value on the right side of the equation in order for the phrase to evaluate to true.
=	The value on the left side *is equal to* the value on the right side of the equation in order for the phrase to evaluate to true.
<>	The value on the left side *is not equal to* the value on the right side of the equation in order for the phrase to evaluate to true.
AND	Logical operator indicating that *values on both sides must be true* in order for the phrase to evaluate to true.
OR	Logical operator indicating that *one of the values on either side must be true* in order for the phrase to evaluate to true.

Table 10-2 lists several keywords that can be combined with the previously mentioned operators to create phrases.

Table 10-2. Common MSI Keywords

Keyword	Description
Version9X	Windows operating system version number for 95, 98, and ME
VersionNT	Windows operating system version number for NT, 2000, and XP
ServicePackLevel	The level of operating system service pack installed
WindowsBuild	The build number of the Windows operating system
SystemLanguageID	The ID for the language of the installed operating system
PhysicalMemory	The amount of Random Access Memory (RAM) in megabytes on the machine
Intel	The version of the processor on the machine

This is by no means an exhaustive list—refer to Visual Studio's Help or http://msdn.microsoft.com for a slew of conditional keywords.

Here's an example of how you might use these keywords and operators together: Perhaps you have three DLLs that perform specific functions depending on the end user's operating system. The first DLL, called THEWIN9X.DLL, should be installed only on Windows 95, 98, and ME. THEWINNT.DLL is for Windows NT version 4.0, and THEWIN2000.DLL is for Windows 2000 and XP machines.

After taking a look at Table 10-2, you can see that it's possible to use the Version9X and VersionNT property values to create conditional phrases. The Microsoft MSDN site, http://msdn.microsoft.com, details the values you use for these properties—find them by searching the MSDN Knowledge Base for *"Operating System Property Values."* For example, the MSDN site tells you that the Version9X property has a value of 400 to indicate Windows 95, 410 for Windows 98, and 490 for Windows ME.

 NOTE *When searching MSDN, be sure to put quotes around the* "Operating System Property Values" *phrase or the site searches for all combination of the words—it can make it much harder to find the proper page.*

After evaluating the chart, you might set your conditions for each of the previously mentioned DLLs to look something like Table 10-3.

Table 10-3. Conditions for Operating System

Object	Condition
THEWIN9X.DLL	Version9X = 400 OR Version9X = 410 OR Version9X = 490
THEWINNT.DLL	VersionNT>=400 AND VersionNT<500
THEWIN2000.DLL	VersionNT>=500

Setting Launch Conditions

You can kill an installation before it ever begins by using launch conditions. This can be important when your product depends on a certain operating system or installed component. By setting a launch condition, MSI gracefully exits from the installation with an informative message box before making any changes to the end user's system.

To set a launch condition, right-click the setup project and choose View ➤ Launch Conditions. An Explorer window tree appears with two folders—Launch Conditions and Search Target Machine.

> **NOTE** *By default, all .NET setup programs include a launch condition using the MsiNetAssemblySupport variable. By including this launch condition, installations don't continue should the .NET Framework not be installed. See the "Redistributing Microsoft .NET Framework Files" section for more information.*

To use the Launch Conditions folder, simply right-click it and choose Add Launch Condition. The Properties window will reflect three new values: (Name), Condition, and Message. Use the (Name) property to identify the new condition. The (Name) property is for description purposes and has nothing to do with the condition itself—feel free to use spaces or any naming pattern desired when naming launch conditions. Use the Condition property to add a conditional phrase—see the previous "Conditional Love" sidebar for more information about creating phrases. Finally, set the Message property to the text that should be communicated to the end user should the condition not be met.

As an example, set your Stock Suite installation to fail if the end user's operating system isn't running Windows 2000 or XP. You can do so by including the launch condition listed in Table 10-4.

Table 10-4. Example Launch Condition

Property	Value
Name	Not_Windows_NT
Condition	VersionNT>=500
Message	You must be running Windows 2000 or Windows XP in order to continue this installation.

Of course, it might be that properties aren't enough to ensure a smooth installation. If the Stock Suite product depends on a certain video driver to be installed, for example, there isn't likely to be a variable that you can use to create a conditional phrase. Instead, you can search for the driver on the end user's machine by right-clicking Search Target Machine and choosing Add File Search. If necessary, you can also search the Registry for particular entries before continuing the installation.

There are quite a few more properties for new objects in the Search Target Machine folder. Use (Name), FileName, Folder, and Property for basic searches. You can fine-tine searches by setting other properties for file versions, sizes, or versions.

Again, the (Name) property is important only as a descriptive title. Set the FileName and Folder properties to indicate which file should exist on the end user's machine in order for the installation to continue. Use [brackets] variables to specify special folders, such as [ProgramFilesFolder] or [SystemFolder].

Finally (and here's the hard part), you have to set an associated launch condition that cancels the installation should the search not be successful. Do this by creating a new launch condition and making up a new association variable—much as you did with the checkbox dialog box earlier in the chapter—and placing it in the launch condition's Condition[1] property. You can call the variable whatever you like—just make sure that no other variables—including built-in Microsoft variables—use the same name.

TIP *Use your company or product name as part of any variable name to ensure its uniqueness. For instance, in the previously described scenario, you might use a variable called STOCKSUITE_VIDEODRIVERCHECK.*

Use the same variable name in the search's Property property.[2] If MSI finds the search file during installation, it sets the variable listed in Property to be true. The launch condition checks the same variable and, if it finds that it's been set to true, allows the installation to continue. Table 10-5 and Table 10-6 demonstrate how you might set up this type or associative search/launch condition.

Table 10-5. Part 1: Using the Search Target Machine Folder

Property	Value
Name	Video_Driver_Check
FileName	VIDEO.DRV
Folder	[SystemFolder]
MinVersion	3.42
Property	STOCKSUITE_VIDEODRIVERCHECK

Table 10-6. Part 2: Creating a Launch Condition

Property	Value
Name	Video_Driver_Check_LaunchCond
Condition	STOCKSUITE_VIDEODRIVERCHECK
Message	You must have the cmReady video driver installed in order for the Stock Suite to work properly. Please install the driver and then run this setup again.

---

1. Could they have named these to be any more confusing?
2. Ibid.

Using Custom Actions

Finally, I'll talk about the ability to add custom actions to your installation. MSI is pretty much limited to adding files or Registry items. By default, you can't use it to run a script on a database or update an installation log file. You can fulfill these tasks, however, by using custom actions to run code from a DLL or other executable.

> **NOTE** *This section details how to create and call code from an executable outside of the MSI database and, as such, is designed for more advanced users. The section presents example code using Microsoft's proprietary C# language.*

Right-click the setup project and choose View ➤ Custom Actions to find the four available custom actions: Install, Commit, Rollback, and Uninstall. Each of these folders represent separate "moments in time." When the setup program reaches an appropriate point in the installation, MSI runs the actions listed in the applicable custom action folder.

MSI calls the Install node actions just before it copies files and other objects to the end user's machine. After all objects have been successfully installed, it calls the Commit node actions. If the installation is cancelled for any reason before it has finished, MSI runs the actions listed in the Rollback folder. Finally, the Uninstall node actions are called—surprise!—during the uninstallation of the program.

Before you use the custom actions folders, however, you have to create an application or DLL that can be called by MSI. To learn about custom actions, in this section you'll create a console application that creates a basic installation log file on the end user's system.

Start by adding a new project to your Stock Suite solution. Use the Console Application template under the Visual C# Projects folder and call the newly created project SETUP_SS.[3]

Once you've created the project, change the code in the CLASS1.CS file so that it looks like Listing 10-1.

---

3. The SS listed in the project name refers to *Stock Suite*.

TIP *Use a console application configuration as you design and code custom actions so that a DOS-style box appears when MSI launches the action. Then, should the code not work as expected, you can at least be sure that the custom actions have actually run. After you've finished debugging the custom actions, copy the code to a new windowless application project so that custom actions are seamless to the end user.*

Listing 10-1. The SETUP_SS Project CLASS1.CS Example File

```csharp
using System;
using System.IO;

namespace SETUP_SS
{
    /// <summary>
    /// Summary description for Class1.
    /// </summary>
    class Class1
    {
        /// <summary>
        /// The main entry point for the application.
        /// </summary>
        [STAThread]
        static void Main(string[] args)
        {
            foreach (string s in args)
            {
                switch (s)
                {
                    case "install":
                        install();
                        break;

                    case "commit":
                        commit();
                        break;

                    case "rollback":
                        rollback();
                        break;
```

```
                        case "uninstall":
                            uninstall();
                            break;
                    }
                }
            }

            static void install()
            {
                TextWriter tx = new StreamWriter("C:\\SETUP_SS.TXT", true,  ⏎
                    System.Text.Encoding.Default);
                tx.WriteLine("The \"install\" custom action has been called.");
                tx.Close();
            }

            static void commit()
            {
                TextWriter tx = new StreamWriter("C:\\SETUP_SS.TXT", true,  ⏎
                    System.Text.Encoding.Default);
                tx.WriteLine("The \"commit\" custom action has been called.");
                tx.Close();
            }

            static void rollback()
            {
                TextWriter tx = new StreamWriter("C:\\SETUP_SS.TXT", true,  ⏎
                    System.Text.Encoding.Default);
                tx.WriteLine("The \"rollback\" custom action has been called.");
                tx.Close();
            }

            static void uninstall()
            {
                TextWriter tx = new StreamWriter("C:\\SETUP_SS.TXT", true,  ⏎
                    System.Text.Encoding.Default);
                tx.WriteLine("The \"uninstall\" custom action has been called.");
                tx.Close();
            }
        }
    }
```

This is a pretty simple program. First, it checks for the existence of install, commit, rollback, or uninstall command-line parameters. If found, the DLL updates a log file located at C:\SETUP_SS.TXT to indicate that the desired action took place.

Once you've written the code, right-click the SETUP_SS project and choose Build to ensure that it has no problems that need to be addressed. Now that you've built the executable, you need to associate it with a custom action.

First, go back to the setup project and the Custom Action pane. In this particular case, you'll add the same action to each node with slightly differing parameters. Right-click the top-level tree item entitled Custom Action and choose Add Custom Action from the pop-up menu. Now add the primary output from the SETUP_SS project to the Application Folder item. This will populate each of the separate custom actions. Alternatively, you can right-click each custom action separately and choose Add Custom Action.

Second, you need to set two properties for each custom action. The first property is Arguments. This property contains a string that's passed to your executable as a command-line parameter during the installation. Use the respective arguments in Listing 10-1 for each action. For instance, the Argument property for the Install action should be install, the Commit action's argument should be commit, and so on.

Lastly, change the InstallerClass property to false. Installer classes are useful because they're written with rollback functionality built into them. Unfortunately, they require too much detail for this chapter so your SETUP_SS.EXE program will not allow automatic rollback. In this case, the InstallerClass property must be set to false, or your custom actions will not work correctly.

As you test your install, notice that a DOS-style box flashes twice. The log file created by your application, located at C:\SETUP_SS.TXT, indicates that the custom actions were called correctly.

Redistributing the Microsoft .NET Framework Files

Even though much has improved in new versions of Visual Studio, there's still a bit of a sting when it comes to deploying .NET Framework applications. You must make sure that the .NET Framework common language runtime exists on the end user's machine before installing your application. If you find that the Framework hasn't yet been installed, you need to either do so yourself or guide your end users in its setup.

NOTE *If using a third-party installation tool such as InstallShield or Wise, the Framework is automatically installed. Feel free to skip this section.*

For the poor SCM in the past, this meant picking and choosing which DLLs needed to be installed into the SYSTEM directory. Nowadays—whew!—you simply need to point your users to a single MSI installable object. The entire .NET Framework runtime is available through a file called DOTNETFX.EXE.

NOTE *Depending on the third-party applications that your developers have chosen to integrate with applications, it may still be necessary to install DLLs. In these cases, however, Microsoft has done a good job of providing MSI packages for groups of important system files. If forced with a choice between copying separate DLLs to a user's system and forcing a prerequisite installation of a service pack or framework package, it's much preferable to force the installation of the service pack.*

The .NET Framework is installed by default on the professional and server versions of Windows 2000 and XP. For earlier versions of Windows, however, it's necessary for the installation to check for the Framework's existence. If your installation determines that the Framework isn't installed on the user's system, it should halt and inform the user how to do so. The default MSI integration in Visual Studio automatically halts the installation for you.

You have several ways to install the .NET Framework package on an end user's system. The best way is to use a third-party installation tool—they've done all the work for you. If that method isn't available as an option, the following are a few other methods:

- You can instruct the user to utilize the Windows Update feature, located at http://v4.windowsupdate.microsoft.com, to download the installation package.

- Depending on your application's use, IT administrators can push the Framework onto client machines using a software deployment tool before they install the application.

- You can provide the DOTNETFX.EXE redistributable file on your application's installation media CD.

- You can create a program that adds the Framework to the end user's machine before running your application's setup. This is by far the most complicated scenario—but the steps to do so are detailed at Microsoft's MSDN website; use your browser to navigate to http://msdn.microsoft.com and search for the words *.NET Framework bootstrap*.

NOTE *End users must have administrative privileges to install the .NET Framework redistributable package.*

If you choose to include the Framework as a redistributable package on your CD media, keep in mind that it's possible Microsoft has updated the Framework with bug fixes or improvements since the CD was burned. Your README file should indicate to the user that a check for updates is in order.

To download the redistributable version of the .NET Framework for placement on a CD, navigate to http://msdn.microsoft.com and search for DOTNETREDIST.EXE. Once downloaded, however, *don't* redistribute the package in its current state. Instead, double-click the DOTNETREDIST.EXE executable on an in-house computer and save the output file, DOTNETFX.EXE, to a directory that mimics your media CD. Alternatively, the package is also available on the Visual Studio .NET Framework Software Development Kit (SDK) CD in a directory called DOTNETREDIST located at the CD's root—however, you can be assured that this won't be the latest version of the Framework.

NOTE *Microsoft makes it clear that you must own a valid Microsoft .NET Framework SDK license, available with your purchased copy of Visual Studio, in order to distribute the Framework package.*

You can install the Framework redistributable package on the following operating systems as long as Internet Explorer 5.01 or higher and MSI 2.0 or higher exists on the machine:

- Windows 98 and Windows 98 Second Edition

- Windows ME

- Windows NT 4.0 with Service Pack 6A (Workstation and Server)

- Windows 2000 (Professional, Server, and Advanced Server)

- Windows XP (Home, Professional, .NET Server)

Depending on the application being deployed, servers may also require the installation of MDAC 2.7 and Internet Information Services (IIS).

Using InstallShield

So you've looked at the "free" tool that comes with Visual Studio and decided for whatever reason that it just doesn't do it for you. If you've got some cash, you have several other choices for creating installations on the Windows operating system.

InstallShield Corporation, founded in 1987, is generally considered the industry leader for installation tools. It has recently branched out into providing system administration tools that can repackage applications and resolve potential conflicts prior to deployment.

At the time of this writing, InstallShield has several product offerings for installations. These products vary in sophistication, and, as you may expect, the products with the most flexibility tend to be the most expensive:

Developer: This product provides a frontend to the MSI API. In addition to the basic MSI features mentioned earlier in this chapter, Developer also provides the ability to redistribute the MSI installer, the .NET Framework, ActiveX Data Object (ADO) components, and other popular Microsoft system objects. In addition to creating typical MSI installations, Developer optionally allows install writers to script installations using InstallScript, a proprietary language that users may know from previous incarnations of InstallShield products. Developer installations that use InstallScript still exploit MSI for much of their functionality.

Express: This is the entry product to the InstallShield line—a product that might be called *Developer, Jr*. Its key benefits are its ease of use and relatively low cost. Because it doesn't provide the scripting capabilities of Developer, Express is a completely MSI-based product. In other words, most of what you can do with Express, you can do with the free version of MSI that comes with Visual Studio—albeit sometimes with a great deal of difficulty. In addition to being able to quickly package the .NET Framework and other redistributables, Express provides a wizard-based creation tool that allows installation writers to quickly create a usable installation. With a price point that's almost 75-percent off the Developer or Professional tools, Express is worth checking out for less-complicated installation procedures.

Professional: This product is the update to the script-based InstallShield product that has been around for the last decade. The bright side to using this tool is that legacy installations can easily be updated, and there's no need to start from scratch. The downside to using this product is its incompatibility with the feature-rich MSI functionality. Because the Manufacturer Suggested Retail Price (MSRP) of this product is more than $1,000 (though upgrades are available for less), I recommend using an MSI-based tool in its stead if starting an installation from scratch.

NOTE *In order to be eligible for the "Optimized for Enterprise" logo provided by Microsoft, you must use an MSI-based installation tool. Professional and Developer installations using InstallScript might not be the tools to use to meet this requirement. Eligibility for the basic Windows XP logo is still available to script-based installation programs.*

MultiPlatform: If creating installations for a product that spans several operating systems, MultiPlatform might be the right tool for the job. Its exploitation of the Java language allows an installation to have a consistent look and feel regardless of the platform on which it's being installed. Supported platforms include many flavors of Unix and Linux as well as Windows. This type of power is expensive, however, both in terms of financial cost and the possible loss of operating-specific installation features included with MSI, the Sun package technology, and Linux RPM.[4]

Creating a Setup in Four Hours (or Less) Using InstallShield Express

All of InstallShield's products are available as evaluation downloads from its Web site at http://www.installshield.com. Any installations created with the evaluations are fully featured but hobbled by a message indicating that the install was created with a free version of the software. Let's take a moment to try out these products by creating installations for the Stock Suite product using Express and Developer—the MSI-based installation tools.

After downloading and installing the last version of Express,[5] try building a new setup by using its Visual Studio integration. After loading the Stock Suite

---

4. The folks at InstallShield have assured me that there's no loss of any operating-system-specific functionality when using the MultiPlatform product.

5. The example included in this section was created with InstallShield Express 4.0.

solution in Visual Studio, right-click it in Solution Explorer and choose Add ➤ New Project. Navigate to the InstallShield Express Projects folder and choose the Project Wizard. Before clicking OK, be sure to name the project appropriately and choose a proper destination folder. In this case, name the project *IS_Express* and use the default destination folder.

Configure the installation's functionality by using the InstallShield Project Wizard. Click Next at the splash screen, and the Application Information screen appears, as displayed in Figure 10-12. Change the application name, version, and default install location as directed by the edit boxes. The default install location refers to where the application should be installed on an end user's machine.

NOTE *Be aware that some of the InstallShield Wizard dialog boxes aren't as intuitive as they could be. For instance, in the Default Destination Folder edit box, it could be assumed that the Program Files Folder, Your Company Name, and Your Product Name are variables that will be filled in automatically by the wizard. Although Program Files Folder is indeed a variable (as indicated by the brackets surrounding it), the others aren't. Be sure to change these values to reflect your company and product names as necessary. If you do make a mistake, however, don't worry about it. Express is forgiving and will let you change any properties using the Visual Studio integration interface at a later time.*

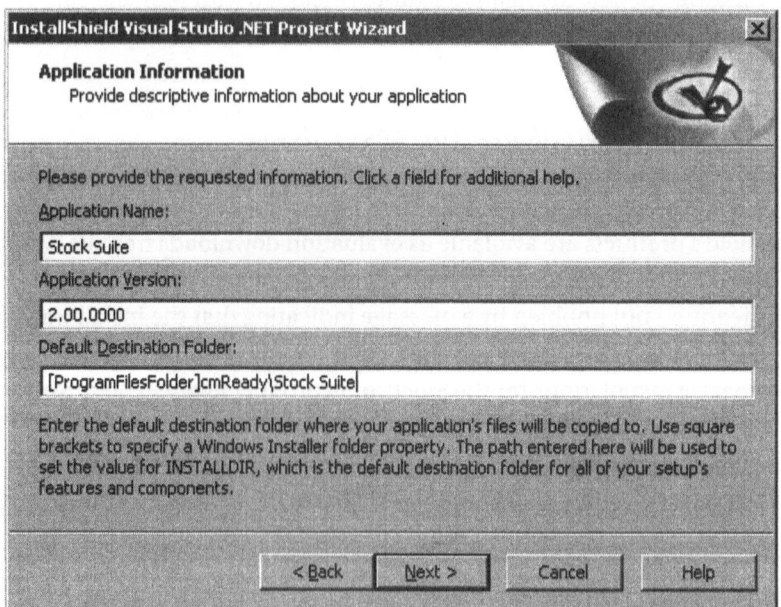

Figure 10-12. Adding application information using the InstallShield Express Project Wizard

Click Next, and a screen will ask if you'd like to enable your product to receive updates via the InstallShield update service. This is a pay-per-customer service provided by InstallShield to ease the pain of providing patches and service packs to its customers. This service is both set up and paid for separately. You won't be using this functionality for the example project in this chapter, so uncheck the Enable checkbox and click Next.

The next screen asks you for your company name, phone number, and Web address. This information is displayed to customers via the Add/Remove Programs Control Panel. The company name is also used as the base point for your product's Registry tree of information. This name should be consistent with any other products you may have created and distributed.

After you've clicked Next on the Company Information screen, the Application Features screen appears. As displayed in Figure 10-13, use this screen to divvy up the product into installable parts or, as InstallShield calls them, features. Use the spreadsheets you created at the beginning of this chapter and remember to approach this task from the customer's perspective.

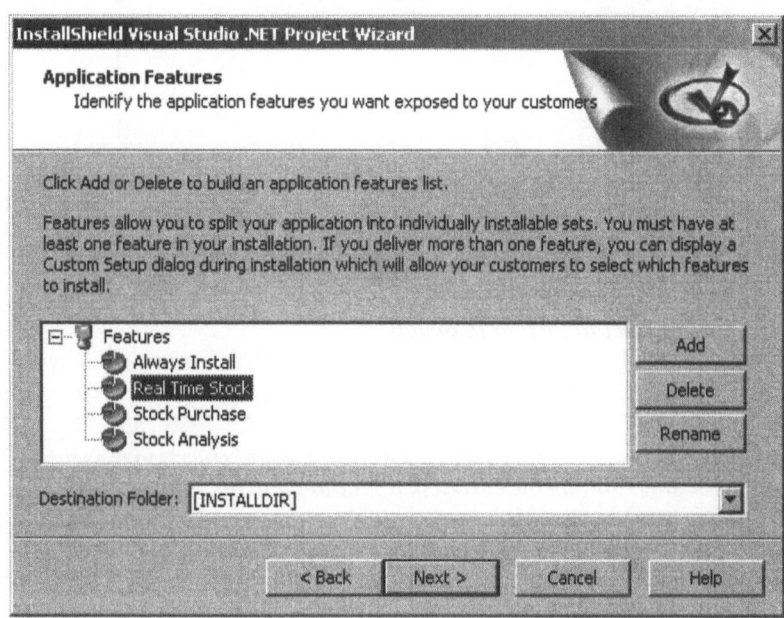

Figure 10-13. Including installable application features using the InstallShield Express Project Wizard

---

TIP *For all top-level features, make sure that the Features item in the tree is highlighted before selecting the Add button. Otherwise, features will be added as children beneath the currently selected object.*

Other than optionally specifying different destination directories for each of your installable parts, there's no need for any other customization at this time—you're simply informing the wizard of the installable parts' existence. Click Next to continue.

On the Visual Studio Project Outputs screen, as displayed in Figure 10-14, specify which files make up each feature. Designate these files as outputs as you did with the default MSI integration discussed earlier in this chapter.

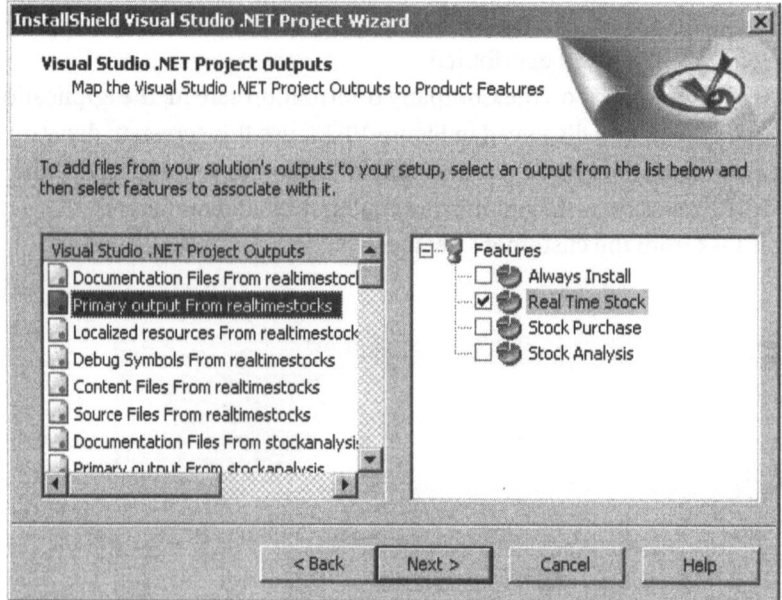

Figure 10-14. Choosing executable files to install

 NOTE *If you're asked to navigate the file system to add objects to the setup, you're probably running the wizard in a solution that doesn't contain any other projects. Although this is an acceptable way to create an installation, it means that the steps in this example may not always be applicable to your solution.*

While navigating down the list of Visual Studio .NET Project Outputs on the left side of the screen, check the features with which that particular object should be installed. It's likely that many of the outputs—such as the debug symbols—won't be included in the installation. Simply keep all the features unchecked for those outputs. For outputs that are needed by multiple components, check all of the features for which the output should be installed. For outputs that should always be installed regardless of which features the user has chosen, check the **Always Install** checkbox. You can leave the other features unchecked if the Always Install checkbox is chosen—the object will still always be installed.

Use the Application Files screen to add non-project-related files from the file system to the project. For instance, if you were writing an office suite program, your word processor might have an associated set of templates that should be installed on the user's system but wouldn't be included in any of the projects of the solution. Keep in mind that files should be added to each feature as listed in the drop-down combo box. For instance, if the Stock Purchase component has an associated Help file called PURCHASE.HLP, use the drop-down combo box to highlight the Stock Purchase feature and then use the Add Files button to search the hard drive for the file. Figure 10-15 displays this example.

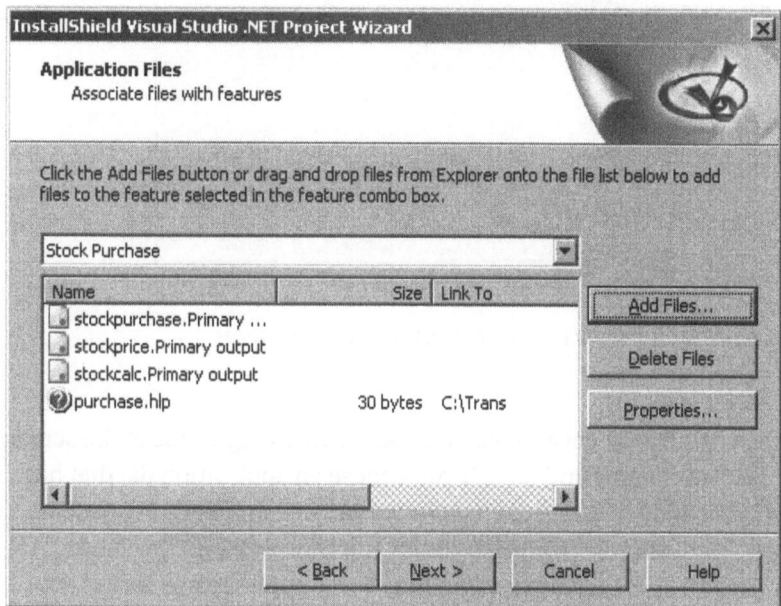

Figure 10-15. Choosing nonexecutable files to install

If you choose to set specific attributes for any of your outputs or files, highlight them now and click the Properties button. The screen that appears allows you to set system attributes (such as making a file read-only or hidden) or allow for applicable Component Object Model (COM) registration. Be sure to consult your engineers whenever changing these specifications (or, in some cases, not changing them)—this can sometimes severely limit your project's functionality.

After clicking Next, your next step is to create shortcuts for objects as necessary. Again, the user interface of this dialog box isn't always the most intuitive—to add a shortcut, right-click a folder in the left window and choose New Shortcut from the pop-up menu, as displayed in Figure 10-16.

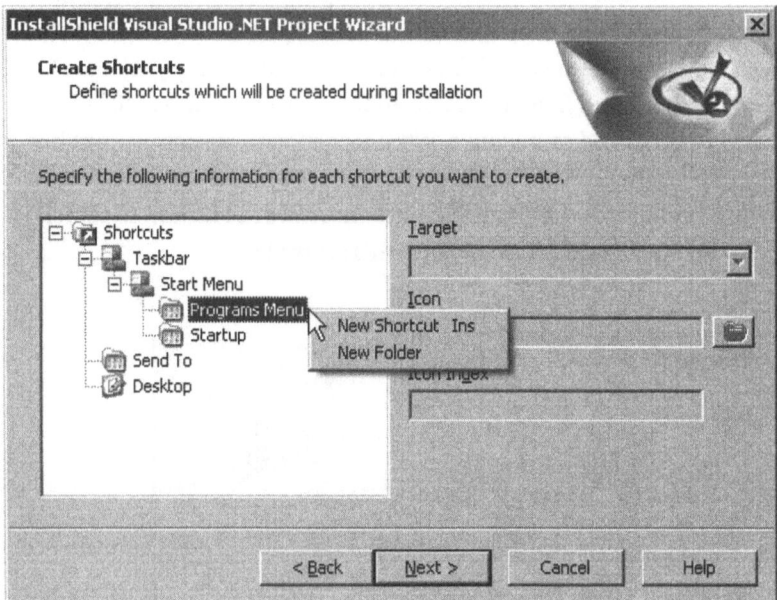

Figure 10-16. Creating shortcuts to install with the pop-up menu

Once created, use the Target and Icon edit boxes on the right side of the screen to specify the shortcut's name and look. If you choose an application file that has multiple icons embedded in it, use the Icon Index edit box to specify which icon should be used. The index will be one based (for you zero-using programmer types out there), so use 1 for the first icon in the file, 2 for the second, and so on.

You're almost done! Just a couple more steps. Use the next dialog box to add Registry information. For instance, you might want to set a couple of default values for your Stock Analysis tool. If you did this by hand using the REGEDIT tool, these default values might look like those displayed in Figure 10-17.

When you worked with the Visual Studio MSI integration, you set these values by hand using a Registry-like tree. You'll have that same ability in InstallShield Express after the wizard completes. If you like, however, you can specify Registry values now by writing what are known as *REG files*. You must write these files in a specific format, as displayed in Listing 10-2.

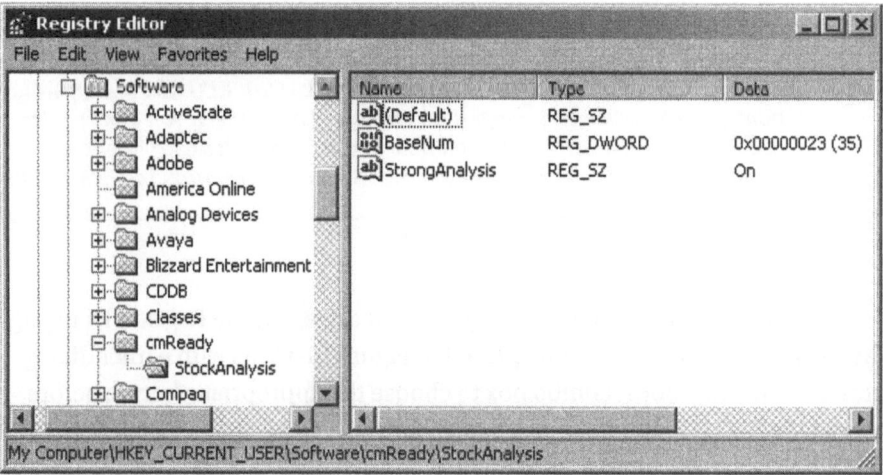

Figure 10-17. Using RegEdit to display Registry values

Listing 10-2. An Example of a REG File

```
Windows Registry Editor Version 5.00

[HKEY_CURRENT_USER\Software\cmReady\StockAnalysis]
@=""
"StrongAnalysis"="On"
"BaseNum"=dword:00000023
;
```

TIP *Typing this information yourself is the hard way to create this file. Instead, try using the REGEDIT default Registry editing tool to manually add whatever default values you'd like to include in the Registry and then export them back out to a text file. Choose Start ➤ Run and type REGEDIT followed by a Return. When the tool opens, navigate to the proper location for your values and add them. When finished, highlight the key that contains those values and choose File ➤ Export to create a Registry file on your file system. Make sure you only export the information you need by clicking specific keys—any child keys that fall under the highlighted key will also be added to the new REG file.*

CAUTION *The Windows Registry isn't a toy with which to trifle. You can severely damage your Windows operating system by making a mistake while editing the Registry. Worse, by making a mistake with REG files and installations, you can severely damage your end user's machine. If you don't understand how the Registry works and how to use it, consult an experienced Windows programmer before changing Registry information in installations.*

Once you've created a REG file on your hard drive, use the Registry Data page to associate it with a feature, as displayed in Figure 10-18. As with earlier dialog boxes, use the drop-down combo box to choose the appropriate feature before filling in the REG File edit box.

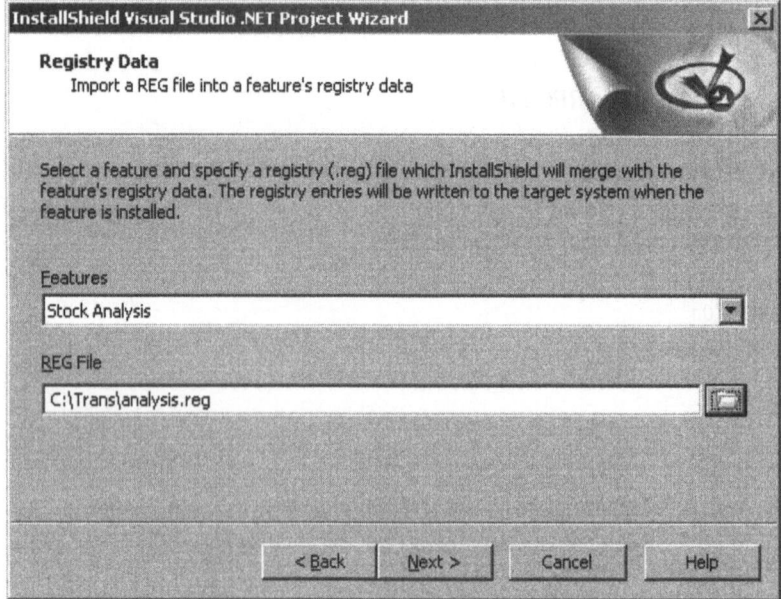

Figure 10-18. Specifying REG files to be installed

Use the final wizard step to add optional dialog boxes to the installation. For instance, include the dialog boxes that display a license agreement, ask for specific customer information, and show a "ready" dialog box by checking their appropriate checkboxes. You'll configure these more completely after the wizard finishes because you can't set several properties here.

After a summary screen, the InstallShield wizard exits, and you'll have a project named IS_Express in the Solution Explorer. This new project is quite different from that of a C# or other project. The objects listed aren't source files as you know them. Instead, the project virtualizes sets of properties together into logical groups—somewhat akin to the windows you used with the Visual Studio MSI setup tools. Figure 10-19 displays an example of the IS_Express window. The right side of the window is the familiar Solution Explorer. But now the top section of the left pane displays a set of properties relevant to the highlighted InstallShield listing in the Solution Explorer. Express always displays the help in the bottom-left window pane.

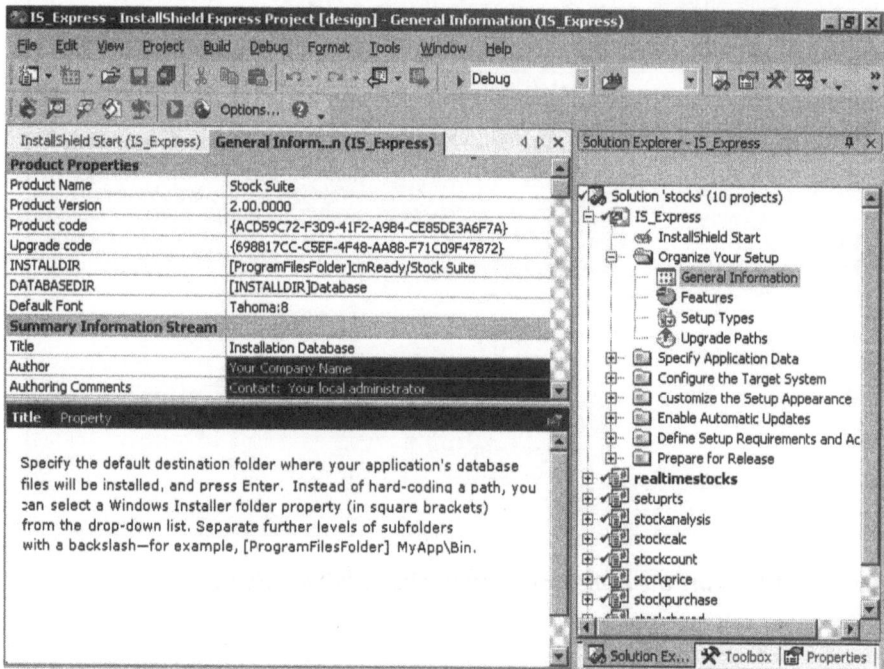

Figure 10-19. Viewing a setup project in the InstallShield Express Visual Studio integration

Your last step in configuring the installation is to navigate through all the properties and double-check all of the settings. Although the InstallShield wizard gave you a good start, it didn't require you to fill in several important fields.

The notable changes you make in this step are to update the general information page, set descriptions for the features, remove the "minimal" setup type, and let the license dialog box know where your End User License Agreement (EULA) text file is located on the local hard drive. Feel free to explore and change any desired settings. At this point, you might also want to explore the stand-alone IDE that was installed with the Express package, as displayed in Figure 10-20. Start the IDE by clicking the Start button and navigating to the InstallShield program group.

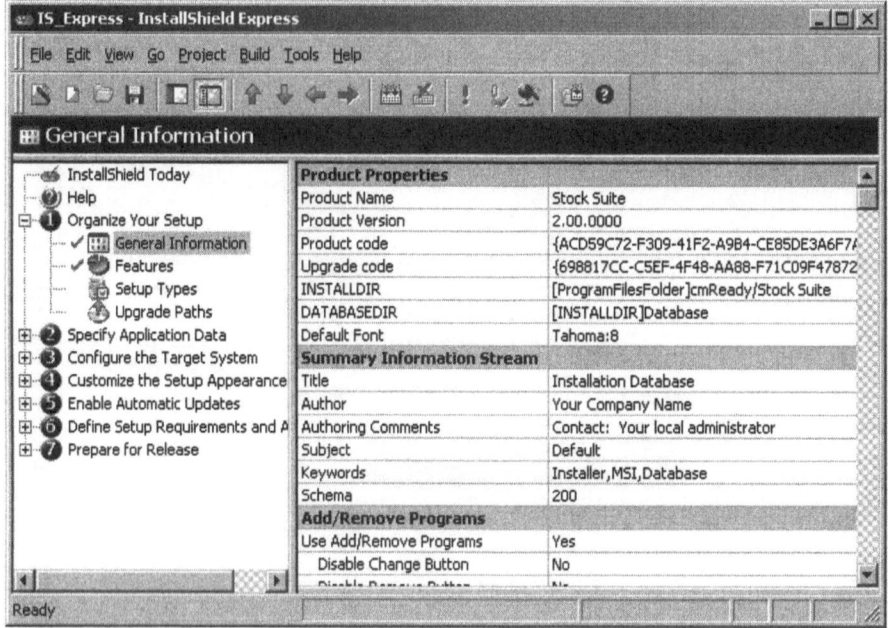

Figure 10-20. Viewing the same project in the InstallShield Express IDE

Once you've created the installation, it's time to build and test it. First, open the Configuration Manager dialog box and specify via which output media you plan to distribute the application. InstallShield Express supports distribution via several media types including CD-ROM, DVD-ROM, and Web download. If the installation will span disks (such as when distributing on a floppy disk), InstallShield automatically splits the installation into multiple parts as necessary. For your project, pick the CD-ROM installation. Figure 10-21 displays how the release configuration for your solution might appear.

NOTE *Don't forget to put the installation at the end of the build order or to make it the startup project! For more information about the Configuration Manager and build orders, see Chapter 9, "Builds for Windows .NET."*

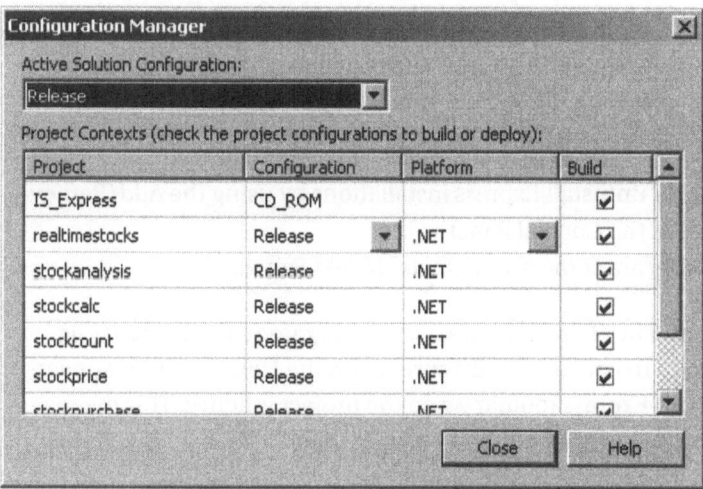

Figure 10-21. Changing propeties using the Configuration Manager

Once you've set the active configuration and chosen CD_ROM for your IS_Express project, you can build the product from within Visual Studio using one of three ways:

- The first is to choose the Build ➤ Build Solution menu item. This builds all of the release components in the solution and then packages them into the installation as defined in the active configuration.

- The second way to build is to right-click the installation project itself and choose Build.

- Finally, you can also open the Prepare for Release folder in the installation project and choose the Build Your Release item.

NOTE *If using project outputs, you must build the installation from within Visual Studio. The Express IDE is unable to compile and build .NET components.*

Once built, there are a couple of ways to test the new setup. First, you can choose the Prepare for Release folder under the installation project and choose the Test Your Release item. This allows you to navigate through the user interface without actually installing any components on your hard drive. Alternatively, you can use the Debug ➤ Start menu item to run the application. Keep in mind that, by default, you can only uninstall Express installations by using the Add/Remove Program Files feature in the Control Panel.

Lastly, the following are some tips on InstallShield Express:

Use the Help icon: The Help for Express isn't integrated into the dynamic Visual Studio Help. To access it, make sure to use the Help icon that appears on the InstallShield Express toolbar when the project is active. This means that it's not possible to use F1 context-sensitive help.

You'll have to stick to one language: You can't create multilanguage installations with InstallShield Express. The language you choose in the Setup Wizard is the language with which you're stuck. It's possible to import Express installations into the Developer product that support multilanguage installations. Of course, you could create multilanguage installations by simply copying the existing project and then changing the string tables, but this isn't a good solution according to SCM standards. Frankly, if you need to have a multilanguage installation, Express isn't the tool for you.

Forget source control: Visual Studio's source control via SourceSafe doesn't work with the Express product.

You can't reorder dialog boxes: Although it's possible to select or deselect user interface dialog boxes, there's no way to reorder them using Express. If this is a requirement, you'll need to switch to the default Visual Studio MSI integration or another product. Developer supports both the reorder of dialog boxes and the creation of custom dialog boxes.

You have to use the InstallShield branding: As included with all InstallShield products, the Express EULA requires that you not change or remove the InstallShield branding or copyright information. The term *branding* refers to the InstallShield name that's displayed in several dialog boxes of the installation. The marketing spin from the InstallShield folks is that customers trust the InstallShield label and that the branding makes both the developer and the customer feel more comfortable—though I bet the marketing aspect of the branding play a part in the way it writes the license. Many development houses choose not to allow third-party software to brand their products. In this case, you'll need to switch to the default Visual Studio MSI integration or to one of the Wise products discussed later in this chapter.

.NET is installed automatically: The Microsoft .NET Framework is installed automatically with an Express installation when it isn't found on an end user's machine. This is a handy feature that isn't available through the default Visual Studio MSI integration without putting in some effort. I found that Install-Shield Express tried to reinstall the .NET Framework on the same machine where the components were built—an action that seems rather redundant. Although it's possible that the installation was simply checking versions of the Framework's components without changing the system, it was an extremely time-consuming process that I couldn't cancel or avoid.

Getting More Options—Using InstallShield Developer

At first glance, InstallShield Developer doesn't appear to be all that different from Express. The Setup Wizard is similar to that of Express, and you've still got the choice to engage MSI as your installation engine. And that's where most of the similarities end. The Developer interface offers quite an increase in customization and features. Some of the additional features include the following:

- A visual dialog box editor

- An installation debugger

- A direct MSI editor

- Visual Studio source control integration

- Multilanguage installations available at an additional price

I suggest that the most significant difference between Developer and Express is the ability to use InstallShield's scripting mechanism as the install's engine in addition to MSI.[6] This allows a level of customization not possible with the Windows Installer—including the inclusion of 100-percent custom dialog boxes. By using InstallScript, MSI doesn't fade completely out of the picture...InstallShield

---

6. InstallShield recommends that the basic MSI setup project be used in most cases and that InstallShield scripting be used only in special cases.

still calls it for much of its basic functionality. Developer supports both scripting and typical MSI installations. You might choose a nonscripting Developer scenario for multilanguage support or if a dialog box reorder is necessary.

NOTE *To be eligible for the "Optimized for Enterprise" logo provided by Microsoft, you must use an MSI-based installation tool. Professional and Developer installations using InstallScript aren't the tools to use to meet this requirement. Eligibility for the basic Windows XP logo is still available to script-based installation programs.*

The scripting language in the latest version of Developer[7] is similar to the InstallScript available in previous incarnations of InstallShield. Unfortunately, folks new to the technology may suffer when choosing to go down this road—even simple tasks are often daunting. For example, adding a default, noncustom dialog box to the installation must be accomplished completely through scripting. Luckily, InstallShield provides a default script and has many examples on its support site and in documentation. A complete InstallScript language reference is also included when Developer is installed.

Listing 10-3 displays a complete Developer script and the steps that can be taken to add a new dialog box, use strings tables for multilanguage support, and put up a customized "ready-to-install" dialog box. Bolded text indicates where I made changes to the default code provided by InstallShield.

NOTE *All custom and some provided dialog boxes require the InstallScript engine.*

Listing 10-3. An Example Developer InstallScript Script Used for the StockSuite Product Installation.

```
//////////////////////////////////////////////////////////////////////////////
//  File Name:      Setup.rul
//  Description:    InstallShield script
//  Comments:       This script was generated based on the selections you made in
//                  the Project Wizard.  Refer to the help topic entitled "Modify
//                  the script that the Project Wizard generates" for information
//                  on possible next steps.
//////////////////////////////////////////////////////////////////////////////
```

---

7. The example included in this section was created with InstallShield Developer 8.0.

```
////////////////////////////////////////////////////////////////////////
// Both the IDS_C_WINDOWTITLE and IDS_C_SDWELCOMETITLE objects
// were added to the English string table as follows:
// IDS_C_WINDOWTITLE = "cmReady Stock Suite 2.0"
// IDS_C_SDWELCOMETITLE = "Welcome to the cmReady Stock ↵
//     Suite 2.0 setup program.  Click "next" to install and use this product."
////////////////////////////////////////////////////////////////////////


// Include header files
#include "ifx.h"

/////////////////////// string defines ////////////////////////////

/////////////////////// installation declarations ////////////////////
// ----- DLL function prototypes -----
    // your DLL function prototypes


// ---- script function prototypes -----
    // your script function prototypes


    // your global variables


////////////////////////////////////////////////////////////////////////
//
// FUNCTION:    OnFirstUIBefore
//
// EVENT:       FirstUIBefore event is sent when installation is run for the first
//              time on given machine. In the handler installation usually displays
//              UI allowing end user to specify installation parameters. After this
//              function returns, FeatureTransferData is called to perform file
//              transfer.
//
////////////////////////////////////////////////////////////////////////
function OnFirstUIBefore()
    number nResult,nSetupType;
    string szTitle, szMsg;
    string szLicenseFile, szQuestion;
    string szName, szCompany;
    string szFile;
    string szTargetPath;
    string szDir;
    string szFeatures, szTargetdir;
    number nLevel;
```

```
            LIST    listStartCopy;
            LIST    list;
            number  nvSize;
            number  nUser;


//NON INSTALLSHIELD DEFAULT CODE STARTS HERE
            string szSetupType;
//NON INSTALLSHIELD DEFAULT CODE ENDS HERE


begin
            // TO DO: if you want to enable background, window title, and caption bar title
            // SetTitle( @PRODUCT_NAME, 24, WHITE );
            // SetTitle( @PRODUCT_NAME, 0, BACKGROUNDCAPTION );
            // Enable( FULLWINDOWMODE );
            // Enable( BACKGROUND );
            // SetColor(BACKGROUND,RGB (0, 128, 128));
            SHELL_OBJECT_FOLDER = @PRODUCT_NAME;
            nSetupType = TYPICAL;
            szDir = INSTALLDIR;
            szName    = "";
            szCompany = "";


Dlg_Start:
            // beginning of dialogs label


Dlg_SdWelcome:


//NON INSTALLSHIELD DEFAULT CODE STARTS HERE
            //This code gets strings from the currently loaded language
            //string table and places them in variables.
            szTitle = @IDS_C_WINDOWTITLE;
            szMsg   = @IDS_C_SDWELCOMETITLE;
//NON INSTALLSHIELD DEFAULT CODE STARTS HERE


            nResult = SdWelcome( szTitle, szMsg );
            if (nResult = BACK) goto Dlg_Start;


Dlg_SdLicense:
//NON INSTALLSHIELD DEFAULT CODE STARTS HERE
            //This code tells the Installer which license file to use
            //when displaying the license textbox.  The SUPPORTDIR
            //variable indicates that I've dropped the license.txt file
            //into the Support Files window listed under Behavior
```

```
    //and Logic.  Respective text files should be dropped into
    //each language supported by your instllation.
    szLicenseFile - SUPPORTDIR ^ "license.txt";
//NON INSTALLSHIELD DEFAULT CODE ENDS HERE

    szTitle    = "";
    szMsg      = "";
    szQuestion = "";
    nResult    = SdLicense( szTitle, szMsg, szQuestion, szLicenseFile );
    if (nResult = BACK) goto Dlg_SdWelcome;


Dlg_SdShowInfoList:
    //sk
    szFile = SUPPORTDIR ^ "readme.txt";
    list = ListCreate( STRINGLIST );
    ListReadFromFile( list, szFile );


//NON INSTALLSHIELD DEFAULT CODE STARTS HERE
    //This code gets strings from the currently loaded language
    //string table and places them in variables.
    szTitle = @IDS_C_WINDOWTITLE;
//NON INSTALLSHIELD DEFAULT CODE ENDS HERE

    szMsg      = "";
    nResult = SdShowInfoList( szTitle, szMsg, list );
    ListDestroy( list );
    if (nResult = BACK) goto Dlg_SdLicense;


Dlg_SdCustomerInformation:


//NON INSTALLSHIELD DEFAULT CODE STARTS HERE
    //This code gets strings from the currently loaded language
    //string table and places them in variables.
    szTitle = @IDS_C_WINDOWTITLE;
//NON INSTALLSHIELD DEFAULT CODE ENDS HERE

    szMsg      = "";
    nResult = SdCustomerInformation( szTitle, szName, szCompany, nUser );
    if (nResult = BACK) goto Dlg_SdShowInfoList;


Dlg_SdAskDestPath:


//NON INSTALLSHIELD DEFAULT CODE STARTS HERE
```

```
        //This code gets strings from the currently loaded language
        //string table and places them in variables.
        szTitle = @IDS_C_WINDOWTITLE;
//NON INSTALLSHIELD DEFAULT CODE ENDS HERE


    szMsg   = "";
    nResult = SdAskDestPath( szTitle, szMsg, szDir, 0 );
    INSTALLDIR = szDir;
    if (nResult = BACK) goto Dlg_SdCustomerInformation;


Dlg_SetupType:


//NON INSTALLSHIELD DEFAULT CODE STARTS HERE
        //This code gets strings from the currently loaded language
        //string table and places them in variables.
        szTitle = @IDS_C_WINDOWTITLE;
//NON INSTALLSHIELD DEFAULT CODE ENDS HERE


    szMsg       = "";
    nResult = SetupType ( szTitle , szMsg , "" , nSetupType , 0 );
    if (nResult = BACK) then
        goto Dlg_SdAskDestPath;
    else
        nSetupType = nResult;
        if (nSetupType != CUSTOM) then
          szTargetPath = INSTALLDIR;
           nvSize = 0;
           FeatureCompareSizeRequired(MEDIA,szTargetPath,nvSize);
           if (nvSize != 0) then
               MessageBox( szSdStr_NotEnoughSpace, WARNING );
               goto Dlg_SetupType;
           endif;
        endif;
    endif;


Dlg_SdFeatureTree:
    if ((nResult = BACK) && (nSetupType != CUSTOM)) goto Dlg_SetupType;


//NON INSTALLSHIELD DEFAULT CODE STARTS HERE
        //This code gets strings from the currently loaded language
        //string table and places them in variables.
        szTitle = @IDS_C_WINDOWTITLE;
//NON INSTALLSHIELD DEFAULT CODE ENDS HERE
```

```
        szMsg       = "";
        szTargetdir = INSTALLDIR;
        szFeatures = "";
        nLevel = 2;
        if (nSetupType = CUSTOM) then
            nResult = SdFeatureTree(szTitle, szMsg, szTargetdir, szFeatures, nLevel);
            if (nResult = BACK) goto Dlg_SetupType;
        endif;

Dlg_SdStartCopy:

//NON INSTALLSHIELD DEFAULT CODE STARTS HERE
    //This code gets strings from the currently loaded language
    //string table and places them in variables.
    szTitle = @IDS_C_WINDOWTITLE;
//NON INSTALLSHIELD DEFAULT CODE ENDS HERE

    szMsg    = "";
    listStartCopy = ListCreate( STRINGLIST );
    //The following is an example of how to add a string(szName) to a
list(listStartCopy).
    //eg. ListAddString(listStartCopy,szName,AFTER);

//NON INSTALLSHIELD DEFAULT CODE STARTS HERE
            //This code creates a string array which will be loaded into the
            //textbox for the Ready to Copy dialog box.  The customer's
            //name, company and install directory will be displayed.  The
            //customer can cancel or continue at this point depending on
            //what they read on this dialog box.
            ListAddString(listStartCopy, "Stock Suite 2.0 Setup", AFTER);
            ListAddString(listStartCopy, "", AFTER);
            ListAddString(listStartCopy, "CUSTOMER INFORMATION", AFTER);
            ListAddString(listStartCopy, "Customer Name = " + szName, AFTER);
            ListAddString(listStartCopy, "Customer Company = " + szCompany, AFTER);
            ListAddString(listStartCopy, "", AFTER);
            ListAddString(listStartCopy, "INSTALL INFORMATION", AFTER);
            ListAddString(listStartCopy, "Install Directory = " + INSTALLDIR,
AFTER);
            switch (nSetupType)
                case CUSTOM:
                    szSetupType = "Custom";
                case TYPICAL:
```

```
                                szSetupType = "Typical";
                        case COMPACT:
                                szSetupType = "Compact";
                endswitch;
                ListAddString(listStartCopy, "Install Type = " + szSetupType, AFTER);
    //NON INSTALLSHIELD DEFAULT CODE ENDS HERE

        nResult = SdStartCopy( szTitle, szMsg, listStartCopy );
        ListDestroy(listStartCopy);
        if (nResult = BACK) goto Dlg_SdFeatureTree;

        Enable(STATUSEX);

        return 0;
    end;


    /////////////////////////////////////////////////////////////////////////////
    //
    //   FUNCTION:     OnMaintUIBefore
    //
    //   EVENT:        MaintUIBefore event is sent when end user runs installation that
    //                 has already been installed on the machine. Usually this happens
    //                 through Add/Remove Programs applet. In the handler, installation
    //                 usually displays UI allowing end user to modify existing
    //                 installation or uninstall application. After this function
    //                 returns, FeatureTransferData is called to perform file transfer.
    //
    /////////////////////////////////////////////////////////////////////////////
    function OnMaintUIBefore()
        NUMBER nResult, nType;
        STRING szTitle, szMsg, svDir, svResult, szCaption;
    begin
        // TO DO: if you want to enable background, window title, and caption bar title

        // SetTitle( @PRODUCT_NAME, 24, WHITE );
        // SetTitle( @PRODUCT_NAME, 0, BACKGROUNDCAPTION );
        // SetColor(BACKGROUND,RGB (0, 128, 128));
        // Enable( FULLWINDOWMODE );
        // Enable( BACKGROUND );
    Dlg_Start:
        Disable(BACKBUTTON);
        nType = SdWelcomeMaint(szTitle, szMsg, MODIFY);
        Enable(BACKBUTTON);
```

```
    if (nType = REMOVEALL) then
        svResult = SdLoadString(IFX_MAINTUI_MSG);
        szCaption = SdLoadString(IFX_ONMAINTUI_CAPTION);
        nResult = SprintfBox(MB_OKCANCEL,szCaption,"%s",svResult);
        if (nResult = IDCANCEL) goto Dlg_Start;
    endif;

    nResult = NEXT;

Dlg_SdFeatureTree:
    if (nType = MODIFY) then
        szTitle = "";
        szMsg = "";
        nResult = SdFeatureTree(szTitle, szMsg, INSTALLDIR, "", 2);
        if (nResult = BACK) goto Dlg_Start;
    endif;

    switch(nType)
        case REMOVEALL: FeatureRemoveAll();
        case REPAIR:    FeatureReinstall();
    endswitch;

    Enable(STATUSEX);
end;
```

The following are some final tips on InstallShield Developer:

Integrates gracefully with Visual Studio: I found that Developer's integration into the Visual Studio environment is much better than that of Express. This especially includes the support of a project's right-click functionality.

Provides mulilanguage support: One language comes for free with Install-Shield Developer. Support for 32 other languages is available for an additional cost from InstallShield. Custom dialog boxes or strings, of course, aren't included in purchased language packages. In those cases, string tables are used for complete translations.[8]

Gives you debugging capabilities: InstallShield Developer comes with a fully featured debugging tool—this is especially helpful when using the scripting engine of the program.

---

8. From my understanding, there are some branding strings that aren't included in the string table and are only available through language package purchases. These strings will appear in English when installation occurs on different language Windows operating systems.

Brands you with the InstallShield name: Again, as with all InstallShield products, the Express EULA requires that you not change or remove the Install-Shield branding or copyright information. The term *branding* refers to the InstallShield name that's displayed in several dialog boxes of the installation. The marketing spin from the InstallShield folks is that customers trust the InstallShield label and that the branding makes both the developer and the customer feel more comfortable—though I bet the marketing aspects of the branding play a part in the way they write the license. Many development houses choose not to allow third-party software to brand their products. In this case, you'll need to switch to the default Visual Studio MSI integration or to one of the Wise products discussed later in this chapter.

Offers redistribution packages: A bevy of system file redistribution packages are available for inclusion in your installation by using a point-and-click interface.

Using Wise

If InstallShield owns the majority of the install market,[9] Wise is generally known as the upstart competitor. Started by a couple of guys in a garage back in 1992, the creators of Wise wanted to provide an easy-to-use alternative to InstallShield, which was then completely script based, considered relatively difficult to use, and held the Windows install monopoly. Wise began as a shareware program but became so popular that the product became an official offering in the late 90s.

At the time of this writing, Wise has several product offerings for installations:

Wise for Visual Studio .NET: Like InstallShield, Wise integrates cleanly into the Visual Studio .NET IDE. According to the marketing spin, Wise is the only third-party installation software that has partnered with Microsoft, thereby making its integration more robust and easier to use than that of the "limited Visual Studio add-in"[10] provided by its competitor.[11]

---

9. Neither Wise nor InstallShield officially track market share—however, representatives from both companies told me that InstallShield owns a majority of the market. From the information I've gathered both from the reps and other sources, it appears that InstallShield has about 60 percent of the Windows market and Wise about 30 percent. These numbers won't hold up in court—I think pulling out the teeth from the people-in-the-know might have been easier than getting an answer to this question. I even started to wonder if I had unearthed some strange Watergate-style installation coverup.

10. Their words—not mine.

11. InstallShield strongly disputes this claim and states that its integration has been at least as strong as Wise's since April 2002.

Wise for Windows Installer: This is the separate integrated development environment that has the same functionality as Wise for Visual Studio .NET. The only real difference between the two products is that this is a completely stand-alone product and can't take advantage of some Visual Studio features.

> **NOTE** *Unlike the equivalent products of InstallShield, Wise Corporation doesn't provide the separate IDE and Visual Studio integration in one package at a single price point. You must buy each product separately.*

Wise Installation System: This is a continuation of the legacy Wise script-based product line that has been on the market for many years. If you're starting your installation from scratch, it's advisable that you start with either the Visual Studio .NET or Windows Installer versions of Wise.

Wise for Visual Studio .NET[12]

I'll put the cards on the table here—Wise touts that the comparative ease of use of its tools is a large differentiating factor between it and the InstallShield Developer product. This is generally true. There's no need to script—even for customized dialog boxes—and you can do almost everything via a point-and-click interface. This product, however, still adheres to one of the basic rules of software: As the power of a tool increases, so does the difficulty of its use. I personally wouldn't say that Wise for Visual Studio .NET is "easy to use." I was, however, able to put out a fairly customized installation for the Stock Suite in just a few hours.

> **NOTE** *Wise products are available for evaluation download via the Wise Web site at* http://www.wise.com.

There's a major difference between the two competitors: The MSI-enabled Wise products aren't procedural in the same way as the script-based InstallShield Developer. Although they do have scripting ability, the scripts are object oriented in nature and are used only at particular times—much like the MSI custom actions discussed earlier in the chapter.

---

12. This evaluation used Wise for Visual Studio .NET 4.2.

Figure 10-22 displays the first and only dialog box you encounter in the Wise Setup Wizard.

NOTE *As usual, the naming of the new project takes place before the wizard starts. Remember to name your project appropriately when choosing which project to create.*

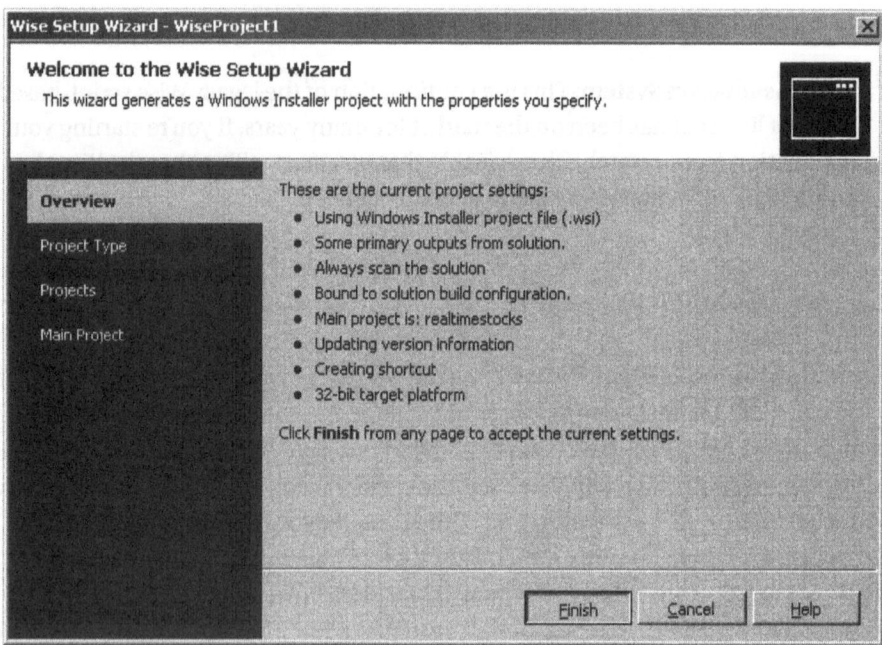

Figure 10-22. Using the Wise Setup Wizard

Use the four tabs to the left of the dialog box to choose the basic options—such as which projects in the solution should be included in the installation. But that pretty much covers it for the wizard—after clicking Finish, you're thrown directly into the tool itself. This is a shame because much of the tool isn't intuitive. Wise would be wise (okay, bad joke) to include an InstallShield-like wizard that allows you to set most of an installation's basic options.

On the positive side, Wise's integration with Visual Studio is indeed impressive. Although InstallShield has small imperfections with its add-in compatibility, Wise looks like it's always been a part of the tool. From accessing the Help all the way to building setup projects, you can access almost all of Wise's functionality through the usual Visual Studio methodologies. Only its debugger appears to be a separate application.

The integration is split into three different modes. The first is the Installation Expert, as displayed in Figure 10-23. In contrast to its name, it's not the "expert mode" as you might expect. This is the beginner's step-by-step creation mode. Much like you did in InstallShield, navigate through the list of properties and set them appropriately for your installation.

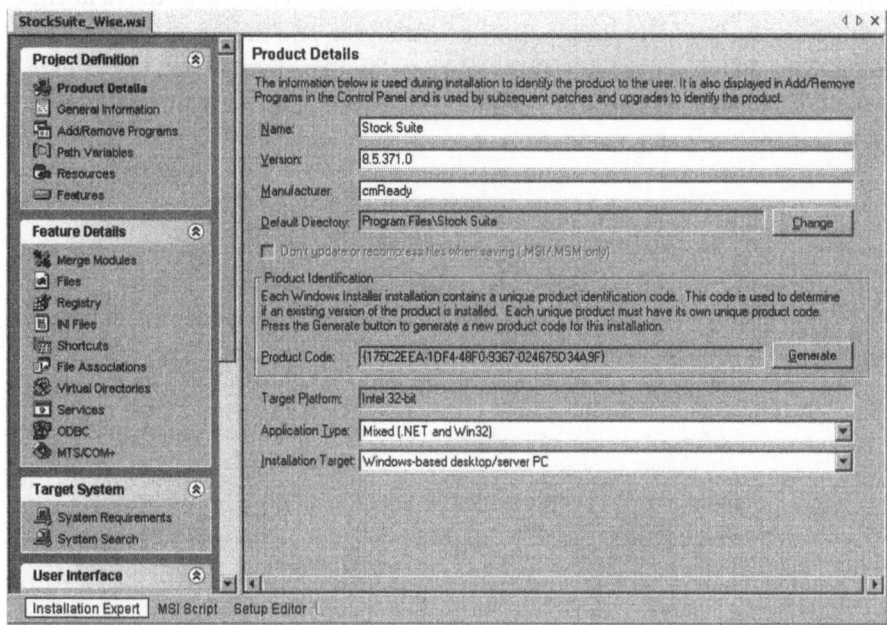

Figure 10-23. Using the Installation Expert mode of Wise for Visual Studio .NET

Change the title, manufacturer, and default directory in the Product Details screen as displayed in Figure 10-23. Note that the version is set automatically—it's tied to the default project in the solution (which in this case is the Real Time Stock Ticker).

NOTE *Setting the default directory on this screen doesn't automatically cascade the change throughout the installation. In fact, in one of my largest criticisms of this product, I was often unable to find a simple way to change properties without making the same change numerous times throughout the interface.*

After navigating to and filling in properties on the screens located in the Product Details and General Information sections of the Installation Expert, it's time to define the installable parts (hereafter known in this section as Wise *features* to be consistent with the product's user interface) of your setup. This isn't as easy as it might seem—by default, Wise automatically gathers all of the outputs created by the solution into a single feature called Complete. You have to undo this default action to split up the application properly.

Navigate to the Features screen of the Project Definition section. Using the Add button, create five separate Wise features—the shared objects, the Real Time Stock Ticker, the Stock Purchaser, the Stock Analyzer, and the Stock Calculator. Add them as children to the currently existing Complete feature—the Complete choice should still install the entire suite. Once completed, the Features screen should look similar to Figure 10-24.

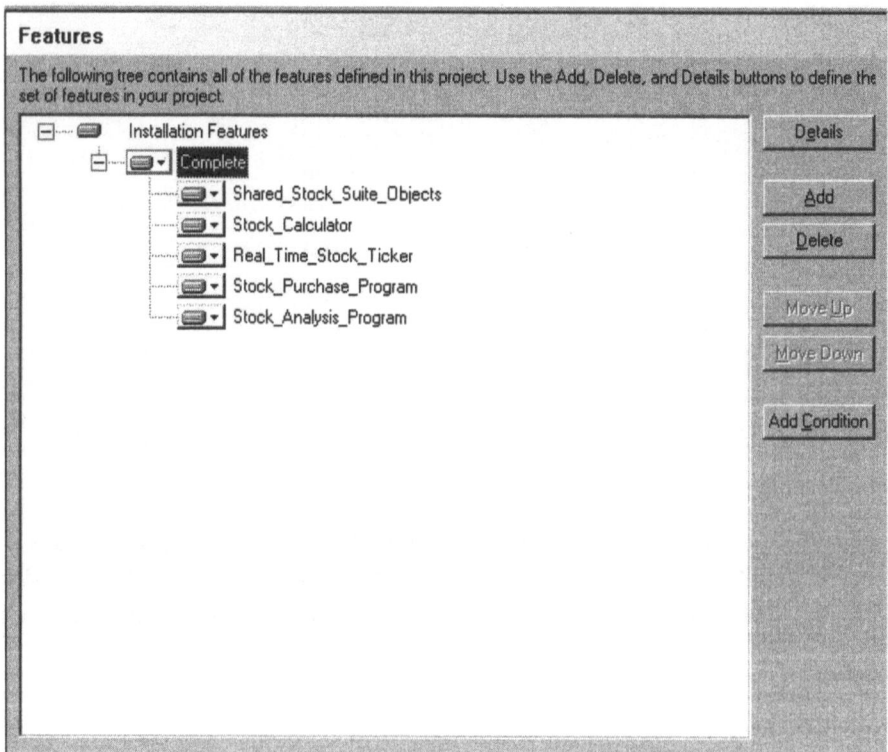

Figure 10-24. Specifying features using Wise's Installation Expert

Unfortunately, there's no easy way from within the Installation Expert to set which files are applicable to which Wise features. This change affects how the rest of the install takes place, so you have to change to Setup Editor mode before continuing. The Setup Editor consists of several tabs that allow you to make changes to the installation in a more power-user-friendly manner. These tabs include the ability to turn on and off dialog boxes, create and change your Wise features, and detail how and under what conditions files should be installed.

Let's concentrate on the Features tab for a moment. This tab allows you to update properties that are out of sync because of the changes you made earlier. First, you need to move the project outputs associated with the Complete feature to the respective features you just created. Do this by navigating to the Components file folder listed directly underneath the Complete feature and dragging and dropping the objects as necessary to the new features. After moving the files, choose to view the details on the shared objects feature and click the Required Feature checkbox so that it's always installed.

NOTE *It's my opinion that installations created with Wise show installable parts/features in a more pleasing manner than either InstallShield or the default MSI integration of Visual Studio. This allows you to list the calculator as a removable feature instead of automatically including it with the Stock Analyzer and Stock Purchaser programs.*

Figure 10-25 displays how the Features tab might look after accomplishing this goal. Once your files are properly associated with features, you need to correct another problem that developed because of an earlier change. By default, Wise decided that the Program Files install directory for your product would be the same name as that of your solution: stocks. This isn't a professional title for the product, so change the default directory to *Stock Suite* on the Product Details screen of the Installation Expert's Project Definition section.

Alas! This change doesn't propagate automatically throughout your installation. All of your Wise installation features still point to the original STOCKS directory and must be changed by hand. To do this, right-click the Wise feature and choose Details. A dialog box appears where you can set a descriptive phrase that describes the Wise feature and that also gives you the ability to designate a new installation directory. Change all the directories to match the one you set earlier: Program Files\Stock Suite.

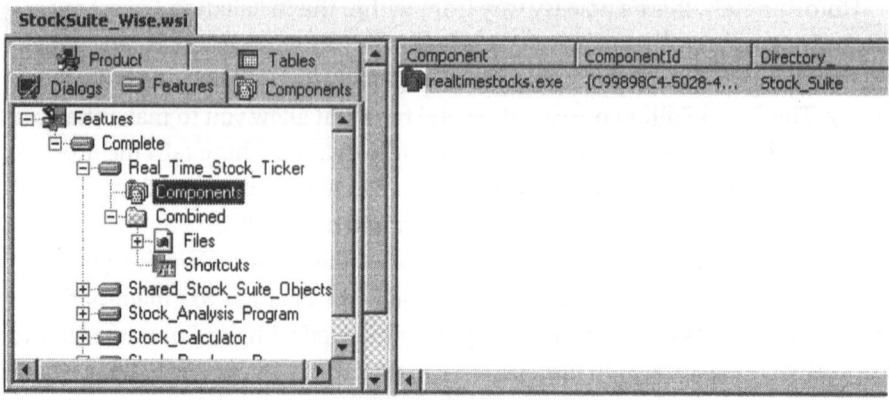

Figure 10-25. Specifying features using Wise's Setup Editor mode

While you're in Setup Editor mode, make a few other quick changes. First, create the shortcuts that should appear for your applications after installation. To do so, right-click any Wise feature and choose New ➤ Shortcut. This creates a shortcut object beneath the feature and pops up a helper wizard. On the first dialog box of the wizard, choose the File in This Installation radio button—this allows you to specify the project outputs associated with this feature rather than a file from the file system. On the second page of the wizard, choose the executable for which you want to create a shortcut. Wise doesn't give you an opportunity to choose a "friendly" name for your shortcut in the wizard. Instead, you make that change afterward by double-clicking the newly created shortcut and changing the Name property to whatever you want.

After creating the shortcuts, it's time to improve the user interface. First, click the Dialogs tab. Much like in the Visual Studio default MSI integration, this displays a tree whose roots contain different kinds of installations—the Install, Maintenance, and Administrative sets of dialog boxes are listed. The Install set refers to the default end user installation. The Administrative set is what administrators see when installing from the network. The Maintenance set holds the user interface that appears if the product is already installed—in this case, an uninstall or repair are offered to the end user.

For the purposes of this example, concentrate on the Install set dialog boxes. In real life, of course, you'd make sure the dialog boxes for all three trees work properly.

After clicking Install Dialogs to expand its tree if necessary, add the Select Features dialog box. With this dialog box, you can choose which Wise Features to install. That's the only dialog box you're going to add for the time being, but because you have the user interface editor open, go ahead and personalize some of the interface dialog boxes. Double-click a dialog box—any dialog box—to make it appear in the editor. Go ahead and change the banner for the dialog box; use your company's bitmap by double-clicking it, choosing the Graphic tab, and then clicking the Set button to find the proper bitmap on your hard drive.

TIP *You can also choose to set pictures anchored on the left side of dialog boxes instead of the top if you like that look better.*

Unlike the default MSI integration in Visual Studio, you aren't required to perfectly size the bitmap—the dialog box editor stretches it to fit. You can choose only bitmaps for this task. If you have other types of images, you must convert them using a program such as Adobe Photoshop before adding them to the project.

You can customize all dialog boxes in Wise without the need for script—a significant difference from the way InstallShield Developer handles the same task. Like the example displayed in Figure 10-26, change the branding located near the bottom of the screen from Wise Corporation to your company name. Be sure to extend the line object next to it to align with the newly sized text. This particular change is small—if you make other changes, be careful that you don't accidentally lose functionality by deleting required text or choice objects.

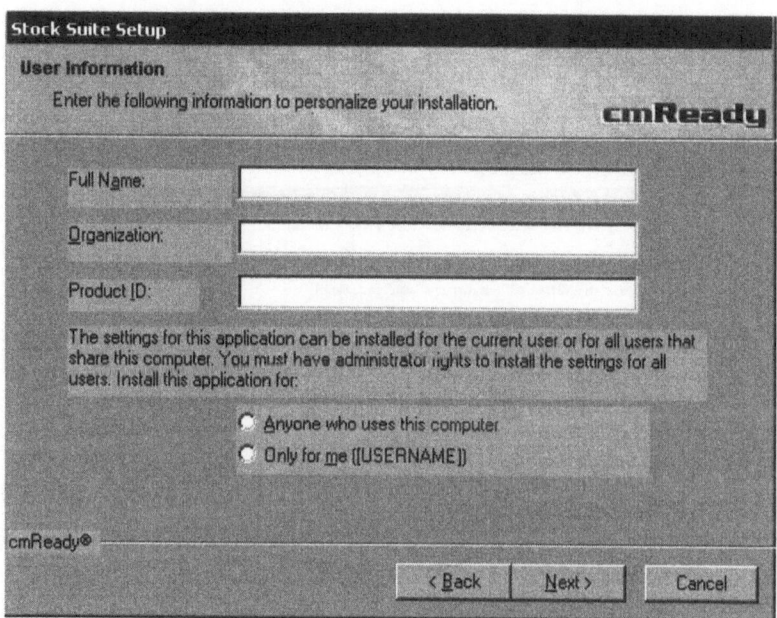

Figure 10-26. Editing the User Information screen of the Stock Suite Setup dialog box

And now for the bad news—you must make that same change on every dialog box you include in the installation. However, it's a small price to avoid another company branding the product.

TIP *Double-click graphical objects in the user interface editor to display the object's x and y coordinates, width and height, respectively. Then you can make the same movement or size change in more than one dialog box by copying and pasting values in other dialog boxes. This assures the consistency of your installation's look as the user navigates through it.*

After you've made any desired aesthetic changes to the dialog boxes, finish the user interface by opening the License Dialog box editor and then double-clicking the text box located in the center. Cut and paste your company's license information into the text box. The box supports rich text—so feel free to format it using your favorite word processor.

You've now completed customizing your installation's user interface. You could have also added custom dialog boxes as necessary to gather information from your users. Had you chosen to do so, you could've used the MSI Script mode, as displayed in Figure 10-27, to instruct Wise how to display and react to it.

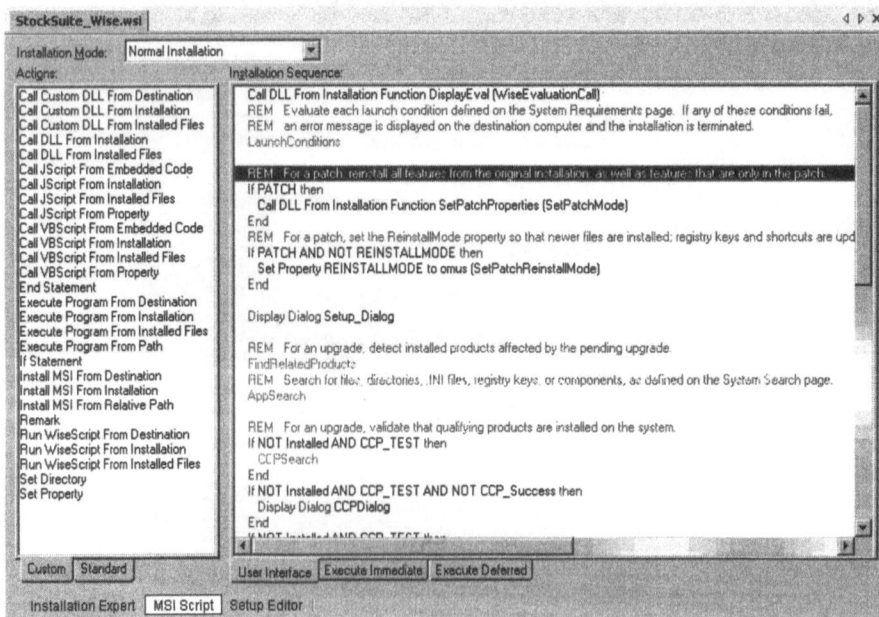

Figure 10-27. Using MSI Script mode in Wise for Visual Studio .NET

Although still somewhat procedural in nature, MSI script isn't typical script. Instead of typing the code, double-click a command to the left of the editor to display a dialog box with options for the command. After filling and closing it, Wise adds a text statement that reflects the command in MSI script on the right side of the window. From this point forward, you must always double-click that line to bring up the command dialog box for any changes you want to make. You can copy and paste code listed in this screen to other locations within Wise but, unfortunately, not outside of the application. For those used to coding via the keyboard, this can be a bit of a culture shock.

The three tabs near the bottom of the MSI Script mode screen relate to "moments in time" in the setup process. The Execute Immediate script runs as the installation starts. The Execute Deferred script runs just before the installation finishes. The User Interface script runs as the dialog boxes display. Each default script has many conditionals based upon whether the installation is an upgrade, uninstall, or other nonstandard setup—so be careful to place commands in the proper location.

Wise also allows using Windows JScript or VBScript to carry out some custom actions. Earlier in the chapter, you created a console application to support custom actions using default MSI. You can still make calls to outside applications if you'd like to do so, but it's much easier to use an interface such as this.

Once you've completed creating the Wise installation, build and run it using the default Build and Debug commands in Visual Studio. The Wise debugger starts automatically when run in debug mode—this allows you to step through code as necessary to root out errors.

That does it for the Wise tutorial. However, I do have these parting thoughts:

Avoid reordering dialog boxes: It's possible to reorder the dialog boxes as created by the Setup Wizard; however, my technical contact at Wise advises against it—it's easy to accidentally break the default installation's flow.

Provides mulilanguage support: Five (count 'em!) languages are included by default with the Wise for Visual Studio .NET product. This includes all strings present in the default dialog boxes—just remember to translate any strings you may have created yourself. To add your own strings, switch to the Installation Expert mode, navigate to the Languages screen listed under the Release Definition section, and click the Strings button.

Remember to add the .NET Framework: The .NET Framework and MSI tool installations aren't included by default with installations created with Wise. To add them to your installation, use the Build Options screen in the Release Definition section of the Installation Expert mode. It's not possible to bundle the .NET Framework and/or the MSI Installer tool in an MSI file, so if you choose to include them in your installation, you must allow Wise to build a setup executable file. It's possible to specify which version of the Framework to include, but Wise automatically downloads the latest version for you if desired.

Watch for the binaries: The Visual Studio SourceSafe integration works fine. Keep in mind that, by default, Wise includes the project output from your other projects as members. If you choose to add the Wise install to your source, you might accidentally check in large and unnecessary binary object files.

Installations for Linux

Although they share quite a few similarities, the Linux and other Unix operating systems often differ in their methods of installing software.

The lack of a common Registry-type system database and the ability to create powerful command-line scripts mean that installations can take the form of simple text files that simply copy files to their proper location. Of course, there are so many different hardware architectures to support in the Linux/Unix world that binary files are often not included as part of deployments. Instead, "installation" packages, especially open-source products, consist of source and makefiles that the end user prepares. Of course, the lack of an uninstall or any sort of rollback capabilities leaves a lot to be desired.

Introducing RPM

Sun and some Linux vendors have taken steps to make software installation and uninstallation more efficient by introducing databases that keep track of software installed on their operating systems. I'll talk about one tool in particular—the Linux installation tool called RPM.

RPM—short for RPM Package Manager[13]—has become the standard for many Linux-flavored environments. I discuss it in this section because it has been ported to many different operating systems, including Sun Solaris and Microsoft Windows. Although this doesn't necessarily mean that the same installation packages can be used on all the operating systems, it does mean you can present your products to the end user with a common interface. Keep in mind, of course, that the RPM packager software needs to be installed on the end user's machine in order for these packages to be used. Although it's common for the packager to be installed by default on many Linux systems, it's less commonly found on Solaris and almost never on Windows.

---

13. In the old days, it stood for the Red Hat Package Manager. The name changed, however, as it became more of a standard Linux project.

RPM allows your end users to install application files from the command line and the graphical programs provided in some operating systems. This robust tool keeps track of an application's version as well as its files for easy uninstall or upgrade. In addition, you can set up package dependencies in order to inform end users of other packages that might need to be applied before your application is installed. In many cases, installing a RPM[14] package is as easy as typing this:

```
rpm --install [package-name]
```

---

14. I'm using RPM version 4.1.1 on Red Hat Linux 8.0.

Once installed, an RPM package is uninstalled by typing the following:

```
rpm --erase [package-name]
```

For the full functionality of RPM, refer to its associated MAN pages or type the following at the command line:

```
rpm --help
```

Creating installation packagers with RPM may seem a little overwhelming at first. It's true that it's always a bit more challenging to work in nongraphical environments, but it's not nearly as difficult as it appears. These two simple rules apply to building RPM packages:

- You must have access to your application's code to build either source or binary RPM packages.

- When creating binary packages, you must be able to build the source for all of the hardware architectures and operating systems that you want to support.

Creating an RPM Package

It's time to create a sample RPM installer package. To follow this example, you'll need to be on a Unix-flavored operating system with the RPM package manager and the standard GNU C compilers installed. I created this example on an Intel-based machine with Red Hat 8.0 installed as the operating system.

 NOTE *So far I've used uppercase letters to denote directories and filenames. Because this section concerns Linux, which is a file case-sensitive operating system, I'll leave file and directory names lowercase so that they match the examples.*

Creating the Source Tree

When creating an RPM package, the first thing you want to do is gather your product's source into a single directory and create a makefile that builds the source into an application.

NOTE *For more information regarding makefiles and building in the Linux world, see Chapter 8, "Basic Builds."*

First, create a directory called rpm-example and place the source and makefile into it. It doesn't matter where this directory lives on your drive. The project you're going to make installs two small executable files. Listings 10-4, 10-5, and 10-6 display the C code for these executables and their associated makefiles. Specifically, Listing 10-4 displays hello.c, Listing 10-5 displays welcome.c, and Listing 10-6 displays the makefile. Be sure to create them in the rpm-example directory.

Listing 10-4. hello.c

```c
#include <stdio.h>

int main()
{
    printf("An RPM example!\n");
}
```

Listing 10-5. welcome.c

```c
#include <stdio.h>
int main()
{
    char szName[128];
    printf( "\n\nPlease enter your name: " );
    gets( szName );
    printf("Hello %s!  Welcome to the RPM example!\n\n", szName);
}
```

Listing 10-6. makefile

```
all: build
build:
        cc -c welcome.c
        cc -c hello.c
        cc -o welcome_rpm_example welcome.o
        cc -o hello_rpm_example hello.o
install:
        cp welcome_rpm_example /usr/bin
        cp hello_rpm_example /usr/bin
clean:
        rm *.o
        rm *_example
```

 NOTE *The makefile should reflect paths relative to its position to the source. In Listing 10-6, the C files have no parent path attached to them—that's because the makefile and the C files reside in the same directory. This distinction is important to the RPM compiler.*

These programs don't do much—they simply output some text to the console. They will, however, be sufficient to demonstrate how to create an RPM package. Go ahead and ensure they build by changing to the rpm-example directory and compiling the files by typing make at the command line.

Tarring the Source

After you've confirmed that the source has been built properly, collect the source files into a TAR file (also known as a *tar ball*). This is a single file that contains many other files—it's analogous to a Windows ZIP file without the compression. Using a TAR file, you can easily transport collections of directories and files.

Before you create the TAR file, be sure to delete the object files you created in your test build by typing make clean in the source directory.

NOTE *From this point forward, you may have to be logged in as root to follow these instructions. The root account has administrator privileges on Linux and other Unix-flavored operating systems. If you don't have root access on the machine for which you're building the RPM, try to create a similar directory structure in your home directory and test build the RPM there.*

For this example, you should follow basic RPM standards by placing the TAR file you created in the special directory designed for RPM source tar balls. On my Red Hat Linux 8.0 machine, this directory is called /usr/src/redhat/SOURCES, but this may differ depending on your installed operating system. Be sure to check with your operating system distributor for the proper RPM build directory.

NOTE *If you don't have rights to the SOURCES directory, it's still possible to create an RPM package. Simply emulate the directory structure in another directory. Be aware that you will not be able to test the installation of your package if you don't have the appropriate rights.*

Navigate to the parent directory of rpm-example and create the TAR file by typing the following:

```
tar cvf /usr/src/redhat/SOURCES/rpm-example.tar rpm-example
```

Don't forget the second rpm-example parameter! It's the directive that tells TAR which files to add to the new rpm-example.tar file. If your source tree had child directories, the same command would recursively add the entire tree to the TAR file.

After creating the tar ball, compress it using the GNU ZIP application:

```
gzip /usr/src/redhat/SOURCES/rpm-example.tar
```

Navigate to the /usr/src/redhat/SOURCES directory to confirm the existence of the rpm-example.tar.gz file. You may find other files in that directory—it's the standard place where source tar balls are stored—but just leave them be.

Creating the SPEC File

You've now created a makefile for your source and made sure it builds properly. You've also packaged it and readied it for the RPM build tool. Before you can build the RPM package, however, you must create a text file that tells the packager how to build the application. These files, typically known as *SPEC files*, are placed in the /usr/src/redhat/SPECS directory.

> **NOTE** *Again, the directory on your operating system may differ. Most of these directories (for instance, the SPECS directory mentioned previously) are likely to be in the same relative position to whatever parent directory you may find on your machine. Simply substitute out the /usr/src/redhat directory with the proper directory for your operating system.*

The SPEC file consists of contextually grouped sections. The first section of the file is called the *preamble* and allows you to tell RPM general information about your package. This general information includes the following fields:

- **Summary:** A one-line description of the application.

- **Name:** The name of the package. Try to be unique with this field—otherwise, your application may interfere with others of the same name.

- **Version:** The release version number of the product.

- **Release:** The release number for the package—but not necessarily the product. For instance, if you were to release an incomplete package, you might need a new package that contains the same "release." In that case, increment this field.

- **Copyright:** Any copyright information regarding this product. For instance, GPL or ©2002 by cmReady.

- **Group:** The group that the package will belong to in a group packager. Examples might be Games, Text Editors, or Utilities. See your operating system's distribution notes for more information.

- **Source**: This is the name of the compressed TAR file containing the source for the product. It should exist in the SOURCES directory as directed earlier in this section and shouldn't be pathed.

- **URL**: The Uniform Resource Locator (URL) where the source distribution is available for download by the general public.

- **Distribution**: The operating system distribution for which the application has been created. In many cases, this can be left blank if you don't plan to be distributed by a major product line.

- **Vendor**: The name of the company or person who created the application.

- **Packager**: The name and email of the person/entity who created the package.

Create a file called rpm-example.spec in the /usr/src/redhat/SPECS directory and add the preamble text from Listing 10-7.

Listing 10-7. The Preamble for the RPM-Example SPEC File

```
#
# Example spec file RPM-Example...
#
Summary: A program that does absolutely nothing but demonstrate RPM!
Name: rpm-example
Version: 1.0
Release: 1
Copyright: GPL
Group: Applications/Sound
Source: rpm-example.tar.gz
URL: http://www.cmready.com
Distribution: Example Linux
Vendor: cmReady, Inc.
Packager: Sean Kenefick <skenefick@cmready.com>
```

The second section of the SPEC file contains a paragraph detailing the product description. Try to keep your description to five or so lines long. The text doesn't wrap automatically, so use the Return key periodically to keep lines shorter than 75 characters. From this point on in your SPEC file, you need to place section titles in the SPEC file with a preceding percentage sign (%). Listing 10-8 details the "description" section.

Listing 10-8. The Description Section for the rpm-example SPEC File

```
%description
It really does nothing except show how RPM works.  Really.  That's
all.  I don't suggest running it unless you want to see it work.
```

The prep section contains information and whatever steps might be necessary to prepare for the build of the source. You might use the prep section to clean up any object files that exist before starting a new build. For instance, you're going to build your application in the /usr/src/redhat/BUILD directory—again, the BUILD directory is a standard—so you want to clean up whatever builds you might have previously created before the source is made again.

 NOTE *Yeah, yeah, yeah…you've never built your source in the BUILD directory so there are no previous builds to clean up! Absolutely true. But in the future, there could be. If you build the source into a package today but need to update the package tomorrow, today's build would still exist in the BUILD directory and would need to be removed. In a time travel scenario worthy of a* Star Trek: The Next Generation *episode, you're planning for future previous builds that will need to be removed when you're building in the "future present." Just be careful not to cause a tremor in the space-time continuum.*

The prep section allows you to use operating system commands as if you were writing a script file. Use the typical rm command to clan the directory. Afterward, use the zcat command to uncompress the source tar balls into the BUILD directory so the source is ready to be built. Listing 10-9 displays both of these steps.

Listing 10-9. The Prep Section for the rpm-example SPEC File

```
%prep
rm -rf $RPM_BUILD_DIR/rpm-example
zcat $RPM_SOURCE_DIR/rpm-example.tar.gz | tar -xvf -
```

NOTE *Notice the introduction of the $RPM_BUILD_DIR and $RPM_SOURCE_DIR variables? These are provided to you for free by RPM and don't need to be declared—hence one of the reasons why you want to use the standard RPM directories. If you're using a nonstandard directory path, you'll have to change these variables in your SPEC file. Keep in mind that this can break the RPM when it runs on an end user's machine.*

Use the build section of the SPEC file to specify the commands RPM should use to build the product. Luckily, the build steps for this product are pretty simple. As displayed in Listing 10-10, the specific steps you'll instruct RPM to follow include changing the source directory and then building the executables by calling the MAKE utility. Keep in mind that these steps are specific to this makefile and set of source—different applications may have different steps.

Listing 10-10. The Build Section for the rpm-example SPEC File

```
%build
cd $RPM_BUILD_DIR/rpm-example
make
```

You've now instructed RPM how to build the source. The next step is to instruct the tool on how to install the product on an end user's machine. As displayed in Listing 10-11, use the install section of the SPEC file to fulfill this goal. Again, you'll simply call the makefile, which has detailed install instructions in it.

Listing 10-11. The Install Section for the rpm-example SPEC File

```
%install
cd $RPM_BUILD_DIR/rpm-example
make install
```

Almost done! The last step in creating the SPEC file is to add a files section. This section tells RPM which application files should be installed on the end user's machine. RPM stores this information on the end user's machine, so it can easily uninstall or upgrade the application as necessary. Because the two executables are installed to /usr/bin, indicate such in the files section, as displayed in Listing 10-12.

Listing 10-12. The Files Section for the rpm-example SPEC File

```
%files
/usr/bin/welcome_rpm_example
/usr/bin/hello_rpm_example
```

NOTE   *The files section can be a little confusing because you must specify every file by the location in which it will be installed and not where it's built. In addition, the installation instructions you specify in the install section must reference the file and the path. In the previous example, the makefile installs a file entitled welcome_rpm_example to the /usr/bin directory. The files section must list it exactly as the install will output it—otherwise, the file will not be copied.*

TIP   *Copy all the files being "installed" to a single outputted directory by listing only the directory name. For example, typing /usr/bin by itself under %files in Listing 10-12 would achieve the same ends. On the other hand, if the install section of the makefile had 12 files being installed to /usr/bin, you'd want to specify only the files you want copied.*

Listing 10-13 displays the rpm-example.spec file in its entirety.

Listing 10-13. The Complete rpm-example SPEC File

```
#
# Example spec file RPM-Example...
#
Summary: A program that does absolutely nothing but demonstrate RPM!
Name: rpm-example
Version: 1.0
Release: 1
Copyright: GPL
Group: Applications/Sound
Source: rpm-example.tar.gz
URL: http://www.cmready.com
Distribution: Example Linux
Vendor: cmReady, Inc.
Packager: Sean Kenefick <skenefick@cmready.com>

%description
```

It really does nothing except show how RPM works. Really. That's
all. I don't suggest running it unless you wish to see it work.

```
%prep
rm -rf $RPM_BUILD_DIR/rpm-example
zcat $RPM_SOURCE_DIR/rpm-example.tar.gz | tar -xvf -

%build
cd $RPM_BUILD_DIR/rpm-example
make

%install
cd $RPM_BUILD_DIR/rpm-example
make install

%files
/usr/bin/welcome_rpm_example
/usr/bin/hello_rpm_example
```

NOTE *SPEC files have many more properties that you can use. For more
information about them and more detailed RPM instructions, refer to the
RPM standards organization Web site at* http://www.rpm.org.

Building the RPM

Whew! The hard part is over. You've gathered the source together and told RPM
how to make, package, and install it to an end user's machine. Your last task is to
build the installer package. Change into the /usr/src/redhat/SPECS directory and,
as displayed in Listing 10-14, use the RPM package creation utility, RPMBUILD, to
build your package. Use the -ba parameter to specify that you want to build both
binary and source packages. I'll talk about source packages at the end of this section.

Listing 10-14. The RPMBUILD Output from rpm-example.spec

```
$ cd /usr/src/redhat/SPECS
$ rpmbuild -ba rpm-example.spec
```

Listing 10-15 displays the output you might receive from the RPMBUILD command on Red Hat Linux 8.0.

Listing 10-15. The RPMBUILD Output from rpm-example.spec

```
$ rpmbuild -ba rpm-example.spec
Executing(%prep): /bin/sh -e /var/tmp/rpm-tmp.104
+ umask 022
+ cd /usr/src/redhat/BUILD
+ LANG=C
+ export LANG
+ rm -rf /usr/src/redhat/BUILD/rpm-example
+ zcat /usr/src/redhat/SOURCES/rpm-example.tar.gz
+ tar -xvf -
rpm-example/
rpm-example/welcome.c
rpm-example/hello.c
rpm-example/makefile
+ exit 0
Executing(%build): /bin/sh -e /var/tmp/rpm-tmp.104
+ umask 022
+ cd /usr/src/redhat/BUILD
+ LANG=C
+ export LANG
+ cd /usr/src/redhat/BUILD/rpm-example
+ make
cc -c welcome.c
cc -c hello.c
cc -o welcome_rpm_example welcome.o
welcome.o: In function `main':
welcome.o(.text+0x2e): the `gets' function is dangerous and should not be used.
cc -o hello_rpm_example hello.o
+ exit 0
Executing(%install): /bin/sh -e /var/tmp/rpm-tmp.104
+ umask 022
+ cd /usr/src/redhat/BUILD
+ LANG=C
+ export LANG
+ cd /usr/src/redhat/BUILD/rpm-example
+ make install
cp welcome_rpm_example /usr/bin
cp hello_rpm_example /usr/bin
+ /usr/lib/rpm/redhat/brp-compress
```

```
+ /usr/lib/rpm/redhat/brp-strip
+ /usr/lib/rpm/redhat/brp-strip-comment-note
Processing files: rpm-example-1.0-1
Finding  Provides: /usr/lib/rpm/find-provides
Finding  Requires: /usr/lib/rpm/find-requires
PreReq: rpmlib(PayloadFilesHavePrefix) <= 4.0-1 rpmlib(CompressedFileNames) ↵
    <= 3.0.4-1
Requires(rpmlib): rpmlib(PayloadFilesHavePrefix) ↵
    <= 4.0-1 rpmlib(CompressedFileNames) ↵
    <= 3.0.4-1
Requires: libc.so.6 libc.so.6(GLIBC_2.0)
Checking for unpackaged file(s): /usr/lib/rpm/check-files %{buildroot}
Wrote: /usr/src/redhat/SRPMS/rpm-example-1.0-1.src.rpm
Wrote: /usr/src/redhat/RPMS/i386/ rpm-example-1.0-1.i386.rpm
```

You should be aware of the important notes output during the build process. The first is that RPMBUILD detected several dependencies that must exist on your end users' machines before this package can be installed. In this case, these packages are extremely common and are likely included in the original operating system distribution. If they weren't, you might distribute those packages with your own application (when licensed to do so) or note the dependency on the download page of your Web site.

Another interesting fact is that you built two RPM packages as part of this process. RPM has placed the first, called rpm-example-1.0-1.src.rpm, into the /usr/src/redhat/SRPMS directory. The second, called rpm-example-1.0-1.i386.rpm, has been placed into the /usr/src/redhat/RPMS directory. You can distribute either of these packages to customers—the end result is always that the application gets installed on their systems. The important distinction between the two files, however, is that the rpm-example-1.0-1.src.rpm package doesn't contain binary files. It contains the source necessary for RPM to build and install on the end user's machine using the SPEC file instructions. Many Linux/Unix users prefer to receive source RPMs so they can evaluate the source for security flaws and distribute it to different hardware architectures. The second file, rpm-example-1.0-1.i386.rpm, contains only binaries. Keep in mind that the binaries can only be installed on machines with the same operating system and hardware architecture as the one from which you built the package.

CAUTION *If you distribute the rpm-example-1.0-1.src.rpm file to your customers,* you distribute your source in its entirety to anyone who might want to see it. *In other words, don't distribute source RPM packages if you're trying to protect your company's intellectual property through secrecy. You can use the* -bb *parameter with RPMBUILD to build only binary packages.*

Once created, distribute your RPM packages in all the usual ways—including posting the package to your Web site or placing it on a distributable CD.

Summary

This chapter discussed how to create installations for both Windows and Unix/Linux-flavored operating systems.

Specifically, I spoke about the following:

- How Microsoft introduced the MSI.

- The default MSI integration in Visual Studio and how to use it with your other projects to create a robust installation.

- Third-party installation tools such as InstallShield and Wise. I also detailed the usage of their most popular products.

- The RPM tool for Linux and Unix machines.

- How to best redistribute the Microsoft .NET Framework to your customers.

CHAPTER 11

Deployment and Build Afterthoughts

So the work is finished, and the project is ready to go out the door. Get out the champagne!

Well...not quite. Of course, a celebration is always required after large projects are completed—but you've missed an important part of the software delivery process—*delivering the product to the customer.*

In addition to the delivery model that your team chooses for your software, you need to take several steps to ensure that the product gets to customers safely. Unlike automated builds, most of the steps involved with releasing the product are manual. As I've discussed in previous chapters, all manual steps must be part of a strong process—be sure to create a document that spells out every task to be fulfilled.

Be sure to practice your deployment procedures periodically. Choose a build that's planned for an internal release—such as one going to the quality team for testing—and test your checklist to make sure you haven't omitted any necessary steps. Update your document often and, as with all important documents related to the build, make sure you keep it in your source control database so you can access previous versions of the document.

Deploying Applications

Software applications are typically delivered in one of three ways:

- The electronic method of delivery—using the Internet or a private network to get the product to customers—is becoming more ubiquitous as the public buys high-bandwidth connections.

- A bit more old-fashioned, but still in wide use, is the transfer of the product via a physical media such as a DVD-ROM, CD-ROM, or floppy disk.

- And, lastly, some products are personally delivered (and installed) by consultants to customer sites.

Predicting the Future of Delivery Media

The electronic and physical methods of transferring products to customers will probably alternate in popularity as the years go by. The convenience and low cost of electronic delivery will, of course, ensure its continuance. But as software applications bloat (and they will), customers will become resistant to downloading products until the speed of Internet connections improve. In the meantime, these bulky products will ship on new larger-format physical media.

Regardless of the delivery method, you should create a checklist for deploying a product and strictly adhere to it during the release process.

Creating a Deployment Checklist for Applications

As discussed earlier, coming up with a strong process for releasing a product is as important as any other task discussed in this book. This section helps you create a checklist for your process document.

 NOTE *This checklist relates to software applications delivered directly to customers. If you're deploying a Web product, you may want to refer to the "Creating a Deployment Checklist for Web Applications" section featured later in this chapter.*

The first tasks on the checklist are performed (by other people for the most part) long before the product is ready for release. Work with your development managers and architects to ensure that these items are completed in a timely manner by bringing up these tasks early in the development process:

Run all code through a code checker: Find a utility that searches for problems with code before they show up as bugs in your product. An example of this type of product is PC-Lint for C++ (available at parent company Gimpel Software's Web site at http://www.gimpel.com). Utilities such as this are especially important when your team uses languages that allow developers to manage memory.

Check the spelling and grammar of the user interface: Someone who has done a little copyediting in the past should check the entire user interface for grammatical and spelling errors. If you'd rather, of course, you can wait until they're pointed out in magazine reviews.

Peer review all code: No one item ever causes as much contention as code reviews. Some developers complain that code reviews are unnecessary—developers should be trusted to do their jobs, shouldn't they? Of course, if this were the case, you wouldn't need a quality team. People make mistakes. Code reviews by peers can catch many problems before they show up as show-stopping bugs.

Ensure that the product has been properly globalized (and localized): Does your product have a market in France, for example? If so, be sure to prepare the product properly. *Globalizing* the product (also known as *internationalizing*) means to prepare it for other languages. An example of globalizing the product is to avoid hard-coding text strings in the source. Instead, keep them in a separate file that you can easily hand off to a translator (which is the second phase, known as *localizing* the product). The developers should also use built-in operating system localization mechanisms to reference dates, numbers, and currency.

Secure the product as necessary: Whether it's with a registration key or by using a licensing server, there are many ways to ensure that pirates can't board your ship and steal your booty. See the "Ahoy There, Matey! Avoiding the Pirates" section later in this chapter for more information.

The next set of tasks should be completed when the release build—also known as the *gold* or *gold candidate* release—is created and placed at a final staging location:

Perform a file check: Whether it's too many files or too few, the wrong amount is just…wrong. Get out your file list and make sure both the master image and the final installed product contain the files you expect.

Fulfill a checksum to ensure that what was tested is what's mastered: Determining that the released build wasn't ever really tested can mean your job. Work with the quality group to ensure that the master staging area contains the same files as the last build that was tested. Use file versions (if available), date/time stamps, and file sizes to fulfill this task. Several freeware comparison tools can complete a quick checksum or a more time-consuming full-difference scan on your product.

Properly date stamp your files: It may only seem like a nicety, but file date/time stamping all files in a release can help your technical support team solve problems with customers later. Several freeware tools can fulfill this task. Remember to date/time stamp the files *before* gathering them into an installation package.

Install the product one last time and fulfill a standard smoke test: Do this just to be on the safe side. The quality group may undertake this task, but you'll want to make sure to check it off your list after it's been completed.

If you're releasing binaries electronically, consider using a digital signature: Crackers (the more nefarious form of hacker) are always looking for new ways to infiltrate computers. An easy way for them to do this is to break into your File Transfer Site (FTP) site and overwrite your binaries with nasty replacements. Protect yourself and your customers by digitally signing your product before placing it on an FTP server. Then post the signatures on an unconnected Web site. Several utilities—many of which follow the Pretty Good Privacy (PGP) standard—allow users to compare these posted signatures to binaries and verify file integrity. Alternatively, you can use an MD5 algorithm product to post a checksum-like hash of your product for the same type of comparison.

Virus scan your product: Possibly the most important task you can undertake when releasing your product is to virus scan both the master media and the final installed product. Little can sully a company's reputation faster than releasing a product with a virus. You might consider running more than one competing scan on your product—after all, you can't be too careful, and each virus database is different. And don't stop at release time—just because you didn't find a virus today doesn't mean it doesn't exist. Go back and periodically scan previous releases to ensure that you find newly recognized viruses you may have already released to customers.

Celebrate: Okay, *now* you can get out the champagne. After several months of stress and long hours, it's crucial that you enjoy your success.

Deploying Web Products

So there's no confusion, let's begin this discussion by differentiating between Web products and Web content sites. Web products follow many of the same rules as applications—they perform specific sets of services and are typically updated infrequently. Examples of Web products are Google or sites where you buy movie tickets. Sure, content on the site may change every so often—such as when a new movie shows up in theaters or when the site has a new featured advertiser—but new content rarely requires the site to be redeployed. The logic that runs the site is treated as a product and follows a typical product cycle.

Web content sites, on the other hand, are like newspapers or magazines—their main service is to deliver information. Examples of Web content sites are CNN and your favorite local newspaper. These types of sites may not be applicable to the issues discussed in the following sections because they're generally updated many times a day and follow a different development process.

WORD OF THE DAY

vīrus, n.

The early bird gets the worm.

I've discussed how scanning for viruses at release time can significantly lower the risk of infecting your customers with something nasty. But where did these nasty bugs come from anyway? Not many people were even aware of them until Melissa—a virus named for its author's favorite neighborhood exotic dancer—made its appearance in the late 90s.

You might be surprised to know that self-replicating viruses made their first appearance in the early 80s and were hypothesized in 1949.

Many claim that the first known viruses infected Apple II when users tried to use pirated games. Others claim they made their first appearance on closed systems such as the Univax 1108. Regardless, the first virus to really make a splash was created by two Pakistani brothers named Alvi in 1986.

How do I know that the origins of the virus? Because the authors put their company name on it. The Alvis wrote the virus in response to the widespread theft of their product. Called the Brain virus, it flashed across the screens of anyone who attempted to use the Alvi's proprietary product without license:

*Welcome to the Dungeon (c) 1986 Basit * Amjad (pvt) Ltd. BRAIN COMPUTER SERVICES 730 NIZAM BLOCK ALLAMA IQBAL TOWN LAHORE-PAKISTAN PHONE: 430791,443248,280530. Beware of this VIRUS.... Contact us for vaccination....*[1]

This virus put fear into the technical folks in America. "When we were contacted by *Time* magazine," said one of the brothers, "we were extremely surprised at [the] panic [the virus] had caused."[2] They were proud to attach their name to the virus because it only attacked those who had stolen their copyrighted material.

Wouldn't it be nice if modern viruses took such a high road? As the years have passed, the modern equivalents to Brain are much more dangerous and clever. They're also equal-opportunity attackers—they'll get you whether you've been good or bad. It's been claimed that such worms as Melissa and I LOVE YOU have cost businesses more than $20 billion.

So throw your master release disk in the CD-ROM drive and start a scan—just to ease *my* mind.

Exploring Strategies for Web Sites

Although Web products go through similar (though probably more frequent) development processes as regular operating-system applications, the following sections discuss a few things you may want to consider when deploying your site.

---

1. From the Brain Computer Services Web site at http://www.brain.net.pk.
2. Ibid.

Picking a Domain Name

It's obvious that in today's market a Web product must have a Uniform Resource Locator (URL) domain name to be successful. Domain names (such as cnn.com or google.com) assign human-readable names to the less-friendly Internet Protocol (IP) addresses that networks understand. In a nutshell, domain names make it a whole lot easier for your customers to find your site.

Although buying a domain for your product may seem pretty straightforward, there are a few gotchas you'll want to avoid:

Make the name as easy as possible: Yes, it sounds obvious, but pretty much all the easy three- to six-letter domain names are long gone. Try to avoid long names such as pleaseremembertopetmydog.com[3] because multitudes of separate words are more difficult to type without spaces and punctuation.

Try to acquire similar domains: If your domain name reflects a trademark or company name, you might also want to pick up the .net and .org domains in addition to the basic .com. Otherwise, those with less morality might try to skim your business by attracting folks to these other domains.

Research domain resellers: Although Network Solutions[4] may be the most popular domain name registrar on the Internet, it's by no means the only one. You may find significant savings by researching domain name registrars before purchasing—especially if you have sets of domains to buy.[5] Keep in mind, however, that different retailers have differing levels of service and experience. Fulfill the proper due diligence before contracting.

Guard your reseller account information and password closely: Your domain is like a permanent phone number. If it's a descriptive, easy-to-type domain, nasty folks might try to steal it by duping domain resellers into changing ownership. One stolen domain that has recently been in the headlines (I won't name it to avoid causing you possible offense) cost the original owner approximately $6 million!

---

3. My apologies to whomever might acquire the pleaseremembertopetmydog.com domain. As of this writing, it's available.

4. Network Solutions is a subsidiary of VeriSign (http://www.verisign.com).

5. I don't want to open myself to lawsuits here, but doing a quick Google search for "domain name registration" showed an 80-percent difference in price between the industry leader and an up-and-coming vendor.

Avoid spam: Providing your name, address, phone number, and email address when you buy domains can lead to an avalanche of spam. Consider this and provide contact information accordingly. Many system administrators set up separate mail accounts and post office boxes to avoid the onslaught. Some domain resellers now allow you to opt out of marketing lists they sell to third parties.

Getting Listed in Search Engines

Getting listed on Google is sometimes as easy as publishing your site. And sometimes, it's a lot harder than it should be. There are reasons why search engines might miss your product or company. Here are some hints:

Link your site: Because most search engines use automated robots to find sites by exploiting links, they might miss you if no one links to you. Get your friends to link to your site whenever possible. Better, your marketing department should try to get listed in Internet trade publications.

Use an Internet Service Provider (ISP) that submits sites to search engines: Some ISPs will submit your site to search engines as part of the basic hosting fee.

Submit if you can: Most search engines have a submission process for new sites. These submissions, however, can get overwritten by the next robot search. Refer to the first item in this list to avoid this problem.

Watch for third-party search engine submitters: If necessary, it's possible to purchase directory submission services. Be aware that many of these sites charge a large fee for a service you can pretty easily provide yourself. *Caveat emptor!*

Use the Robot Exclusion Protocol (REP): You may want to exclude pages on your site from being indexed by the major search engines. In this case, you can use REP to indicate which parts of your site should be avoided. Refer to http://www.robotstxt.org for more information. Note that this is a voluntary service—unethical robots, such as those searching for email addresses to spam, simply ignore REP.

Watch your frames: Some search engines can't find metadata placed inside frames. Be sure that the main frame has company and product information that can be indexed.

Keeping Things Speedy and Compliant

Slow-loading pages are a drag for both you and your customers. Studies show that users will wait an average of seven seconds before they click somewhere else. The following tips show how you can keep your site moving:

Use the Secure Sockets Layer (SSL) protocol sparingly: Performance suffers when SSL encryption negotiations take place between a Web client and a Web server. You may want to use SSL only on pages that require privacy—such as a login page or a page that accepts credit cards. But use discretion—some sites may require this type of privacy on every page.

Get rid of extra white space: Web clients, such as Internet Explorer and Netscape Navigator, process every character that might appear in a Hypertext Markup Language (HTML) file—even if it's only to throw away extra spaces or carriage returns. Consider using utilities that will strip unnecessary white space from text documents before publishing your site.

Use persistent connections: Network communication is the main contributor to Web latency. By eliminating the repetitive "handshake" that must take place between a Web client and server, users can see pages much more quickly. Both Internet Explorer and Netscape Navigator support this feature, as do most Web servers. The Apache group states that using its Keep-Alive server feature can result in speeding up the delivery of Web pages by 50 percent.

Comply with current standards: By ensuring that your site is compliant with World Wide Web Consortium (W3C) standards, your company can rest assured that your product will work with whatever W3C-compliant browser the customer may want to use. Consider running your site's pages through a tool such as Bobby (http://bobby.watchfire.com) to expose compliancy problems in the code.

Exploring Strategies for Databases

A mistake that many companies make is to ignore setup procedures for connected production databases. The following are some tips:

Back it up: With a Web product, the data held in the database is often more important than even the source. Make sure the database is properly maintained and backed up nightly.

Put database changes under revision control: Almost every database allows the ability to script changes to data models and insert base data. These text scripts should be added to source control and treated as if they were source. Just like the rest of the product, you should be able to rebuild the database at a moment's notice.

Treat database changes as if they were code changes: Any change to the database's model should go through the typical development cycle. A test database machine should be available to the quality group, and changes should be thoroughly tested before being deployed to a production environment.

Treat the Database Administrator (DBA) as a developer: Any rules applied to the developers should also be applied to the guys and gals who work on the database. This includes smoking their work on test machines and following appropriate checkin regulations.

Consider requiring rollback capabilities: Because you can't really start from scratch every time you have a new release, the data in the testing and production environments can greatly differ. A seemingly insignificant change to the data model that passed muster on the test machine can cause havoc when it's deployed to customers. By having a rollback database script (as well as labeled code) available when the site is to be deployed, you can be assured a return to the site's previous incarnation should a problem rear its ugly head.

Creating a Deployment Checklist for Web Applications

Just as if they were typical applications, Web products need to be deployed using a strong process. It's important to create a list where you can check off items as you complete them. You may want to fulfill the following tasks before deploying your site:

Perform a file check: Whether you're deploying a Web product or a regular application, get out your file list and make sure the master staging arena contains the files you expect.

Check the links and spelling: Luckily, Web sites are easy to patch. But there are still few errors that look as unprofessional as misspelled words or broken links. Web creation products such Macromedia Dreamweaver can often spell check HTML and verify all of a site's links.

Fulfill a checksum to ensure that what was tested is what's mastered: Compare your master staging area to the one tested by the quality group. Use file versions (if available), date settings, time settings, and file sizes to fulfill this task. Several freeware comparison tools can complete a quick checksum and perform a more time-consuming full-difference scan on your product.

Properly date/time stamp your files: Changing the date and time stamp on files before they're copied to the Web server can greatly help when it comes time to debug a problem. Be sure to use a copying tool that will preserve the date stamp as the files are transferred to the production Web site.

If releasing binaries electronically, consider using a digital signature: As discussed more thoroughly in "Creating a Deployment Checklist for Applications," use a signature or hashing tool, such as MD5, to instill confidence in your customers.

Virus scan your product: Any binaries available for download to customers—including word processing and spreadsheet documents—should be virus checked before being transferred to the production machine.

Start fresh: To ensure you don't accidentally provide a mechanism for cracker entry, be sure to completely delete all pages of a previously installed version of your Web product (but not necessarily the data in the database!) before releasing the new site. Unfortunately, this means the computer on which the site is located must be unavailable during the deployment phase. Consider using more than one machine for Web access to your customers—that way, one can be downed for new installations while the other(s) stay active.

Celebrate: Yep, make sure you get some champagne, too!

After the Product Ships...

Your job doesn't end when the product ships. Several tasks might come up once the product is out the door.

Providing Patches and Service Packs

It's a rare product that doesn't need a touchup after it has been released. Whether the problem is as serious as data corruption or as innocuous as a misspelled word in the user interface, you want your customers to be satisfied. The following are some ideas to consider:

Service patch first, service pack second, and service release last: Some quick definitions first: A *patch* is generally considered a single file or set of files that are individually installed to fix a specific defect. A *service pack* is a group of files that updates numerous bugs. And a *service release* is a rebuild of the entire product with numerous bug fixes. Unless yours is a small product or you find a catastrophic bug in the product after shipping, there's typically no reason to rerelease the entire product for small changes. Your customers will generally thank you if they can simply copy over a file or two instead of going through the process of uninstalling/reinstalling the application.

Trickle down all fixes: A service release should contain all the fixes in all the appropriate service packs (which contain all of the previous patches). Forcing your customers to install patch after patch is just another way to annoy them. An exception to this rule is when certain patches are localized to certain customers.

Use a patch delivery system: Even if it's only to patch a single file, look professional to your customers and provide a binary delivery system instead of forcing them to install multitudes of single files. For Windows, the InstallShield, Wise, and WinZip companies all provide tools that allow you to provide collective patches of bug fixes. On the Unix/Linux side, use RPM Package Manager (RPM) or a shell script to fulfill the same functionality.

Suggest an architecture that's easily updateable: Work with your architects to design the product so that new features can be delivered through metadata such as Extensible Markup Language (XML) instead of through binary updates. Sending out a text file as an update to your product is clean and easy.

Provide a Web update tool: One of the finest features to come out of the Windows operating system in the past few years is the ability to quickly update computers via an easy-to-access Web site. Consider providing a similar feature to your customers that will automatically check and update their systems with product enhancements and patches.

Get in the distribution: Both Microsoft and Linux distributors provide the ability to distribute hardware drivers through their Web update tools. If providing such a hardware solution, consider talking to the respective companies about providing your drivers for such update tools. Keep in mind that Linux distributions may require your product be open source before such inclusion can take place.

Properly build and version patched components: Any patched components should go through the typical automated build process. If your build was designed correctly, it should be able to build a single component (and its dependencies) using a single command. On operating systems where it's possible, each patched file should have its minor or build version number properly incremented.

Update the product's version number: Every time you create a service pack or release, you should increment the minor version of the product. This version change should then be reflected appropriately in the About box, if there is one, so customers can easily determine which packs have been applied to their computers. By updating the new version number in the Windows Registry or an applicable text file, you could design the About box to populate this information automatically.

Follow the typical deployment checklist for each patch, service pack, or service release: If it's going out the door, you should fulfill all of the tasks listed in the appropriate deployment checklist section of this chapter.

Ahoy There, Matey! Avoiding the Pirates

Regardless of the delivery method your company may have chosen to release the product, you'll want to protect it from theft once it has been released.

In the old days, media products lost some of their luster when they were stolen—for instance, cassette tapes made from record albums suffered from a loss of sound quality. Photocopies of books faded and looked blurry.

That paradigm has completely changed in the digital age. In most cases, every copy made of music, text, or software is the same as the original. This has led many companies to research ways they can limit access to their products. For instance, some products require a license server or a registration key. Other products nag users until a license is purchased. Even others expire or become crippled until the user produces a credit card.

You can perform the following tasks to avoid being pirated:

Track serial numbers: If there's a way for you to identify users through serial numbers, you might be able to figure out who placed a registration key on one of the popular pirate sites.

Watch out for the backlash: Many folks may consider a demand for identifying information to be an invasion of their privacy. Others get annoyed if they must insert a CD-ROM each time they use a product. Consider the backlash your product may suffer should you add security measures.

Test your application's security: The best way to plunder software is when its creator leaves an open hole to exploit. For instance, Web product manufacturers should make sure that users must log into the site securely instead of being able to jump to restricted pages simply by typing a URL. Application creators should consider what kind of information they provide in logs and whether debugging information is accidentally handed to end users when using the product.

Obfuscate your source: Don't accidentally give your source away for free. For instance, it's possible to open .NET applications and see the code line by line! Available utilities make almost any language's code more difficult to read. These utilities remove unnecessary white space, change the names of functions so it's difficult to know what they do, and generally scramble source code to make it harder to steal. See Chapter 9, "Builds for Windows .NET," for more information about obfuscating your code.

Summary

This chapter helped you create processes for deploying and shipping your applications, whether they're typical applications or Web products. The topics I spoke about included the following:

- Creating deployment checklists for both applications and Web products

- Understanding the importance of virus scanning your product

- Exploring strategies to help you successfully deploy Web sites

- Learning how to treat database model changes

- Creating service patches, packs, and releases

- Lessening the chances for theft of your product

Index

R

-r maint_1_1 parameter, 140
-R option, 198
-r parameter, 132, 135, 140
RAID mechanism, 155
RAS (Remote Access Services), 67
RCS (Revision Control System), 83, 87
README files, 27, 43, 344, 363
Ready to Copy dialog box, 383
RealTimeStock setup project, 341
recovering from catastrophe. *See* backing up and restoring
redirect operator (>), 271
redistributing binary files and third-party programs, 221–22
REG files, 370–71, 372
REGEDIT (Registry editing tool), 371
Registry objects, 353
regressions, 31
Release field, 402
Release folder, 375, 376
release manager, 23, 41
release_tag parameter, 117
releases, naming, 61–62
Remote Access Services (RAS), 67
remote locations (CVS), 145–47
Remote Protocol model (CVS), 106
removing
    files (SourceSafe), 167–68
    users (SourceSafe), 162
renaming
    directories/files (CVS), 102
    users (SourceSafe), 162
REP (Robot Exclusion Protocol), 417
Report command, 175
Requests for Changes (RFCs) in functionality, 39
Restore Wizard, 196
restoring projects. *See* backing up and restoring
results pane, of SourceSafe client, 164
revision control, 45, 418–19
Revision Control System (RCS), 83, 87
RFCs (Requests for Changes) in functionality, 39
RIGHTS.DAT file, 204
rituals, 17
rm command, 404
RoboHelp, 235
Robot Exclusion Protocol (REP), 417
rollback capabilities, 419
Rollback command, 175
Rollback folder, 358
RPM Package Manager, 231, 243
    building RPM, 407–10
    creating RPM Package, 398–407
        creating source tree, 399–400

creating SPEC File, 402–7
overview, 398
tarring the source, 400–401
RPMBUILD command, 408, 409
rtag command, 139
runtime considerations for objects, 233

S

sales representatives, 79
Samba, 196
sandbox, 119
Save data to file command, 194
SCCS (Source Code Control System), 83
schedules
    challenges of, 28–29
    and large changes, 217
    task schedule, 223–28
        daily tasks, 224–25
        monthly tasks, 226–27
        overview, 223–24
        quarterly tasks, 229–30
        weekly tasks, 225
SCM lab, 209–28
    best practices for SCM, 215–23
        branching and merging, 216–18
        builds, 218–20
        labels and versions, 220–21
        overview, 215–16
        redistributing binary files and third-party programs, 221–22
        tools, 223
        workspace, 216
    creating SCM guide for developers, 211–15
    stocking, 209–11
    task schedule, 223–28
        daily tasks, 224–25
        monthly tasks, 226–27
        overview, 223–24
        quarterly tasks, 229–30
        weekly tasks, 225
SCM (Software Configuration Management). *See also* SCM lab
    dilemmas of, 9–15
        build dilemma, 10–12
        deployment dilemma, 12–13
        source control dilemma, 9–10
        versioning dilemma, 14
    Golden Rules of, 15
SCM (Software Configuration Manager)
    overview, 21
    relationship with development and quality groups, 36–40
    SCM positions, 32–35
SCP (Secure Copy) tool, 66
scripting languages, 8